WOMEN AND WEAPONS IN THE VIKING WORLD

WOMEN AND WEAPONS IN THE VIKING WORLD

AMAZONS OF THE NORTH

LESZEK GARDEŁA

OXBOW | books
Oxford & Philadelphia

Published in the United Kingdom in 2021 by
OXBOW BOOKS
The Old Music Hall, 106–108 Cowley Road, Oxford, OX4 1JE

© Oxbow Books and the author 2021

Hardback Edition: ISBN 978-1-78925-665-9
Digital Edition: ISBN 978-1-78925-666-6 (epub)

A CIP record for this book is available from the British Library

All rights reserved. No part of this book may be reproduced or transmitted in any form or by any means, electronic or mechanical including photocopying, recording or by any information storage and retrieval system, without permission from the publisher in writing.

Printed in Malta by Melita Press

Typeset by Lapiz Digital Services

For a complete list of Oxbow titles, please contact:

UNITED KINGDOM
Oxbow Books
Telephone (01865) 241249
Email: oxbow@oxbowbooks.com
www.oxbowbooks.com

UNITED STATES OF AMERICA
Oxbow Books
Telephone (610) 853-9131, Fax (610) 853-9146
Email: queries@casemateacademic.com
www.casemateacademic.com/oxbow

Oxbow Books is part of the Casemate Group

Front cover: Photo by Rebeca Franco Valle

In memory of
Sæbjørg Walaker Nordeide

Contents

List of figures x
List of tables xiv
Acknowledgements xv

1. Introduction: the methodological and theoretical framework 1
   Entering the Viking world ... of the dead 1
   Funerary diversity 4
       Cremation graves 5
       Inhumation graves 5
   Lost identities and elusive grave goods 5
   Warriors and warrior ideals 9
   Sex and gender in the Viking Age 12
   Amazons of the North: the scope of the book 12

2. Historiography 17
   Researching women in the Viking Age 17
   Warrior women in Old Norse studies and Viking archaeology 22

3. Women and weapons in medieval textual sources 27
   Armed women in *Gesta Danorum* 27
   Armed women in Old Norse Literature 30
   Women and weapons in the *Íslendingasögur* 30
       Freydís Eiríksdóttir 30
       Þórdís Súrsdóttir 31
       Auðr and Þuriðr 32
       Þórhildr Vaðlækkja 32
       Not only axes and swords: understanding women's weapons 33
   Women and weapons in the *fornaldarsögur* 34
       Hervör Bjarmarsdóttir 34
       Þornbjörg Eiríksdóttir 35
       Other armed women in the *fornaldarsögur* 36
   Armed women in Old Norse mythology 37
       Valkyrjur, disir, fylgjur 37
       Skaði 38
       Þorgerðr Hölgabrúðr 38
       Female Giantesses as grinders of war and bearers of arms 39
   Armed women of the Viking Age in non-Scandinavian medieval sources 40
       Æthelflæd of Mercia 40
       Women and war in the account of John Skylitzes 41
   Women with weapons in medieval literature: more than literary embellishments 41

4. Women and weapons in Viking archaeology: the burial evidence ... 47
    Female graves with weapons ... 47
        Swedish female graves with weapons ... 47
        Norwegian female graves with weapons ... 57
        Danish female graves with weapons ... 69

5. Interpreting the arsenal of armed women ... 81
    Women and axes in the Viking Age ... 81
        Axes in the Viking Age ... 81
        Axes in Viking Age funerary contexts ... 81
        Miniature axes ... 82
        Interpreting axes in Viking Age female graves ... 84
        Women and axes in textual sources and folklore ... 85
        Women and axes in the Viking Age: conclusions ... 86
    Women and swords in the Viking Age ... 86
        Swords in the Viking Age ... 86
        Swords in Viking Age funerary contexts ... 87
        Women and weaving swords ... 88
        Women and swords in iconography ... 89
        Miniature swords ... 91
        Interpreting swords in Viking Age female graves ... 91
        Women and swords in Old Norse sources ... 92
        Women and swords in the Viking Age: conclusions ... 93
    Women and spears in the Viking Age ... 94
        Spears in the Viking Age ... 94
        Spears in Viking Age funerary contexts ... 94
        Women and spears in iconography ... 95
        Miniature spears ... 95
        Interpreting spears in Viking Age female graves ... 95
        Women and spears in Old Norse sources ... 100
        Women and spears in the Viking Age: conclusions ... 100
    Women and shields in the Viking Age ... 100
        Shields in the Viking Age ... 100
        Shields in Viking Age funerary contexts ... 101
        Women and shields in iconography ... 102
        Miniature shields ... 102
        Interpreting shields in Viking Age female graves ... 103
        Women and shields in Old Norse sources ... 104
        Women and shields in the Viking Age: conclusions ... 104
    Women, bows and arrows in the Viking Age ... 105
        Bows and arrows in the Viking Age ... 105
        Bows and arrows in Viking Age funerary contexts ... 105
        Interpreting bows and arrows in Viking Age female graves ... 106
        Women, bows and arrows in Old Norse sources ... 107
        Women, bows and arrows in the Viking Age: conclusions ... 107
    Women, riding equipment and horses in the Viking Age ... 108
        Riding equipment in the Viking Age ... 108
        Riding equipment and horses in Viking Age funerary contexts ... 108
        Interpreting riding equipment and horses in Viking Age female graves ... 108
        Women and horses in Old Norse sources ... 110
        Women, horses and riding equipment in the Viking Age: conclusions ... 111

6. Women and weapons in Viking Age iconography 117
    The so-called 'valkyrie brooches': distribution and materiality 117
        (Re)interpreting the so-called 'valkyrie brooches' 118
        Freyja and a warrior woman? 119
        Sigurðr and Brynhildr/Sigrdrífa 121
    Other iconographic representations of armed females in Viking Age Scandinavia and England ... 122

7. Women with weapons: a cross-cultural phenomenon 125
    Warrior women in prehistoric times 125
    Female cross-dressers in early modern Europe 127
    The Amazons of Dahomey 129
    Women in the First and Second World Wars 132
    Emerging patterns and conclusions 133

8. Amazons of the North? Women and weapons in the Viking world 137
    Women and weapons in Viking archaeology 137
    Women and weapons in medieval texts 139
    The way of the warrior: past and present 140

Appendix 143
References 149

List of figures

Fig. 1.1. Hjalmar Stolpe (1841–1905). Public domain. — 2
Fig. 1.2. Holger Arbman (1904–1968). Public domain. — 2
Fig. 1.3. Haakon Shetelig (1877–1955). Public domain. — 3
Fig. 1.4. Viking Age cemetery at Lindholm Høje, Jylland, Denmark. Photo by Leszek Gardeła. — 6
Fig. 1.5. Viking Age cemetery at Hringsdalur, Iceland. Photo by Leszek Gardeła. — 6
Fig. 1.6. Grave goods and their 'mixed messages' according to Heinrich Härke. Image by Leszek Gardeła. — 9
Fig. 1.7. A Viking Age warrior as interpreted by re-enactor Jakub Zbránek. Photo by Jan Zbránek. Courtesy of Marobud re-enactment group. — 10
Fig. 4.1. An engraving of grave Bj. 581 published in *Ny Illustrerad* Tidning. Public domain. — 48
Fig. 4.2. Hjalmar Stolpe's (a) and Holger Arbman's (b) plans of grave Bj. 581. Image (a) from the Birka papers in the ATA archive. Image (b) from Arbman 1943: 189. — 50
Fig. 4.3. Silver cap mounts from Bj. 581 (a) and Bj 644 (b) at Birka and an analogous find from Shestovitsa (c). Image (a) from Statens Historiska Museum online database. Image (b) after Arbman 1940: Taf. 94. Image (c) after Kovalenko, Motsya, Syty 2012: 335. Edited by Leszek Gardeła. — 50
Fig. 4.4. Human bone from Bj. 581, clearly marked with ink. Image from the Statens Historiska Museum online database. — 51
Fig. 4.5. Plan of grave Bj. 581 with the weapons highlighted in grey: sword (a), axehead (b), spearhead (c), spearhead (d), battle knife (e), arrowheads (f), shield bosses (g). Based on Arbman 1943: 189 and edited by Leszek Gardeła. — 52
Fig. 4.6. Gaming pieces from Bj. 581. After the Statens Historiska Museum online database. Photo by Charlotte Hedenstierna-Jonson. — 54
Fig. 4.7. Artistic reconstruction of the Nordre Kjølen grave. Illustration by Mirosław Kuźma. Copyright Mirosław Kuźma and Leszek Gardeła. — 59
Fig. 4.8. Image from the Bayeux tapestry showing the ruler with an inverted sword, probably serving as a symbol of power and authority. Illustration by Leszek Gardeła. — 61
Fig. 4.9. The Oseberg ship during excavations in 1904. From Brøgger, Falk, Shetelig 1917a: 76. — 63
Fig. 4.10. The burial chamber onboard the Oseberg ship. From Brøgger, Falk, Shetelig 1917a: 32. — 63
Fig. 4.11. Two axes from the Oseberg grave. After Grieg 1928: 162. — 63
Fig. 4.12. Artistic reconstruction of the Mårem grave. Illustration by Mirosław Kuźma. Copyright Mirosław Kuźma and Leszek Gardeła. — 66
Fig. 4.13. Artistic reconstruction of the Løve grave. Illustration by Mirosław Kuźma. Copyright Mirosław Kuźma and Leszek Gardeła. — 68
Fig. 4.14. Iron staffs from Hilde, Kvåle and Gausel in Norway, probably serving as ritual accoutrements in the practice of *seiðr*. All three staffs were found in burial contexts together with shield bosses and other goods. Photos by Leszek Gardeła. — 69
Fig. 4.15. Artistic reconstruction of the Gerdrup grave. Illustration by Mirosław Kuźma. Copyright Mirosław Kuźma and Leszek Gardeła. — 70
Fig. 4.16. Needle case and iron pin from Gerdrup. Photo by Leszek Gardeła. — 71
Fig. 4.17. Spearhead from Gerdrup. Photo by Leszek Gardeła. — 71

Fig. 4.18.	Artistic reconstruction of grave BB from Bogøvej. Illustration by Mirosław Kuźma. Copyright Mirosław Kuźma and Leszek Gardeła.	72
Fig. 4.19.	Strike-a-light from Bogøvej. Redrawn by Leszek Gardeła on the basis of Grøn, Hedeager Krag, Bennike 1994: 121.	73
Fig. 4.20.	Axe from Bogøvej (a) and a selection of axes from Central Europe representing Nadolski's type Va: Czarna Wielka, Poland (b), Końskie, Poland (c), Końskie, Poland (d). Redrawn by Leszek Gardeła on the basis of Grøn, Hedeager Krag, Bennike 1994: 120 and Nadolski 1954: 257. Not to scale.	73
Fig. 4.21.	Artistic reconstruction of grave A505 from Trekroner-Grydehøj. Illustration by Mirosław Kuźma. Copyright Mirosław Kuźma and Leszek Gardeła.	75
Fig. 4.22.	Copper alloy arrowhead, spearhead or staff from grave A505 from Trekroner-Grydehøj. Photo by Leszek Gardeła.	76
Fig. 5.1.	Artistic reconstruction of the Svingesæter grave. Illustration by Mirosław Kuźma. Copyright Mirosław Kuźma and Leszek Gardeła.	83
Fig. 5.2.	An example of using an axe in a magic ritual in Finland in 1910. From Holck 1996.	85
Fig. 5.3.	Viking Age weaving sword from Sanddal. Photo by Leszek Gardeła.	89
Fig. 5.4.	Selection of anthropomorphic female(?) figurines carrying swords from Gammeltoften, Denmark (a), Skodsebølle, Denmark (b), Rostock-Dierkow (c), Unknown location in Jylland, Denmark (d), Rutland, England (e) and a fragment of the Oseberg tapestry portraying a sword-carrying female (f). Photos (a), (b) and (d) by the National Museum of Denmark. Photo (c) courtesy of Sebastian Messal. Photo (e) from the Portable Antiquities Scheme Database. Drawing (f) based on an illustration by Sofie Krafft and edited by Leszek Gardeła.	90
Fig. 5.5.	Sword-carrying figures on a picture stone from Tängelgårda on Gotland. Based on Nylén and Lamm 2003: 67 and edited by Leszek Gardeła.	91
Fig. 5.6.	Selection of Viking Age miniature swords: Dragedyssegård, Denmark (a), Kalmergården, Denmark (b), Nørholm, Denmark (c), Gamborg Vest, Denmark (d), Voel II, Denmark (e), Hoby, Denmark (f), Engsiggård, Hodde, Denmark (g), Stavnsager, Denmark (h). Photos by the National Museum of Denmark, edited by Leszek Gardeła.	92
Fig. 5.7.	Artistic reconstruction of the Ballateare grave. Illustration by Mirosław Kuźma. Copyright Mirosław Kuźma and Leszek Gardeła.	96
Fig. 5.8.	Selection of Viking Age miniature spears: Helgö, Sweden (a), Västerljungs, Sweden (b), Bruzelius collection, Sweden (c), Birka Svarta Jorden, Sweden (d), Birka grave Bj. 581, Sweden (e), Birka grave Bj. 944, Sweden (f), Tissø, Denmark (g), Trelleborg, Denmark (h). Photos (a–d) after Arrhenius 1961: 148, 148, photo (e) after the Statens Historiska Museum Online Database, drawing (f) from Arbman 1943: 370, photos (g–h) by Leszek Gardeła.	97
Fig. 5.9.	Spear-carrying figure on a matrix from Torslunda. Creative Commons. CC-BY.	98
Fig. 5.10.	Armed figures in animal costumes from the Oseberg tapestry: figure (a) has a shield and a spear, and figure (b), possibly a woman (as indicated by the trailing garment), is equipped with a shield. The photos (c-d) depict a scene with a female figure holding an unusual spear or staff. Images (a-b) based on Hougen 1940: 104 and redrawn by Leszek Gardeła. Photos (c-d) by E.I. Johnsen, MCH. Used by kind permission.	99
Fig. 5.11.	Carved stone from the Isle of Man probably portraying Óðinn and the wolf Fenrir. Notice the winged spear held by the god. Photos by Leszek Gardeła.	99
Fig. 5.12.	Authentic reconstruction of a Viking Age round shield. The shield is built as part of a project led by Rolf Warming (Society for Combat Archaeology) in collaboration with Trelleborg Viking Fortress (National Museum of Denmark) based on new research data (Warming, Larsen, Sommer, Ørsted Brand, Pauli Jensen 2020). Photographer: Tom Jersø/The Viking Shield Project. Used by kind permission.	101
Fig. 5.13.	Selection of Viking Age miniature shields: Birka grave Bj. 533, Sweden (a), Birka grave Bj. 825, Sweden (b), Birka grave Bj. 835, Sweden (c), Birka grave Bj. 963, Sweden (d), Birka grave Bj. 987, Sweden (e), Truso/Janów Pomorski, Poland (f). Photos (a–e) by Gabriel Hildebrand (Collections of the Statens Historiska Museum), photo (f) by Leszek Gardeła.	103
Fig. 5.14.	Viking Age trefoil brooches are modelled on Carolingian strap distributors. The photo shows a replica of one such item from Östra Påboda in Söderakra socken in Småland, Sweden. Replica by Mikołaj Organek (Organek Arts and Crafts). Photo by Jacek Gajak. Used by kind permission.	104

Fig. 5.15. The curious arrowhead, spear or staff from grave A505 in Trekroner-Grydehøj (a) and similar arrowheads from the nomadic world: Bruszczewo, Poland (b), Trepcza, Poland (c), Trepcza, Poland (d), Łazy, Poland (e). Photo (a) by Leszek Gardeła. Drawings (b–e) based on Świętosławski 2006: 92 and edited by Leszek Gardeła. 107

Fig. 5.16. Magyar grave from Przemyśl, Poland. Redrawn by Leszek Gardeła after Koperski 2004: 91. 109

Fig. 5.17. Reconstruction of the horse bridle from Løve. Redrawn by Leszek Gardeła after Resi 2013: 119. 110

Fig. 6.1. Selection of miniatures depicting a rider and an armed figure: Tissø, Denmark (a), Hedeby, Germany (b), Ribe, Denmark (c), Stentinget, Denmark (d), Bylaugh, England (e), Truso/Janów Pomorski, Poland (f). Photos (a) and (d) by the National Museum of Denmark, photos (b), (c) and (f) by Leszek Gardeła, photo (e) by Norwich Castle Museum & Arts Gallery, used by permission. 118

Fig. 6.2. Detail of the runestone from Ockelbo in Gästrikland, Sweden showing two figures playing a board game. Drawing by Leszek Gardeła. 119

Fig. 6.3. The obverse and reverse of the double miniature from Tissø. The reverse has two well-preserved closed loops; this constructional feature implies such artefacts were probably used as pendants and/or appliques. Photo courtesy of Mads Dengsø Jessen. Edited by Leszek Gardeła. 119

Fig. 6.4. The 'welcoming scene' on a Gotlandic picture stone from Tjängvide I. Notice the rider in baggy trousers and the standing figure holding a horn. In some regards the imagery resembles the double figurines from Denmark. Photo by Leszek Gardeła. 120

Fig. 6.5. Selection of standalone armed miniature figures: Hårby, Denmark (a), Galgebakken/Vrejlev, Denmark (b), Wickham Market, England (c), Cawthorpe, England (d), Søllested, Denmark (e). Photos (a) and (e) by the National Museum of Denmark, photo (c) from the Portable Antiquities Scheme Database, photo (d) from Hall 2007 and photo (b) by Leszek Gardeła. 122

Fig. 7.1. The Mino around 1890. Public domain. 130

Fig. 7.2. Group photograph of 'Amazons of Dahomey' taken during their stay in Paris. Public domain. 130

Fig. 7.3. Seh-Dong-Hong-Beh, a leader of the Dahomey warrior women. Public domain. 131

Fig. 7.4. Milunka Savić (1892–1973). Public domain. 132

Fig. 7.5. Female paramedics at Moniuszki Street during the Warsaw Uprising in 1944. Public domain. 134

Fig. 7.6. Tunnel guides near Malczewskiego Street during the Warsaw Uprising in 1944. Public domain. 134

Fig. 7.7. Participants of the Warsaw Uprising on a tank near Okopowa Street. Public domain. 135

Plate section

Plate 4.1. Weapons from Bj. 581: sword (a–b), battle knife (c), spearheads (d–e), axehead (f), arrowheads (g), shield bosses (h). After the Statens Historiska Museum online database. Photos by Christer Åhlin. Plate assembled and photos edited by Leszek Gardeła.

Plate 4.2. Plan of the Klinta grave. Redrawn by Leszek Gardeła after Schultze 1987: 59.

Plate 4.3. Iron staff (a–d) and axehead (e) from Klinta. Notice the house-shaped terminal on top of the staff. Photos (a–d) by Leszek Gardeła. Photo (e) after the Statens Historiska Museum online database.

Plate 4.4. Weapons from Nordre Kjølen: sword (a–b), axehead (c), bent spearhead (d), arrowheads (e), whetstone (f), file (g). Photos by Leszek Gardeła.

Plate 4.5. Grave goods from Frafjord: axehead (a), shield boss (not to scale) (b), horse bits (c), wool comb (d), weaving sword (e), shears (f). Photos by Leszek Gardeła.

Plate 4.6. Grave goods from Sanddal: oval brooches (a–b), silver wire chain (c), whetstone (d), thirteen white stones possibly used as gaming pieces (e). Photos by Leszek Gardeła.

Plate 4.7. Grave goods from Sanddal: axehead (a–d), sickle (e), weaving sword (f), horse bits (g), wool comb (h), strike-a-light (i). Photos by Leszek Gardeła.

Plate 4.8. Grave goods from Terum: axehead/wood-working tool (a), arrowheads (b), file (c), spindle whorls (d), knife (e), fragmented oval brooch (f), glass beads (g), chain link (dog leash?) (h), shears (i), copper alloy bracelet (j). Photos by Leszek Gardeła.

Plate 4.9. Plan of the Aunvoll grave. Based on an original field drawing by Lars Stenvik (courtesy of the NTNU) and edited by Leszek Gardeła.

Plate 4.10. Grave goods from Aunvoll: shears (a), gaming pieces (b), round stone (c), bead (d), whetstone (e), sickle (f), knife (g), comb (h). Photos by Leszek Gardeła.

Plate 4.11. Weapons from Aunvoll: sword (a–d), spearhead (e–f). Photos by Leszek Gardeła.

Plate 4.12. Plan of the Mårem grave. Based on Engh 2009: 152 and edited by Leszek Gardeła.

Plate 4.13. Selected grave goods from Mårem: oval brooches (a), textile fragments found underneath one of the oval brooches (b), copper alloy container with gold flakes inside (c), round brooch decorated in the Borre style (d), silver ring (e), axehead (f), sickle (g). Photos (b–c), (g) by Leszek Gardeła. Photos (a), (d–f) from the Unimus database.

Plate 4.14. Plan of the Løve grave. Redrawn by Leszek Gardeła after Resi 2013: 118.

Plate 4.15. Plan of the Gerdrup grave. Redrawn by Leszek Gardeła after Christensen 1982: 23.

Plate 4.16. Plan of grave BB from Bogøvej. Redrawn by Leszek Gardeła after Grøn, Hedeager Krag, Bennike 1994: 34.

Plate 4.17. Plan of grave A505 from Trekroner-Grydehøj. Redrawn by Leszek Gardeła after a grave plan kindly supplied by Jens Ulriksen.

Plate 4.18. Plan of the Oens grave. Redrawn by Leszek Gardeła after a grave plan kindly supplied by Charlotta Lindblom.

Plate 5.1. Plan of the Svingesæter grave. Redrawn by Leszek Gardeła after Schetelig 1911: 5.

Plate 5.2. Grave goods from the Svingesæter grave: copper alloy miniature axe (a–c), glass beads (d), oval brooches (e–g) (notice the textile remains on the reverse), key (h), needles (i–j). Photo by Leszek Gardeła.

Plate 5.3. Miniature axe from Svingesæter (a) and its modern replica (b) created by Grzegorz Pilarczyk (Pilar Art). Photos by Leszek Gardeła.

List of tables

Table 1.	List of (possible) female inhumation graves from Viking Age Norway furnished with swords, spearheads, axeheads and arrowheads	143
Table 2.	List of (possible) female cremation graves from Viking Age Norway furnished with arrowheads and shield bosses	145
Table 3.	List of (possible) female inhumation graves from Viking Age Denmark furnished with spearheads and axeheads	146
Table 4.	List of female inhumation graves from Viking Age Sweden furnished with martial equipment	147
Table 5.	List of (possible) female cremation graves from Viking Age Sweden furnished with spearheads, axeheads and arrowheads	147

Acknowledgements

This book is the final outcome of the most challenging and at the same time most rewarding project in my academic career so far. Originally entitled *Amazons of the North: Armed Females in Old Norse Literature and Viking Archaeology*, the project ran in the years 2018–2019 and was generously supported by the German Academic Exchange Service (DAAD P.R.I.M.E.) with funds from the German Federal Ministry of Education and Research (BMBF) and the European Union.[1]

I spent the first year of the project at the Department of Archaeology, History, Cultural Studies and Religion (AHKR) at the University of Bergen where I worked under the mentorship of Professor Sæbjørg Walaker Nordeide, one of the leading Norwegian archaeologists and expert on the Viking Age. From the very beginning of my stay in Bergen, Professor Nordeide's belief in me and my *Amazons* project gave me strength and confidence and guided me towards my goal. I remember always being in awe of her kindness and generosity, beautiful qualities which one does not witness often enough in today's world. The informal talks and seminars with other colleagues at the AHKR also contributed to the quality of my time in Norway and to the eventual shape of this book, and it is therefore my pleasure to give my sincere thanks to Randi Barndon, Heidi Lund Berg, Anne Drageset, Marte Mokkelbost and Joseph Ryder for their great companionship. The image that graces the cover of this book was taken by Rebeca Franco Valle, a talented researcher and artist also from the AHKR, and I am deeply indebted to her for this outstanding work.

The year I spent in Bergen was a profoundly formative period when many things changed for the better in both my professional and private life. The outstandingly supportive and stimulating academic environment at the AHKR contributed immensely to my productivity, while the magnificent Nordic scenery I could see whenever I looked out the window of my cliffside apartment at Skivebakken kept me immersed in the atmosphere necessary to write a book about the Viking Age. These wonderful experiences will always remain in my heart.

After a year in the north, I returned to Germany – the country that soon became my new home – to commence the textual stage of my project at the Department of Scandinavian Languages and Literatures at the University of Bonn. My host was Professor Rudolf Simek, with whom I had collaborated on a range of Viking-related projects before. Working with Professor Simek is always a great privilege and I will forever remain indebted to him for his kindness, enthusiasm and undying support. During my time in Bonn, I also had a number of opportunities to discuss my thoughts and findings pertaining to the *Amazons* project with my German colleagues and I wish to especially acknowledge the kind help and advice I received from my dear friend Matthias S. Toplak. Not only did he read the entire manuscript of this monograph ahead of its official submission but also provided many valuable comments which improved my arguments and the overall quality of the text. Over the last couple of years we have worked on a number of Viking projects and I look forward to many more in the future. I am also indebted to my family and international colleagues who have either read and commented on parts of this work or provided their good advice, support and encouragement: Joonas Ahola, Gunnar Andersson, Maths Bertell, Henrik Brinch Christiansen, Clare Downham, Mads Dengsø Jessen, Matthias Egeler, Ann Kristin Engh, Marianne Hem Eriksen, Frog, Jóhanna Katrín Friðriksdóttir, Igor Górewicz, Daniela Hahn, Wilhelm Heizmann, Dustin Arne Hemmerlein, Charlotte Hedenstierna-Jonson, Judith Jesch, Kamil Kajkowski, Klaudia Karpińska, Tommy Kuusela, Mirosław Kuźma, Carolyne Larrington, Christina Lee, Charlotta Lindblom, Marianne Moen, Luke John Murphy, Simon Nygaard, Peter Pentz, Peter Vang Petersen, Neil S. Price, Ben Raffield, Keith Ruiter, Einar Selvik, Daniel Sävborg, Trine Sørbøen, Barbara Turzańska, Marianne Vedeler, Rolf Warming, Izabella Wenska, Howard Williams, Tomáš Vlasatý, Jakub Zbránek and Jan Zbránek.

I would also like to express my sincere thanks to the whole team at Oxbow Books, especially Julie Gardiner, Felicity Goldsack, Declan Ingram and Jessica Scott for their excellent assistance and support during the process of producing this book.

Since I am one of those archaeologists who likes to take every opportunity to personally see and examine the archaeological finds they write about in their books and articles, I spent a substantial part of the *Amazons* project studying artefact collections in museums in Scandinavia and Germany. I thoroughly enjoyed these experiences and I wish to express my heartfelt gratitude to the curators at the University Museum of Bergen, Museum of Cultural History in Oslo, Archaeological Museum in Stavanger, Norwegian University of Science and Technology/NTNU Vitenskapmuseet in Trondheim, Historical Museum of Northern Jutland, Museum of Southwest Jutland and the Archaeological Museum Schloss Gottorf for making my research stays both pleasant and fruitful. In particular, I wish to acknowledge the kind help of Hanne Lovise Aannestad, Torben Trier Christiansen, Zanette Tsigaridas Glørstad, Torkel Johansen, Terje Masterud Hellan, Volker Hilberg, Brita Hope, Mari Høgestøl, Birgit Maixner, Mette Højmark Søvsø, Morten Søvsø and Melanie Wrigglesworth.

Presenting new discoveries and ideas at seminars and international conferences is a hugely important part of the academic lifestyle. In that regard, the years 2018–2019 were remarkably intensive for me, as I took part in over a dozen scholarly events in Denmark, Germany, Iceland, Norway, Poland, Slovakia, Sweden and Switzerland. I should like to express my thanks to their organisers and participants for the constructive critique and advice they gave me and for reassuring me that the path I decided to take with this project was really worth pursuing.

There have also been other stimulating developments in my professional life arising from the *Amazons of the North* project which have helped me to fulfil my childhood dreams of becoming involved with historical movie production. In 2018, I was invited to present the results of my ongoing academic work in two documentaries focusing on Viking Age women. Originally filmed for the Travel Channel (*Legends of the Lost*) and the Smithsonian Channel (*Viking Warrior Women*), they are now widely available on various media platforms around the world. Although I had previously appeared in traditional and online media, these were actually my first experiences with full-scale TV productions and I owe deep thanks to Lauren Deuterman, Sebastian Peiter and their teams for introducing me to the exciting nuances of professional movie making. In 2019, I was also invited to appear as an expert in a National Geographic documentary on *Viking Warrior Women* and in a special programme for the Swedish Television (SVT) called *Vetenskapens Värld*, both of which provided further opportunities to hone my skills in presenting archaeology to the wider public. In the course of the *Amazons* project I was also interviewed by a number of international newspapers and recorded two podcasts on women and weapons for Medievalists.net and The History of Vikings. My cordial thanks go to Danièle Cybulskie and Noah Tetzner for their friendly and very professional approach. In the meantime – with the expert help of my fiancé Mira Fricke – I also produced a short video portraying my museum-based work in Norway. Mira also accompanied me on several fieldtrips to investigate the dramatically beautiful Viking Age landscapes of Scandinavia. I have very fond memories of all our travels.

Following two years of stimulating but very intensive archaeological endeavours in Norway and Germany, and after an additional year which was necessary to complete the manuscript of this book, I can now breathe a sigh of relief. As I write these words on a cold January morning, one of the most complex projects I have ever commenced is drawing to an end. I feel fortunate to have had the opportunity to follow in the footsteps of the 'Norse Amazons' and I am immensely grateful to all the people and institutions who have helped me along the way – my colleagues at work, my friends outside the remit of professional academia and especially my dearest Mira who gave me all her love and support whenever I was in doubt of my abilities to ever finish this book and when my seasonally reoccurring 'Slavic melancholy' was taking its toll.

The largest debt of gratitude, however, I owe to Professor Sæbjørg Walaker Nordeide who passed away before she could see the final outcome of my work. Without her enthusiasm towards my research and her kind invitation to launch the *Amazons of the North* project at the University of Bergen the trajectory of my current life would have been very different indeed. She will forever remain in my thoughts as an outstanding Mentor, a dear Friend and a genuinely good person. I therefore wish to dedicate this work to her memory.

Leszek Gardeła
January 2021, Berlin

Notes

1   FP7-PEOPLE-2013-COFUND – grant agreement n° 605728.

Chapter 1

Introduction: the methodological and theoretical framework

Over the last several years we have been the hearers and witnesses of a surge of exciting discoveries shedding new light on the lives of Viking Age women. In particular, the 2017 re-interpretation of a richly furnished chamber grave Bj. 581 from Birka in Uppland, Sweden, formerly hailed as the grave of a high-ranking *male* warrior, created quite a commotion in the field of Old Norse and Viking studies: as a result of aDNA analyses, the occupant of the grave was identified as biologically female. Immediately after the release of the first academic paper discussing the implications of this re-assessment – provocatively entitled 'A Female Viking Warrior Confirmed by Genomics' – international media picked up the topic and turned it into a global sensation. While numerous history afficionados enthusiastically welcomed these new results, others began to wonder if the Birka case provided actual proof of the existence of 'Viking warrior women' or if the data had been stretched or even deliberately manipulated to fit a particular agenda or vision of the past. In the context of our current Digital Age it should not come as a surprise that alongside heated debates among non-professional history enthusiasts in social media, the first lengthy academic responses to the new interpretation of Bj. 581 were also published online on private websites and blogs. It soon became clear that members of the international scholarly community were divided in their opinions regarding the identity of the individual from Birka; while some accepted at face value the idea that this person was an active warrior, others remained sceptical and reserved.

This book offers a new approach to the broad theme of women and weapons in the Viking world. However, in exploring the intricacies of female participation in martial activities and in discussing the multifarious circumstances that led human and supernatural women to take up arms, it aspires to be more than a study of medieval female warriors. By adopting an interdisciplinary methodology, involving first-hand investigations of archaeological finds and thorough analyses of textual sources, cross-cultural phenomena and folklore, an argument is proposed that Viking Age women's associations with weapons were remarkably nuanced and extended beyond the spheres of conflict and war. In the following pages we will encounter women who used weapons as potent symbols manifesting inheritance, authority and power, and we will investigate the lives and deeds of ambiguous female characters who used weapons in ritual practices enabling them to invoke fear, transform their appearance and see into the future.

One of the main entryways into these complex topics and pre-Christian worldviews from which they arise is the exploration of mortuary remains; somewhat paradoxically, careful analyses of the burial record allow the most intimate insight into the lives of past individuals, providing us with rich details concerning the deceased themselves and the world(s) they were immersed in. We shall therefore begin this study with a journey into the world of the dead.

Entering the Viking world ... of the dead

There is a general consensus in today's international research on funerary archaeology that graves can provide valuable insights into many aspects of life in the past and that they have the capacity to convey important information not only about the fluid notions of social status, identity, migration, economy, cultural interaction, ritual practice and religious belief, but also about the biological condition of the deceased person and of the wider society they were immersed in.[1] Since a substantial part of the present monograph will deal with finds from Scandinavian funerary contexts, especially from Sweden and Norway, it is essential to begin with an outline of the past and present research trajectories pertaining to this material.

The aforementioned site of Birka on the island of Björko on Lake Mälaren in Uppland, Sweden occupies an iconic place in Viking studies. In the late 1800s, a man of many talents named Hjalmar Stolpe (1841–1905) arrived on Björko to study amber and was immediately drawn to the numerous mounds that dotted its landscape (Fig. 1.1).[2] Intrigued by what they could hold, Stolpe soon began his excavations that led to the discovery of dozens of opulently furnished Viking Age graves. Before long, the island of Björko turned out to be identical with Birka, an important Viking Age

Fig. 1.1. Hjalmar Stolpe (1841–1905). Public domain.

port-of-trade mentioned in several medieval textual sources including Rimbert's *Vita Anskarii* and Adam of Bremen's *Gesta Hammaburgensis Ecclesiae Pontificum*.[3]

In the course of his work, Stolpe introduced innovative methods of excavation and recording. Today, in addition to an impressive collection of finds encompassing literally thousands of objects, the documentation from his work at Birka consists of notebooks, separate notes, sketches and plans. It is worth pointing out that Stolpe was one of the first European archaeologists to use graph paper to record graves and their contents *in situ*.[4] Detailed plans of the Birka burials, showing their internal structure, the position of the human remains and the accompanying artefacts are invaluable sources of information for any studies of Viking Age mortuary practices. One could only wish other sites discovered across Scandinavia in the nineteenth century would be documented to equally high standard.

Although many positive things can be said about Stolpe's excavations at Birka, in approaching his findings today, it is essential to be critically aware of some of the more problematic aspects of his work – aspects that, to a certain extent, may also influence the scholarly perception and interpretation of the contents of the famous chamber grave Bj. 581.

According to surviving records, Stolpe was not always present at the site and recorded some of the Birka finds *after* they had been excavated by his peasant workers, meaning that (due to the workers' lack of professional expertise or 'archaeological awareness') some details of the discovered graves might have been omitted or simply 'lost in translation'. Furthermore, it is now a well-known albeit disturbing fact that in the course of his work at Birka, Stolpe used dynamite, for instance to make his way through the tight stone packaging that covered some of the burial chambers. Notably, this was also the case with Bj. 581; the grave was marked by a stone so large that it was impossible to move it by hand and thus Stolpe had to blow it to pieces.[5] It is unknown whether (or to what extent) this procedure damaged the grave's contents.

As the years went by, scholars working with the Birka material relied heavily on Stolpe's documentation, sometimes adding their own observations or amendments to it. In the 1940s, Swedish archaeologist Holger Arbman (1904–1968) released a two-volume catalogue of the Birka graves excavated by Stolpe, a truly massive publication which still today forms the standard reference work for anyone dealing with the mortuary archaeology of this site (Fig. 1.2).[6] Arbman's catalogue includes numerous grave plans reproduced in black-and-white on the basis of Stolpe's field drawings (many of which were originally made in colour). However, as some scholars have critically noted, 'not all the drawings are accurate reproductions of Stolpe's sketches and they do not necessarily represent the contents of the boxes correctly [*i.e.* boxes with the archaeological finds stored in museum collections today – LG]'.[7] In 2018, Fedir Androshchuk published a critical response to the 2017

Fig. 1.2. Holger Arbman (1904–1968). Public domain.

paper on the re-interpretation of Bj. 581, where he noted a number of divergences that exist between the different plans of this grave.[8] However, these issues were soon clarified in a 2019 study by Neil Price *et al.* who demonstrated convincingly that there are no reasons to doubt the integrity of the grave's contents.[9] We will consider this case in more detail in Chapter 4, but it is important to keep these various nuances in mind.

Since the twentieth century, many Viking Age burial sites have been discovered in Sweden.[10] Interdisciplinary research projects have also led to new observations regarding the structure and extent of the Birka cemeteries and to the re-excavation of some of the graves originally discovered by Stolpe.[11] New insights into the life and death of Sweden's Viking Age population have also been gained as a result of osteological, isotope and genetic analyses.[12] Regional studies, such as the important work of Fredrik Svanberg from 2003, focusing specifically on south-east Scandinavia have certainly helped to embrace and comprehend a substantial body of the available data, at the same time introducing interesting interpretational perspectives.[13] Although these different studies have certainly nuanced our understanding of the diversity and meaning of mortuary practices in this part of Scandinavia, we still have to wait for the publication of a detailed overarching overview of the massive corpus of material stemming from funerary contexts.

As in the case of Sweden also Norwegian Viking Age graves and burial practices began to attract public and academic attention in the nineteenth century.[14] Unsurprisingly, many of the earliest discoveries were made by farmers, landowners and other amateurs who were curious about the contents of old mounds and/or who accidentally came across artefacts and human remains during agricultural work. Regrettably, these amateurs' lack of expertise in handling and recording archaeological remains often resulted in the loss or omission of significant information about the graves' external and internal construction and wider contexts. In the words of Heinrich Härke, 'to European antiquarians of the eighteenth and nineteenth century, the search for prehistoric cremation urns and the excavation of Bronze and Iron Age barrows was primarily a treasure hunt'.[15] Rigorous excavation methodologies started to be employed on a wider scale only in the early twentieth century when archaeology in Norway became a professional academic discipline. This not only led to a substantial increase in the number of artefacts but also to a better understanding of the Viking Age and other historic and prehistoric periods.

Haakon Shetelig (1877–1955) was one of the key catalysts of change in Viking Age archaeology in Norway and his outstanding work quickly received international acclaim (Fig. 1.3). In his foundational book *Vestlandske graver fra jernalderen* released in 1912, Shetelig stated that: 'In Norway we have a rather extraordinary assemblage of burial finds from the three hundred and fifty years covered by the Viking Age, so rich over this relatively short time that in most Norwegian museums it is quantitatively stronger represented than the finds from all previous periods of the Iron Age combined'.[16] Although his main goal was to provide merely an overview of the material, Shetelig set the bar very high for other contemporary scholars working in the field of Viking studies, creating new standards of publishing graves. This was due to the fact that he was not only a prolific writer and a skilled field archaeologist who took part in some of the most iconic excavations and research projects in Norway (*e.g.* Oseberg, Myklebostad, Kvalsund), but also because he was competent in working with museum collections both in his homeland and abroad. Although more than 100 years have passed since the release of *Vestlandske graver i jernalderen*, the book still remains a standard source of reference for anyone researching the Viking Age in Norway.

Despite the substantial size of the find corpus, many of the objects analysed by Shetelig were poorly preserved, fragmented or damaged in other ways – all this, together with the fact that Viking studies were still at a nascent stage, strongly affected his interpretations, sometimes resulting in misleading conclusions. Furthermore, the absence or poor preservation of osteological material from Norwegian Viking Age graves created serious problems in establishing the biological sex of the deceased. Following traditional research paradigms, Shetelig was therefore compelled to consider weapons (swords, shields, axes, spears and arrowheads) as diagnostically 'male' goods, whereas objects of domestic use (*e.g.* spinning and weaving tools as well as other utensils) he considered as items characteristic of women. In so doing, he remained rather inconsistent and somewhat Victorian in his approach. These 'double standards' are

Fig. 1.3. Haakon Shetelig (1877–1955). Public domain.

very clear in his attempt to explain the presence of cooking utensils in both male and female graves: 'The reason can be that cooking utensils were included in male graves just as indispensable commodities, whereas in the case of female graves they represented something that referred to the actual work women were involved in'.[17] The impact such biased interpretations had on the field of Viking studies could be felt very strongly over the next several decades after the release of his foundational book.

At the time of publication Shetelig's monograph was doubtlessly ground-breaking, but other than providing a list and fairly comprehensive descriptions of selected Viking Age graves from Western Norway hardly any attention was devoted to the performative aspects of funerals, the meaning-content of graves (broadly understood) and the symbolism of objects buried with the dead. The same can be said about the work of the aforementioned scholars from Sweden, especially Stolpe and Arbman. The research paradigms they adhered to should not come as a surprise, however, since European archaeology in the early twentieth century was mainly focused on cultural, chronological and typological classification of artefacts and much less attention was devoted to explorations of past identities and symbolism. Next to nothing was therefore said about the phenomenological aspects of burial practices, something that later became a hallmark of post-processual approaches to mortuary remains.[18] Lacking an interdisciplinary angle, Shetelig's book also did not include any specialist analyses of artefacts and paid no attention to the possible correlations between archaeological finds and surviving medieval written accounts (*e.g.* Old Norse, Latin and Arabic texts) and folklore.

Similar interpretative frameworks to those employed by Shetelig and his contemporaries prevailed for a considerably long time in Viking scholarship. Until the late 1980s, all around Scandinavia and Iceland the major academic focus concentrated on portable grave goods and here for the most part on visually attractive objects made of metal, such as weapons and jewellery.[19] Typology, dating and the economic value of objects were considered to be of crucial importance, and there was much less academic concern about the dead as individuals and about the diverse ways in which they had been treated during the funeral. Remarkably little attention was thus devoted to the symbolic meanings of mortuary practices and there were hardly any discussions about the wider spatial and ideological context of individual graves and cemeteries as a whole.[20] Today, in more theoretically driven archaeologies, all these issues have become matters of key importance.

Over the last two decades or so a number of important regional overviews of Viking Age burial traditions have been published, contributing to a more comprehensive and sophisticated understanding of Norse societies and their death-ways. Among others, these include the work of scholars like Silke Eisenschmidt (on chamber graves and other burial traditions in Denmark),[21] Lena Thunmark-Nýlen (on Gotlandic burial customs)[22] and Fredrik Svanberg (on ritual systems in south-east Scandinavia).[23] In 2014, Anne Pedersen published a thorough overview of Danish Viking Age graves with weapons and equestrian equipment, thereby substantially increasing our knowledge not only of warrior culture, but also of the complex processes of state formation in which militarised elites had a crucial part to play.[24] In 2015, the cemeteries and graves of Scandinavian immigrants in Ireland were thoroughly reassessed in the impressive work of Stephen Harrisson and Raghnall Ó Floinn,[25] and similar work was also commenced by Dirk Steinforth with regard to Viking Age mortuary practices on the Isle of Man.[26] In 2014–2020, a series of publications thoroughly reassessing the burial customs of Scandinavian settlers in Central Europe and in the area of present-day Poland was released by Leszek Gardeła, raising international awareness of this largely overlooked part of the Viking world.[27] Theoretically driven discussions on Norse burials were successfully initiated in a series of influential studies by Neil Price, who highlighted the intricate links funerary rituals share with poetry and drew attention to the role of time and motion in these ceremonies.[28] Mnemonic aspects of Norse mortuary customs were emphasised on a number of occasions by Howard Williams who also introduced a very useful concept of 'mortuary/material citations'.[29] Analyses of specific graves and burial practices conducted in the chapters that follow will draw heavily on these new perspectives. With this historiographic background in mind, we can now move on to the important issue of funerary diversity in the Viking world.

Funerary diversity

The people of the Viking Age could pass away as a result of various circumstances – some met their end during travels, expeditions and battles, while others died from sickness, old age or unfortunate accidents. One aspect of Viking Age mortuary practices that is constantly emphasised by today's scholars is their intrinsic diversity – in the words of Neil Price, 'no two burial tableaux are exactly the same'.[30] Nevertheless, despite the immense variability with regard to the external and internal composition of Viking Age graves, extant textual and archaeological sources make it clear that there existed at least two basic ways of dealing with the dead in the Viking world: cremation and inhumation. While the remains of these two customs can be identified archaeologically, it is highly probable that some of the Norse dead were dealt with in other ways which rarely left tangible traces. For instance, whole or cremated bodies could be disposed of in rivers, lakes, wells, bogs or the sea. It is not unlikely that sometimes corpses were left to decompose in the open landscape, too; this may have resulted from various logistical and/or economic difficulties that the mourners experienced or from other circumstances which necessitated the treatment of the dead in a non-normative manner. Such cases are usually difficult or impossible to identify today using archaeological methods, which makes it challenging to assess if and how frequently they occurred in the past.

In discussing the associations between women and weapons in the Viking Age, the present study will draw mainly on archaeological finds from cremations and inhumations. The contents of these particular graves are discussed in Chapters 4 and 5, but in order to better understand their broader context, it is first crucial to outline a bigger picture of cremation and inhumation rituals in ninth- and tenth-century Scandinavia.

Cremation graves

Cremation is a visually spectacular form of dealing with the cadaver. A considerable amount of labour is necessary to prepare and orchestrate such burials.[31] The act of burning the body is often preceded by a series of ritual acts that require the active engagement of mourners (*e.g.* the deceased person's relatives), but also the knowledge and expertise of religious specialists and the help of other people. Drawing on comparative evidence from various cultural milieus around the world, we may surmise that the activities leading up to the culminating act of cremation (and inhumation, too) may include – among other things – washing and clothing the cadaver as well as the recital of prayers and/or the singing of songs.[32] Afterwards, the body is transported to the place of burial, sometimes in a special procession.[33] When the pyre is finally lit, the reduction of the body to ashes can take up to several hours. Medieval textual and archaeological sources suggest that funerals involving cremation were visually dramatic and memorable events.

In the Viking world people of all genders could be subject to cremation. Extant archaeological evidence suggests that bodies were burnt on wooden pyres and/or various other constructions (including vehicles such as wagons, boats and ships) often in the company of portable goods (*e.g.* weapons, jewellery, utensils and vessels) and sometimes together with other living beings (animals, humans).[34] After the burning process, when the fire died down and the bones were reduced to ash, the remains would be collected (perhaps also washed) and buried in the ground, scattered in the open landscape (in fields or forests) or thrown into the water.

The exact details of the handling and treatment of human cremains are not always clear from the archaeological record, but it is possible to make the general observation that bones were commonly deposited loose in earthen pits or in organic or non-organic containers (*e.g.* in vessels made of clay, wood or metal or in textile or leather bags). The pits were often filled with a selection of objects and/or animals that had previously laid on the pyre. It is important to note, however, that not all items found in cremation graves bear traces of fire, meaning that they were subject to other physical and ritual processes than the human bodies.

In Viking Age Scandinavia, the external appearance of cremation graves could take the form of earthen mounds or cairns, sometimes with additional features such as stone settings (in some cases forming elaborate patterns) or posts (Fig. 1.4). Many mounds were relatively small, but some could reach the height of several metres. This 'funerary architecture' might have served as important landmarks and tangible mementoes of the dead, encouraging and facilitating various forms of post-funerary interactions.

Inhumation graves

The rite of inhumation essentially involves burying the body whole, without subjecting it to fire. Among Viking Age Scandinavians, inhumation took many forms and was remarkably varied on both local and supra-local scales.[35] This diversity depended on a wide range of factors such as the wealth of those responsible for the act of burial and/or the deceased person, but also on local customs and beliefs as well as the availability of specific building material. The dead could be placed in simple earthen pits without any container for the body or they could be laid in coffins, chests, boats, wagons and – in some parts of the Viking world – in special underground 'rooms' known as chamber graves. Inside such graves a wide assortment of goods could be placed, ranging from weapons to jewellery, utensils, textiles, vessels and sometimes even animals, either whole or fragmented. The external appearance of inhumation graves could take many forms – they could either be completely flat and unmarked on the surface of the cemetery or covered by earthen mounds or stone cairns (Fig. 1.5). Some graves had external geometrical stone settings (occasionally in the shape of ships of boats), but archaeological excavations in different parts of the Viking world have also revealed the remains of canopies, fences and wooden posts, all erected with some deliberate purpose in mind.

Despite this remarkable diversity of Viking Age cremation and inhumation graves, both on a micro and macro scale, and regardless of the fact that each case is unique in its overall composition and has a different story to tell, it is still possible to trace some recurring patterns and general trends in how the dead were treated upon death. Careful observation of these patterns can inform and sophisticate our interpretations, leading to a better understanding of their underpinning meanings.

Lost identities and elusive grave goods

In attempting to interpret graves from the distant past, we must always remember the old cliché that 'the dead don't bury themselves'[36] and bear in mind that it is always the living who make the final decisions regarding the funeral.[37] Graves, therefore, do not reflect the identities of the deceased in an undistorted way – similar to poems, they are filled with metaphors and allusions the unveiling of which

Fig. 1.4. Viking Age cemetery at Lindholm Høje, Jylland, Denmark. Photo by Leszek Gardeła.

Fig. 1.5. Viking Age cemetery at Hringsdalur, Iceland. Photo by Leszek Gardeła.

requires considerable caution and an interdisciplinary set of skills.³⁸

Although commonly accepted today, such approaches to funerary remains were unheard of in the nineteenth and early twentieth centuries when all across Europe archaeology started to be acknowledged as a fully-fledged academic discipline. As emphasised above, at that point in time prehistoric and medieval graves were usually seen in a very straightforward way – with their main focus on artefacts, most archaeologists were convinced that graves and grave goods accompanying the dead mirrored the social identities, roles, professions, cultural affiliations and religious beliefs of the buried people.³⁹ It was often the case in Scandinavian archaeology that when a male grave with military equipment was found, this person would be immediately considered a 'warrior' and the weapons would be typically regarded as his prized possessions as well as markers of social status, prestige and prowess in battle.⁴⁰ In the same vein, female graves with opulent furnishings were seen as belonging to women of very high social standing, for example princesses, queens and/or religious leaders.⁴¹ Similar views, although still endorsed by some scholars in Scandinavia and elsewhere in Europe, have been subject to strong criticism from numerous international researchers, especially Heinrich Härke⁴² and Howard Williams.⁴³ Drawing on sociological and anthropological inspirations, Härke in particular has made a significant contribution to the studies of the messages and meanings conveyed by graves and grave goods in the Early Middle Ages – the theoretical and methodological underpinnings of his work have also strongly influenced the analyses conducted in the following chapters of the present study concerning female graves with weapons.

In one of his recent articles, Härke has explicitly admitted that 'the interpretation of artefacts found in prehistoric and early historical grave contexts is anything but straightforward'.⁴⁴ He has also highlighted the fact that – due to unfavourable soil conditions and poor preservation of organic remains – modern reconstructions of and inferences about early medieval graves tend to be based predominantly on objects made of durable materials, especially ferrous and non-ferrous metals. These limitations are necessary to bear in mind also in the context of the main topic of the present study, since many of the allegedly female graves that will be subject to scrutiny in the following chapters do not contain *any* organic remains.

With a critical awareness of the above problems, and following Härke's observations, we shall now review and discuss some of the most common interpretations of grave goods employed by archaeologists working on early medieval burial customs. This will serve to illustrate the multivalence and multidimensionality of material culture from mortuary contexts – aspects that are of crucial importance in approaching female graves with weapons.

***

As Härke notes, the oldest archaeological interpretation of grave goods is as 'equipment for the hereafter'. In this perspective, objects buried with the dead were intended to be used by them in the otherworld and/or on the journey that led there.⁴⁵ There is strong textual, ethnographic and archaeological support for this idea in China but also in some parts of the early medieval world, including Anglo-Saxon England and Scandinavia. However, as Härke interestingly points out:

> A problem for archaeologists is that even where objects are thought to be required in the hereafter, they would not always be deposited in the grave. For example, the Lober of Ghana do not bury weapons of the dead with their former owners; they display them during the funeral, assuming that this makes them available in the hereafter.⁴⁶

It is not unlikely that also in the Viking world certain types of items were placed in graves so that the deceased could use them in the hereafter. Many scholars have argued that such may have been the role of wagons, boats and ships in cremation and inhumation burials.⁴⁷ There is no way to be certain, however, if other items with the same symbolic purpose were displayed during the funeral but eventually never made their way into the grave. Based on the famous account of the Arab traveller Ibn Fadlān, who witnessed a spectacular funeral of a Rus noble at the Volga, we can surmise that some of the Norse dead (at least those stemming from the elite) were laid to rest only with a selection of their possessions: one third of their belongings was donated to the family, one third was used to cover the costs of production of funerary garments and one third was spent on alcohol to be used during the burial ceremony.⁴⁸ It remains obscure whether any or all of these redistributed goods were displayed during the funeral or used in some other ritualistic manner in the course of the accompanying ceremonies.

Referring to Germanic law, some scholars have suggested that grave goods could represent 'inalienable property' of the dead.⁴⁹ In Härke's view, however, this idea can be misleading when dealing with early medieval burials, since certain types of objects may have been passed down for generations, thereby becoming 'collective possessions'. Excavations have shown that practices involving the deliberate reopening of graves and manipulations of their contents were commonplace across the Viking world.⁵⁰ Written sources, such as the Old Norse sagas and eddic poetry, provide further hints as to the possible symbolic underpinnings of these practices, vividly describing ritualised acts of (re)entering graves to acquire heirlooms (especially weapons) regarded as potent symbols of inheritance. In the following chapters of this book we shall look more closely at one such case from *Hervarar saga ok Heiðreks konungs* where a cross-dresser named Hervör acquires the sword of their deceased father from his mound.

The *potlatch* phenomenon, where 'the ostentatious destruction of accumulated wealth confers prestige and influence', is another idea some scholars refer to when trying to unravel the meaning of grave goods.[51] The deposition of objects in funerary contexts is thus seen as a form of competition, whereby the objects are intended to display active claims to social position and identity.

Aside from subscribing to the ideas of grave goods as 'equipment for the hereafter', 'inalienable property of the dead' and 'potlatch', many archaeologists tend to perceive grave goods as 'indicators of rank, status, and identity'.[52] In this perspective, the quantity and quality of objects accompanying the dead, as well as the overall splendour of the funeral are supposed to reflect the individual's position in the society. By analogy, ritual acts and material culture accompanying modern funerals of military officers, prominent politicians and members of royal families are likewise intended to display – and in some cases even exaggerate and/or fabricate – these individuals' social importance.

Another idea is that grave goods serve as metaphors for specific bygone events or to give an overall impression of the person's life. For instance, foreign objects discovered in graves 'may be meant to express a distant origin, real or imagined'.[53] Closely connected to the concept of grave goods as metaphors is also the idea that objects acquire their own biographies by association with people.[54] Therefore, as Härke sees it, 'the deposition of such items in a grave would link two biographies, the object's and the deceased's, and give the latter additional status'.[55] In the early medieval context, swords in particular might have served such a role,[56] and we will discuss this and other related themes more comprehensively in Chapter 5.

Grave goods can also be perceived as gifts, either to the deceased or to the deities, for instance those that have some role in facilitating the journey to the otherworld.[57] In the early medieval world, coins found in graves are sometimes interpreted (not necessarily correctly) as payment for the safe passage to the other side, echoing the ancient idea of Charon's Penny.[58]

Items discovered in inhumation and cremation graves, especially vessels for food and drink as well as various cooking utensils, can also be plausibly interpreted as the remains of or allusions to the funeral feast.[59] Animals in funerary contexts can likewise be seen in this light, although archaeologists are often tempted to perceive them as sacrifices, especially when the remains belong to large mammals like horses or cattle.[60]

It is noteworthy that in some societies, objects tend to be buried with the dead with the intention to avoid 'pollution' or potential damage they could cause. While such concepts are fairly common in Africa (especially in connection with items used by people dealing with witchcraft), it remains uncertain whether or to what extent they could be applied to explain aspects of burial practices in the Viking world. Perhaps some iron staffs, found in female graves and interpreted as implements used in *seiðr* magic, could be perceived as 'polluted' objects, especially if they are found bent, broken or covered with stones.[61] This is only a tentative hypothesis, however, since the deliberate destruction of staffs could simply reflect the desire to render them useless for potential robbers. Alternatively, the acts of 'killing' and/or 'transforming' these objects could make them 'available' for the deceased in the afterlife (if the afterlife is seen as a place where everything is 'inverted'). Closely related to the concept of pollution is also the custom of placing apotropaics in graves, for instance to ensure the dead would not return to haunt the living. This may have been the role of stones or boulders laid directly over the bodies as noted in some cemeteries in Scandinavia, Anglo-Saxon England and elsewhere in Europe.[62]

Härke also argues that some objects may be placed in graves because otherwise they would remind the living of the deceased.[63] Their deposition is thus seen as an act of forgetting that helps to sever the ties between the living and the dead.

Overall, Härke strongly discourages scholars from trying to perceive grave goods only in light of one of the ideas discussed above and emphasises that categories like 'equipment for the hereafter', 'inalienable property' etc. serve purely for analytical purposes and should not be regarded as strictly separate: even within one burial assemblage various objects could signal various meanings.[64] These 'mixed messages', as Härke calls them, are particularly vivid in the case of elite graves, but it is not unlikely that the same composite meanings were attributed to goods deposited in less opulent burial contexts (Fig. 1.6).

In approaching the issues discussed above, we should be wary that 'the same practice can mean different things in different periods and places',[65] and thus it is necessary to always pay close attention to the historical, social and geographical context. Bearing in mind all of the above, Härke concludes his discussion on the meaning of grave goods in these words:

> The surest means of identifying motives for the deposition of grave goods are textual sources from the respective period. Where these are lacking [...], the best approach is a careful contextual analysis of all correlations: what was deposited, when, where, with what, with whom and how does it vary across geographical regions and chronological periods? The emerging patterns may then be used to suggest interpretations of grave goods, but such inferences are only ever likely to apply to a particular society, or even community, at a particular point in time. Whatever their background in specific cases, grave goods were not simply intended to help the dead on their journey to the hereafter and in the afterlife [...], nor are they mirrors of life in the past.[66]

Härke's observations on the multivalent nature of early medieval burial practices have strong implications for the studies of what archaeologists tend to call 'weapon burial' (essentially any grave containing military equipment)[67] – a mortuary phenomenon that lies at the core of the present

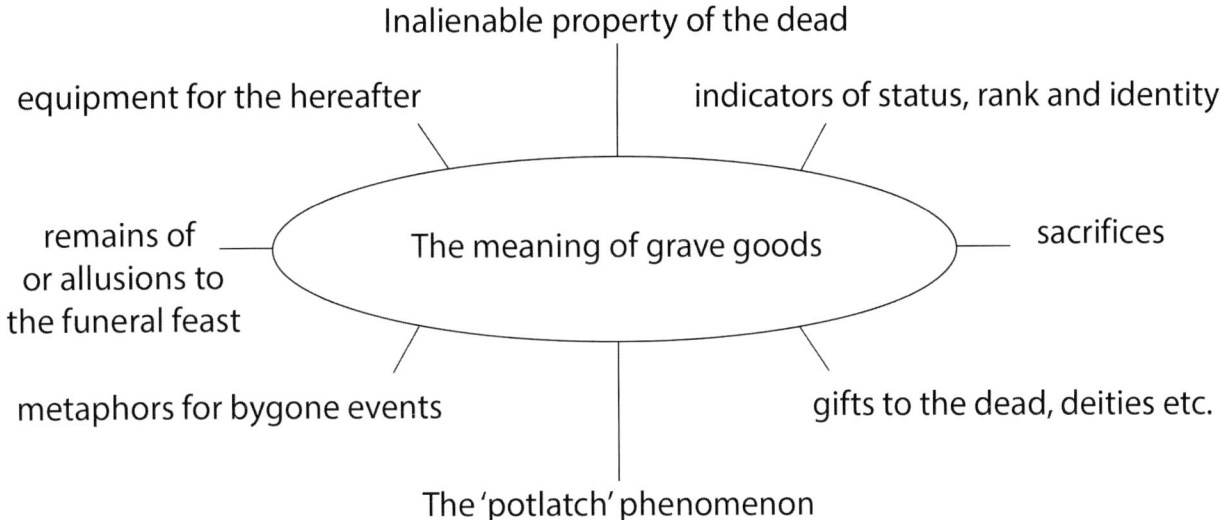

Fig. 1.6. Grave goods and their 'mixed messages' according to Heinrich Härke. Image by Leszek Gardeła.

book and one that Härke himself has explored in the 1990s in a series of influential studies.[68]

After a thorough analysis of the weapon burial rite in Anglo-Saxon England, Härke arrived at the conclusion that weapons in early medieval graves (regardless of the biological sex of the dead) *cannot* be regarded exclusively as indicators of status and warrior identity of the deceased. His view is motivated by the observation that weapons in funerary contexts are not found exclusively with adults but also with children and other people who would have been unable to effectively use them in combat. Härke's ideas are commonly known in Anglophone scholarly milieus, but they are not always thoughtfully considered in international scholarship pertaining to Viking Age Northern Europe.[69] Similarly to Anglo-Saxon England, also in Scandinavia and Iceland weapons are buried in a wide plethora of ways (as regards their specific position and relation to the deceased and other grave-contents) and with people representing various age and gender groups. These cases strongly indicate that – regardless of the biological sex and socially constructed gender of the dead – weapons *cannot* always be seen in the same way and as indicators of active warriors. It is with these ideas and caveats in mind this book shall approach the broader topic of women and weapons in the Viking Age.

Warriors and warrior ideals

The term 'warrior' has already appeared a number of times in the preceding pages. It is also commonly employed in numerous other studies pertaining to the Viking Age. This should not come as a surprise, since it is difficult or perhaps even impossible to discuss this turbulent and pivotal period in history without referring to warfare. And yet, although the term 'warrior' can be encountered so frequently in archaeological studies (especially when talking about graves furnished with weapons), scholars rarely see the need to define what they actually mean when they use it. The significance of the term 'warrior', therefore, is often implied, but not explained directly.

In Viking Age Scandinavia only free people could legally carry weapons (Fig. 1.7). These individuals had the capacity to use them for their own private needs or for the greater purposes of a group or warband they were part of. In the late ninth and tenth centuries and in the period of state formation, more specialised warrior groups started to emerge. Closely bound to a prominent leader, they often had access to high quality military and equestrian equipment which served as material markers of their distinct identity.[70] In the course of time, these groups developed into what in today's parlance we would call 'national armies'.[71] Medieval textual sources preserve traces of specific vocabulary pertaining to warriors.[72] In Old Norse tradition, terms like *drengr*, *bróðir* and *félagi* are often used to indicate warrior status and membership in a group of people engaged in warfare.[73] We can encounter these names in the sagas but also in runic inscriptions commemorating people who fought and fell in armed clashes and large-scale battles in the Viking world.

In a recent thought-provoking article devoted to warriors, warrior ideals and 'weapon graves', Kerstin Odebäck sees and defines Viking Age 'warriors' contextually, as people associated with life in strongholds and urban milieus who use weapons and share similar worldviews.[74] However, her basic definition of a 'warrior' is 'a person who actively participates in conflict or has actively taken part in conflict'. A 'warrior ideal', on the other hand, is something 'spiritual, intangible, desirable and exemplary'.[75] As Odebäck argues, in the specific cultural context of the Viking world, this ideal was conveyed through stories and myths and also 'performed'

Fig. 1.7. A Viking Age warrior as interpreted by re-enactor Jakub Zbránek. Photo by Jan Zbránek. Courtesy of Marobud re-enactment group.

on a variety of occasions, including funerals and other ritual practices. Like Härke, she is cautious in immediately equating people buried in weapon graves with warriors (in the strict sense of the word) and emphasises the dynamic and transformative aspects of funerary practices. Very much in the vein of previous arguments proposed by Härke pertaining to Anglo-Saxon funerary practices, she believes that in Scandinavian Viking Age graves the deposition of military equipment was not always intended to materialise *warrior identities* but rather *warrior ideals*. The latter concepts can be variously understood by people orchestrating the burial. For instance, in addition to having connotations with the sphere of religion, they might reflect the deceased person's and/or the mourners' ideas of themselves and/or (sometimes unfulfilled) aspirations, including claims to power. In other words, weapons in graves are *not just* or *not only* weapons – they can also allude to other things and ideas, too. Odebäck exemplifies this claim by drawing attention to the use of shields in Viking Age cremations and inhumations, where they are subject to a variety of ritual acts that transform them and give them (and their contexts) new meanings.[76] For instance, in some graves shield bosses are employed as 'receptacles' for bone remains, arrowheads, knives, elements of riding equipment and other goods, thereby resembling vessels made of metal and clay. In view of her studies of the weapon burial rite in Viking Age Scandinavia, Odebäck – similarly to Härke, Williams and other scholars – is hesitant to consider weapons in graves as markers of a warrior identity of the deceased but rather sees them as potential references to all kinds of *ideas* associated with the warrior ideal.

In approaching the issue of warrior identity *versus* warrior ideal in mortuary archaeology, it is therefore critically important to always situate the studied material in context. This again echoes Härke's call for the necessity to each time ask 'what was deposited, when, where, with what, with whom and how does it vary across geographical regions and chronological periods?'[77] Similar contextual and conceptual approach to the warrior idea can be seen in one of the core articles on the Bj. 581 grave from Birka. Therein, Price *et al.* argue that in the Viking Age:

> To be a warrior was, at least in part, a social construct, and not necessarily directly connected to entering actual combat. If such a thing applied to the person in Bj. 581, we do not know exactly how this operated, and it is possible that we are just seeing the high-end 'straight-to-Valhöll' option from the Birka funeral directors, but it would have made this individual a warrior nonetheless.[78]

In their paper, Price *et al.* emphasise that in dealing with individuals such as the person buried in grave Bj. 581, it is essential to avoid generalisations and to 'question our assumptions and categories. What constitutes a weapon or a warrior, and how might we tell? What links do we make between buried individuals and the items accompanying them?',[79] they ask. These are all important and valid questions, especially in relation to the studies conducted in this monograph.

So how can we (and can we at all?) define the term 'warrior' for the purposes of the present study and in the specific historical setting of the Viking Age? Is a warrior any person who uses weapons to defend themselves and/or attack others? Or does the status of a warrior apply only to those who undergo specific military training, who are sworn to a leader and who regularly go on expeditions? Is there an age limit that defines when one can and cannot become a warrior, and are there any gender restrictions as to who can and cannot enter the war path? It would be much easier to provide answers to these questions if we were discussing modern societies, especially those that have strictly defined laws pertaining to military affairs. In the case of the Viking Age that occupies us here, these issues are not so straightforward.

Extant textual sources such as the Old Norse sagas and other medieval accounts written in Latin and Arabic, although abounding with references to weapons and warriors, do not really provide a clear answer as to what it meant to be a warrior in the Viking Age. If we were to rely on the specific vocabulary – such as the aforementioned terms *drengr*, *bróðir* and *félagi* – and the contexts in which it is used, we could say to be a warrior is to actively take part in combat. But how did one become a warrior? And was this path open for anyone, regardless of their age and gender?

Jómsvíkinga saga,[80] a textual source from the thirteenth century which creatively combines literary imagination and supernatural characters with actual historical figures and events, may potentially provide a glimpse of the rules and ideals that members of a Viking warband had to subscribe to. The saga preserves the laws of the Jómsvikings – warriors who lived somewhere on the southern coast of the Baltic, possibly in the area of present-day Poland – which define who could become part of their group. According to these laws, no one who was under eighteen and over fifty years old could join the warband. Its members could never flee from their enemies and they were obliged under oath to avenge the death of their companions. By law, nobody could speak words of fear or be afraid. Stirring up strife was strictly forbidden as well as spreading any news without first informing the leader of the group. All goods acquired as a result of raiding were to be carried to the banner. Nepotism was also forbidden.

In the context of the main theme of the present study, it is worthy of note that women were explicitly forbidden to stay in Jómsborg, the famous fortress of the Jómsvikings. While it is difficult to determine whether (or to what extent) these rules reflect the ideals of actual warriors of the Viking Age or whether they are merely a literary creation of the composer of the saga, they do provide a point of reference as to how the warrior ideal was understood or imagined in the Norse intellectual milieus of the thirteenth century.

It is interesting to note that although the law of Jómsborg explicitly forbids men under the age of eighteen to join the warband, other Old Norse texts – such as the *Íslendingasögur* and *fornaldarsögur* (sagas of Icelanders and legendary sagas) – mention *much* younger individuals (both male and female) who reach for weapons and even participate in killings.[81] Together with the fact that military equipment is occasionally found in graves of adolescents and alongside the fact that objects interpreted as children's toys found in Scandinavia and elsewhere in Viking Age Europe often allude to aspects of warfare (*e.g.* wooden swords, boats etc.),[82] it is clear that – willingly or not – infants and juvenile individuals would have been exposed to warrior lifestyles or at least to ideas, stories and myths about them. The immersion of children in this specific cultural and ideological context may have spurred some of them to pursue the life of active warriors, even from a very young age. We do not know for sure if there existed any specific 'rites of passage' that facilitated a transformation into a Viking warrior. One account that could shed some light on our speculations is the aforementioned *Jómsvíkinga saga* (ch. 22–23), where a twelve-year-old boy named Vagn is initially refused admission to the warband (on the grounds of his age), but then proves his worth by winning a battle contest and is eventually officially admitted to the group.

In view of the above, when discussing the manifold identities of Viking Age individuals, this book will refrain from providing one rigid definition of the term 'warrior'. The term 'warrior' will thus not be seen as exclusive to people who actively participated in armed conflict and/or representatives of specific age or gender groups. Instead, it will be seen as something fluid and relying on the specificities of a particular social, historical and geographical context.

Sex and gender in the Viking Age

In discussing the associations between women and weapons in the Viking world, it is critical to address Norse approaches to sex and gender. These themes can be investigated based on a range of sources including archaeological finds and extant texts such as eddic poetry, sagas and other medieval accounts written in Latin and Arabic but also by referring to modern theoretical approaches.

On a very basic level, in sociological and anthropological studies sex tends to be understood as a biological essence, whereas gender is perceived as a social category.[83] It is often argued that the latter has a performative character and can be subject to change. Ethnographic research shows, however, that the boundaries between sex and gender, at least in some societies, could actually be blurred and that some cultures do not subscribe to the binary division into male and female individuals.[84]

Based on extant sources concerning the Viking Age, it is possible to surmise that Norse societies comprised individuals who were essentially characterised as either male or female. These categories were not always static, however, and Norse women and men could on occasion be regarded by their contemporaries as either 'masculine' or 'effeminate' respectively, especially if they performed acts characteristic of the opposite sex and/or displayed traits that breached the conventional norms. Old Norse texts imply that when men or women dressed or behaved in a subversive way this would lead to serious consequences, involving social ostracism or other acts of punishment. At the same time, however, it appears that in the case of some people subversive behaviour (*e.g.* wearing clothes characteristic of the opposite sex or performing acts of magic which brought associations with sexual deviance) was sanctioned by the special role these individuals played in their society; in particular this appears to have been the case of some ritual specialists (especially those dealing with *seiðr* magic) and members of the highest echelons of the social elite. According to Old Norse texts, people who for various reasons committed acts of sexual transgression or behaved in a subversive way were labelled as *blauðr*, *argr* and *ergi*, with the two latter terms bearing negative connotations of sexual perversion.[85]

As David Clark and Jóhanna Katrín Friðriksdóttir argue with regard to representations of male and female characters in the Old Norse textual corpus: 'women and men are not, on the whole, represented as diametrically opposed to one another'.[86] They further add that 'the role of women in sagas of various genres is important: female characters are often explicitly valued for wisdom, sound counsel, and support, in both private matters and public' and they make the important observation that 'often, we see female characters behaving just as "badly" – cunningly, deceitfully – as male ones, refusing to accept their family duty and the wishes of their male kin, or subverting the traditional, passive gender roles they are accepted to fulfil'.[87] These important issues, as well as the scholarly perceptions of different female roles and incarnations, will be discussed more thoroughly in the next two chapters of this monograph.

Amazons of the North: the scope of the book

The term 'Amazons' used in the title of this book echoes the semi-legendary warrior women who roamed the Black Sea area in the early Iron Age. The classic description of these women's lifestyles – apparently in their own words which they uttered in a conversation with Scythian men – is provided by the ancient Greek historian Herodotus who lived in the fifth century BC:

> We would find it impossible to live with your [*i.e.* Scythian] women, because our practices are completely different than theirs. We haven't learnt women's work. We shoot arrows, wield javelins, ride horses – things which your women never have anything to do with. They just stay in their wagons and

do women's work; they never go hunting or anywhere else either. We would find it impossible to get along with them.[88]

Further in his work, Herodotus speaks of these women's marriage customs, observing that 'no young woman may marry until she has killed a male enemy. Inability to fulfil this condition means that some of them die of old age without being married'.[89] He also remarks that the Amazons wear the same clothes as men do.[90]

In a recent and probably most thorough scholarly exploration of these warrior women's lives entitled *The Amazons: Lives and Legends of Warrior Women Across the Ancient World*, Adrianne Mayor has defined three categories of 'Amazons' that emerge from the contexts of history, Greek myths and non-Greek settings.[91] They include:

- Real nomadic horsewomen archers of the steppes
- Amazon queens Hypolite, Antiope and Penthesilea and other Amazons of classical mythology
- Women warriors in non-Greek traditions from the Black Sea to China

In the case of the Viking world, we can also encounter examples of female warriors or weapon wielding women (real or imagined) in three different, although not necessarily mutually exclusive, categories of material:

- Texts concerning 'real' human figures and 'supernatural' female characters wielding weapons
- Archaeological discoveries of female graves with military equipment
- Iconographic sources portraying armed female figures

This monograph aspires to extract various portrayals of armed women from these diverse categories of textual, archaeological and iconographic sources. In critically weaving them together, an attempt will be made to reveal how the idea of the warrior woman was understood, conceptualised and verbally and visually expressed and performed in the Norse cultural sphere. Having now discussed the methodological and theoretical framework adopted for the present study, we are armed with the necessary apparatus to venture deeper into the topic of women and weapons in the Viking world. In order to situate the ensuing debate in an adequate historiographic context, Chapter 2 will provide a critical overview of past and present research of women's lives and roles in the Viking Age, commenting on the various trajectories these studies have taken over the course of the last one hundred years. This chapter is also intended to demonstrate that Viking scholarship does not function in a vacuum and that certain research themes and trends tend to reflect, consciously or not, wider changes occurring in modern societies. Since most of the current discussions surrounding the topic of women and weapons (or women warriors specifically) in the Viking Age draw from Old Norse and other medieval literature, Chapter 3 will provide a thorough analysis of Old Norse textual sources that depict weapon-wielding women. These captivating female figures belong both to the human and supernatural world and – as we shall see – their motivations to reach for weapons vary considerably. In order to provide a wider cross-cultural context for the core debate, the accounts of their lives and deeds will be compared to and contrasted with stories recorded in several non-Norse sources. Chapter 4 is an investigation of the complete corpus of Viking Age female graves furnished with weapons, with an especial focus on their contexts and morpho-metric features of their contents. Building on this material, Chapter 5 considers the various symbolic or metaphorical meanings weapons may have played in Viking Age funerary practices. Since the idea of the armed woman is seen not only in Old Norse texts and burial contexts but also in iconography, Chapter 6 offers an analysis of a broad range of figural representations of weapon-bearing figurines found across Scandinavia and the wider Viking world; in particular, it aims to discuss their different types and distribution and to explore their possible links to Old Norse texts and burial evidence. Chapter 7 serves as a window into the much broader world of female warriors, tracing women's roles in martial activities since deep prehistory until the present day. Using selected case studies from different time periods, it also investigates a wide plethora of circumstances that have motivated female individuals to enter the war path. The final chapter brings all these different strands of textual and material evidence together to offer a new perspective on women and weapons in the Viking world.

Notes

1. For recent discussions on the broadly understood archaeology of death and burial, see Arnold & Wicker 2001; Parker Pearson 2003; Nilsson Stutz & Tarlow 2013. On public engagements with funerary archaeology, see also Williams & Giles 2016; Williams *et al.* 2019.
2. On Hjalmar Stolpe's rich biography and work at Birka, see Eriksson 2015.
3. Tschan 2002.
4. Jensen 2018: 176–179; Price *et al.* 2019: 183.
5. Price *et al.* 2019.
6. Arbman 1940; 1943.
7. Androshchuk 2018: 48.
8. Androshchuk 2018.
9. Price *et al.* 2019.
10. See, for example, Thunmark-Nylén 1998–2006; Carlsson 1999; Andersson 2005b; Artelius 2005; Rundkvist & Williams 2008 with further references.
11. See, for example, Andersson *et al.* 2015.
12. Kjellström 2012; 2016; Hedenstierna-Jonson & Kjellström 2014; Ahlström Arcini 2018; Price *et al.* 2018.
13. Svanberg 2003.
14. See, for example, Rygh 1885; Schetelig 1905.
15. Härke 2014: 41.

16 Shetelig 1912: 173: 'Vi har i Norge et ganske overordentlig rikt materiale av gravfund fra halvtredje hundre aar som vikingetiden omfatter, saa rikt at denne forholdsvis korte tid i de fleste norske museer er kvantitativt sterkere representert end alle forutgaaende perioder av jernalderen tilsammen'.
17 Shetelig 1912: 175: 'Grunden kan tænkes at være den at kjøkkentoiet for manden er kommet med i graven bare som en uundværlig nodvendighetsartikel, for kvinden derimot som noget der horte med til hendes helt personlige virke'.
18 See, for example, Tilley 1994; Williams 2006; Nordeide 2011; Nordeide & Brink 2013 with further references.
19 See, for example, Petersen 1919; 1928; Brøndsted 1936; Arbman 1940; 1943; Ramskou 1950; Thorvildsen 1957; Gräslund 1980; Kristján Eldjárn & Adolf Friðriksson 2000.
20 Cf. Gräslund 1980.
21 Eisenschmidt 1994; 2004. See also Arents & Eisenschmidt 2010a; 2010b.
22 Thunmark-Nylén 1998–2006.
23 Svanberg 2003.
24 Pedersen 2014a.
25 Harrison & Ó'Floinn 2015.
26 Steinforth 2015a; 2015b.
27 Gardeła 2014a; 2015b; 2016c; 2019a; 2020b.
28 Price 2002; 2008a; 2010b; 2012b; 2014; 2019.
29 Williams 2016.
30 Price 2012a: 82.
31 On cremations in the past, see Thompson 2015; Cerezo-Román et al. 2017 with further references.
32 See, for example, Williams 2006; Gardeła 2020c.
33 On processions in the Viking Age, see Nygaard & Murphy 2017. On time and motion in Viking Age funerary practices, see Price 2014 with further references.
34 For overviews of cremation graves in the Viking Age, see Ramskou 1950; Holck 1986; Svanberg 2003; Price 2008b with further references.
35 For overviews of Viking Age inhumation graves, see Brøndsted 1936; Sellevold et al. 1984; Eisenschmidt 1994; Kristján Eldjárn & Adolf Friðriksson 2000; Svanberg 2003; Price 2008b; Pedersen 2014a with further references.
36 Jordan 2009: 99.
37 E.g. Härke 1990; 1992a; 2014; Williams 2003; 2006; Sayer & Williams 2009.
38 E.g. Carver 1998; Price 2010b.
39 E.g. Nicolaysen 1882; Rygh 1885; Mørck 1901; Shetelig 1912. For an overview of these trends in European early medieval archaeology, see Härke 2014.
40 E.g. Nicolaysen 1882; Grieg 1947.
41 E.g. Brøgger et al. 1917a; 1917b; Brøgger & Shetelig 1927; 1928; Christensen et al. 1992. See also Nordström 2006.
42 See, for example, Härke 1990; 1992a; 2014.
43 See, for example, Williams 2006.
44 Härke 2014: 44.
45 Härke 2014: 45.
46 Härke 2014: 45.
47 See, for example, Müller-Wille 1969; 1985; Aannestad & Glørstad 2017 with further references.
48 Montgomery 2000; Mackintosh-Smith & Montgomery 2014.

49 Härke 2014: 45–46. On problems with the concept of 'inalienable property', especially with regard to early medieval graves, see also Kars 2013.
50 On grave reopening and interactions with the dead in Old Norse literature and Viking archaeology, see, for example, Beck 1978; Gjerpe 2005a; 2007; Soma 2007; Bill & Daly 2012; Hofmann 2015; Gardeła 2016a; Klevnäs 2016; Wenn 2020 with further references.
51 Härke 2014: 46.
52 Härke 2014: 47.
53 Härke 2014: 48.
54 On biographies of things and the idea of personhood, see Kopytoff 1986; Fowler 2004; Hodder 2012 with further references.
55 Härke 2014: 49.
56 On the concepts of sword biography and personhood, see especially the work of Brunning 2019.
57 Härke 2014: 49–50.
58 Suchodolski 2015.
59 Härke 2014: 50.
60 See, for example, Müller-Wille 1972; Gräslund 2004; Weigand 2008; Jennbert 2011; Karpińska 2018; Toplak 2019a with further references.
61 For a more detailed discussion of this idea, see Gardeła 2016b.
62 Reynolds 2009; Gardeła 2013a; 2017b.
63 Härke 2014: 52.
64 Härke 2014: 52–53.
65 Härke 2014: 54.
66 Härke 2014: 54
67 Odebäck 2018.
68 Härke 1990; 1992b; 1997.
69 Although see Pedersen 2014a: 240; Odebäck 2018: 65.
70 See, for example, Randsborg 1980; Pedersen 2014a; Raffield et al. 2016 with further references.
71 Halpin 2008: 11.
72 For a discussion of warrior-related nomenclature in medieval Western and Central Europe, see Bogacki 2007; Halpin 2008: 11–12.
73 On the term *drengr* see, for example, Jesch 2009: 73; Odebäck 2018: 67.
74 Odebäck 2018: 66.
75 'Begreppet krigare definieras har som en person som aktivt deltar i krig eller har erfarenhet av aktivt deltagande i krig. Ideal definieras som något andligt, immateriellt, önskvärt och förebildligt. "Krigare" kan därmed betraktas som praktik och "krigarideal" som symbolik'. Odebäck 2018: 66.
76 Odebäck 2018: 71–74.
77 Härke 2014: 54.
78 Price et al. 2019: 192.
79 Price et al. 2019: 194.
80 For various translations and editions of *Jómsvíkinga saga*, see Blake 1962; Hollander 2000; Finlay & Þórdís Edda Jóhannesdóttir 2018.
81 For instance, according to *Jómsvíkinga saga* (21) a boy named Vagn Ákason killed three men when he was nine years old. Later on he participated in plundering expeditions and raided the shores (*Jómsvíkinga saga*, 22), activities which provided

him with weapons, armour and other provisions. Eventually, he joined the famous band of the *Jómsvíkingar* (Jómsvikings).

82 On Viking Age toys, especially those that resemble weapons, see Gardeła 2012a; Raffield 2019.
83 Sørensen 2004.
84 See, for example, Price 2002; 2019.
85 On the concepts of *nið* and *ergi*, see Ström 1973; 1974; Solli 1999b; Blain & Wallis 2000; Price 2002: 210–223 with further references.
86 Clark & Jóhanna Katrín Friðriksdóttir 2016: 336.
87 Clark & Jóhanna Katrín Friðriksdóttir 2016: 336.
88 Herodotus, Book 4.114. Translation after Waterfield 1998: 272.
89 Herodotus, Book 4.117. Translation after Waterfield 1998: 273.
90 Herodotus, Book 4.116.
91 Mayor 2014: 31.

Chapter 2

Historiography

The history of the Viking Age would be incomplete without women, and yet, at least until the mid-1980s, women were marginalised in academic studies of Old Norse literature and Viking archaeology. In approaching the main theme of this book and in investigating the intricate associations between women and weapons, it therefore feels appropriate to provide an overview of the rapidly developing interdisciplinary field of research pertaining to female lifeways in the North. This endeavour will not only serve a purely historiographic purpose but will also illuminate the historical, socio-political and other circumstances that have inspired past and present research trajectories.

Researching women in the Viking Age

A terrifying horde of bearded warriors disembarking their long-ships to explore, pillage and burn is an image that often springs to mind when thinking about the Vikings. Although the perception of the Viking world has undergone significant transformations since the National Romantic period (a time when Viking history became a strong component of national identity in Scandinavia and Iceland as well as an important point of reference in other European countries),[1] some people today still hold the opinion that the period between the eighth and eleventh centuries AD, commonly known as the Viking Age, *belonged* to men, and that women were merely passive and silent companions of their proactive husbands. Such a clichéd perception of Norse societies, with an unsophisticated understanding of women's roles, is now largely dismissed in professional academia, especially due to the increased interest in feminist perspectives among philologists, cultural historians, scholars of religion and archaeologists. The scholarly community has certainly come a long way since the National Romantic period, and thus in the following it is worth recalling some of the major milestones and trajectories in the field of gender research within Old Norse and Viking studies that form the foundations of today's understanding of the Viking world.

In the 1970s, after many decades of relegating Norse women to the confines of the household and dismissing or simply failing to notice their agentive potential 'outside the threshold',[2] Old Norse and Viking scholars eventually began to explore women's lives with more attention, acknowledging their prominence in the wider social arena as, *inter alia*, resourceful matriarchs, craftspeople, travellers and traders.[3] Around this time also supernatural female entities inhabiting Old Norse worldviews and mythical landscapes were subjected to scholarly scrutiny.[4] These new research initiatives, in part inspired by the second wave of the feminist movement of the 1960–1970s and involving investigations of written and archaeological sources (predominantly burial evidence), revisited and revised some of the dominant androcentric views of the Viking Age and convincingly demonstrated that Norse women were actively involved in a wide repertoire of activities, both inside and outside the domestic sphere. By organising a series of seminars and conferences centred on women in prehistory and the Middle Ages, the University of Stavanger in Norway played a crucial part in these developments, challenging and ultimately changing former scholarly paradigms and agendas.[5] In the intervening years these important initiatives also affected other Scandinavian and non-Scandinavian countries, gradually raising awareness of previously marginalised issues and untapped research themes.

Norwegian archaeologist Liv Helga Dommasnes is doubtlessly among the pioneers of sophisticated studies into the roles of Viking Age women as well as one of the crucial figures in the development of gender perspectives in Scandinavian archaeology.[6] As early as 1979 Dommasnes released a ground-breaking methodological article where she discussed the value of archaeological finds in illuminating the lives of Viking Age women.[7] She further expanded her views on the potential of burial evidence in addressing social roles and ranks in a series of studies published in the 1980s and 1990s.[8] In these publications, Dommasnes highlighted the complex nature of mortuary archaeology and openly acknowledged the problem that in Norway human bones are rarely available for specialist analyses, something that is partly due to unprofessional excavation techniques adopted by nineteenth and early twentieth century scholars and partly results from acidic soil conditions.⁹ Relying on comparative material from other areas of the Viking world where bone preservation is more favourable (*e.g.* Birka in Uppland, Sweden),¹⁰ Dommasnes concluded that it is safe to say that Norwegian graves with oval brooches typically belonged to biological women. Although she fairly admitted that elements of male costume and attire were less consistent in the Viking Age, she nevertheless assumed that graves with military equipment belonged to men, a claim she substantiated by referring to medieval laws containing passages claiming that weapons were emblematic of 'free men'.¹¹ However, it is noteworthy that even at this initial stage of research into aspects of gender in the Norse past, Dommasnes acknowledged the possibility that on some occasions Viking Age women could be buried with weapons.¹² Furthermore, by collating extant medieval laws, saga literature and archaeological material, she emphasised that women could exercise considerable power in their own right. Her comprehensive studies of graves from several regions in Norway led her to the conclusion that in this part of Scandinavia 'more women obtained high rank in the ninth century than in any other period' and that 'the number of high ranking women was at all times higher in the coastal areas than in the interior'.¹³ In her view, the elevated social position of these women resulted largely from their participation in the household economy in the role of housewives and administrators.¹⁴

In looking at Dommasnes' work today, it appears that in her early publications she often adhered to the idea that personal ornaments, weapons and tools discovered in funerary contexts reflected 'at least some of the more important duties of the deceased in life'.¹⁵ This is a fairly balanced opinion, but one that – to a certain extent – assumes that graves and their contents are 'mirrors of life', a view that in more recent scholarship has been seriously contested (see Chapter 1).¹⁶ For instance, in one of Dommasnes' articles, the presence of a pair of weight-scales in a (possibly) female grave from Hoppestad in Sogn og Fjordane, Norway has been seen to indicate that this person was 'a female merchant'.¹⁷ This interpretation does not have to be incorrect, but the fallacy of its underpinning interpretative framework – possibly inspired by culture-historical and functionalist perspectives – lies in the fact that it dismisses or simply fails to acknowledge the possibility that grave goods could hold symbolic meanings and/or that rather than reflecting the identities of the dead the grave goods might instead mirror the identities and aspirations of the mourners who participated in the funeral. As noted already in Chapter 1, this is also something to bear in mind when discussing graves with weapons, regardless of the biological sex of the deceased.

Soon after the release of Dommasnes' foundational articles, more scholars dealing with Viking and medieval Scandinavia started to contribute to the emerging field of research on Norse women. For instance, the 1980s saw the publication of Nanna Damsholt's work on the role of Icelandic females in the production of homespun cloth¹⁸ as well as a series of studies by other Old Norse philologists, historians of religion and archaeologists, most notably Lise Præstgaard Andersen,¹⁹ Carol Clover,²⁰ Else Mundal,²¹ Gro Steinsland,²² Anne Stalsberg²³ and Birgit Strand,²⁴ aspects of which will be taken up in detail in the following chapters of this book. Here, it is worth pointing out Stalsberg's pioneering work which introduced Northern and Western European scholars to the corpus of Viking Age artefacts used by women in the Rus area. The presence of typically Scandinavian jewellery (*e.g.* oval, round, equal-armed and trefoil brooches) as well as the occurrence of weights and/or scales in female graves in these far-flung places in Eastern Europe was interpreted by Stalsberg as evidence of Norse women's active participation in long-distance journeys and cross-cultural trade networks. Stalsberg's publications from the 1980s and 1990s also offered nuanced approaches to notions of cultural identity and religious belief in diasporic contexts,²⁵ and thus – in many regards – were way ahead of their time.

Aside from a range of papers written by individual scholars concerned with women's lifeways in the North, the 1980s also saw the emergence of Scandinavian research groups specifically dedicated to gender in the past. In 1983, an interdisciplinary conference was held in Bergen, concentrating on the position of females and their diverse roles in the North in a long-term perspective. The papers from this event were published in a modest but important edited collection entitled *Kvinnearbeid i Norden fra vikingtiden til reformasjonen* (*Women's Work in the North from the Viking Age to the Reformation*).²⁶ Among other things, the articles in this volume illuminated the roles of Viking and medieval women as healers and ritual specialists, but the analyses relied predominantly on textual sources, without paying much regard to other kinds of evidence, even though archaeologists were among the editors of the collection.²⁷

Several years still had to pass for scholars to fully realise the benefits of employing interdisciplinary methodologies in explorations of women's lives in the past. A significant step forward was made in the mid-1980s when researchers from the University of Bergen, together with scholars from other institutions in Norway (especially the University Museum of Stavanger), established a scholarly society and initiated the publication of a new academic journal called *K.A.N.* or *Kvinner i Arkeologi i Norge* (*Women in Archaeology in Norway*) specifically dedicated to feminist perspectives in archaeology – this was, in fact, the world's first journal with this particular scope.²⁸ In the intervening years, *K.A.N.* served as a forum for discussion and dissemination of the latest advancements in the field of gender studies in Northern Europe and beyond.

Truly ground-breaking changes in research on Viking Age women came in 1991 when Judith Jesch released her seminal and now classic book entitled *Women in the Viking Age*. In the opening sections of her monograph, Jesch made a critical remark concerning the persistent absence of women in contemporary narratives of the past:

> Every man is born of a woman and most also have sisters, lovers, wives or daughters. Even the bad old warriors who terrorised Europe had females in the family, like the more domesticated traders and craftsmen who, we are told, represent the other, pleasanter, side of viking activities. Yet, in all the books written about the Viking Age, there is little mention of these females who undoubtedly existed (and the tendency in such books that do mention women to lump them together with children in a subchapter just reinforces the impression that 'vikings' were adult males).[29]

As blunt as these words may sound, generally speaking this indeed *was* the state of Viking scholarship in the early 1990s. However, since the release of Jesch's work – a book which, as a matter of fact, became the first-ever full-length English language study of women's lives in the Viking Age – the image of the Norse past started to undergo considerable transformation eventually leading to an exponential growth of interest in the scholarly exploration of different facets of female activities, roles and material culture. Thus, Jesch's monograph certainly achieved its goal in bringing the previously 'invisible'[30] women of the Viking Age into the spotlight. Her pioneering study covered practically all aspects of the female life-course, with separate sections dedicated to archaeological evidence, runic inscriptions as well as art and texts pertaining to human and supernatural female figures. Overall, after thirty years since its original release, *Women in the Viking Age* is still an outstandingly interdisciplinary book, demonstrating Jesch's competence in critically dealing with an impressive array of sources, even those that lay outside of her academic specialism. Importantly, Jesch succeeded in demonstrating that extant archaeological finds and textual sources are in concert in their portrayal of Norse women as individuals who performed a plethora of activities, not merely those associated with household chores. To illuminate those different female roles, substantial attention in Jesch's study was dedicated to women of power and to those individuals whose prominent social status can be glimpsed through investigations of surviving burial evidence (*i.e.* Viking Age female graves with opulent furnishings), runic inscriptions as well as Old Norse and other medieval texts. Furthermore, Jesch paid close attention to women on the move and investigated their lives as travellers, explorers and colonists in distant lands. Interestingly, the final part of her study briefly looked at women warriors, focusing especially on their portrayals in the renowned account of Saxo Grammaticus but also in other medieval sources pertaining to the Norse cultural milieu (for a comprehensive analysis of these texts, see Chapter 3).

The majority of Old Norse textual accounts employed in Jesch's discussions of Norse women were drawn from the corpus of the *Íslendingasögur* or Family Sagas, with the important caveat that these sources were used:

> not for whatever kernel of genuine history they may or may not contain, but because our modern view of the Viking Age is so utterly entangled with our knowledge of the sagas. No other source is so colourful, so detailed, so seductive in its realism.[31]

In discussing the stories of armed women from medieval literature, in the following chapters of the present study I will subscribe to similar views on the nature of Old Norse texts, remaining critically aware that the details they convey cannot be regarded as undistorted reflections of the past, but that they may occasionally hold some historical value.

In writing her book Jesch consciously left out some categories of written sources, such as those that illuminate the legal position of the female part of the Norse population, and she also refrained from discussing the images of women in so-called kings' sagas and *fornaldarsögur* (legendary sagas). However, it was not before long when these themes were covered by other international academics. Only four years after the first release of Jesch's monograph, Jenny Jochens published a book centred on women in Viking and medieval Scandinavia and Iceland. Entitled *Women in Old Norse Society*, this ground-breaking study investigates aspects of marriage, reproduction, leisure and everyday female work before and after the religious conversion in Iceland as portrayed in Old Norse literature (especially in sagas and Eddas) and legal texts. The main difference to Jesch's monograph is that this work more explicitly applies gender analysis and feminist theory to shed light on the female part of Norse society. A meticulous and detailed study predominantly intended for academic audience, Jochens' book soon became an important cornerstone in research on aspects of gender in the North.[32] Today, however, some interdisciplinary scholars would probably disagree with Jochens' conclusion that 'the Norse world was profoundly patriarchal' and that 'the human ideal that was most admired and to which both men and women aspired was more masculine than feminine'.[33] According to Jochens' understanding and interpretation of written sources, Norse women were generally not allowed to actively perform political and juridical roles and they could not:

> act as chieftains (*goðar*), judges, or even witnesses; they were not allowed to prosecute, except in minor personal matters concerning themselves and their daughters, and even here they could not act directly but had to seek the mediation of male relatives. Although women owned property, it was under male administration.[34]

As we shall see further below, in the intervening years some of these claims were subject to revisions. Interdisciplinary studies of archaeological, iconographic and textual materials revealed convincing cases of women who – under certain circumstances – could indeed perform roles and duties conventionally ascribed to men.

In 1996, only one year after the release of *Women in Old Norse Society*, Jochens produces yet another book specifically dedicated to female roles in Viking and medieval Scandinavia and Iceland.[35] Entitled *Old Norse Images of Women*, this important follow-up volume is focused on 'divine' and 'human' female figures in Old Norse literature, the former being created by human imagination in the period before, during and after the religious conversion and the latter being at least in part based on real living people. In investigating these different female figures, Jochens focuses her attention on their four specific 'images', namely: the warrior woman, the prophetess/sorceress, the avenger and the whetter. The dividing line between these images is obviously blurry, and medieval literature includes cases of women who acted in several of these different guises.

It is worthy of note that for the purposes of her analyses Jochens referred not only to Old Norse texts but also to other sources, for example the accounts of Adam of Bremen and Saxo Grammaticus. In some instances, archaeological finds were also consulted although not to the extent Jesch had earlier employed them in her own book.[36] In this way, Jochens' monograph also became an important step towards the development of multidisciplinary approaches to the Viking Age, something that has become a hallmark of medieval research today.

Over the next decade or so, several international scholars followed in the footsteps of Judith Jesch and Jenny Jochens, conducting further in-depth studies of women in Old Norse literature and archaeology.[37] In addition to new research on human figures, also supernatural women became the topic of thorough scholarly investigations. Building on her earlier studies into female supernatural beings in the North,[38] in 1993 Lotte Motz[39] wrote extensively about sorceresses, giantesses, trolls and other female entities in Norse mythology and Germanic folklore in her thought-provoking monograph *The Beauty and the Hag: Female Figures of Germanic Faith and Myth*. Two years later, Britt-Mari Näsström released a detailed study concerning Freyja, portraying her as 'the great goddess of the North'.[40]

The beginning of the twenty-first century opened up a whole new chapter in the history of gender research in Viking and Old Norse scholarship. One of the most important contributions to this dynamically developing field was a 2002 volume edited by Sarah M. Anderson and Karen Swenson entitled *Cold Counsel: Women in Old Norse Literature and Mythology*.[41] With a title echoing a well-known episode from *Brennu-Njáls saga* (where one of the saga protagonists – who has been goaded by a woman named Hildigunnr to take revenge – utters the famous words: 'Cold are the counsels of women'), and including over a dozen papers by international researchers from Europe and the USA, the volume drew attention to a plethora of previously underappreciated or completely untapped themes in Old Norse gender research – for instance, the lives and achievements of female skalds[42] – but also helped nuance existing discussions on what women did, 'what they said or wrote, how they were represented, and what roles they occupied in their culture as a whole'.[43] In the same year another volume on Old Norse women, but with a major focus on their mythological images, was edited by Rudolf Simek and Wilhelm Heizmann.[44] Entitled *Mythological Women* and dedicated to the memory of Lotte Motz, one of the most prominent researchers in the field of Old Norse religious studies, this important collection brought together stimulating articles on female deities, *valkyrjur*, *dísir* and other supernatural women,[45] as well as an interesting study of armed females in Old Norse and Latin medieval sources.[46]

Also in 2002 archaeologist Neil S. Price produced his doctoral dissertation *The Viking Way: Religion and War in Late Iron Age Scandinavia*,[47] a book which immediately and deservedly received international acclaim and is now considered to be one of the most important contributions to the field of Viking studies ever released.[48] In this ground-breaking work, Price offered an in-depth multidisciplinary exploration of a very specific aspect of Old Norse religious belief, namely the practice of magic known as *seiðr*.[49] By critically collating textual sources, archaeology and cross-cultural ethnography (to an extent that had previously never been attempted in Viking studies), he was able to provide convincing arguments for the identification of *seiðr* practitioners and the tools of their trade in the archaeological record. Price's monograph soon became a cornerstone of all new studies into Old Norse magic and religion broadly understood but it also substantially refined the scholarly understanding of female roles in the North. *Seiðr* magic, which lies at the core of Price's investigations, was a typically (though not exclusively) female craft, and most of the archaeological finds that probably served as ritual accoutrements used in *seiðr* come from women's graves. In discussing the burial evidence and collating it with textual and ethnographic sources, *The Viking Way* also challenged former scholarly ideas of gender and gender transgression in the Old Norse world, demonstrating that the concepts of 'masculine' and 'feminine' were not as clear-cut as previous researchers had thought.

Brit Solli's monograph on Old Norse magic entitled *Seid: Myter, sjamanisme og kjønn i vikingenes tid* (*Seid: Myths, Shamanism and Gender in the Viking Age*), also released in 2002, differs significantly from Price's study in that it largely focuses on highlighting the queer nature of the god Óðinn and other *seiðr* practitioners.[50] Although some of her interpretations of archaeological finds (*e.g.* so-called holy white stones and the Oseberg burial) might seem farfetched, due credit must be given to Solli for bringing to wider academic attention the queer aspects of Old Norse gods and the sexual ambiguity of human sorcerers.

After the publication of Solli's book, a new generation of philologists, historians of religion and archaeologists pursued research on Old Norse women and produced stimulating works challenging old academic dogmas and providing nuanced insight into female lives, activities and material expressions thereof. In 2007, issues of gender and queerness in the North were investigated in erudite detail and in a broad historical perspective in Ing-Marie Back Danielsson's doctoral dissertation entitled *Masking Moments: The Transitions of Bodies and Beings in Late Iron Age Scandinavia*, a thought-provoking (and in some regards slightly controversial) work centred on visual representations of human and non-human bodies on gold foils (so-called *guldgubber*) and other ritual objects.[51] In this work, Back Danielsson offered a different vision of Viking Age 'mental landscapes' than Neil Price but one that is certainly worthy of discussion.

Lena Elisabeth Norrman's *Viking Women. The Narrative Voice in Woven Tapestries* published in 2008 represented another interesting contribution to the field of gender research in Old Norse and Viking studies.[52] Norrman focused predominantly on the active role of Norse women in weaving practices, and she demonstrated that through this laborious work female individuals were able to express their thoughts and feelings in an unburdened and original way. Using the Swedish Överhogdal tapestries as one of her main case studies, Norrman argued that Viking Age weaving can be perceived as a form of 'text' and that the process of making textiles was as a highly performative act, endowing women with a special kind of 'voice' and an opportunity to carry poetic traditions in visual form through generations.

The intricate relationships between women and textile work were something that drew significant attention from researchers in the first decade of the twenty-first century, and it is noteworthy that some of them – even though they were working independently and in different countries – arrived at largely similar conclusions. Eldar Heide, for instance, devoted a series of articles,[53] as well as his 2006 doctoral thesis,[54] to a multidisciplinary exploration of *seiðr*, arguing that the idea of spinning (a domestic practice typically associated with women) – together with all of its practical and symbolic undertones – formed an essential conceptual component of Old Norse magic. Heide was also the first scholar to observe that iron staffs discovered in Viking Age female graves from Denmark, Norway and Sweden (previously identified by Neil Price as possibly belonging to *völur* and other magic workers) resembled distaffs, long staff-like items typically made of wood and serving as essential implements in the production of threads.[55] Intricate associations between women, spinning and weaving were also investigated by Karen Bek-Pedersen in a series of articles and especially in her book *The Norns in Old Norse Mythology*, the first thorough scholarly exploration of some of the most enigmatic supernatural female beings.[56] Ingunn Ásdísardóttir's volume on the goddesses Frigg and Freyja, released in 2007, also includes sections dedicated to women and *seiðr*.[57]

The recent studies of Jóhanna Katrín Friðriksdóttir are some of the most stimulating contributions to international research on human and supernatural female figures in the Viking world. In addition to a series of eloquent and thought-provoking articles,[58] her two books *Women in Old Norse Literature: Bodies, Words and Power*[59] from 2013 and *Valkyrie: The Women of the Viking World*[60] from 2020 are both rich in detail, meticulously researched and raising new and important questions. The former study embraces a very broad corpus of textual sources, ranging from the *Íslendingasögur* to *fornaldarsögur* and *riddarasögur*, in an attempt to shed new light on women's agency in both human and supernatural domains, while the latter publication skilfully interweaves a variety of textual and archaeological sources to paint a detailed picture of the female life-course. Both volumes are significant contributions to the field of Old Norse and Viking studies and are highly recommended to anyone interested in the lives of women in the medieval North both within and beyond the pages of medieval manuscripts.

It is fair to say that over the last decade academic interest in Viking Age women has grown exponentially. This has found its expression in a surge of articles that concern practically all aspects of female lives as well as in the publication of several edited collections. Particularly noteworthy is a volume edited by Nancy Coleman and Nanna Løkka entitled *Kvinner i vikingtid* (*Women in the Viking Age*) released in 2014 and resulting from an interdisciplinary conference organised in 2012 at Høgskolen i Telemark at Bø, Norway which gathered over 100 participants.[61] The editors have assembled an impressive array of papers written by prominent authors representing a variety of academic disciplines including textual studies, runology, archaeology and history of religions. The opening chapter of the volume, written by Nanna Løkka, provides a concise and critical overview of the changes that have occurred over the last three centuries in the understanding of women in Old Norse and Viking studies.[62] Further sections of the book are centred on women in the sagas,[63] female presence at Norse assemblies,[64] women's roles as sorceresses and traders,[65] the significance of landscape analyses in deepening the scholarly understanding of gender roles in the Viking Age,[66] women in early towns,[67] female textile production,[68] women's identities and names[69] and other themes. Overall, this is a highly stimulating volume which – together with a plethora of full-colour illustrations of Viking Age sites and finds as well as reproductions of Norse-inspired paintings created by nineteenth- and twentieth-century European artists – presents a truly multi-faceted image of women in the Viking Age.

After the success of *Kvinner i vikingtid*, in 2017 Nanna Løkka together with Karoline Kjesrud released yet another edited volume on women in Viking and medieval Scandinavia. This time, however, as reflected in the book's title *Dronningen i vikingtid og middelalder* (*Queens in the Viking Age and the Middle Ages*), the main focus was on women of power, especially in their role as rulers but also as other prominent players in the social arena, including sorceresses, religious specialists and keepers of tradition.[70] As in the case of the former volume, this one also has an interdisciplinary scope, embracing contributions from researchers representing such diverse fields as textual studies, archaeology, religious history and iconography.

The image of the powerful woman – especially in her role as a ruler and religious specialist – is one that currently receives especial attention from academics. The work of Marianne Moen, including her published MA and PhD theses[71] as well as several articles,[72] emphasises it very strongly, urging the more traditionalist scholars to reconsider their contention that women had merely marginal roles in the Viking Age. The added value of Moen's approach is its theoretical depth combined with a commanding knowledge not only of the archaeological material but also its wider landscape context. Although at times provocative, Moen's publications certainly deserve to be widely read and discussed.

Warrior women in Old Norse studies and Viking archaeology

This concise review of over two hundred years of research has demonstrated how Norse women have been gradually emerging from the shadows of history to finally gain the recognition they fully deserve. From their initial perception as passive housewives to acknowledging them as proactive traders, craftspeople, powerful matriarchs and sorceresses, the images of Viking Age women have certainly taken many guises, and we are only now beginning to see them with appropriate clarity. We should never forget, however, that our current understanding of Viking Age women lies on the foundations laid out by several generations of academics – the implementation of the latest revisionist perspectives on Norse women would have been impossible without the combined efforts of textual scholars, historians of religion, archaeologists and other specialists. As we have seen, at least until the late 1980s interdisciplinary perspectives were rarely implemented in Old Norse textual scholarship and Viking archaeology, and researchers rarely and reluctantly attempted to transcend the boundaries of their specialist fields. Fortunately, this situation started to change in the 1990s, especially in the advent of post-processualism, reaching its peak in the first two decades of the twenty-first century, the modern Digital Age, where interdisciplinarity is not only advised but absolutely necessary for the research field to advance.

In thinking about the history of research on Norse women, we can see how it has come to reflect the multifarious transformations in theoretical and intellectual currents within the wider field of Viking Age studies as well as within the humanities at large. The current global fascination with the image of the Viking Age woman as a warrior is not only the result of the ground-breaking re-interpretation of grave Bj. 581 at Birka and the international success of the History Channel TV Series *Vikings*. It is also – and perhaps predominantly – the prolonged outcome of the aforementioned developments in the field of Old Norse and Viking studies as well as (at least to a certain degree) a reflection of the current *Zeitgeist* in Europe and beyond. In looking back at scholarly publications from the twentieth century that centred on the lives of Norse women, we can notice that some of them, at least cursorily, actually did take up the theme of women warriors and/or investigated the relationship between women and weapons. In other words, although the recent revaluation of grave Bj. 581 from the cemetery at Birka as that of a 'female Viking warrior'[73] has become an international sensation, the idea that medieval women occasionally used weapons and engaged in martial activities *is not* really a novelty in Viking studies.

Thorough survey of Scandinavian academic literature shows that the history of archaeological discoveries of alleged 'Viking warrior women' or 'shieldmaidens' actually began *more* than one hundred years ago. The starting date is August 1900 when the son of a farmer from Nordre Kjølen in Aasnes, Hedmark, Norway made a decision to excavate an old mound located in the vicinity of his home.[74] Using the basic working tools available to him – and having no prior experience in the recovery of archaeological finds – the man revealed what later turned out to be a hugely important Viking Age grave containing a human skeleton accompanied by a full set of weapons (a sword, an axehead, a set of arrowheads and a shield) and the remains of a horse. Some time after this remarkable discovery was made, a professional archaeologist was called in to see the site at Nordre Kjølen, but at this point the skeletal material and all of the archaeological finds had already been removed from their original context. Due to the amateur nature of the 'excavation', no plans and drawings had been made, but fortunately, the farmer and his son still remembered how the different objects and skeletal remains had been originally arrayed in the grave and shared this knowledge with the archaeologist. After the initial professional documentation of the grave good assemblage was made, for a while the artefacts from the mound continued to remain in the farmers' possession, but following an unfortunate fire at Nordre Kjølen, which led to the complete destruction of the iron shield boss, they were eventually donated to the museum in Kristiania/Oslo.

The human and animal bones from Nordre Kjølen were exceptionally well preserved by Norwegian standards, which made it possible to conduct specialist analyses of them. To everyone's surprise, however, anthropological studies revealed that the deceased person was not a man – as one would normally expect at that time, based on the 'martial nature' of the grave contents – but actually a young woman.[75] In their published reports, Gustav Guldberg, the osteologist who was responsible for the osteological examination, and Gustav Mørck, the archaeologist who documented the artefacts, were in agreement that the buried person had probably lived her life as a 'shieldmaiden'. This conclusion is explicit in the final paragraphs of Mørck's article:

> I ethvert fald synes dette fund fra Aasnes at være et sikkert vidnesbyrd om, at skjoldmøer har eksisteret i den virkelige historie, og sagaernes taushed om dem kan da skrive sig fra, at de er fortale længe efter begivenhederne og i tider med en anden opfatning af sømmelig optræden end i vikingetiden.[76]

> In any case, the discovery from Aasnes appears to testify to the idea that shieldmaidens really existed in history, and that the sagas' silence about them results from the fact that they were written in much later times and with a different perception of events that had taken place in the Viking Age.[77]

Notwithstanding the controversial circumstances surrounding the discovery of the Nordre Kjølen grave, this bold interpretation is still taken for granted in publications of some Old Norse and Viking scholars.[78] A detailed and critical discussion of this remarkable grave – based on a first-hand re-examination of its contents – will be provided in Chapter 4.

Aside from Nordre Kjølen, also other *allegedly* female graves discovered in Norway in the nineteenth and twentieth century contained military equipment. Some of them were cursorily discussed in scholarly publications released in the 1980s and 1990s while others are mostly known from museum yearbooks.[79] In an article published in 1987, Liv Helga Dommasnes argued that the presence of 'male' objects in several female graves in western Norway could indicate that 'these women had taken over more responsibilities than those usual to a housewife, responsibilities traditionally belonging to a man'.[80] In her opinion, especially in Sogn og Fjordane, an area known to have had significant links with Western Europe (especially with the British Isles and Ireland), women might have taken up traditionally masculine roles when the men were away on Viking expeditions and/or when all their relatives had died:

> It is therefore suggested here that high rank for women in the Late Iron Age was related to their role in established agricultural life. If a woman achieved rank comparable with men, it was because she had taken over one or more traditional male roles; she was allowed to do this when male energy was needed elsewhere, for example in trade or in warfare.[81]

In Dommasnes' opinion, this interpretative scenario can be supported by the fact that the richest female graves (including those containing military equipment) are typically located in coastal areas – *i.e.* places from which ships would have departed on Viking voyages and military expeditions overseas. Another argument in support of this theory is that the most opulent female graves in Norway are dated to the ninth century, which is precisely the time of turbulent state formation as well as a period of increased Viking activity and constant warfare both in the local arena and in foreign lands.

In light of these arguments, Dommasnes' interpretation seems highly probable, but only if we adhere to the idea that women stayed at home while men were away and that they had no desire nor chance to themselves engage in overseas trade and warfare *and* if we choose to perceive grave goods as direct indicators of rank and social role of the deceased.

Within the field of Old Norse textual scholarship of the 1980s the notion of women warriors or shieldmaidens (as they are sometimes called in the sagas) was investigated in some detail by Lise Præstgaard Andersen in her pioneering book entitled *Skjoldmøer – en kvindemyte* (*Shieldmaiden – a Mythical Woman*).[82] Intended primarily for students and the general public, Præstgaard Andersen's study mainly focused on the exploration of textual sources pertaining to armed women in the Norse world – *i.e.* eddic poems, the *fornaldarsögur* (legendary sagas) and Latin accounts (*e.g.* Saxo Grammaticus' *Gesta Danorum*). Despite its modest size, the book was fairly broad in scope, additionally situating the phenomenon of the armed woman in the context of folktales and contemporary discussions surrounding sexuality and feminist studies. The overall impression arising from this work, however, is that Lise Praestgaard Andersen considered the warrior women of medieval and renaissance literature as largely fictitious characters.

Apart from Lise Præstgaard Andersen, Judith Jesch is among the first scholars who in their work devoted more than cursory comments to the notion of warrior women in the medieval North. In *Women in the Viking Age*, Jesch touched upon the famous passages from Saxo Grammaticus *Gesta Danorum* which describe women in Denmark who preferred 'conflicts instead of kisses, tasted blood not lips' and 'sought the clash of arms rather than the arm's embrace'. Jesch argued that these accounts had little to do with historical reality and contended that in writing his work and in creating these vivid descriptions of fierce women warriors Saxo drew his inspiration from classical accounts of Amazons.

Jenny Jochens' book from 1996 embraced a selection of written accounts on warrior women deriving from different genres of Old Norse literature – *i.e.* eddic poetry, sagas of Icelanders (*Íslendingasögur*), legendary sagas (*fornaldarsögur*), chivalric sagas (*riddarasögur*) and kings' sagas (*konungasögur*). In discussing these texts, she concentrated her attention on the most memorable characters like Sigrdrífa/Brynhildr, the shieldmaidens Sigrún and Sváva, Hervör and her grandmother, Þornbjörg etc. Interestingly, and by way of contrast to most other textual scholars, in discussing the figure of Hervör in *Hervarar saga ok Heiðreks konungs* and her participation in the battle between Goths and Huns, she made the following observation:

> The presence of a fully-fledged maiden warrior in a poem of such ancient provenance is noteworthy and lends credibility to the notion that Germanic women may have participated in war, at least under specific circumstances.[83]

This shows that already in the mid-1990s – long before the (re)discovery of several Viking Age female graves with weapons in Scandinavia and elsewhere in Europe – some textual scholars fathomed the possibility that 'under specific circumstances' Germanic women could have actively participated in armed conflict.

Not much was said about warrior women immediately after the publication of the abovementioned monographs, and it took several years for scholars to seriously return to the topic. In 2002, Lise Præstgaard Andersen released a paper entitled 'On Valkyries, Shield-maidens and Other Armed Women – in Old Norse Sources and Saxo Grammaticus', providing a useful overview of some of the Latin and Old Norse sources featuring armed female characters.[84] The tone of her article, similar to her monograph from 1982, reveals her scepticism towards the existence of shieldmaidens and other female warriors beyond the literary and fantastic sphere. In Præstgaard Andersen's view, these women only appear in what she calls 'non-realistic sources'. However, like most of the previous studies cursorily dealing with Norse women and the sphere of war, this publication is focused solely on textual materials and disregards archaeological finds or comparative evidence from non-Scandinavian cultural milieus.

In 2006, Lydia Klos also took up the topic of armed women in the Viking world.[85] Her article is certainly worthy of attention in that it can be regarded as the first truly interdisciplinary approach to the theme of women and war in the medieval North. Including a comprehensive overview of the core written sources (*e.g.* eddic poetry, Old Norse sagas, mythological accounts but also laws and Latin texts), Klos' paper also provided some important remarks on relevant archaeological finds from the Viking Age. Although she did not delve into too much detail in her discussion of particular sites and objects, Klos highlighted the numerous source-critical problems that the search for archaeological traces of warrior women might evoke. For instance, she critically noted the challenges in dealing with mortuary remains and assessing the biological sex of the deceased. She also drew attention to the fact that (in the absence of osteological analyses) many graves with weapons have often been automatically – and thus potentially incorrectly – ascribed to men. Fully acknowledging these various source-critical issues, Klos nonetheless demonstrated the existence of several apparently female Viking Age graves with weapons. Contrary to her predecessors, however, she was reluctant to immediately ascribe a 'female warrior identity' to the deceased and rightly noted that weapons in funerary contexts could also have had non-martial connotations.[86] For instance, as Klos argued, spears might have been effectively used for hunting, while axes might have been employed as tools. Overall, Klos's study certainly set the stage for more nuanced and source-critical investigations into the motif of armed women in the Viking world, and illuminated the benefits of approaching the topic in an interdisciplinary way.

Around the time when literary scholars like Lise Prastgaard Andersen and Lydia Klos released their works on armed women in the Viking Age, the same themes began to be explored more thoroughly by archaeologists, especially by Peter Vang Petersen[87] and Neil Price.[88] In a range of articles Petersen focused his attention on miniature metal objects depicting a 'welcoming scene', which – in his view – represented two armed *valkyrjur*. To support this interpretation he referred to Old Norse sources, in particular the famous poem *Darradarljóð* interpolated in *Brennu-Njáls saga*. Possible iconographic and literary portrayals of the *valkyrjur* were also an important theme in Price's in-depth analysis of the religious underpinnings of Viking Age warfare – we will return to these issues and the growing body of scholarship pertaining to them in Chapter 6.

The impressive and erudite doctoral dissertation written by Michaela Helmbrecht in 2011, entitled *Wirkmächtige Kommunikationsmedien. Menschenbilder der Vendel- und Wikingerzeit und ihre Kontexte*, was also a hugely significant contribution to the study of the relationships between women, weapons and war in the Viking Age, as it embraced a substantial corpus of Viking Age miniatures depicting what appear to be armed female figures.[89] Helmbrecht's analyses were conducted with admirable source-critical attention (based on first-hand analyses of many of the finds), leading to important conclusions and revisions of previous misconceptions surrounding this group of objects. Various aspects of Helmbrecht's work will be taken up more extensively in Chapter 6, so they are only mentioned in passing here.

Only one year after the release of Helmbrecht's book, Viking scholars and the general public were thrilled to learn about the discovery of a previously unknown type of miniature – a tiny three-dimensional representation of an anthropomorphic character holding a sword and shield.[90] The knotted ponytail of this remarkable figure, as well as the details of its long garment, led to the immediate contention that it portrayed a *valkyrja*. This is still the prevalent and preferred interpretation but, as we shall see in Chapter 6, it should not be taken for granted.

Partly in response to these new developments and partly arising from my earlier studies into unusual mortuary behaviour in the Viking Age (the subject of my doctoral dissertation from 2012 as well as a series of articles),[91] in 2013 I published a paper entitled '"Warrior-women" in Viking Age Scandinavia? A Preliminary Archaeological Study'.[92] Despite its considerable length, this publication was intended merely as a pilot investigation, with an overarching aim to provide a survey of archaeological evidence for female graves with weapons in Viking Age Scandinavia. Numerous positive responses to this work spurred me to pursue the topic of women with weapons in a more comprehensive manner. Therefore, in 2015–2018, I released a series of publications concerning female graves with weapons[93] and miniature finds depicting what appear to be weapon-wielding women,[94] and I also examined selected Old Norse and Latin textual sources portraying armed female heroines.[95] Following up on this, in 2018, together with Kerstin Odebäck, I published an article investigating miniature shields, a group of intriguing objects found in funerary contexts, hoards and settlements in Scandinavia which appear to be strictly associated with Norse women.[96] The outcomes of these various preliminary studies will be discussed more extensively in the chapters that follow.

The re-investigation of the Bj. 581 grave, together with the international media buzz surrounding the official announcement of its results in late 2017,[97] coincided with the grant award that I received from the DAAD allowing me to initiate the *Amazons of the North* project. In the intervening years leading to the completion of the present monograph, other international scholars have also discussed the idea of women and weapons in the Viking Age in their articles,[98] books[99] and undergraduate theses.[100] Concurrently, there has also been an almost overwhelming surge of online publications touching upon related themes. All these different inquiries into the roles of Viking Age women, conducted by specialists representing such diverse but not mutually exclusive fields as philology, archaeology, history of religion and cultural anthropology, have one thing in common – they illustrate the necessity of approaching the motif of women and weapons in the Viking world in a multidisciplinary manner.

In the hope to present an unprejudiced and multifaceted image of the relationships between women and weapons in the Viking Age, and in recognition of the diversity of material and textual sources, the present study thus employs an original collage of theories and methods. Given that much of former research has centred on medieval textual sources that have largely inspired more recent archaeological interpretations of female graves with weapons, I am compelled to begin my investigation with a source-critical appraisal of Old Norse and other written accounts pertaining to armed women.

Notes

1. On the reception of the Vikings and the Viking Age in nineteenth- and early twentieth-century Europe, see Arwill-Nordbladh 1991; Roesdahl & Meulengracht Sørensen 1996; Haavardsholm 2004; Gardeła 2019f; Meylan & Rösli 2020.
2. For early and mid-twentieth-century pioneering contributions to the study of female roles in the North, drawing mainly on Old Norse textual sources, see von Schweringen 1909; Rittershaus 1917; Krappe 1926; Krause 1926; Heller 1958.
3. Bruder 1974; Næss 1974; Dommasnes 1979.
4. Mundal 1974.
5. Lundström & Foldøy 1995.
6. On Dommasnes' significant contribution to gender archaeology, see also Sørensen 2004: 18.
7. Dommasnes 1979.
8. Dommasnes 1982; 1987; 1991.
9. It is noteworthy that even today these factors typically lead to the situation where ideas about past peoples' biological sex as well as their roles and ranks are inferred based on objects that accompany them in their graves.
10. Arbman 1940; 1943.
11. Dommasnes 1987: 65–67.
12. Dommasnes 1987: 75.
13. Dommasnes 1987: 72.
14. Dommasnes 1987: 74.
15. Dommasnes 1987: 65.
16. See, for example, Härke 1990; Williams 2006; Williams & Sayer 2009.
17. Dommasnes 1987: 74.
18. Damsholt 1984.
19. Præstgaard Andersen 1982.
20. Clover 1986.
21. Mundal & Steinsland 1989.
22. Steinsland 1985.
23. Stalsberg 1987.
24. Strand 1980.
25. See, for example, Stalsberg 1987: 92–94 for an interesting and balanced discussion of the social implications of wearing Scandinavian female jewellery in a culturally foreign environment, mainly in the Rus' area.
26. Andersen *et al.* 1985.
27. Guðrún P. Helgadóttir 1985; Steinsland 1985.
28. Dommasnes 1999: 29; Næss 2006: 17–18.
29. Jesch 1991: 3.
30. Jesch 1991: 3. Following Jesch's study, several other works in the field of Viking studies have used the term 'invisible women' – see, for instance, Stalsberg 2001.
31. Jesch 1991: 4.
32. See the reviews of Jochens' work in Ebel 1997.
33. Jochens 1995: 162.
34. Jochens 1995: 163.
35. Jochens 1996.
36. Jochens 1996: 108.
37. See, for example, Clover 1993; Steinsland 1996; Wolf 1996; Tsigaridas 1998; Wicker 1998. A useful overview of the state of archaeological research on women in Viking Age Scandinavia was published by Næss 1994.
38. Motz 1975; 1980a; 1980b; 1981; 1988.
39. Motz 1993.
40. Näsström 1995. See also Näsström 1996.
41. Anderson & Swenson 2002.
42. Straubhaar 2002.
43. Anderson 2002: xiii.
44. Simek & Heizmann 2002.
45. Simek 2002.
46. Præstgaard Andersen 2002.
47. Price 2002.

48 A revised and expanded edition of Price's book appeared in 2019. See Price 2019.
49 For previous studies on *seiðr*, see Strömbäck 1935; 2000; Ohlmarks 1939a; 1939b; Buchholtz 1968; Dillmann 1993; 1994; Słupecki 1998; Dubois 1999 with further references.
50 Solli 2002. See also her articles on related themes published in Norwegian and English: Solli 1998; 1999a; 1999b; 2008.
51 Back Danielsson 2007.
52 Norrman 2008. Some of the themes explored in her 2008 book were touched upon in her earlier publications – see, for example, Norrman 2000; 2004; 2005.
53 Heide 2006a; 2006b.
54 Heide 2006c.
55 On the symbolic and functional connection between *seiðr* staffs and distaffs, see also Milek 2006; 2012; Gardeła 2008; 2009; 2016b.
56 Bek-Pedersen 2011. See also her previous work which focuses on women and weaving: Bek-Pedersen 2007; 2008.
57 Íngunn Ásdísardóttir 2007.
58 Jóhanna Katrín Friðriksdóttir 2009; 2010; 2012.
59 Jóhanna Katrín Friðriksdóttir 2013.
60 Jóhanna Katrín Friðriksdóttir 2020.
61 Coleman & Løkka 2014.
62 Løkka 2014.
63 Auður Magnúsdóttir 2014.
64 Sanmark 2014.
65 Sørheim 2014.
66 Moen 2014.
67 Hedenstierna-Jonson & Kjellström 2014; Pedersen 2014b.
68 Pritchard 2014; Thomsen 2014.
69 Coleman 2014; Jesch 2014.
70 Kjesrud & Løkka 2017.
71 Moen 2011; 2019a; 2019c; Lund & Moen 2019.
72 Moen 2019b.
73 Hedenstierna-Jonson *et al.* 2017.
74 Mørck 1901.
75 Guldberg 1901.
76 Mørck 1901: 74.
77 Translation by Leszek Gardeła.
78 Jochens 1996: 108; see more nuanced discussions in Klos 2006; 2007; Gardeła 2017c; 2018b; 2019c; Gardeła & Toplak 2019; Jóhanna Katrín Friðriksdóttir 2020: 63–64.
79 Dommasnes 1982: 77–78; 1987: 75.
80 Dommasnes 1987: 75.
81 Dommasnes 1987: 75.
82 Præstgaard Andersen 1982.
83 Jochens 1996: 100.
84 Præstgaard Andersen 2002.
85 Klos 2006. See also her follow-up article Klos 2007.
86 Klos 2006: 31–32.
87 Petersen 2005. See also his earlier work concerning a 'valkyrie figurine' from Ribe – Petersen 1992b. Similar artefacts are discussed in more detail in Chapter 6.
88 Price 2002.
89 Helmbrecht 2011.
90 Henriksen & Petersen 2013.
91 Gardeła 2012c; 2012d; 2013a; 2013d.
92 Gardeła 2013b.
93 Gardeła 2017a; 2017c.
94 Gardeła 2015a; 2016d; 2018a.
95 Gardeła 2018b.
96 Gardeła & Odebäck 2018.
97 Hedenstierna-Jonson *et al.* 2017. See also a follow-up study of Bj. 581 by Price *et al.* 2019 and a short commentary by Hedenstierna-Jonson 2018.
98 McLeod 2019; Raffield 2019.
99 See, for example, Moen 2019a: 104–107; Jóhanna Katrín Friðriksdóttir 2020: 56–71.
100 See, for example, Lund 2016; Redon 2017; Zappatore 2017.

Chapter 3

Women and weapons in medieval textual sources

Drawing predominantly on written sources stemming from Scandinavian and Icelandic cultural contexts, this chapter will offer a thorough exploration of medieval texts pertaining to armed women in the medieval North. In order to situate these varied accounts and their protagonists into a wider cross-cultural perspective, attention will also be given to relevant texts from the British Isles and Eastern Europe.

Armed women in *Gesta Danorum*

Contemporary discussions concerning armed women in medieval textual sources often refer to the following vivid passage preserved in Saxo Grammaticus' *Gesta Danorum*,[1] a twelfth–thirteenth century work describing the semi-legendary history of Denmark:

> Fuere quondam apud Danos foemine, que formam suam in uirilem habitum conuertentes omnia pene temporum momenta ad excolendam militiam conferebant, ne uirtutis neruos luxurie contagione hebetari paterentur. Siquidem delicatum uiuendi genus perose corpus animumque patientia ac labore durare solebant totamque foeminee leuitatis mollitiem abdicantes muliebre ingenium uirili uti seuitia cogebant. Sed et tanta cura rei militaris notitiam captabant, ut foeminas exuisse quiuis putaret. Precipue uero, quibus aut ingenii uigor aut decora corporum proceritas erat, id uite genus incedere consueuerant. He ergo perinde ac natiue conditionis immemores rigoremque blanditiis anteferentes bella pro basiis intentabant sanguinemque, non oscula delibantes armorum potius quam amorum officia frequentabant manusque, quas in telas aptare debuerant, telorum obsequiis exhibebant, ut iam non lecto, sed leto studentes spiculis appeterent, quos mulcere specie potuissent.

> There were once women in Denmark who dressed themselves to look like men and spent almost every minute cultivating soldiers' skills; they did not want to allow the sinews of their valour to lose tautness and be infected by self-indulgence. Loathing a dainty style of living, they would harden body and mind with endurance and toil, rejecting all the fickle pliancy of girls and compelling their womanish natures to act with a virile ruthlessness. They courted military expertise so earnestly that anyone would have guessed they had unsexed themselves. Those especially who had forceful personalities or were tall and elegant tended to embark on this way of life. As if they were forgetful of their true selves they put toughness before allure, aimed at conflicts instead of kisses, tasted blood, not lips, sought the clash of arms rather than the arm's embrace, fitted to weapons hands which should have been weaving, desired not the couch but the kill, and those they could have appeased with looks they attacked with lances.[2]

Further in his *Gesta Danorum*, Saxo mentions the names of several warrior women and provides intriguing details regarding their physical appearance, the weapons they allegedly used and the lifestyles they lived. These armed female heroines feature particularly prominently in the chronicler's description of a great battle that ensued at Brávellir (or Bråvalla)[3] in Östergötland between the armies of King Haraldr hilditönn (Harald Wartooth) of Denmark and King Sigurðr Hringr (Sigurd Ring) of Sweden. With hundreds of warriors involved, the battle was apparently so brutal and loud that the clashing of blades could be heard miles away. The image of medieval warfare that the chronicler unfolds before the reader, with the hurling of spears filling the air with a din and with the stream of blood from men's wounds drawing a mist across the sky, is both poetic and terrifying. According to *Gesta Danorum*, among the numerous warriors present on the battlefield at Brávellir were three outstanding women – Hetha, Visna and Vebiorg – all of whom were – in Saxo's words – endowed with 'manly courage'. We learn that Hetha fought on the right flank of King Haraldr's army and Visna was a standard bearer, but it is especially worth recalling how Saxo portrayed Visna and the men who fought bravely by her side:

> Wisnam uero, imbutam rigore foeminam reique militaris apprime peritam, Sclaua stipauerat manus. Cuius precipui Barri ac Gnizli satellites agnoscuntur. Ceteri uero ex eadem cohorte corpus clypeolis tecti prelongis ensibus aeriique coloris parmulis utebantur. Quas belli tempore aut in tergum repellentes aut impedimentorum gerulis dantes abiectis pectorum munimentis expositisque ad discrimen omne corporibus districtis Martem mucronibus intenderunt.

> E quibus Tolcar atque Ymi precipui claruere. Post quos Toki Iumensi prouincia ortus cum Otrico, cui agnomen Iuuensis erat, illustris agnoscitur.
>
> Visna was a woman hard through and through and a highly expert warrior; her chief followers among the band of Wends who thronged about her are known to have been Barre and Gnisli. The remainder of this company bore small shields in front of their bodies and used very long swords; these sky-coloured shields they pushed round behind them in time of war or gave to their bearers, so that, having cast away all protection from their breasts and exposed their persons to every danger, they would plunge into the fight with blades drawn. Among them the most shining lights were Tolke and Imme. After these, Toki, born in the province of Julin, is known to fame together with Otrik, called the Young.[4]

Later in *Gesta Danorum* Saxo speaks of Hetha and her companions in these words:

> At Hetha promptissimis stipata comitibus armatam bello centuriam afferebat. Cuius primi fuere Grimar ac Grenzli. Post hos Ger Liuicus, Hama quoque et Hunger, Humbli Biarique regum fortissimo memorantur. Hi persepe duellis foeliciter gestis insignes late uictorias edidere. Itaque memorate uirgines non modo comiter, sed etiam pugnaciter culte terrestres in aciem copias ductauere.
>
> Now Hetha, encircled by ready comrades, brought to the war a century of armed men. Their captains were Grimar and Grenzli; next, Ger of Livonia, Hama and Hunger, Humli and Biari are remembered as the most courageous of the princes; these would very often wage duels successfully and far and wide win outstanding victories. So the two women I have mentioned, graceful in their battle gear, led their land forces to combat.[5]

The third warrior woman, Vebiorg, fought with equal bravery until she was eventually shot with an arrow by a certain Thorkil from Telemark.

One striking detail in the two descriptions cited above is that the female heroines are accompanied by warriors stemming from non-Scandinavian cultural milieus: Visna has Wends or Western Slavs among her followers and Hetha fights alongside a certain Ger from Livonia, an area of today's Latvia which in the Viking Age was inhabited by Baltic tribes. The presence of foreign warriors in warbands led by women could simply be a literary embellishment intended to add an exotic flavour to Saxo's description, but it is not unlikely that in some regards these details hark back to something that actually had basis in historical reality. As we shall see in the following chapters, some female graves with weapons discovered in Scandinavia include a range of objects from distant lands, suggesting that either these women or the people who buried them had ties with Central and Eastern Europe.

The dramatic battle at Brávellir culminated with King Haraldr's death, and soon a spectacular funeral was prepared for him. Later, the victorious King Hring was entreated by the Danes to appoint Hetha to rule the land. Although in *Gesta Danorum* Saxo speaks highly of the women who fought at Brávellir, praising their expert training and brave deeds on the battlefield, he seems to be particularly impressed by another female warrior called Lathgertha. Saxo is so intrigued by this woman that he not only describes her involvement in armed conflict but also provides remarkably detailed information about her biography, physical appearance and outstanding beauty.

The story of Lathgertha is closely bound up with the life of a famous Viking called Regnerus (in other textual sources also known as Regner Lothbrog and Ragnarr loðbrók).[6] Soon after Regnerus inherits his throne, he learns that his grandfather Sigvarth, king of the Norwegians, has been killed by a Swedish ruler named Frø. Driven by a strong desire for revenge, Regnerus sets out on a journey to find the slayer. We first encounter Lathgertha when she arrives to Regnerus' camp in Norway together with a group of other women who 'had lately suffered abuse to their bodies or feared that their chastity was in imminent danger'.[7] Interestingly, Saxo notes that out of these concerns the women dressed themselves as men. He then introduces Lathgertha in these words:

> Inter quas affuit et Lathgertha, perita bellandi foemina, que uirilem in uirgine animum gerens immisso humeris capillitio prima inter promptissimos dimicabat. Cuius incomparabilem operam admirantibus cunctis-quippe cesaries tergo inuolare conspecta foeminam esse prodebat.
>
> Among these [abused women – LG] had appeared Lathgertha, a skilled female fighter, who bore a man's temper in a girl's body; with flocks flowing loose over her shoulders she would do battle in the forefront of the most valiant warriors. Everyone marvelled at her matchless feats, for the hair to be seen flying down her back made it clear that she was a woman.[8]

As soon as Regnerus has laid the killer of his grandfather in the dust, he begins his attempts to woo Lathgertha. He is so deeply impressed by her skills in battle as well as by the fact that she is of 'distinguished foreign birth'[9] that he becomes desperate to win her affection. Winning Lathgertha's hand in marriage turns out to be an onerous task, however, and Regnerus must first overcome a series of obstacles. Being fully aware of Regnerus' feelings towards her, Lathgertha orders a bear and a hound to protect her house. These animal guardians prove to be no serious threat to Regnerus, however, as he effortlessly pierces the first one with his spear and twists and throttles the gullet of the other. Before long, Lathgertha agrees to marry Regnerus and they have two daughters (whose names remain unknown) and a son named Fridlev. According to Saxo, the family spends the next three years in peace.[10]

Regnerus' and Lathgertha's marriage ends fairly quickly – he falls in love with another woman named Thora and divorces Lathgertha. Regardless of this course of events, and the fact that Lathgertha eventually marries another man, she still has strong feelings for Regnerus and remains loyal to him. Her devotion to her former husband is best seen when Regnerus finds himself in need of support in battle against King Haraldr Klak and when without hesitation Lathgertha provides him with a fleet of one hundred and twenty ships. Saxo goes on to describe in detail her bravery as well as her somewhat unusual and impressive fighting technique:

> Lathgertha quoque teneris membris incomparabilem sortita spiritum trepidantis militie studium specioso fortitudinis exemplo correxit. Militari namque discursu inopinatorum terga circumuolans socialem metum in hostilia castra conuertit. Ad ultimum laxata Haraldi acie atque ipso per summam suorum stragem fugato, quum domum ex acie reuertisset, spiculo, quod toga occultauerat, noctu mariti iugulum attentauit totiusque potentie eius ac nominis summam inuasit. Insolentissimus namque foemine spiritus absque uiro regnum gerere quam fortune eius communicare iocundius duxit.

> Lathgertha too, with a measure of vitality at odds with her tender frame, restored the mettle of the faltering soldiery by a splendid exhibition of bravery. She flew round the rear of the unprepared enemy in a circling manoeuvre and carried the panic which had been felt by the allies into the camp of their adversaries. Finally, when Harald's line had given way, his troops been massacred in abundance and their leader put to flight, she returned home from the battle; that night she stuck a dart, which she had concealed beneath her gown, into her husband's throat, thereby seizing for herself his whole sovereignty and title. This woman, of the haughtiest temperament, found it pleasanter to govern a realm alone than share the fortunes of her husband.[11]

Lathgertha's peculiar behaviour on the battlefield, and especially her ability to 'fly', has been interpreted by some scholars as displaying associations with supernatural female beings from Old Norse mythology. For instance, Judith Jesch has argued that this 'shows her kinship with the valkyries of the Helgi poems' and that Saxo must have been well aware of the existence of such women in Norse pre-Christian worldviews.[12] Regrettably, the Danish chronicler says nothing more about the further course of Lathgertha's life, but of all female warriors he portrays in his *Gesta Danorum* she is certainly the one who steals the spotlight.

Among other women who transformed themselves into female warriors, Saxo also mentions Alvild, the daughter of the king of Götaland. As a child Alvild was apparently endowed with such beauty that her father veiled her face with a robe 'to prevent her fine looks arousing anyone's passions'[13] and he also gave her two poisonous snakes,[14] which would act as protectors of her chastity. One day, a suitor named Alf appeared, and using his wit managed to overcome the challenge and kill the bloodthirsty animals. Although Alvild thought highly of this man, her mother had a different opinion and did not consider him as a candidate worthy of her daughter's hand. Disappointed about the unfortunate turn of events, Alvild chose to undergo a radical transformation of her appearance and lifestyle. As Saxo writes:

> Ita Aluilda ad Danici iuuenis contemptum adducta uirili ueste foemineam permutauit atque ex pudica admodum puella ferocem piratam agere coepit. Compluribus quoque eiusdem uoti puellis in commilitium adscitis eo forte loci peruenit, ubi piratarum agmen amissi bello ducis interitum deplorabat. A quibus ob forme pulchritudinem piratice princeps creata maiores muliebri uirtute res edidit.

> Once Alvild had been prevailed upon to despise the young Dane, she changed into man's clothing and from being a highly virtuous maiden began to lead the life of a savage pirate. Many girls of the same persuasion had enrolled in her company by the time she chanced to arrive at a spot where a band of pirates was mourning the loss of their leader, who had been killed fighting. Because of her beauty she was elected the pirate chief and performed feats beyond a woman's courage.[15]

Alf decided to pursue Alvild and set out on a long voyage. One day he reached Finland and found her fleet there. As soon as Alvild caught sight of unfamiliar ships, she 'shot off to encounter them, judging it wiser to burst on an enemy than lie waiting for him'.[16] Soon, a sea battle broke out and both Alvild and Alf fought courageously, each remaining completely unaware of the true identity of the opponent. In the course of the fight, one of Alf's companions named Brokar struck off Alvild's helmet and 'seeing the smoothness of her chin, realised that they ought not to be fighting with weapons but with kisses'.[17] Alf eventually convinced Alvild to change back to female clothing and they soon had a daughter together whom they named Gyrith.

Similar to her mother, Gyrith is described as an intelligent and proud woman who can take matters into her own hands. Saxo mentions that as time went by and when there was nobody but her left alive from the royal stock 'she declared a self-imposed oath of chastity'.[18] In order to protect herself from unwanted suitors, she handpicked a band of warriors to guard her room – a recurring motif that closely resembles the aforementioned cases of Lathgertha (who had a bear and a hound guarding her) and Alvild (who had two snakes to protect her chastity). After a while, however, Gyrith married a man named Halfdan and together they had a son named Harald. Halfdan then set out on an ambitious endeavour to restore the Danish kingdom but eventually fell in battle in Zealand. When Gyrith realised what had happened, she put on male attire and joined the fight. Her son was also among the combatants and as soon as she noticed that his warriors had fled, in fear for his life she lifted him and carried him away from the heat of battle. During this process, the son got shot in the buttocks – something that was obviously regarded as shameful. As Saxo notes, 'Harald consequently reckoned his mother's aid had brought him more embarrassment than assistance'.[19]

Saxo himself openly admits that in writing *Gesta Danorum* his ambition was to 'glorify the fatherland',[20] and as a man educated in France, Italy and Britain he wanted to celebrate the deeds of his forefathers in 'a Roman manner'.[21] In the preface to his work, he enumerates the sources he has used, including poetry, songs, runic inscriptions and various written narratives, claiming that his chronicle:

> relying on these aids, should be recognized not as something freshly compiled but as the utterance of antiquity; this book is thereby guaranteed to give a faithful understanding of the past, not a frivolous glitter of style.[22]

Notwithstanding Saxo's declaration about the authentic and unbiased nature of his work, a substantial portion of his writing is actually little more than a display of his erudition and literary imagination. His accounts of women warriors might possibly serve as literary embellishments, too, echoing ancient writings of classical authors (for instance Herodotus) of which he might have been aware.[23] Interestingly, however, some details of these women's biographies tend to overlap with what we know about real female warriors from other historical periods and different non-Scandinavian cultural areas. Their tomboyish nature, insatiable thirst for adventurous lifestyles and/or romantic motivations to take up arms and fight are all motifs that tend to recur across space and time both in literature and in real life. We will investigate these intriguing parallels more closely in Chapters 7 and 8 of the present study.

Armed women in Old Norse literature

In a general sense, the Old Norse textual corpus is fairly rich with examples of women who reach for weapons. Armed female characters appear in practically all literary genres, from the sagas of Icelanders (*Íslendingasögur*) to legendary sagas (*fornaldarsögur*) and the Eddas, but it is noteworthy that not all of these individuals can be regarded as warriors in the strict sense. Some women reach for weapons only in the face of danger and in moments of serious tension, for example in self-defence or to exercise revenge; others, often dressed as men, engage in armed conflict and display exceptional prowess in battle as actual and active warriors; and some employ weapons or weapon-like objects only in ritual practices. As Jenny Jochens has rightly observed, broadly speaking these remarkable female characters are distributed in 'the three realms of the divine, the heroic, and the human'.[24] In the sections below, we will investigate those Old Norse texts more closely in an attempt to uncover and better understand the different motivations that led human and supernatural women to take up arms.

Women and weapons in the *Íslendingasögur*

For the most part, the *Íslendingasögur* portray the lives of Norse settlers in Iceland as well as their overseas travels and adventures.[25] The focus of these texts is typically on particular families and their members, charting their biographies over one or more generations. Some elements of the fantastic are occasionally present in this genre of Old Norse literature, but overall the sagas tend to give the (sometimes misleading) impression that they portray real people and authentic events from the Viking Age.

The *Íslendingasögur* were composed predominantly in the thirteenth century but they typically refer to the period between the late ninth and tenth centuries. Much ink has been spilled over the possibilities and limitations of using these sources in trying to reveal and better understand the actual historical reality and mentality of the Viking Age, and although some scholars still continue to remain rather critical – arguing that the sagas might occasionally portray real characters but generally ought to be considered as works of fiction – others are more eager to see within them reliable reflections of the past. Over the last two decades or so international researchers have been particularly interested in descriptions of ritual practices preserved in some of the sagas. For instance, interdisciplinary studies, combining textual scholarship, archaeology, iconography and cultural anthropology, have demonstrated that some Old Norse accounts of ritual specialists, their accoutrements and religious practices are actually very strongly rooted in Viking Age reality.[26] As regards the issue of the authenticity of the portrayals of armed women in this genre of Old Norse literature, however, researchers seem to be somewhat more sceptical. In order to nuance the ongoing debates, in the sections below we will investigate and contextualise the motivations of several women who appear in *Íslendingasögur* and who in the course of their lives happen to reach for weapons.

Freydís Eiríksdóttir

Freydís was the illegitimate daughter of *Eiríkr inn rauði* (known to most people today as Eirik the Red), a renowned traveller and explorer who is credited with the discovery of Greenland.[27] According to extant texts, she had a farm at Garðar in Greenland and was married to a man called Þorvardr.[28] The two so-called 'Vínland sagas' in which she appears – *Eiríks saga rauða* and *Grænlendinga saga* – recall that Freydís had a somewhat haughty and domineering nature, and that at times of crisis or danger she had the capacity to act rather ruthlessly. Born into a family whose members were driven by great ambitions, it comes as no surprise that in the course of her life Freydís also had a thirst for adventure and took part in long sea travels; according to the sagas, at one point in her life she even embarked on a journey to Vínland.[29]

We learn from *Grænlendinga saga* that soon after her successful arrival in Vínland Freydís devised a cunning plan and – pretending she was mistreated by a certain Finnbogi who also had recently set foot in Vínland – spurred her husband to repay the dishonour, threatening him with divorce if he would dare to disobey her. Unable to ignore her upbraiding any longer, Þórvardr assembled his men and went to set things straight. When he arrived at the house of Finnbogi and his brother, he found the two men sleeping. He then had them tied up and led outside. Freydís, who came along with her husband, had the men killed immediately. Since only women were left alive and since no one would dare to kill them, Freydís took an axe and murdered them with cold blood. According to *Grænlendinga saga*, this mischievous event left no stain on Freydís and she was 'highly pleased with what she had accomplished'.[30] Although she threatened her companions that if anyone would reveal what had happened she would have them killed as well, in the end, after Freydís returned back to Greenland, word got out, and her brother, Leifr, got deeply upset about these terrible happenings. The saga does not say whether or not Freydís was in any way punished for her deeds, however.

Another instance when Freydís displayed her violent side is recounted in *Eiríks saga rauða*.[31] When Native Americans attacked the Norse camp in Vínland, in contrast to her companions who were ready to escape without putting up a fight, Freydís showed no fear at all. Despite the fact that she was pregnant, she suddenly picked up a sword from one of the fallen Norsemen, bared one of her breasts and smacked the sword with it. Upon seeing this, the attackers were so stunned that they decided to flee. It is noteworthy that the wording of the saga description makes it clear that the woman actually smacks the sword with her breast and not *vice versa* (as some scholars, including the present author, have earlier assumed)[32] – visually, this act would have seemed very striking and would have doubtlessly instilled confusion among anyone seeing it.

The episode when Freydís bares her breasts has been carefully deconstructed in a thought-provoking study by Oren Falk entitled *The Bare-Sarked Warrior*.[33] Falk has also found a number of interesting cross-cultural parallels to the motif of battlefield exposure, the analysis of which has led him to the following conclusion:

> What they [*i.e.* the women who expose themselves in battle and/or use weapons] do, or threaten to do, to their tender flesh is as important as the reminders they supply of its appealing and vulnerable tenderness. Through the interplay of sex and gender in the construction of the bare-sarked warrior, through the violence she directs at herself yet mysteriously unleashes on her foes, she is somehow able to metamorphose the unbearable danger of the Other into manageable risk for the Self.[34]

Þórdís Súrsdóttir

In *Gísla saga Súrssonar* we encounter a woman named Þórdís, who is the daughter of Þornbjörn Þorkelsson Súr and sister of the saga's main protagonist Gísli Súrsson. The saga emphasises her attractive looks but actually does not provide any particulars about her physical appearance.[35] We learn that she marries a man called Þorgrímr Þorsteinsson and receives a farm at Sæbol as her dowry. One day Gísli sneaks into their home and secretly murders Þorgrímr while he is sleeping in bed with his wife. His motivation is to avenge the death of his friend Vesteinn who has been killed by Þorgrímr. Þórdís, who is pregnant with Þorgrímr's child, soon marries another man named Börkr. She suspects that Gísli is responsible for killing her husband and tells Börkr about it who then then files a lawsuit against Gísli. By the sentence of the Þorsnes assembly Gísli is outlawed and forced to hide from people who want to take revenge on him.

Things get nasty when a man called Eyjólfr arrives with his companions at the farm where Gísli lives together with his wife Auðr and their foster-daughter Gúðrid. As soon as they become aware of the intruders, both Gísli and the two women prepare to stand their ground – Auðr and Gúðrid arm themselves with large clubs and wait for the attackers on a ridge.[36] When Eyjólfr comes near, Auðr strikes his arm with her club with so much strength that he staggers back down. Although Gísli fights fearlessly and courageously, he eventually gets killed by the hands of Eyjólfr and his men.

Sometime after all these happenings Þórdís experiences feelings of remorse and devises a cunning plan leading to one of the most memorable episodes in Old Norse literature. One evening, when she is inside a house together with Eyjólfr and other people, she deliberately drops a tray of spoons. The ensuing scene, described in detail in *Gísla saga Súrssonar*, is worth citing in full:

> Eyjólfr hafði lagt sverð þat í milli stokks ok fóta sér, er Gísli hafði átt. Þórðís kennir sverðit, ok er hon lýtr niðr eptir spánunum, þreif hon meðalkaflann á sverðinu ok leggr til Eyjólfs ok vildi leggja á honum miðjum. Gáði hon eigi, at hjaltit horfði upp ok nam við borðinu; hon lagði neðar en hon hafði ætlat, ok kom í lærit, ok var þat mikit sár. Börkr tekr Þórdísi ok snarar af henni sverðit. Þeir hlaupa upp allir ok hrinda fram borðunum ok matnum. Börkr bauð Eyjólfi sjálfdœmi fyrir þetta, ok gerði hann full manngjöld ok kvezk gört hafa mundu meira, ef Berki hefði verr í farit.[37]

> Eyjólfr had laid Gísli's sword between the bench and his feet, and Þórðís recognised it. When she bent down to pick up the spoons, she grabbed it by the hilt and thrust out at Eyjólfr, meaning to strike him in the guts. But she had not noticed the blade-guard which turned upward and caught against the table. Moreover, she struck at him lower than she intended, hitting him in the thigh and thereby wounding him sorely.

> Bork grabbed hold of Þórðís and wrenched the sword away from her, and the others all jumped to their feet and overturned the tables and the food. Börkr left it in Eyjólfr's hands to decide the penalty for this deed, and he claimed full compensation – the same as was imposed for slaying a man – and said he would have demanded more if Börkr had handled this matter less fittingly.[38]

In this case, Þórdis fails to fully avenge the death of her brother and even gets punished for inflicting a serious wound. In the face of Icelandic law, therefore, she is treated exactly like a man. It is interesting to note, however, that the sheer fact that she has used a weapon and has for a moment stepped into a masculine role does not seem to have raised any controversies. This stands in some contrast to what we can see in *Laxdœla saga*, as detailed below.

Auðr and Þuriðr

Although *Laxdœla saga* describes her as 'neither good looking nor exceptional in other ways',[39] Auðr is one of the most memorable female characters of the *Íslendingasögur*. The same saga says that her husband Þórðr had little affection for her and that he married her only because she was wealthy. Nicknamed Bróka Auðr (Breeches Auðr), this woman is known to have caused a controversy in the neighbourhood for wearing breeches with a codpiece and long leggings. Initially, Þórðr did not even notice it himself but when a certain Guðrún made a remark about it, he enquired about the consequences this could have for a woman. Guðrún then commented on the matter in the following words:

> Slíkt víti á konum at skapa fyrir þat á sitt hóf sem karlmanni, ef hann hefir höfuðsmátt svá mikla, at sjái geirvörtur hans berar, brautgangssök hvárttveggja.[40]

> If women go about dressed as men, they invite the same treatment as do men who wear shirts cut so low that the nipples of their breasts can be seen – both are grounds for divorce.[41]

Upon hearing this, Þórðr immediately announced his divorce at the Alþing without even bothering to inform Auðr about his decision beforehand. When the matter was settled, without further ado he asked for Guðrún's hand in marriage. Realising that the true reason for the divorce was not the fact that she had been wearing masculine clothing but because Þórðr had fallen in love with another woman, the following summer Auðr decided to give her unfaithful husband a lesson he would never forget. She yet again dressed in trousers, mounted a horse and rode to Þórðr's new home. When she reached his bed, she was ready to exercise her revenge:

> Þá vakði Auðr Þórð, en hann snerisk á hliðina, er hann sá, at maðr var kominn. Hon brá þá saxi ok lagði at Þórði ok veitti honum áverka mikla, ok kom á höndina hœgri; varð hann sárr á báðum geirvörtum; svá lagði hon til fast, at saxit nam í beðinum staðar. Síðan gekk Auðr brott ok til hests ok hljóp á bak ok reið heim eptir þat. Þórðr vildi upp spretta, er hann fekk áverkann, ok varð þat ekki, því at han mœddi blóðrás.[42]

> She woke Þórðr, but he only turned over on his side when he saw some man had come in. She drew her short-sword and struck him a great wound on his right arm which cut across both breasts. She struck with such force that the sword lodged in the wood of the bed. Auðr then returned to her horse, sprang into the saddle and rode home. Roused by the attack, Þórðr tried to get to his feet, but was weakened by the wound and loss of blood.[43]

When Auðr returned home and told her brothers about what had happened, they agreed that what she had done was right and that her former husband actually deserved much worse. Although from a legal perspective Þórðr had every right to seek compensation, he refrained from pressing any charges, acknowledging that the score between him and his former wife was even.

In this context it is noteworthy that *Laxdœla saga* preserves a roughly similar account of a woman named Þuríðr who has been deserted by her husband and has decided to play a trick on him.[44] Shortly before the man is about to set out on a journey, Þuríðr bores a hole in his ship to slow it down and then, when the man is sound asleep, she takes away his precious sword (named *Fótbítr* – Leg Biter) and instead places her one-year-old baby by his side.

In examining these two cases from *Laxdœla saga*, we can see that both Auðr and Þuríðr exercise their revenge in such a way that symbolically reverses gender roles. Jóhanna Katrín Friðriksdóttir has even suggested that the scene when Auðr wounds her husband with a sword while he is sound asleep in bed could be understood as an act of symbolic penetration,[45] something that – by Viking Age standards – would have brought great shame to a man and even sexual defamation.[46] In this context it is possible to argue that the case of Þuríðr who bores a hole in the ship (something that metaphorically 'injures' the ship's owner and thus affects his ability to embark on a journey, symbolically reducing his agentive potency) and substitutes her husband's sword for a child could reveal a similar conceptual pattern. In both instances gender roles are being inverted, but when Auðr and Þuríðr wield weapons and temporarily 'become men' this does not bring them any shame. The same cannot be said about their husbands, however, who are both stripped of their honour as a result of the women's revenge.

Þórhildr Vaðlœkkja

In discussing the associations between women and weapons in Old Norse literature, it is crucial to pay close attention to a unique passage recorded in *Ljósvetninga saga*. At one point in the story the main hero of the saga, Guðmundr, decides to consult a sorceress named Þórhildr about his and his sons' fate.[47] Upon his first visit, the woman is reluctant to speak and asks Guðmundr to come another time. When the protagonist returns, he finds the sorceress in a somewhat unusual attire, dressed like a male warrior. Because this passage is so special, and also relatively unknown and underappreciated among today's Viking and Old Norse specialists, it is worth citing it in full:

Kona hét Þórhildr ok kölluð Vaðlækkja ok bjó at Naustum. Hon var forn í lund ok vinr Guðmundar mikill. Guðmundr fór á fund hennar ok mælti: 'Forvitni er mér á því mikil, hvárt nökkur mannhefnd mun fram koma fyrir Þorkell hák.' Hon svarar: 'Kom þú í öðru sinni at hitta mik, eina saman.' Síðan liðu stundir. Ok einn morgin reið Guðmundr Heiman snimma einn saman til Vaðla. Ok var Þórhildr úti ok gyrð í brœkr ok hafði hjálm á höfði ok øx í hendi. Síðan mælti hon: 'Far þú nú með mér, Guðmundr.' Hon fór ofan til fjarðarins ok gerðisk heldr þrýstilig. Hon óð út á vaðlana, ok hjó hon fram oxinni á sjóinn, ok þótti Guðmundi þat enga skipan taka. Síðan kom hon aptr ok mælti: 'Eigi ætla ek, at menn verði til at slá í mannhefndir við þik, ok muntu sitja mega í sœmð þinni.' Guðmundr mælti: 'Nú vilda ek, at þú vissir, hvárt synir mínir munu undan komask.' Hon segir: 'Nú gerir þú mér meira fyrir.' Síðan óð hon út á vaðlana, ok hjó hon í sjó inn, ok varð af brestr mikill ok blóðigr allr sjórinn. Síðan mælti hon: 'Þat ætla ek, Guðmundr, at nær stýrt verði einhverjum syni þínum. Ok mun ek þó nú eigi optar þraut til gera, því at engan veg kostar mik þat lítit: ok munu hvártki tjóa við ógnir né blíðmæli.' Guðmundr mælti: 'Eigi mun ek þessa þraut optar fyrir þik leggja.' Síðan fór Guðmundr heim ok sat í virðingu sinni.

There was a woman named Þórhildr, called the Widow of Vodlar [Vaðlækkja], and she lived at Naust. She was still a heathen in spirit and was a great friend of Guðmundr.

Guðmundr went to meet with her and said, 'I am very curious to know whether there will be any vengeance for Þorkell hák.'

'Come to see me another time when I am alone,' she answered.

Some time passed, and early one morning Guðmundr rode off alone to Vodlar. Þórhildr was outside dressed in breeches and with a helmet on her head and an axe in her hand.

She said to him, 'Come with me now, Guðmundr.'

She headed down to the fjord and seemed to grow in stature. She waded out into the shallows and struck her axe into the water, and Guðmundr could observe no change.

Then she came back and said, 'I don't think there will be men to take up vengeance against you. You will be able to keep your honour.'

'Now I would like to know if my sons will escape reprisal,' said Guðmundr.

'That's a more onerous task,' she said.

She then waded out into the shallows and struck a blow in the water. There was a loud crash and the water turned all bloody.

Then she said, 'I think, Guðmundr, that the blow will fall close to one of your sons. I will not exert myself again because I do so at no little cost for myself; neither threats nor coaxing will avail.'

'I will not impose this strain on you ever again,' he said.

Guðmundr returned home and kept his respect.

Ljósvetninga saga (21)[48]

The story recorded in *Ljósvetninga saga* has no close parallels in the corpus of Old Norse literature[49] and it is also the only text which portrays a cross-dressing sorceress using an axe in a prophetic ritual. Such unique accounts, without any close and contemporary parallels whatsoever, tend to be dismissed by scholars and considered merely as products of the vivid imagination of medieval writers.[50] Nevertheless, as we shall see in the following chapters dealing with women's graves with weapons, there are strong reasons to believe that the story of Þórhildr echoes authentic ritual practices of the Viking Age in which axes played the role of important accoutrements.

Not only axes and swords: understanding women's weapons

In summarising her views on some of the saga episodes reviewed above, Kirsten Wolf has made an interesting observation on the specific and recurrent circumstances that spur Norse women to step into what can be regarded as a 'masculine role':

> Þórhildr's case, like those of Auðr and Freydís, involves the absence of a husband: Þórhildr is a widow, Auðr is divorced, and Freydís appears to be contemplating divorce. Without a husband, the woman can no longer be labelled as a wife, with all the subordinating baggage that attends the designation. Through adoption of male dress, the woman, in effect, appropriates to herself the power of the dominant stratum while also displaying her own sexual identity, with the effect that she is free to act in ways never open to her as a woman. The absence of the husband, then, removes the limitations imposed by male control and thus permits the reassignment of female identity.[51]

It is noteworthy that with the exception of Þórhildr and Freydís, the two other aforementioned women who reach for weapons in the *Íslendingasögur* (Auðr and Þórdís) are unsuccessful in achieving their desired goal and only manage to wound their victims instead of actually killing them. As Jóhanna Katrín Friðriksdóttir rightly observes, in Old Norse literature usually the main female strategy to exert influence is by verbally convincing others (typically men) to exercise their will.[52] Another alternative for women, if there is nobody able or willing to help them, is to resort to magic,[53] a motif which we will investigate more closely further below. The women whose deeds we have reviewed above deviate significantly from this pattern.

Aside from the different cases investigated above, the *Íslendingasögur* portray other female characters who occasionally reach for weapons or provide supernatural aid for other people who (in their name) engage in armed conflict. One such case is recounted in *Fóstbrœdra saga* where a woman named Gríma – a rich widow endowed with magic skills – is concerned about her daughter who is being seduced by a womaniser called Þórmódr. Worried that the man would bring her daughter nothing but dishonour, she gives a sword to her slave Kolbakr, fills his garments with hanks of yarn (to protect him from potential injuries), and sends him to another farm. On his way Kolbakr encounters Þórmódr and attacks him. Because Gríma has filled Kolbakr's garments with yarn (something that in the saga is interpreted as providing it with magic qualities, making it impenetrable), Þórmódr is unable to strike back and hurt his opponent. As Jóhanna Katrín Friðriksdóttir concludes: 'Magic is a dangerous and effective weapon available to women that even powerful men are depicted as regarding with apprehension'.[54]

Women and weapons in the *fornaldarsögur*

Fornaldarsögur or Legendary Sagas are replete with fantastic events, supernatural beings and magic.[55] In this saga genre, more than in any other Old Norse sources, the reader can frequently encounter sorcerers, berserkers, monsters and revenants all woven into captivating narratives about enchanted weapons and great adventures in distant lands. Here, too, female warriors feature very prominently, and some of the sagas provide us with a significant degree of detail regarding the course of their lives, allowing us to better understand what motivated these fictitious women to enter the war path. In this section, we will focus on the most evocative examples of armed females from the *fornaldarsögur*, paying especial attention to the famous heroines named Hervör and Þornbjörg.

Hervör Bjarmarsdóttir

Hervör is probably the most renowned female warrior of Old Norse literature. The story of her remarkable life is recounted in *Hervarar saga ok Heiðreks konungs*, a *fornaldarsaga* from the thirteenth century which combines strong elements of the fantastic with some possible echoes of authentic historical events such as the fourth-century battle(s) between Goths and Huns.[56]

Hervör is the only daughter of a famous warrior and berserker named Angantýr. Because her father dies before her birth, she grows up in the house of a jarl. From her early days Hervör displays exceptional physical strength, and instead of engaging in feminine activities like needlework and embroidery, she trains herself in using shield and sword. As we learn from the saga, she also has the tendency to run away to the woods to kill men for her own pleasure. The people from her closest environment are not at all impressed by or pleased with her behaviour and simply consider her evil. As soon as Hervör learns the truth about her father Angantýr, she longs to set out on a journey to search for his grave mound on the enigmatic island of Sámsey (today's Samsø in Denmark), a numinous place that appears in a range of Old Norse texts.[57] Shortly before departure she decides to conceal her long hair under a linen headgear, dons men's clothing and changes her name to Hervard. Hervör's mother helps her in her endeavour and prepares a cloak and kirtle as well as all the necessary equipment a man would need for an expedition. Not long after leaving her home, the heroine finds a group of Vikings and decides to join them – she introduces herself as Hervard and soon becomes their leader. Together with these Vikings Hervör/Hervard finally reaches the island of Sámsey, where she hopes to find the mound of her fallen father. Afraid of the evil creatures that apparently dwell there, her companions are reluctant to take part in Hervör/Hervard's endeavour, and so the female heroine embarks on this quest all by herself. Suddenly, Hervör/Hervard notices fire burning on the mounds and eventually finds Angantýr's grave. She then utters the following words to wake him up and raise him from the dead:

> Vaki þú, Angantýr,
> vekr þik Hervör,
> eingadóttir
> ykkr Sváfu;
> selðu ór haugi
> hvassan mæki
> þann er Sigrlama
> slógu dvergar.
>
> Wake, Angantýr,
> wakes you Hervör,
> Sváfa's offspring,
> your only daughter;
> the keen-edged blade
> from the barrow give me,
> the sword dwarf-smithied
> for Siglami.[58]

In investigating Hervör's first encounter with the Vikings, her journey to Sámsey and the memorable meeting with her deceased father, it is worth drawing attention to how smoothly she is able to shift between her gender identities; shortly before disembarking the ship she was known to her Viking companions as a man called Hervard, and now, when she raises Angantýr from the dead, she introduces herself as a woman. It is, of course, crucial for Hervör to reveal her true identity when meeting her father, because otherwise he would not recognise her and she would be unable to claim her inheritance and its most significant symbol – the sword Týrfingr.

At first Angantýr is reluctant to give away his famed weapon, but ultimately Hervör/Hervard manages to persuade him. He warns her, however, that the sword – the edges of which are poisoned – is cursed and that it will only bring ruin to her and her family. Regardless of this, Týrfingr remains a weapon of great importance and one that is endowed with profound symbolism – Hervör knows very well that she will need it to fulfil her destiny. As Carol Clover has argued:

> Týrfingr is thus more than a sword, more than a phallic symbol, and more than a literary binding device. It is the emblematic representation of the larger patrimony – not only treasures and lands, but family name and ancestral

spirit – that each generation must secure for itself and pass on to the next.[59]

Because Hervör is Angantýr's only child, and thus the only one to inherit, these special circumstances predestine her to step into a masculine role, to continue her life as a man and to become, in Clover's words, 'a functional son'.[60] Failing to retrieve the sword would simply mean the end of her family's line.

We learn from *Hervarar saga ok Heiðreks konungs* that after the memorable encounter with her dead father at Sámsey Hervör/Hervard continues to live a warrior's life. For a while she stays with King Guðmundr of Glasisvellir. One day she assists him in a game of chess (or *tafl*) and then someone suddenly draws Týrfingr from its scabbard without permission. Hervör/Hervard immediately snatches the sword and cuts off the man's head. Surprised and infuriated, the king's men are willing to take immediate revenge, but the king discourages them from trying and gives them the following explanation: 'your vengeance on this man ... will seem smaller than you think, because it is my guess that he is a woman; but I think that with that weapon which she wields her slaying will be dearly bought by every man of you'.[61] Hervör is thus free to leave unharmed and after some further Viking adventures she finally decides to settle down. Later, she marries a man called Höfund and they have two sons whom they name Angantýr and Heiðrek. When her son Heiðrek gets older, she passes the sword Týrfingr to him.[62] Heiðrek then has a daughter whom he names Hervör after his mother. This second Hervör also becomes a female warrior and eventually meets her end in the famous battle between the Goths and Huns.[63]

A peculiar paradox of *Hervarar saga ok Heiðreks konungs* is the inversion of historical chronology: the Viking Age Hervör becomes the grandmother of the Gothic/Germanic Hervör. One reason for this is that the compiler of *Hervarar saga ok Heiðreks konungs* merged several different texts. In trying to provide a sensible explanation, Jenny Jochens has argued that:

> Angantýr's warning that the sword would destroy his daughter's family inspired the prose author to create Hervör as the generational link needed to transmit the fateful Týrfingr from her father to her son in this five-generation dynasty. In the mind of the author, Hervör's position as the only heir born after the decimation of twelve brothers makes her male role necessary, at least for a short period. The author's chronological route is thus biological succession and not historical event.[64]

The life of Hervör/Hervard has been the subject of numerous scholarly debates.[65] Often, the deeds of this remarkable individual and aspects of their ambiguous identity are brought forward in discussions concerning gender and female warriors in the Old Norse world. Recently, however, Miriam Mayburd has also investigated Hervör's nature in the context of *seiðr* magic and concepts like *ergi* and 'queerness'.[66] Mayburd's novel approach is particularly stimulating in that it challenges the traditional scholarly perception of Hervör, where her identity has been typically set within the rigid binary-gender model, and suggest instead that in discussing Hervör's complex identity it is more appropriate to speak of the more fluid idea of 'queerness'. 'Queerness' and 'inter-gender dynamics of sexual abnormality', as Mayburd argues, are crucial to Hervör's success in raising her dead father and in obtaining great power.

Þornbjörg Eiríksdóttir

Hrólfs saga Gautrekssonar, presumably composed in the thirteenth century, provides a fairly detailed account of the lifecourse of another female warrior named Þornbjörg.[67] As in the case of Hervör, the reader first learns about her childhood, which permits a better understanding of the underpinning reasons for the life choices she is about to make later in the story. According to *Hrólfs saga Gautrekssonar*, Þornbjörg was the only daughter of Swedish king Eiríkr and, similar to several warrior women from Saxo Grammaticus' *Gesta Danorum*, she is described as 'unusually good looking and intelligent'.[68] Þornbjörg was brought up at home by her parents and acquired exceptional skills in feminine crafts. However, in the early days of her childhood she also expressed interest in activities that were regarded as more masculine, including horseback riding and fighting with sword and shield. According to the saga, she soon became an expert in using different kinds of weapons, but her father did not approve of her unconventional interests. One day, when he expressed his discontent, Þornbjörg gave him a very bold reply:

> Since you've been given only one life to govern this kingdom and I'm your only child and heir [...] it seems very likely that I'll have to defend it against a few kings or princes once you're gone. It's also hardly likely I'll be very keen to marry any-one against my will if it ever comes to that, and that's why I want to get to know something of the skills of knighthood. It seems to me that would give me a better chance of holding on to this kingdom, with the help of strong and reliable followers. So I want you, father, to put me in charge of some part of your kingdom while you're still alive, so that I can try my hand at government and commanding the men entrusted to me. There's one more point: if any-one asks to marry me and I don't want him, there'll be a better chance of your kingdom being left in peace if you leave the answers to me.[69]

Although Þornbjörg's father was initially not at ease with her audacity, he nevertheless decided to grant her control over a third of his realm. Furthermore, he fortified her residence at Ullarakur and provided her with tough and obedient warriors. Þornbjörg was soon elected king over one third of Sweden and she also took up a new male name, Þórbergr, making sure people would from that moment onwards refrain from calling her a maiden or a woman. Having acquired a new masculine identity, Þórbergr 'started dubbing knights and appointing courtiers, and gave them pay the same as king Eiríkr of Uppsala'.[70]

As time goes by, the saga's main protagonist, Hrólfr, is tempted to try his luck in obtaining Þornbjörg's hand in marriage. Rumours spread that the woman has already turned down several suitors and that she has even had some of them killed 'and others maimed one way or another, some blinded, some castrated, some have had their arms or legs cut off, and she's ridiculed and insulted everybody'.[71] Hrólfr is well-aware of this, but nonetheless decides to take up the challenge and sets out to meet her parents with the intention to present his marriage proposal. Þornbjörg's father is initially reluctant to give him his approval, but later, after he has consulted the matter with his wife, he gives Hrólfr a favourable answer and they finally reach an agreement. Next, Hrólfr travels to see Þornbjörg at Ullarakur where he receives a very cold welcome. Nevertheless, Hrólfr boldly proposes and speaks of his desire to have her as his wife, expressing his hope that she will give strength and support to their realm and rear and increase their offspring. All these words – essentially completely undermining her new masculine identity – infuriate Þornbjörg immensely and soon a fierce fight ensues. Completely outnumbered, Hrólfr is forced to flee and the news about his failure spreads widely bringing him nothing but shame. The ambitious and determined man does not wish to give up, however, and soon gathers new forces to try his luck yet again.

When Hrólfr returns to Ullarakur, he can see that the maiden king has not been idle and that she has prepared herself very well for his arrival – the noise of weapons can be heard everywhere and the fortress is better protected than before. He asks her yet for her hand in marriage but she refuses. Moreover, to silence his words, Þornbjörg starts beating her shield and soon her followers do the same. Seeing no other alternative, Hrólfr commences his attack. The battle is extremely fierce and whatever strategy Hrólfr tries, there is always something to curb his intentions so that he is unable to enter the fortress. When he finally manages to overcome the defences, he finds the fortress all empty and realises that Þornbjörg has escaped using an underground passage. His army then enters the passage and they eventually find themselves in a forest where the forces of the maiden king are waiting. Another fight ensues but yet again the Swedes suffer heavy losses. At some point one of the combatants, Ketill (Hrólfr's brother), manages to get very close to Þornbjörg. He slaps her backside with the flat of his sword and utters the following insult: 'here's how we cure your itching crutch. That's what I call a dirty stroke!'[72] In response, Þornbjörg strikes him with full strength with her axe and knocks him over. Hrólfr then manages to lay his hands on the maiden king and promises to spare everyone's lives if only she agrees to marry him. Þornbjörg finally gives in and embarks

on a journey to Uppsala to seek her father's counsel. When she arrives at her father's court, she ceremoniously lays her shield on the floor, removes her helmet, admits that she has been defeated and succumbs to her father's will. King Eiríkr then gives her the following response:

> We'd be very pleased if you'd stop this fighting and turn to feminine matters in your mother's boudoir. After that, we'd like to marry you to King Hrolf Gautreksson, because we haven't come across his equal anywhere in Scandinavia.[73]

The daughter accepts her father's will, hands over the weapons and begins working at embroidery together with her mother. Soon king Hrólf marries Þornbjörg and together they take rule over her kingdom. After some time has passed, the queen gives birth to two sons who are named Gautrek and Eiríkr. As the years go by, Þornbjörg remains a very good advisor to her husband (including offering her assistance on military matters) but she completely abandons her former lifestyle as an active warrior. Nevertheless, when one day her husband goes missing, driven by romantic concerns, she yet again musters an army, takes her shield and sword and sets out with her twelve-year-old son Gautrek in search for him. This situation resembles the aforementioned event from *Gesta Danorum* when Lathgertha set out to help her husband when he was in need of support in battle.

Other armed women in the fornaldarsögur

In addition to the stories of Hervör and Þornbjörg, the *fornaldarsögur* preserve accounts of other women who take up arms and step into the male role. For instance, *Hrólfs saga kraka* mentions a woman named Ólöf, who is the queen of Saxaland but whom the saga portrays as an army king. She is clad in armour, carries a shield and sword and wears a helmet. However, in contrast to Hervör and Þornbjörg, and despite the fact that she is dressed like a warrior, she does not actively participate in battle.[74]

Another armed woman is mentioned in *Örvar Odds saga*.[75] She is a loyal companion of the king of Garðariki and assists him in all his battles. One day, the king offers her services to Örvar Oddr (the main protagonist of the saga) and compels her to join his expedition. Regardless of the king's high opinion of her, the woman does not perform very well and at one point in the story is afraid to come over a swamp. This disappoints Örvar Oddr so much that he eventually casts the woman into the swamp.

Armed women also appear in an unexpected and unusual manner in a short *fornaldarsaga* known as *Ásmundar saga kappabana*.[76] Here, they show up in the main protagonist's dream, promising him to serve as his prophetic spirits and to defend him against his enemies. Soon everything the women have professed turns out to be true – when the day of the battle comes, weapons cannot cause any serious harm to Ásmund and his sword cuts everything and everyone that stands in his way.[77]

In *Hálfdanar saga Eysteinssonsar* an old sorceress gives the main protagonist named Hálfdan a short sword which is as bright as a polished mirror and which seems to drip venom from its edges (interestingly, before giving the weapon to Hálfdan, the woman had kept it in a rag bag under her pillow).[78] She also assures him that anyone carrying the sword will be victorious as long as the weapon is properly handled. Hálfdan later uses the sword in his adventures and kills several of his enemies with it, including a dragon. The special features of this weapon resemble those of the famed sword Týrfing already mentioned above, but in this particular story the sword does not serve as a potent symbol of inheritance as was the case in *Hervarar saga ok Heiðreks konungs*.

Armed women in Old Norse mythology

From the *dísir*, *fylgjur*, *hamingjur* and *nornir* to the famed *valkyrjur*, the Old Norse mythical landscape was rich with supernatural female beings. These entities were endowed with various powers and capable of providing protection at home and on the battlefield, as well as having the ability to influence human fate. According to extant Old Norse sources, people would address them through special spells and magic formulas, but allegedly some individuals would also meet them in their dreams. Archaeological excavations have also provided tangible evidence for the belief and perhaps also worship of female supernatural beings, as suggested by runic inscriptions mentioning their names[79] and small figurines possibly serving as their visual representations (on these finds, see Chapter 6).

In investigating the different kinds and roles of supernatural beings in Old Norse pre-Christian beliefs, one can frequently encounter female entities that are either directly associated with the martial sphere or those that only occasionally carry weapons. The most prominent among the former are certainly the *valkyrjur* or Valkyries – in fact, no other supernatural entities have such close associations with warfare as they do. But in addition to the *valkyrjur*, also other beings that inhabited the Old Norse conceptual landscapes used weapons – among them were Giantesses, often portrayed as immensely powerful beings additionally skilled in magic arts. Finally, there is also Freyja who, although conventionally associated with fertility and widely understood sexuality, appears to have had a not insignificant connection with the sphere of war; according to the poem *Grímnismál*, half of the warriors slain in battle departed to the enigmatic Fólkvangr, a special otherworldly place ruled over by this goddess. In the sections below we will investigate the nature of a number of supernatural female beings more closely, aiming to find whether and in what sense they resemble the images of armed women from the sources discussed earlier.

Valkyrjur, dísir, fylgjur

The *valkyrjur* are some of the most prominent supernatural female beings in Old Norse literature, and a wealth of information about them can be found in extant texts.[80] They appear in all saga genres as well as in eddic and skaldic poetry. Furthermore, their names are sometimes mentioned in runic inscriptions.

The *valkyrjur* or 'choosers of the slain' are intrinsically associated with the battlefield where their major role is to select warriors who are to be killed. They also have a strong connection with Óðinn, acting as his companions in Valhöll – an otherworldly feasting hall built from spears and shields – where they serve beer to fallen warriors known as the *einherjar* who eat and drink there every evening.

In his impressively thorough examination of the intricate nature of the *valkyrjur*, Neil Price has pointed out the fact that many of their names allude to aspects of violent conflict, such as the dramatic sounds and sights like the clashing of arms, clattering, grinding, pushing, scraping, shaking etc. The compound names of some of the *valkyrjur* also refer to specific types of weapons, mainly spears and shields. One *valkyrja* name, Skegg[j]öld, has been translated to mean 'Axe-Age'.[81] Two names, Hjörþrimul and Skalmöld refer to swords and have been translated as Sword-Noise and Sword-Time respectively.[82] One name, Hjalmþrimul, refers to a helmet and means Helmet-Clatter.[83] It is also worthy of note that *valkyrja* names tend to appear in poetry as metaphors (kennings) for different kinds of weapons like swords, shields and armour.[84]

Price has argued that the typical image of the *valkyrjur* most people have today differs considerably from what is actually conveyed by Old Norse textual sources, and he has also noted that the medieval literary portrayals of the *valkyrjur* have changed over the course of time. Initially, the *valkyrjur* would have been conceptualised as terrible 'female demons of carnage' and only later they 'took on a semi-human aspect, and were depicted as tragic warrior women, doomed by their love for mortal men'.[85] It is also worthy of note that some *valkyrjur* are called *skaldmeyjar*, a term conventionally associated with female warriors belonging to the human world.

One of the most evocative literary sources that displays the intricate associations between the *valkyrjur* and the sphere of war is the Old Norse poem known as *Darraðarljóð* interpolated in *Brennu-Njáls saga*. Extensive research on *Darraðarljóð* – a source to which we will return in Chapter 5 – has shown that although it survives in a saga from the thirteenth century, it is of much earlier tenth-century date and refers to events that occurred in 919. This magnificent piece of Old Norse poetry mentions twelve *valkyrjur* who weave battle on a macabre loom made out of various weapons: human heads serve as weights and entrails substitute for weft and warp. As they weave, the *valkyrjur* sing their song and when their work is finally finished they rip the textile apart and ride away to the south and to the north. Here, the women participate in armed conflict from afar (and perhaps in a purely metaphorical sense) but in other sources – such as the poem *Hákonarmál* – the *valkyrjur* actually/physically take part in the act of killing a king.[86]

According to some Old Norse texts, the *valkyrjur* have the ability to fly and they are shown wearing feathered costumes.[87] For instance, in the prose introduction to *Völundarkviða* they have swan garments. In light of the ambivalent nature of the *valkyrjur*, their association with these animals is by no means surprising – swans are very graceful birds but they can be fierce and aggressive, especially when defending their nests and territories.

An apparently female figure wearing a special kind of headgear(?) in the form of a bird head (perhaps that of a swan?) is shown on the Oseberg tapestry,[88] and one *guldgubbe* from Torring in Denmark bears a representation of a female dressed in what looks like a feathered costume.[89] In this context we may recall Saxo Grammaticus' remark about the unusual fighting technique of Lathgertha who apparently 'flew round the rear of the unprepared enemy in a circling manoeuvre and carried the panic which had been felt by the allies into the camp of their adversaries'.[90] Price has speculated that 'perhaps the "early" *valkyrjur* possessed an innate ability to fly, but also used horses either in the air or on the ground'[91] and he has also made an interesting observation that 'the *valkyrjur* in the heroic poems are re-incarnations of others, moving from supernatural to human forms and back again'.[92] The latter idea could perhaps also explain why some female ritual specialists used weapons, why one of them was actually called 'the angel of death'[93] and why in Anglo-Saxon England they were referred to as *wælcyrge*.[94] There are hints in the archaeological record suggesting that some female ritual specialists occasionally mirrored or re-enacted the deeds of the mythical *valkyrjur* or that they were considered as their human incarnations.

Other supernatural female beings, who share similar traits with the *valkyrjur*, are sometimes encountered in Old Norse texts in the context of violence and battle.[95] For instance, in *Ólafs saga Tryggvasonar en mesta* the *dísir* commence an attack on a hall and in *Brennu-Njáls saga* the *fylgjur* are responsible for creating fog and causing confusion among one group of combatants engaged in an armed conflict. As noted earlier, aside from the *valkyrjur*, *dísir* and *fylgjur*, female beings who wield weapons and actively engage in combat are also found among the Giants. It is to these intriguing women of the Old Norse world of thought that we shall now turn our attention.

Skaði

Skaði is a giantess who features in several Old Norse sources including *Grímnismál* (st 11), *Hyndluljóð* (st 30), *Lokasenna* (st 49–52), *Gylfaginning* (ch. 22–23), *Skáldskaparmál* and *Ynglingasaga*.[96] According to *Skáldskaparmál* (1), when her father Þjázi gets killed by the Æsir, Skaði – in the absence of any male relative to avenge his death – immediately decides to seek retribution. She puts on mail armour and helmet, takes a set of weapons and travels to Ásgarðr. Instead of engaging in a fight, however, the Æsir offer her a settlement and compensation and they also allow her to choose a husband: the rule is, however, that she is only able to see his lower legs. Skaði of course picks the one with the most beautiful legs, hoping that it is Baldr, but – to her disappointment – the man turns out to be Njörðr of Nóatún. Since each of the two partners desperately wants to live in a different place (Skaði wishes to stay in the mountains, while Njörðr wants to be by the sea), their marriage is a complete failure. In the end the couple separate and Skaði continues to live in the wilderness where she enjoys skiing and shooting game.

Based on the admittedly scant textual evidence, we can see that Skaði differs from the human female heroines of the *fornaldarsögur* in that she never engages in actual combat. However, she does seem to have some traits in common with warrior women; she enjoys the wilderness and the harsh mountainous landscapes as well as hunting and using her bow and arrows. Given these characteristics, Rudolf Simek considers her as a Norse counterpart to the Greek goddess Artemis.[97] John McKinnell, on the other hand, rightly observes that in the story of Skaði there is an intriguing reversal of traditional social norms and narrative patterns where it is typically the armed male hero who seeks the bride – here, instead, it is Skaði who takes up the masculine role. McKinnell argues that 'this inversion implies some disgrace for both parties (for Njörðr in allowing himself to be chosen like a woman, for Skaði in her diversion from honourable vengeance into marriage with one of her father's slayers)'.[98]

Þorgerðr Hölgabrúðr

Þorgerðr is one of the most puzzling characters that appears in Old Norse literature. She makes an appearance in several different accounts, predominantly in *Jómsvíkinga saga* (ch. 33) but also in *Brennu-Njáls saga* (ch. 88), *Færeyinga saga*, *Harðar saga* (ch. 19), *Ketils saga hœngs* (ch. 5), *Þorleifs þáttr jarlaskálds* as well as in Þorkell Gíslason's *Búadrápa* and in *Ólafs saga Tryggvasonar* in *Flateyjarbók*. The image of Þorgerðr Hölgabrúðr[99] that emerges from these different sources is not homogenous, however; some accounts suggest she is a kind of goddess who even has her own temples in Gudbrandsdalen in western Norway (*Brennu-Njáls saga*, ch. 88) and southern Iceland, while other texts imply that she should rather be seen as a completely different kind of supernatural being, most probably a Giantess or generally a sort of 'troll-woman'. Extant sources provide limited information about her physical appearance: we know from *Brennu-Njáls saga* that she is tall and that her statue has a headdress, while *Flayteyjarbók* says that she is beautifully dressed. Similar to Skaði, the supernatural female being known as Þorgerðr Hölgabrúðr (portrayed in *Jómsvíkinga saga*) also has a warlike nature but in contrast to the rather passive Skaði she actually displays her agency in combat.[100]

For the purposes of the present discussion it is worth providing a commentary on Þorgerðr's involvement in the battle between the Jómsvíkingar (led by Sigvaldi) and Hákon jarl which broke out at Hjörungavágr in 986. According to *Jómsvíkinga saga*, in order to secure his success in battle Hákon jarl resorts to extreme measures and sacrifices his own seven-year-old son to Þorgerðr in return for her supernatural assistance.[101] During the fight that follows, Þorgerðr, together with her enigmatic sister called Irpa,[102] aid Hákon's warriors with their magic. The fierce battle with the Jómsvíkingar is vividly described in *Jómsvíkinga saga* and the relevant passage is worth citing here:

> Eptir þat ferr jarl aptr til skipa sinna ok eggjar nú lið sitt af nýju, 'ok veit ek nú víst at oss mun sigrs auðit. Ok gangið nú fram at betr því at ek hefi heitit til sigrs oss á þær báðar systr, Þorgerði ok Irpu.' Nú gengr jarl á skip sitt ok búask um af nýju. Ok síðan greiða þeir atróðrinn ok teksk þar nú af nýju inn grimmasti bardagi. Ok því næst tekr veðrit at þykkna í norðr ok dregr yfir skjótt. Líðr ok á daginn. Því næst flugu eldingar ok reiðar, ok því næst gørir á él mikit. Þeir Jómsvíkingar áttu at vega í gegn veðrinu. Þetta él var með svá miklum býsnum at menn máttu varla standask. En menn höfðu áðr farit af klæðunum fyrir hita sakir, en nú tók at kólna. Sœkja þó bardagann frýjulaust. Ok þó at þeir Jómsvíkingar kastaði grjóti eða vápnum eða skyti spjótum, þá bar veðrit þat aptr á þá allt ok þar með vápnagangr sinna óvinna.
>
> Hávarðr höggvandi sá fyrstr Hölgabrúði í liði Hákonar jarls ok margir sá ófreskir menn. Ok þá er líttat linaði élinu sá þeir at ör fló af hverjum fingri flagðinu ok varð maðr fyrir hverri; ok sögðu þeir Sigvalda. Ok hann mælti: 'Eigi þykki mér þá sem vér berimsk við menn eina, en þó er nauðsyn at hverr dugi sem má.' Þá er nökkut linaði élinu heitr Hákon jarl í annat sinn á Þorgerði ok kvezk nú hafa mikit til unnit. Nú tekr í annat sinn at røkkva at élinu ok er nú miklu meira ok harðara en fyrr. Ok þegar í öndverðu élinu þá sér Hávarðr höggvandi at tvær konur eru komnar á skip jarls ok hafa eitt atferli.

After that the earl went back to his ships and encouraged his men anew 'and I know now for certain that we shall be victorious. Go forward more bravely in the knowledge that I have invoked the two sisters Þorgerðr and Irpa for our victory.' The earl went aboard his ship and they made ready again. Afterwards they attacked and fierce fighting broke out once more. And thereupon clouds began to gather in the north and, as the day drew on, they soon covered the whole sky. This was followed by lightning and thunder, accompanied by a violent hailstorm. The Jómsvíkingar had to fight against the storm and the hailstorm was so fierce that men could hardly keep on their feet. Many had taken off their clothes earlier because of the heat, but now it began to freeze. But they fought the battle fearlessly. Though the Jómsvíkingar hurled stones or weapons or shot spears, the storm brought it all back on themselves together with their opponents' weapons.

Hávarðr the hewer was the first to see Hölgabrúðr among Hákon's men, but many others endowed with second sight saw her, too. When the hail let up a little, they saw that an arrow flew from every finger of the witch and each one found its mark. They told this to Sigvaldi. And he said: 'I don't think that we are fighting against men alone, but yet everyone must fight as well as he can.' When the hailstorm slackened somewhat, Earl Hákon called on Þorgerðr a second time reminding her how much he had sacrificed to her. Then the hailstorm began a second time though much harder and fiercer than before. As soon as the storm began Hávarðr the hewer saw that there were then two women on the earl's ship both doing the same thing.[103]

This passage shows unequivocally that the two supernatural women are not only present among the combatants but also take very active part in the fight – Þorgerðr shoots arrows from her fingers and, together with her sister Irpa, she is also responsible for the strange weather phenomena that impede the Jómsvíkingar. It is noteworthy, however, that although the warriors from each of the fighting parties are all affected by the women's supernatural power and magic, not everyone can actually see them, only those who have been endowed with 'second-sight'. The belief that the women are aiding Hákon gives his men the courage to excel and at the same time leads the Jómsvíkingar to fail in their attempts to gain advantage in combat. Here, perhaps, the saga gives us a rare glimpse into the psychological aspects of Viking Age warfare and into the great power of mental manipulation.

Female Giantesses as grinders of war and bearers of arms

Aside from Skaði and Þorgerðr other Giantesses of Old Norse literature are occasionally seen bearing arms and/or actively fighting. Among them are two Giant women called Fenja and Menja[104] who in the eddic poem *Grottasöngr* operate a magic millstone belonging to king Fróði that has the capacity to grind anything the owner desires.[105] The women serve as Fróði's slaves, and as they work, they reminisce and boast about their former deeds:

> Enn vit síðan á Svíðióðo,
> framvísar tvær, í fólc stigom;
> beittom biorno, enn brutom scioldo,
> gengom í gegnom gráserkiat lið.
> Steypþom stilli, studdom annan,
> veittom góðom Gothormi lið;
> vara kyrrseta, áðr Knúi felli.
> Fram heldom því þau misseri,
> at vit at köppom kendar vórom;
> þar scorðo vit scörpom geirom
> blóð ór beniom oc brand ruðom.[106]
>
> And afterwards in Sweden,
> we two fore-sighted ones advanced in the army;

> we challenged bearlike warriors, we smashed shields,
> we marched through the grey-corsletted army.
> We overthrew one prince, we supported another one,
> we gave good Gothorm help;
> there was no sitting quiet until Knúi fell.
> So we went on for some seasons,
> so that we were acclaimed as champions;
> there we scored with sharp spears
> blood out of wounds and reddened the sword.[107]

In many regards the behaviour of the two Giantesses in *Grottasöngr* echoes the work of the twelve *valkyrjur* from *Darraðarljóð*. Here, too, the traditionally domestic practice undergoes a radical transformation and becomes an act of sheer magic – at first the process of grinding is intended to bring peace and prosperity but after a while it becomes linked only with martial violence. The two women who operate the millstone are described as 'mighty' and apparently good-looking, but the poem soon makes it clear that they also have extensive experience in combat. The latter is something Fróði had not realised when he enslaved them. As their song draws to an end, and as their work becomes more and more relentless, Fenja and Menja foresee the end of Fróði's rule and the collapse of his kingdom. In the end, the rageful grinding makes the mill-shafts shudder, the mill-box collapses and the grindstone breaks in two. This striking image, when all is broken into pieces, harks back to the memorable finale of *Darraðarljóð* where the blood-stained textile stretched on a macabre loom is torn apart by the *valkyrjur*.

Armed women of the Viking Age in non-Scandinavian medieval sources

We have now investigated various portrayals of human and supernatural armed women in the Norse cultural context. These individuals are not completely unique to Scandinavia and Iceland, however, and Medieval textual sources stemming from non-Norse parts of Europe preserve accounts of other Viking Age women who wielded weapons and in one way or another engaged in warfare. A comprehensive exploration of all these stories is beyond the scope of this monograph, and for the purpose of the present study it should suffice to point to two particularly evocative cases, namely that of the Anglo-Saxon queen Æthelflæd of Mercia and of the women who engaged in the battle of Dorostolon.

Æthelflæd of Mercia

Æthelflæd was the daughter of Alfred the Great, an Anglo-Saxon ruler famous for his wars against Viking armies that repeatedly invaded England as well as for his social reforms and the construction and reinforcement of boroughs.[108] In contrast to the stories of the Norse female heroines Hervör and Þornbjörg, extant textual sources convey relatively little about Æthelflæd's childhood but we can assume that she was born sometime in 870 or early in 871.[109] Her compound name is unusual in the Anglo-Saxon context and has been translated as 'noble beauty' or 'noble flood', essentially implying that the person bearing it was 'overflowing with nobility'.[110] Since her family belonged to the social elite and since there does not seem to have been any bias against allowing young girls and women to pursue education, Æthelflæd was doubtlessly knowledgeable and literate.[111] However, regardless of her later career as a prominent and successful military leader, there is nothing to suggest that she grew up as a tomboy like some of the Norse women of the *fornaldarsögur*. As Joanna Alpern argues:

> As a girl, she would almost certainly not have been given the training in arms and martial pursuits that were part of the traditional education of male children, and probably spent much of her time in female company with her mother and other noblewomen or a nurse and female attendants.[112]

Around the time when she turned fourteen, Æthelflæd married Æthelred of Mercia, a man probably at least ten years older than her and already accomplished in the sphere of warfare and politics.[113] Because Æthelred suffered from ill health,[114] over the course of twenty-five years of their marriage it was Æthelflæd who gradually had to take on a leading role. After her husband's death in 911 she became the Lady of Mercia, essentially a queen ruling in her own right.

The difficult socio-political circumstances in England in the ninth century, mostly associated with the continuous waves of Norse invasions, compelled the young ruler to take on the additional role of military leader. Similar to her father, to defend her land against Danish attacks she began a programme of fortress building, and over the period of ten years she constructed ten fortified garrisons.[115] The *Fragmentary Annals of Ireland* mention that Æthelflæd was responsible for organising the defence of Chester in 907 against an attack of Danish and Norwegian Vikings commanded by a warlord called Ingimund.[116] As a leader Æthelflæd also orchestrated a number of other military operations, for instance a punitive expedition against the Welsh in 916, as well as a fierce attack on Derby intended to regain control over the town after it had been taken over by Vikings. She was also responsible for leading her forces to the fortress of Leicester – the crew of which eventually surrendered without a fight.

Although Æthelflæd was undoubtedly a skilled leader, extant textual sources do not provide concrete evidence that she participated in armed conflicts as an active warrior. Nevertheless, given the fact that she was regarded as the Lady of the Mercians and that she ruled like a queen at the same time being responsible for military campaigns in the face of constant threat from Norse invaders, it is highly probable that her contemporaries would have regarded her as an embodiment of the 'warrior ideal', even if she never actually used weapons in direct hand-to-hand combat. In all this – similar to some of the warrior women of the sagas surveyed above – Æthelflæd was also a mother to a daughter named Ælfwyn who was likely born in the early years of her marriage with Æthelred.[117] Her case shows that having a child in the Viking Age did not mean that the mother was confined to her home and that if necessary or desired she could take up many other challenges, including those related to the sphere of war.

Women and war in the account of John Skylitzes

In his major work known as *Synopsis of Histories*, Greek historian and high official John Skylitzes included a detailed account of a battle that broke out at Dorostolon (today's Silistra in Bulgaria) in 971 between the army of the Kievan Rus and the Byzantines – a battle in which women allegedly fought alongside men.[118]

The fortress of Dorostolon was seized by the Kievan Rus prince Svyatoslav I who had occupied Bulgaria with his army and had been particularly 'charmed by the fertility of the place'.[119] The fact that the Rus considered Bulgaria as conquered territory was met with disapproval from the Byzantines and this eventually led to armed conflict. Soon, Emperor John commenced an attack on Dorostolon – occupied by Svyatoslav and his people – and sieged it for a period of 65 days. The battle was fierce and violent and involved a series of melees outside the walls, but overall it was the Rus who suffered the most severe casualties; interestingly, Skylitzes mentions that for the first time the Rus were seen fighting on horseback.[120]

Despite various efforts to renew their supplies, including a night-time guerrilla attack on the Byzantines outside the city walls, the Rus defenders were soon struck with severe famine. According to another Byzantine historian, Leo Deacon, in an act of desperation and in the hope to overcome it by resorting to religious measures, the Rus made a sacrifice of chickens and drowned them in the Danube.[121] This came to no avail, however – the Rus forces were largely reduced and in the end, despite all their heroic efforts, they were forced to sign a treaty with the Byzantines.

In the context of our discussion on armed women in the Viking Age, it is worth pointing out that in describing some of the last stages of the battle, Johannes Skylitzes mentions that the Byzantines were surprised that among the dead were also women 'equipped like men'. In his own words, the historian says:

> When the Romans fell on them again, the Scyths were put to fight and ingloriously sought refuge in the city. Many of them fell that day, trodden underfoot by others in the narrow defile and slain by the Romans when they were trapped there. Sviatoslav himself would have been taken too, if night had not fallen and delivered him. [...] When the Romans were robbing the corpses of the barbarians of their spoils, they found women lying among the fallen, equipped like men; women who had fought against the Romans together with the men.[122]

Apart from this brief mention, Skylitzes does not provide any details as regards the identity of these women. We do not know if they were common civilians who simply took up arms in the face of imminent danger or actual female warriors who had had prior experience and training in using weapons. Notwithstanding these uncertainties, this piece of information, in a source completely unrelated to and culturally distant from the Old Norse texts reviewed above, implies that in some circumstances Viking Age women *did* actively participate in armed conflict. It remains completely obscure if these women were of Norse origin, however. Since Svyatoslav's army comprised people from many different cultural milieus, especially nomadic, it is therefore quite possible that if he actually had some warrior women among his troops, these females were of nomadic rather than Norse descent.

Women with weapons in medieval literature: more than literary embellishments

When all surviving Old Norse texts are critically drawn together, what emerges is a complex image of women's association with weapons and the sphere of war. As we have seen, in the *Íslendingasögur* women are rarely portrayed as bearers of arms – they typically reach for weapons (usually swords) to exercise revenge or defend themselves. Only in one unusual instance recorded in *Ljósvetninga saga* an axe is used by a sorceress in a violent prophetic ritual. In the majority of cases, to achieve their goals the women of the *Íslendingasögur* resort to other non-martial measures – they either goad men to fulfil their will (something that often leads to dramatic consequences) or perform magic. It is also noteworthy that whenever women use actual weapons they rarely do so to kill other people (the only exception is Freydís who murders five slaves); they only inflict serious wounds that bring shame to their victims (as in the case of Bróka Auðr and Þórdís) or confuse and frighten their enemies (as in the case of Freydís in the memorable episode in Vínland). Even though the armed women of the *Íslendingasögur* cannot be regarded as warriors in the strict sense, we should acknowledge the fact that they are all individuals endowed with a very strong will and sense of justice who are not afraid to speak their mind and who have the courage and capacity to take matters into their own hands even if this means contravening social norms.

The image of the armed woman in the *fornaldarsögur* is a whole different story, however. Here we encounter actual female warriors who have the capacity and necessary skills to wield various kinds of weapons (swords, shields), command men and exercise royal power in their own right. The captivating stories of Hervör/Hervard and Þornbjörg detailed above show clearly that for some women of the *fornaldarsögur* the path to becoming a warrior is something they choose consciously and willingly. Often, these women tend to display certain predispositions for an adventurous lifestyle from a very early age. As we have seen, already as a child Hervör commenced weapon training and preferred sword and shield to engaging in domestic and typically feminine activities. In modern parlance, we could perhaps consider her as a hyperactive child and we can get the impression that her tomboyish nature was nothing unusual given the particular time and environment where she was raised. However, the saga makes it very clear that the people closest to her were so displeased with her that they simply considered her 'evil'. Certainly, running in the woods and killing purely for pleasure is an act of sadism not heroism. In her later years Hervör undergoes a significant transformation, however, learning to control her fiery nature and eventually settling down to become a mother. Nevertheless, the Viking spirit still continues to run strong in her family and is passed on to her progeny, including her granddaughter. Þornbjörg of *Hrólfs saga Gautrekssonar* is similar to Hervör in many ways – she is also raised by the elite and from the early days of her childhood prefers riding and fighting to practicing typically feminine crafts. Her parents disapprove of this but they ultimately have little choice but to accept her firm decision to step into a masculine role. In ruling her new kingdom at Ullarakur, Þornbjörg does not shy away from violence or even sheer sadism and brutality – some of her unsuccessful suitors are not only left insulted or ridiculed but also blinded, castrated or mutilated in other ways. Like Hervör, after living a life of a warrior, Þornbjörg eventually settles down, marries and gives birth to two children. Nevertheless, when her husband faces danger, Þornbjörg does not hesitate to act and sails overseas to rescue him.

The *Poetic Edda* also preserves accounts of women who take up arms and courageously launch themselves into the fray. We will examine them in further detail in the chapters that follow, but here it is worth pointing to a memorable episode depicted in *Atlamál in grœnlenzko*, a poem likely composed in the twelfth century that retells the dramatic story of a man named Atli, possibly echoing the deeds of the famed Attila the Hun. To defend the life of her brothers, queen Guðrún, who is Atli's wife, throws away her jewellery and cloak (an act that can be seen to symbolise a temporary abandonment of her feminine identity) and with no hesitation reaches for a weapon. Her actions are worth recounting here by citing the relevant stanzas of the poem:

> Sá þá sælborin, at þeir sárt léco,
> hugði á harðræði oc hrauze ór sciccio;
> nǫcþan tóc hon mæki oc niðia fior varði,
> hœg var at hialdri, hvars hon hendr festi.
> Dóttir lét Giúca drengi tvá hníga,
> bróður hió hon Atla, bera varð þann síðan,
> scapþi hon svá scœro, sceldi fót undan.

> Annan réð hon hǫggva, svá at sá upp reisat,
> í helio hon þann hafði; þeygi henni hendr sculfo.[123]

Then the high-born lady saw them play a wounding game,
  she resolved on a hard course and flung off her cloak;
she took a naked sword and fought for her kinsmen's lives,
  she was easy with fighting, wherever she turned her hand.
    Giuki's daughter brought down to fighters,
  she struck at Atli's brother – he had to be carried off:
she shaped her strokes so she cut his leg from under him.
Another she set to strike so that he did not get up again,
  she had him away into hell; nor did her hands tremble.[124]

Aside from portraying these remarkable human female individuals, whose 'hands do not tremble' when they have to take up arms and fight, Old Norse literature and the Norse world of thought was saturated with images of supernatural women who immersed themselves in the sphere of war. In the sections above we have reviewed the nature and deeds of the *valkyrjur* whose compound names often allude to the sights and sounds of armed conflict. Furthermore, we have also seen them as violent and almost demonic entities who have the capacity to influence the outcome of battles. Other supernatural beings that inhabited the Norse imagination, such as the *fylgjur* and the *dísir*, are also occasionally associated with broadly understood warfare. The Giantesses, for instance, tend to participate in martial endeavours in various guises – either directly engaging in battles and aiding warriors with their powerful spells (as in the case of Þorgerðr Holgabrúðr and Irpa in *Jómsvíkingasaga*) or by predicting and magically influencing future conflict (as in the case of Fenja and Menja in *Grottasöngr*). On the other hand, some of their kind, like the Giantess Skaði, display the capacity to bear arms and fight but never actually use weapons for any other purpose than hunting animals.

In discussing all these diverse images of armed and actively fighting women of Old Norse literature, and in critically acknowledging that many of the accounts that concern them were created several centuries after the events, it is easy to relegate them all to the sphere of fiction and to regard them as having no basis in historical reality whatsoever. But if we turn to other medieval sources, created independently of Old Norse literary tradition and stemming from different cultural milieus, we will find within them very similar patterns of the occasional female participation in martial activities. The two case studies reviewed above – namely that of Æthelflæd of Mercia and of the women who fought in the siege of Dorostolon – strongly support the idea that there *could be* some reality behind the stories of armed women that survive in Old Norse literature. Also other historical women of the Viking Age, especially those who stemmed from the highest echelons of society, were occasionally compelled to engage in endeavours associated with warfare and would oversee military operations. For instance, the great Princess Olga, who was the wife of Igor of Kiev, led her army against the Slavic tribe of Derevlians, devised her own impressive strategies and through all these initiatives gained recognition among her companions, regardless of her biological sex.[125]

It thus feels highly unlikely that *all* these medieval accounts, including the famed descriptions of female warriors in Saxo Grammaticus' *Gesta Danorum*, were only inspired by legends of the ancient Amazons and served as curiosa and literary embellishments to entertain the audience. As we shall see in the following chapters of this book, archaeological finds from across Scandinavia provide support for the idea that *some* Viking Age women *did* wield weapons and in one way or another found their place in the martial sphere.

Notes

1. See, for example, Jesch 1991: 176–177; Gardeła 2013b: 305; 2018b: 409–413.
2. Saxo Grammaticus, *Gesta Danorum*, Book VII (6.8). Text and translation after Friis-Jensen & Fisher 2015: 476–478.
3. The famous battle of Brávellir is also described in *Sögubrot af fornkonungum*. For a detailed discussion on this event and a comparison between the different textual sources that mention it, see Ashman Rowe 2010.
4. Saxo Grammaticus, *Gesta Danorum*, Book VIII (2.5). Text and translation after Friis-Jensen & Fisher 2015: 534–537.
5. Saxo Grammaticus, *Gesta Danorum*, Book VIII (2.6). Text and translation after Friis-Jensen & Fisher 2015: 536–537.
6. On Ragnarr loðbrók, see Ashman Rowe 2012 with further references.
7. Saxo Grammaticus, *Gesta Danorum*, Book IX (4.1). Translation after Friis-Jensen & Fisher 2015: 633.
8. Saxo Grammaticus, *Gesta Danorum*, Book IX (4.2). Text and translation after Friis-Jensen & Fisher 2015: 632–633.
9. Saxo Grammaticus, *Gesta Danorum*, Book IX (4.2). Translation after Friis-Jensen & Fisher 2015: 633.
10. Saxo Grammaticus, *Gesta Danorum*, Book IX (4.3).
11. Saxo Grammaticus, *Gesta Danorum*, Book IX (4.11). Text and translation after Friis-Jensen & Fisher 2015: 638–639.
12. Jesch 1991: 180.
13. Saxo Grammaticus, *Gesta Danorum*, Book VII (6.1).
14. On the multi-layered symbolism of snakes in Viking and medieval Scandinavia, see Paulsen 1966; Brunning 2015; Gardeła 2020a. On the significance of snakes in the North, see also Pearl 2014.
15. Saxo Grammaticus, *Gesta Danorum*, Book VII (6.4). Text and translation after Friis-Jensen & Fisher 2015: 472–475.
16. Saxo Grammaticus, *Gesta Danorum*, Book VII (6.5). Translation after Friis-Jensen & Fisher 2015: 475.
17. Saxo Grammaticus, *Gesta Danorum*, Book VII (6.7). Translation after Friis-Jensen & Fisher 2015: 475–477.
18. Saxo Grammaticus, *Gesta Danorum*, Book VII (9.9). Translation after Friis-Jensen & Fisher 2015: 503.
19. Saxo Grammaticus, *Gesta Danorum*, Book VII (10.2). Translation after Friis-Jensen & Fisher 2015: 513.
20. Ellis Davidson & Fisher 2008: 1, 4.
21. Ellis Davidson & Fisher 2008: 2.
22. Saxo Grammaticus, *Gesta Danorum*, Preface (1.3). Friis-Jensen & Fisher 2015: 7.
23. Cf. Jóhanna Katrín Friðriksdóttir 2020: 67.
24. Jochens 1996: 88.
25. On the *Íslendingasögur*, see O'Donoghue 2004; Clover 2005; Vésteinn Ólason 2005; Kristjánsson 2007: 203–298; Simek & Pálsson 2007; Clunies Ross 2010.
26. See, for example, Price 2002; 2019; Gardeła 2016b.
27. For previous discussions on Freydís and her deeds, see Wolf 1996; Jochens 2002: 146–147; Price 2002: 332; Falk 2015; Jóhanna Katrín Friðriksdóttir 2020: 117–119.
28. *Grænlendinga saga*, ch. 1.
29. On Norse journeys to Vínland, see Simek 2016 with further references.
30. *Grænlendinga saga*, ch. 7. Translation after Kunz 1997b: 31.
31. *Eiríks saga rauða*, ch. 11. Einar Ólafur Sveinsson & Matthías Þórðarson 1935.
32. See Price 2002: 332 and Gardeła 2018b: 416 who mistakenly speak of Freydís slapping the breasts with the sword.
33. Falk 2015.
34. Falk 2015: 39.
35. *Gísla saga Súrssonar*, ch. 5.
36. *Gísla saga Súrssonar*, ch. 34.
37. *Gísla saga Súrssonar*, ch. 37. Text after Björn K. Þórólfsson & Guðni Jónsson 1943: 116.
38. *Gísla saga Súrssonar*, ch. 37. Translation after Regal 1997: 48 with my amendments.
39. *Laxdæla saga*, ch. 32. Translation after Kunz 1997a: 43.
40. *Laxdæla saga*, ch. 35. Text after Einar Ólafur Sveinsson 1943: 96.
41. *Laxdæla saga*, ch. 35. Translation after Kunz 1997a: 48.
42. *Laxdæla saga*, ch. 35. Text after Einar Ólafur Sveinsson 1943: 98.
43. *Laxdæla saga*, ch. 35. Translation after Kunz 1997a: 49 with my amendments.
44. *Laxdæla saga*, ch. 30. On this episode, see also Short 2014: 106.
45. Jóhanna Katrín Friðriksdóttir 2020: 57.
46. For a detailed discussion on sexual defamation in Old Norse society, see Meulengracht Sørensen 1983.
47. On Þórhildr, see also Jóhanna Katrín Friðriksdóttir 2013: 51.
48. Text after Björn Sigfússon 1940: 59–60. Translation after Andersson & Miller 1997: 230–231 with my amendments.
49. It is noteworthy, however, that the motif of water turning red occurs twice in *Gesta Danorum* (Book 6). Ellis Davidson and Fischer have compared these 'water omens' to the abovementioned event from *Ljósvetninga saga*. See Ellis Davidson & Fisher 2008: 96.
50. See, for example, Clive Tolley's 2009 hypercritical views on the description of a prophetic *seiðr* ritual in *Eiríks saga rauða* (4). Counterarguments are provided in Gardeła 2016b: 24–26.
51. Wolf 1997: 680.
52. Jóhanna Katrín Friðriksdóttir 2013: 54–55.
53. Jóhanna Katrín Friðriksdóttir 2013: 10.
54. Jóhanna Katrín Friðriksdóttir 2013: 55.
55. On the *fornaldarsögur*, see Ármann Jakobsson *et al.* 2003; Tulinius 2005; Kristjánsson 2007: 341–362; Ney *et al.* 2009; Arnold & Finlay 2010; Clunies Ross 2010: 76–80; Lassen *et al.* 2012 with further references.
56. Turville-Petre & Tolkien 1956: xii–xiii; Tolkien 1960.

57 For a stimulating discussion on Samsø and its symbolically-charged landscape, see Mitchell 2020.
58 *Hervarar saga ok Heiðreks konungs*. Text and translation after Tolkien 1960: 14–15.
59 Clover 1986: 38.
60 Clover 1986: 39.
61 *Hervarar saga ok Heiðreks konungs*, ch. 4. Translation after Tolkien 1960: 20.
62 *Hervarar saga ok Heiðreks konungs*, ch. 4.
63 *Hervarar saga ok Heiðreks konungs*, ch. 10.
64 Jochens 1996: 98–99.
65 See, for example, Fell 1996; Jochens 1996: 97–100; Mayburd 2014.
66 Mayburd 2014.
67 On Þornbjörg, see also Jochens 1996: 100–102; Jóhanna Katrín Friðriksdóttir 2013: 112–113.
68 *Hrólfs saga Gautrekssonar*, ch. 4. Translation after Hermann Pálsson & Edwards 1972: 34.
69 *Hrólfs saga Gautrekssonar*, ch. 4. Translation after Hermann Pálsson & Edwards 1972: 35.
70 *Hrólfs saga Gautrekssonar*, ch. 4. Translation after Hermann Pálsson & Edwards 1972: 36.
71 *Hrólfs saga Gautrekssonar*, ch. 6. Translation after Hermann Pálsson & Edwards 1972: 42.
72 *Hrólfs saga Gautrekssonar*, ch. 13. Translation after Hermann Pálsson & Edwards 1972: 66. As Jochens (1996: 101) notes, this is one of the strongest sexual insults in Old Norse vocabulary.
73 *Hrólfs saga Gautrekssonar*, ch. 13. Translation after Hermann Pálsson & Edwards 1972: 68.
74 On Ólöf from *Hrólfs saga kraka*, see also Jochens 1996: 103.
75 Jochens 1996: 105.
76 For an English language translation of *Ásmundar saga kappabana* and comments on its contents, see Finlay 2010.
77 *Ásmundar saga kappabana*, ch. 7.
78 *Hálfdanar saga Eysteinssonar*, ch. 16. For an English translation, see Hermann Pálsson & Edwards 1985: 171–198.
79 Price 2002: 344.
80 There is a massive body of academic literature on the *valkyrjur*. For some of the most important contributions, see Price 2002: 331–346; Egeler 2011; Boyer 2014 with further references. For concise overviews of their roles and the textual sources in which they appear, see Lindow 2001; Orchard 2002: 376; Simek 2006: 349–350.
81 Price 2002: 340.
82 Price 2002: 339–340.
83 Price 2002: 339.
84 Meissner 1921; Price 2002: 343.
85 Price 2002: 331, 334. See also Simek 2006: 349 who shares similar views.
86 Price 2002: 334.
87 See the prose introduction to the Eddic poem *Völundarkviða* and *Hrómundar saga Greipssonar*, ch. 7.
88 Price 2002: 337; Hedeager 2011: 76–77.
89 Back Danielsson 2007: 212.
90 Translation after Friis-Jensen & Fisher 2015: 639.
91 Price 2002: 335. A *valkyrja* named Sváva who rides a horse through the air and sea is mentioned in the eddic poem *Helgakviða Hjörvardssonar*. According to *Helgakviða Hundingsbana II*, she is later reborn as Sigrún.
92 Price 2002: 335.
93 The term *Malak-al-Maut* or 'Angel of Death' is found in Ibn Fadlān's account of a Rus funeral at the Volga in 922. In Islam *Malak al-Maut* is an angel that takes people's souls after death by the will of Allah. The use of this particular Arab term to refer to a female ritual specialist responsible for the funeral ceremony thus feels very appropriate. This woman may indeed have been conceptualised by the Rus as a human analogue of a mythological *valkyrja*. For further details, see Price 2010b; 2012b: 27. Ibn Fadlān's account in the original language and its English translation is included in Mackintosh-Smith & Montgomery 2014.
94 The term *wælcyrge* is found in several Anglo-Saxon texts. For further details, see Price 2002: 345–346; 2010a.
95 Relevant episodes involving these beings are discussed in further detail by Price 2002: 346–347.
96 On Skaði, see Schröder 1941; Lindow 2001: 268–270; Orchard 2002: 324–325; McKinnell 2005: 62–64; Simek 2006: 286–287 with further references.
97 Simek 2006: 286.
98 McKinnell 2005: 64.
99 It is noteworthy that the name of this supernatural female being is variously rendered in Old Norse sources, for instance as Þorgerðr Hölgabrúðr (*Jómsvíkinga saga*), Þorgerðr Hörgabrúðr (*Harðar saga*), Þorgerðr hörgatröll (*Ketils saga hængs*), Þorgerðr Hörðabruðr (*Fareyinga saga*). See, McKinnell 2005: 82–83.
100 On Þorgerðr Hölgabrúðr, see Storm 1885; Chadwick 1950; Steinsland 1991; Motz 1993: 76–78; McKinnell 2002: 265–272; 2005: 81–85; 2014; Price 2002: 347–349.
101 This information is also interesting in that it demonstrates that Hákon's seven-year-old son was among the jarl's crew and – whether he liked it or not – actually witnessed the battle. We do not know if the boy had any active role in the fighting but the saga nevertheless shows that from a very young age children (especially those who belonged to the social elite) were no strangers to first-hand experiences of warfare. For other examples of children participating in armed conflicts in the Viking Age, see Gardeła 2012a; Raffield 2019.
102 Þorgerðr's sister Irpa – of whom relatively little is known – also appears in *Brennu-Njáls saga*.
103 *Jómsvíkinga saga*, ch. 33. Text and translation after Blake 1962: 36–37 with my amendments.
104 On Fenja and Menja and the etymology of their names, see Simek 2006: 79–80, 211.
105 The story of Grotti is also retold in detail by Snorri Sturluson in his *Skáldskaparmál* (ch. 40).
106 *Grottasöngr*, st 13–15. Text after Kuhn & Neckel 1983: 299.
107 *Grottasöngr*, st 13–15. Translation after Larrington 2014: 253–254 with my amendments.
108 For previous studies on Æthelflæd, see Arman 2018; Downham 2019; Toler 2019: 87–90.

109 Arman 2018: 31.
110 Arman 2018: 32.
111 Arman 2018: 73.
112 Arman 2018: 37.
113 Arman 2018: 83–87.
114 Extant sources do not offer any specific details as regards the nature of Æthelred's illness. See Arman 2018: 137.
115 Toler 2019: 88.
116 Arman 2018: 141–143.
117 Arman 2018: 111–112.
118 Price 2002: 332.
119 *John Skylitzes, A Synopsis of Byzantine History*. Translation after Wortley 2010: 275.
120 Wortley 2010: 286.
121 *The History of Leo the Deacon*, Book IX. Talbot & Sullivan 2005: 193. Interestingly, in the nineteenth century this episode was depicted on canvas by the Polish-Russian painter Henryk Siemiradzki – see Gardeła 2019c for more details concerning this artist's life and his interest in Viking Age history.
122 *John Skylitzes, A Synopsis of Byzantine History*. Translation after Wortley 2010: 289–290.
123 *Atlamál in grænlenzko*, st 49–51. Text after Kuhn & Neckel 1983: 254.
124 *Atlamál in grænlenzko*, st 49–51. Translation after Larrington 2014: 217.
125 On Olga, see Poppe 1992; Kovalev 2012; Downham 2019 with references.

Chapter 4

Women and weapons in Viking archaeology: the burial evidence

In the years following the pathbreaking discovery at Nordre Kjølen (see Chapter 2), numerous lavishly furnished weapon graves were unearthed in Norway[1] and elsewhere in Scandinavia.[2] However, in the vast majority of cases osteological analyses showed that the deceased were biologically male,[3] leading scholars to surmise that in Viking Age mortuary contexts weapons were typically associated with men. In line with this hypothesis, and given the fact that due to unfavourable soil conditions in Northern Europe (especially in Norway) skeletal remains rarely survive in a state which permits conclusive osteological analyses to be conducted, it became a norm to arbitrarily determine the sex and gender of the dead based on objects that accompanied them in their graves. The idea that weapons were typically male attributes and that jewellery was characteristic of women thus found a strong foothold in Viking archaeology. This chapter seeks to demonstrate and discuss exceptions from this pattern.

Even if we were to dismiss the grave from Nordre Kjølen on the grounds of the controversial circumstances of its discovery and recording, there are still other examples in Viking Age funerary archaeology showing unequivocally that occasionally women *were* buried with martial equipment.[4] Interestingly, not only full size weapons are found in female graves but also their miniature variants in the form of ferrous and non-ferrous pendants and appliques probably endowed with amuletic properties.[5] It is also noteworthy that some types of female jewellery – for instance trefoil brooches – display strong and obvious militaristic connotations, confirming that female associations with the broadly understood martial sphere were remarkably manifold.[6]

Since some of the graves that will be scrutinised in this chapter are devoid of well-preserved bone material, thus making specialist osteological analyses impossible to conduct, it is their internal and external features as well as their artefactual assemblages that have been taken as indicators of the deceased person's sex and gender. The author is fully aware of the theoretical and methodological concerns or even controversies this approach may evoke; therefore, to minimise the risk of error, in the following discussion a 'weapon grave' lacking well-preserved skeletal material is cautiously considered as a female grave only if the size and layout of the grave implies that it belonged to a single individual (thus dismissing the possibility of double burial) and if the grave contains at least several types of typically female objects such as brooches and/or bead necklaces and/or spinning and weaving utensils. Artefact-based presumptions regarding the biological sex and gender of the deceased can be misleading (*e.g.* it is theoretically possible, although difficult to prove, that some of the graves analysed below actually belong to biological men who were dressed like women *and* buried with weapons), but because in the vast majority of osteologically sexed Viking Age graves jewellery and textile implements have been proven to be associated with biological women,[7] this approach to the archaeological material feels justified. The information on the contents of the graves discussed here is summarised in the Appendix at the end of the volume.

Female graves with weapons

This section surveys all Viking Age female graves furnished with actual weapons and/or multifunctional objects such as arrowheads and axes. In examining this diverse body of material, close and critical attention has been devoted to the find circumstances and the deliberate arrangement of the grave goods in relation to the deceased. Together with an exploration of other nuances of the burial record, and with a focus on its symbolic meanings, this survey is intended to provide solid foundations for further multidisciplinary analyses which will be conducted in Chapter 5.

Swedish female graves with weapons
Grave Bj. 581, Birka, Uppland
Over the last several years, grave Bj. 581 from Birka has received outstanding international attention, but before commenting further on its recent (re)interpretation, according to which the deceased was a Viking warrior,[8] we shall first review this grave's wider historical context and the somewhat controversial circumstances of its discovery.

Fig. 4.1. An engraving of grave Bj. 581 published in Ny Illustrerad Tidning. Public domain.

In the period spanning the ninth and tenth centuries, the island of Birka located in Lake Mälaren in Uppland, Sweden was a renowned and thriving emporium with a diverse population stemming from different corners of the then known world. Frequent visitors to Birka included, among others, Western and Eastern Slavs, Magyars and the multi-ethnic group of people known as the Rus.[9] Archaeological excavations and non-invasive prospection surveys that have been conducted at Birka since the nineteenth century have revealed several different burial sites[10] as well as special harbour areas and a hillfort with a hall building probably serving as a garrison.[11] The material culture of the Birka graves, as well as the numerous artefacts discovered around the island, are often of exceptionally high quality, demonstrating that many of the town's permanent and temporary inhabitants were wealthy, well-connected and widely travelled.[12] Importantly, the Birka finds leave no doubt that the town was inhabited by a martial society.

Discovered in 1879 by the Swedish scholar Hjalmar Stolpe and his co-workers, Bj. 581 is one of nearly 3000 graves that have been identified at Birka. It was situated in a cemetery to the north of the fortified area on a natural terrace overlooking the lake. The authors of the recently published reinterpretation of Bj. 581 strongly emphasise that in the Viking Age this would have been a very prominent location amplifying the special status of the deceased individual.[13] It is noteworthy that the graves in the closest vicinity of Bj. 581 were also furnished with martial equipment and objects of high material value (*e.g.* graves Bj. 495, Bj. 496, Bj. 585).[14]

Resembling an underground room or house, Bj. 581 can be categorised as a so-called chamber grave. In the Viking Age (but also in the preceding periods) such funerary architecture was an ostentatious marker of prestige, something that is additionally underlined by the fact that the building process was a laborious endeavour which required considerable economic input.[15]

One key feature of chamber graves – which must be seriously taken into account whenever one attempts to interpret their contents today – is that it was possible to access them even long after the funeral; this would have created opportunities for all kinds of interactions between the living and the dead, involving *inter alia* the removal, displacement and even destruction of objects and bodies.[16] As already noted in Chapter 1, grave disturbance was commonly practiced in the Viking world, including the cemeteries at Birka. Surviving textual and archaeological sources demonstrate that the motivations behind the reopening of graves were manifold and that these acts were not always intended to gain material wealth: sometimes graves were accessed to establish supernatural contact with the deceased, to obtain special or 'enchanted' objects (*e.g.* family heirlooms), to perform magic or to maim or annihilate the dead.[17] It is unknown if grave Bj. 581 from Birka has ever been reopened and its contents manipulated, but this scenario cannot be ruled out completely.

The available field documentation of Bj. 581 permits a fairly detailed reconstruction of the layout of the skeletal remains and accompanying goods at the time of their discovery. In approaching this material, however, we should be wary of the fact that actually two different plans of the grave were prepared by its excavator Hjalmar Stolpe, one of which was also recreated by an artist and released in a Swedish newspaper *Ny Illustrerad Tidning* (Fig. 4.1). Holger Arbman noted this fact in 1943 in his seminal monograph on the Birka graves saying that: 'Von diesem Grab gibt es zwei Pläne, beide von Stolpe, die aber nicht in allen Punkten übereinstimmen' ('There are two plans of this grave, both made by Stolpe, which do not match in all points').[18] The differences in the drawings are actually quite significant and concern the position of the skeleton and the types of objects that accompanied the dead person. Furthermore, in carefully examining the archival records today, we can notice that there must have been some confusion regarding the type of the sword buried in Bj. 581: in each of the plans the weapon looks different.[19] Due to the various issues with the documentation, the plan eventually included in Arbman's publication was based on Stolpe's second and final sketch, presumably the one most accurately representing the actual contents of Bj. 581 (Fig. 4.2). However, in writing up the grave's description, Arbman noted that some of the finds from the grave could not be identified and that they were missing in the museum collections.

These are not the only hinderances pertaining to the famous Birka grave. In the 1970s and 1980s, specialists like Berit Vilkans[20] and Greta Arwidsson[21] argued that Bj. 581 could have held the remains of not one but actually two individuals. A discussion of their views was omitted in the 2017 publication by Charlotte Hedenstierna-Jonson and her team, who expressed their conviction that the grave in question belonged only to a single individual.[22] While Hedenstierna-Jonson *et al.* may indeed be right in their claims, it is nevertheless vital to be critically aware of the various controversies surrounding this grave before drawing any conclusions about the identity of its occupant.

In light of the above, it is also worthy of note that in an article commenting on the recent reinterpretation of Bj. 581 Fedir Androshchuk drew attention to the striking parallels between this grave and another Viking Age chamber grave discovered in 2006 at Shestovitsa in Ukraine.[23] Even though the Shestovitsa grave was disturbed at some point in the past (meaning that some of its contents might have been removed), its surviving assemblage very closely resembles the contents of Bj. 581. Most remarkably, the grave from Shestovitsa included a silver cap-mount, which happens to be a direct analogy to the cap-mount found at Birka (Fig. 4.3). The main point of Androshchuk's discussion, however, was not to demonstrate artefactual analogies, but to highlight the possibility that the Shestovitsa grave

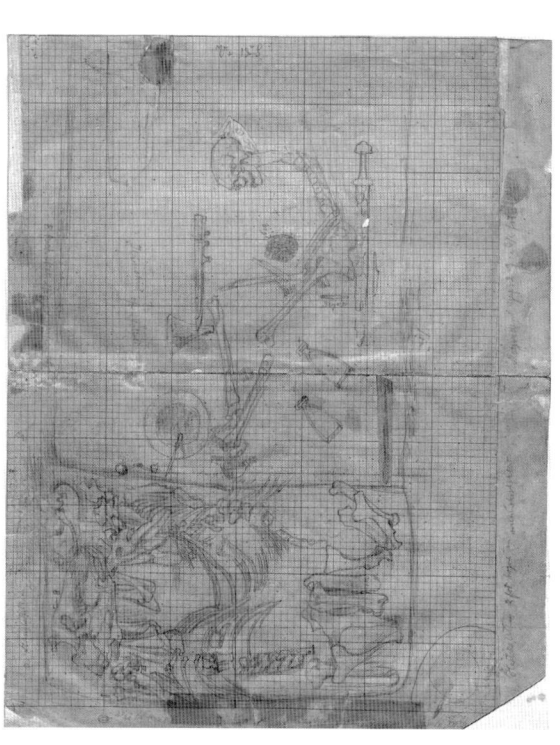
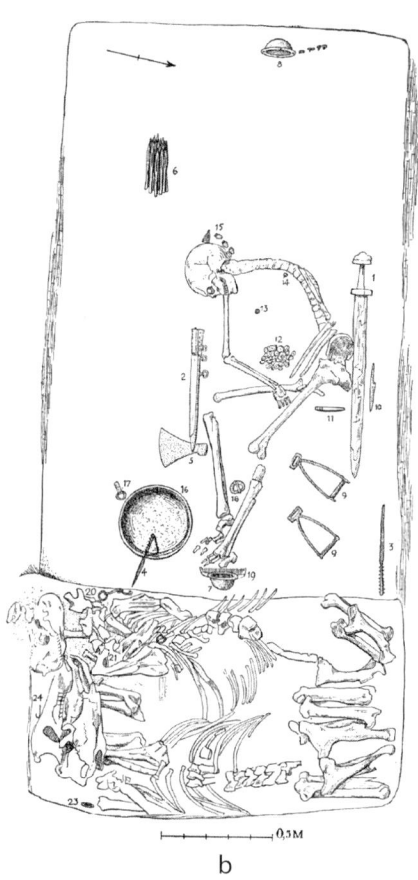

Fig. 4.2. Hjalmar Stolpe's (a) and Holger Arbman's (b) plans of grave Bj. 581. Image (a) from the Birka papers in the ATA archive. Image (b) from Arbman 1943: 189.

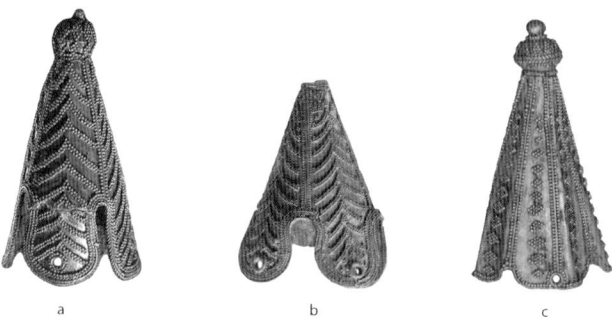

Fig. 4.3. Silver cap mounts from Bj. 581 (a) and Bj. 644 (b) at Birka and an analogous find from Shestovitsa (c). Image (a) from Statens Historiska Museum online database. Image (b) after Arbman 1940: Taf. 94. Image (c) after Kovalenko, Motsya, Syty 2012: 335. Edited by Leszek Gardeła.

originally contained the remains of two individuals, a male and a female. In his view, this lends even further support to the hypothesis that the remarkably similar grave Bj. 581 from Birka was a double grave.

After a wave of heavy criticism from a number of international scholars and some members of the general public[24] – who suggested that Bj. 581 was originally a double grave and/or that the authors of the 2017 study had studied the wrong skeletal material – in 2019 Neil Price, Charlotte Hedenstierna-Jonson and other members of their international team released a follow-up article where they responded to the critique and clarified their previous arguments.[25] Their paper was supplemented by a separate online document containing further information detailing the wider context of Bj. 581 and the methods of its recording and analysis. In this important study Price *et al.* show convincingly that the surviving bones, which they have subjected to careful osteological, isotopic and genetic analyses, doubtlessly belong to grave Bj. 581 (they are also clearly labelled with ink – Fig. 4.4), and that there is no reason to think that they had been mixed up. The claim that Bj. 581 included two individuals has thus been rejected, and Price *et al.* have demonstrated that the additional bone (femur) in one of the boxes belongs to a female individual (or a teenager of indeterminate sex) from another grave; this bone is also labelled with ink and bears the number 'Bj. 854'. The bottom line is that Price *et al.* maintain their initial argument from 2017 and express the opinion that Bj. 581 *is* the grave of a female warrior:

The person in Bj. 581 was buried in a grave full of functional weapons and war-gear (and little else), in close proximity to other burials with weapons, next to a building saturated with weapons, outside the gate of a fortress. Furthermore, the interment took place at a time when the hillfort and 'garrison' were at their zenith. Many other interpretations of both funerary treatment and gender are possible, but Occam's razor would suggest that to reach for them as a first resort is to attempt to 'explain away' what seems to be the most obvious and logical conclusion. In our opinion, Bj. 581 was the grave of a woman who lived as a professional warrior and was buried in a martial environment as an individual of rank.[26]

Price *et al.* also raise an important point by saying that in interpreting the identity of exceptional individuals from the past, and the person from Bj. 581 was doubtlessly one of them, we must 'question our assumptions and categories'.[27] They emphasise the difficulties in deciding what constitutes a weapon and a warrior and 'how to extrapolate from archaeologically recorded individuals to society in general'.[28] Relativity is an important factor here, as well as the fact that our current perceptions of the Viking Age, including how we conceptualise 'warriors' (see also Chapter 1), are probably very different from how everyday Viking Age reality was understood by the people who actually lived in this period of history. Remaining critically aware of these and other concerns let us now investigate the contents Bj. 581 more closely in an attempt to find out if there are any features of this grave that have skipped the attention of previous scholars.

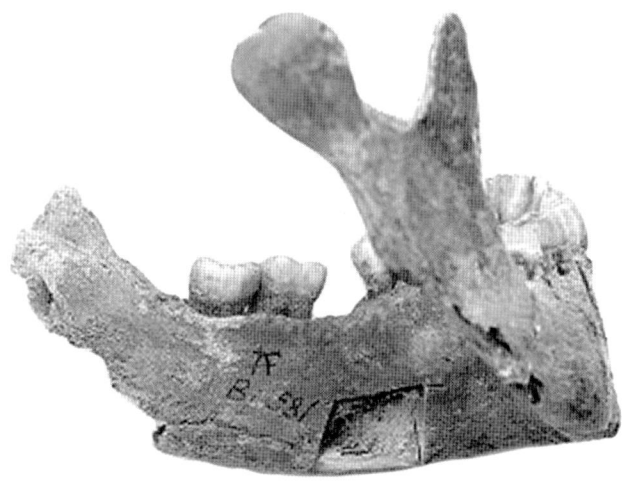

Fig. 4.4. Human bone from Bj. 581, clearly marked with ink. Image from the Statens Historiska Museum online database.

According to Holger Arbman's seminal publication, Bj. 581 included the following finds (Fig. 4.5 and Plate 4.1): an iron sword decorated with copper alloy,[29] a battle knife (sax) in a scabbard with copper alloy fittings (ca. 51 cm long), an iron spear with a socket ornamented with copper alloy (42.6 cm long), another spearhead with silver and copper decorations (34 cm long), an axehead (ca. 20 cm long), 25 arrowheads (ca. 12–15 cm long), two shield bosses (ca. 13.5 cm and 15.5 cm in diameter and ca. 6 cm high), iron fittings (perhaps rim-fittings), two stirrups (22.2 cm and 23 cm long), an iron knife (today no longer preserved), a whetstone (13.1 cm), 28 gaming pieces made of antler, three dice made of antler, three weights, a quarter of an Arabic silver coin (Samanid dirham of Nasr ibn Ahmad dated to AD 913–933), a ringed pin, silver fittings for a hat, a copper alloy bowl, an iron ring, a large iron buckle and an antler comb. In addition to these artefacts, grave Bj. 581 was furnished with riding equipment: horse bits, iron rings, four horse crampons made of iron and an iron hook. Iron fittings (probably from a chest) were also found as well as iron fittings of a gaming board. Arbman also mentioned that among the items associated with this grave were a copper alloy buckle, ca. 40 fragments of a glass mirror, a miniature spear made of iron (5.3 cm long)[30] as well as three small pins made of tin (ca. 1 cm long).[31]

At first glance, other than being an example of a richly furnished chamber grave, there appears to be nothing unusual about the contents of Bj. 581. Assuming that Stolpe's second grave plan is correct, we can also notice that the layout of the military equipment in Bj. 581 did not deviate significantly from the normative positioning of weapons in Viking Age inhumations at Birka – the sword, with the point of its blade directed towards the foot-end of the grave, was by the left side of the buried person, while the axehead and the battle knife lay to the right. At the feet of the deceased lay a copper alloy bowl, a spearhead and a pair of stirrups. In the same area was also a raised platform constructed out of clay with two horse skeletons (a mare and a stallion) on top of it. One of the two shields probably stood at the western wall of the chamber while the other shield lay or stood at the person's feet. The second spear was also at the foot-end of the grave and by the left side of the deceased.

Remembering Härke's valuable advice on how to approach and interpret burial remains,[32] in discussing Bj. 581 one should pay close attention not only to the morphometric and chronological aspects of the grave goods buried with the deceased, but also to *how* and *where* exactly these different objects had been placed. First, we shall consider the position of the weapons – the sword, the battle knife (sax), the two shields and the two spearheads. Afterwards we will move on to investigate the possible meaning(s) of the gaming pieces and the copper alloy bowl.

In Viking Age inhumations swords are typically placed on the proper right-hand side of the body.[33] In the case of

Fig. 4.5. Plan of grave Bj. 581 with the weapons highlighted in grey: sword (a), axehead (b), spearhead (c), spearhead (d), battle knife (e), arrowheads (f), shield bosses (g). Based on Arbman 1943: 189 and edited by Leszek Gardeła.

the graves from Birka, the vast majority of swords were also deposited in this manner.³⁴ Bj. 581 is special as it is one of only three graves (the other being Bj. 850 and Bj. 977) with the sword on the proper left-hand side of the deceased person. Interestingly, in two other potentially female weapon graves from Norway (Nordre Kjølen in Hedmark and Aunvoll in Nord Trøndelag – see below) swords were also laid by the left side of the bodies. Could this have signalled something peculiar about these weapons and/or the identity of the dead? Was this how swords in the Viking world were 'supposed' to be buried with women? We will return to this motif further below.

Another noteworthy aspect of Bj. 581 is the fact that it contained two shields and two spearheads, something that is rather uncommon in Viking Age Sweden where weapons are rarely duplicated in single graves. Burials including multiple shields are more popular in Norway,³⁵ a custom that has recently been interpreted as a means to display respect and/or allegiance to the deceased.³⁶ In the case of Bj. 581, the presence of two shields and two spearheads could, perhaps, lend credence to the idea that the grave was originally intended to hold two bodies. Because the Birka grave had a chambered construction, which could be reopened and accessed, the potential removal of the second individual might have occurred at some point in the Viking Age, perhaps even shortly after the burial. Alternatively, if no grave disturbance had occurred, the complete decomposition of the body could have been the reason why the remains of the second individual were never found during Stolpe's excavation. It must be highlighted, however, that even if the duplicate shields and spears were to indicate that Bj. 581 was originally a double grave, this could mean that *both* of the buried individuals were afforded with weapons and that they *both* had similar social status. In other words, this scenario *does not* challenge nor dismiss the idea advocated by Neil Price and Charlotte Hedenstierna-Jonson that the woman was 'buried like a warrior' – whether she actively participated in warfare is, of course, another question.

In discussing the two spears from Bj. 581 it is noteworthy that one of them was located at the foot-end of the grave with its point directed towards the elevated clay platform with the remains of two horses. This position of the weapon might indicate that it had been thrust into the grave as part of a special ritual. Andreas Nordberg³⁷ and Neil Price³⁸ have argued that acts of thrusting weapons into graves might have been performed with the intention to 'dedicate' the deceased to Óðinn – the people buried in such graves might have failed to meet their end in battle and therefore the mourners might have wanted to bury them in a manner that would ensure they reached the 'appropriate' otherworld for warriors. A textual expression of this idea can be found in Snorri Sturluson's *Ynglinga saga* in an episode that describes how Óðinn is marked with a spear before he dies; this unprecedented ritual act sets an example for those who wish to join the god in the afterlife and – according to the same saga – it is later re-enacted in connection with Njörðr's passing.

Another aspect of Bj. 581 worth (re)considering is the symbolic role of the gaming pieces (Fig. 4.6). Hedenstierna-Jonson has argued that their presence in the grave might indicate that the deceased woman was 'a high-ranking officer'.³⁹ While this may have been the case, we have to acknowledge the fact that board games and gaming pieces are not at all uncommon in Viking Age funerary contexts, both in Scandinavia and in other parts of the Viking diaspora, and that they tend to be found together with male and female individuals representing different social classes.⁴⁰ In light of this evidence, the claim that in Viking Age funerary contexts gaming pieces and gaming boards served solely as indicators of military rank is stretching the evidence – both archaeology and extant textual sources imply that their meanings were manifold. Furthermore, it is clear from Old Norse literature that playing strategy games, such as *hnefatafl*, was not only a strictly male activity – several women stemming from different social strata are portrayed in extant sources as actively engaging in this pastime.⁴¹ There are some textual hints, however, implying that the ability to play games was among the skills nobles were required to master. A perfect illustration of this idea is the twelfth-century poem by Earl Rögnvaldr of Orkney:⁴²

> Tafl em ek örr at efla,
> íþróttir kannk níu,
> týnik trauðla rúnum,
> tíð er mér bók ok smíðir.
> Skríða kannk á skíðum,
> skýtk ok roe'k, svát nýtir,
> hvárt tveggja kannk hyggja
> harpslátt ok bragþáttu.
>
> I am quick at playing chess,
> I have nine skills,
> I hardly forget runes,
> I am often at either a book or craftsmanship.
> I am able to glide on skis,
> I shoot and row so it makes a difference,
> I understand both the playing of the harp and poetry.⁴³

Aside from the association of board games with the social elite, there are reasons to believe that gaming pieces and gaming boards were conceptually linked to the idea of fate.⁴⁴ This can be inferred from the eddic poem *Völuspá* in which the Norse gods are merrily and carelessly playing a game in the meadow until three supernatural women arrive and announce an impending 'Nordic apocalypse' – Ragnarök:

> Tefldo í túni, teitir vóro –
> var þeim vettergis
> vant ór gulli –
> unz þriar kvómo
> þursa meyiar,
> ámátkar miök,
> ór iötunheimom.

Fig. 4.6. Gaming pieces from Bj. 581. After the Statens Historiska Museum online database. Photo by Charlotte Hedenstierna-Jonson.

They played chequers in the meadow,
They were merry –
For them there was no
Want of gold –
Until there came three
Ogres' daughters,
Of redoubtable strength,
From Giant Realms.[45]

In stanza 58 of *Völuspá*, which mentions a new world after the apocalyptic horrors of the Ragnarök, the lost gaming pieces are found in the grass, a motif that might perhaps symbolises that a new game (of life) has begun:

Þar muno eptir
undrsamligar
gullnar töflor
í grasi finnaz,
þærs í árdaga
áttar höfðo.

There will once more
the miraculous
golden chequers
be found, in the grass,
those that in the old days
they had owned.[46]

The sources reviewed above show that the symbolic connotations of gaming pieces and gaming boards in Viking archaeology and Old Norse literature were varied and fluid. We will never know for certain what exactly they meant to the deceased person from Bj. 581 and to those who orchestrated the burial, but we should certainly remain open to several alternative interpretations, rather than arguing that they were just symbols of rank in a martial environment.

It is worth highlighting that aside from weapons and gaming pieces grave Bj. 581 was furnished with a copper alloy bowl. Analogous luxurious objects are known predominantly from Gotland and Denmark but also from Central and Western Europe, including the area of today's Germany and Poland.[47] A few exemplars of such bowls have also been discovered in Finland, Norway, Russia and the Sambia Peninsula, but they are generally very rare in these areas. According to the results of a series of recent extensive studies by Andrzej Janowski, at the present moment around 170 early medieval copper alloy bowls are known from Europe. They are typically found in very high status graves, where they are usually (but not exclusively) laid at the feet of the deceased. Some examples are undecorated – and this is also the case of the find from Bj. 581 – but others have intricate geometric, floral, anthropomorphic and/or zoomorphic imagery. There are good reasons to believe that bowls with religious imagery were associated with Christian rituals, perhaps serving as liturgical washing basins, but they could have had other applications as well. In light of the specific furnishings of Bj. 581, and in view of the fact that the grave displays traces of evidently pagan acts (*e.g.* seated burial, thrust spear), it is unlikely that the bowl from this grave had Christian connotations; it is rather more probable that it represented a prized possession of the deceased or that it belonged to the mourners who decided to place it in the grave with some special intention in mind. One interesting detail that emerges from recent studies of graves with copper alloy bowls is that in funerary contexts they seem to have been associated predominantly with men.[48] In view of this, the presence of the bowl in Bj. 581 can be seen as yet another indication of the ambiguous identity of the grave's occupant.

A few brief remarks must also be added here concerning the riding equipment found in Bj. 581. Interestingly, the grave contained a set of stirrups but lacked spurs. In Viking Age funerary contexts stirrups usually co-occur with spurs, forming a standard set that would have been used by heavily armed equestrian warriors.[49] The lack of spurs can be explained in at least two ways – they might have been removed from the grave at some point after the burial ceremony or the owner (presumably the incumbent of Bj. 581) preferred an eastern, nomadic style of riding in which case the spurs would have been unnecessary. Together with the rare silver hat cap (with parallels in Kievan Rus), the lack of spurs amplifies the idea that the deceased person (and/or those who conducted the burial) had strong eastern connections.

Let us now recapitulate the above observations. It is beyond doubt that grave Bj. 581 is exceptional in all sorts of ways and that it can be approached from many different angles. If Charlotte Hedenstierna-Jonson, Neil Price and their team are right in their assumptions that Bj. 581 was actually a single grave of a biological woman – and indeed their 2019 study is very convincing in that regard – we must still remain open to alternative interpretations. In view of the ongoing debate surrounding weapon graves in early medieval Europe, some scholars will certainly remain sceptical of the idea all people buried with weapons – including the occupant of Bj. 581 – actively participated in warfare or broadly understood martial activities.[50]

Regardless of the various source-critical issues pertaining to Bj. 581, we must embrace the obvious fact that most weapons in the Viking Age were designed and manufactured with the deliberate intention to make them effective in combat. Is impossible to gauge, however, whether every person who owned a weapon actually had the opportunity to use it for martial purposes. The presence or lack of trauma on the individuals buried in weapon graves should also be taken with a pinch of salt and should not be used as a decisive argument for or against their warrior status. The life of a Viking warrior – similarly to the life of any other weapon-wielding person in past and present societies – did not necessarily have to involve engaging in actual physical combat and did not have to end in a violent way on the battlefield. We will return to these themes in the following chapters of this book.

Klinta, Öland

The Klinta grave belonged to a woman who had probably been burnt on a pyre *together* with a man.[51] However, after the cremation process was completed, the remains of the two individuals were separated and buried in two different graves (59:2 and 59:3), each of which was constructed in a unique way. The woman's remains were placed inside a ceramic urn and interred in an earthen pit. Afterwards, the pit was filled with numerous items including a silver pendant (probably an import from Eastern Europe or Asia), a copper alloy jug, a copper alloy basin, two copper alloy brooches (Jan Petersen's type 51), two copper alloy cruciform mounts, two copper alloy rings, two copper alloy strap ends, a copper alloy trapezoidal mount, two copper sheets with runic inscriptions, two pairs of iron shears, two iron knives, an iron wood-working cramp, an axehead (bearded, slim-bladed and driven vertically into the pit), an L-shaped key, 25 fragments of an iron chain, two fragments of iron hook-eyes, 151 beads (carnelian, rock crystal, glass and glass paste), an iron ring with four Þórr's hammers, over 30 fragments of iron mounts (probably from a bucket), a brooch or reins-distributor made of copper alloy, fragments of copper alloy and melted droplets, over 40 fragments of iron mounts and two rowan berries (Plate 4.2). The largest object placed inside the pit was an iron staff with a lavishly decorated handle (Plate 4.3).[52] Additionally, the pit contained the remains of a bird, probably a chicken.[53]

When all these different grave goods had been deposited, the pit was sealed with a hexagonal lid made of twigs and bracken and afterwards additionally covered with clay. During the excavation, directly above the pit a layer of debris from the pyre was found, containing a range of small objects such as (among other things) an Abbasid silver coin, a glass linen smoother, fragmented jewellery, partially preserved riding equipment and hazelnut shells.

Due to its exceptionally rich assemblage, including items with uncontested religious connotations (*e.g.* the iron Þórr's hammer ring)[54] and an elaborately decorated iron staff, several scholars have interpreted the Klinta grave as belonging to a Viking Age sorceress or *völva*.[55] In his seminal book Neil Price drew attention to the interesting fact that both the female and the male graves 59:2 and 59:3 contain items that are commonly associated with the opposite sex:[56] in the case of the woman's grave, the most glaring of these objects is the axehead. The curious nature of this item is additionally emphasised by the fact that it represents a type with a relatively thin and long beard that was uncommon on Öland and which would have been quite old already at the time of its deposition in the grave. Another puzzling detail is that the axehead was found stuck vertically in the burial pit, a practice resembling the thrusting of spears and other weapons which – as we have seen above – appears to have been connected with Óðinnic rituals. We shall discuss the intricate symbolism of Viking Age axes in Chapter 6.

Mound A24 at Lake Dalstorp, Västergötland

Mound A24 discovered at Lake Dalstorp in Vastergötland represents another peculiar example of a female grave with weapons.[57] Built entirely of sand, the mound stood about 1 m high and was about 7 m in diameter. Excavations have shown that it had been initially erected in the Migration Period and that it was reused in the Viking Age. The details of the mound's stratigraphy, as well as its contents, reveal that the tenth-century funeral took a considerable amount of time.

Meticulous excavation methods have allowed scholars to reconstruct the course of events that occurred during the burial ceremony, offering a glimpse into somewhat atypical mortuary acts. The Viking Age funeral involved a cremation, probably on a pyre, but it is unknown if the burning process was conducted *in situ* or somewhere else. After the fire died, the human remains, probably of a female individual, were scattered on the surface of the mound to form a thin oval layer. The bones were then mixed with a number of objects (ten knives, comb fragments, brooches and beads – probably those that had been laid on the pyre together with the deceased) and spread on the surface to form an oval-shaped layer. Later, as many as five intentionally twisted and bent spearheads were driven vertically into this layer. In the opinion of Tore Artelius who excavated this outstanding grave:

> The deposition pattern reveals that these spearheads cannot be described as either personal belongings or as gifts to the dead. The way in which they were placed in the grave had some functional religious significance to the participants. Like religious symbols in general, the spears *did* something at the burial by the lake.[58]

Remarkably, the spears showed no traces of having been affected by fire,[59] which implies that they probably had not been placed on the pyre together with the deceased person. Their role, as Artelius argues, was therefore not as grave goods *per se* but rather as apotropaic items intended to serve a very specific purpose. The elaborate and premeditated nature of the ritual acts conducted at Dalstorp is further amplified by the fact that after some time had passed and after the grave had been covered by soil, someone dug a small pit in the middle of the mound and placed two oval brooches, a piece of garment and a knife inside it. The deliberate deposition of these items in that very spot can be seen as part of a prolonged cremation burial, but it can potentially represent yet another female grave.

The presence of as many as five spears in the cremation layer can be variously interpreted. One plausible explanation is that the spears served to hold the woman down in her grave and prevented her from rising – the spears would therefore have played an apotropaic role. Although the use of weapons for this purpose is relatively rare in Scandinavia, similar customs have been noted in eleventh–twelfth-century Finland where spears were used as coffin nails to hold the restless dead in place.[60] Another peculiarity of the Dalstorp grave – and one that might also have apotropaic connotations – is that it contained a large number of knives. According to Artelius, in Scandinavian folklore knives were used to safeguard the society from revenants: for instance, placing them on graves prevented the dead from walking.[61] Analogous ideas can be found in other medieval societies in Europe, for instance among the Slavs.[62] In conclusion, the very unusual position of the spears, the liminal location of the grave, and the presence of several knives are all strong indications that the people who conducted the funeral at Dalstorp feared the grave's occupant and devised special apotropaic acts intended to keep this person at rest. All these features make this grave unique, but they certainly do not permit us to interpret it as the grave of a female warrior. As Artelius concludes:

> After the traditional burial the woman had been put to death one more time by driving the spears down through her remains. Through this action, the living sought to create an assurance that order would be restored and maintained. For some reason this woman has been associated with characteristics that might have negatively affected the community order.[63]

Nennesmo, Finnveden

In the Viking Age cemetery at Nennesmo in Finnveden two cremation graves possibly belonging to women contained arrowheads. Grave 4 was furnished with two arrowheads, four indeterminate iron fragments and a casket handle, and it also held the cremated remains of a dog and pig.[64] Grave 22 from the same site had much more opulent furnishings and contained at least three arrowheads, a knife, eight copper alloy fragments, a nail, four mounts with rivets, a fragmented clasp, a copper alloy needle, a fire steel(?), 121 indeterminate iron fragments and a pottery shard.[65] Additionally, the grave held the remains of three different animals: a horse, a cow and a dog. Regrettably, no further information about these graves has been published, and the sexing of the deceased seems to have been made solely on the basis of the artefactual assemblages. All this significantly hinders their interpretation, meaning that they cannot be seriously regarded as potential female warrior graves.

Arrowheads in possible female graves on Gotland

Among thousands of Viking Age graves on the Baltic island of Gotland, several have been found to contain the remains of possible women buried with arrowheads. Grave 1:31/1952 from the cemetery at Barshalder Roes, Grötlingbo sn. contained a single arrowhead, a fish-shaped pendant, glass beads and various iron fragments, which probably were originally part of a chest. In addition, some burnt and unburnt bones were found there.[66] Another possible woman's grave with an arrowhead was identified in the cemetery at Laxare, Boge sn. (grave 9). This grave contained a fish-head shaped pendant – a characteristic element of Gotlandic female costume – a comb as well as various iron fragments and five pottery shards.[67]

In the Viking Age cemetery at Ire, Hellvi sn., as many as three cases of possible female graves with arrowheads have been noted, all of which are cremations. The assemblage of grave 173A from Ire, comprising tweezers (typically associated with women in Gotlandic funerary traditions), a knife, a comb, iron fragments and two arrowheads, strongly suggest that the deceased person was biologically female.[68] Grave 196 from the same site – in the fill of which a single arrowhead was discovered – might also be that of a woman, as indicated by the presence of animal-head brooches and a disc-on-bow brooch.[69] A fragmented arrowhead was found in grave 374 together with a disc-on-bow brooch, a copper alloy bracteate, fragmented copper alloy fish-head shaped pendants, five glass beads and a number of other goods – again, the funerary assemblage gives a strong impression that the deceased person was female.[70] Grave 498 from Ire held two arrowheads, an animal-head brooch, a tongue-shaped pendant, a small knife, a comb, a fragmented bucket (iron handle), two iron crampons as well as various fragments of iron.[71] Although there are good reasons to consider these different Gotlandic graves as belonging to women, it is unjustified to formulate a hypothesis that these individuals had lived their life as active warriors. All graves discussed above contain only one or two arrowheads, a fact which strongly implies that rather than representing martial equipment *par excellence* they held very different meanings probably disassociated from the martial sphere – they might have, for instance, referred to hunting activities or even served as amulets. We also cannot exclude the possibility that in some cases the arrowheads were deliberately shot into the grave as part of some special funerary act (perhaps similar to the thrusting of other weapons like spears, axes and swords) or even that they ended up in the grave completely by accident, swept from the surface during backfilling.

Norwegian female graves with weapons

Nordre Kjølen, Hedmark

The external structure of the Nordre Kjølen grave had the form of a mound standing around 3 m tall and with a 15 m diameter at the base.[72] According to Mørck's description, it seems that it was one of several burial monuments which all formed a small cemetery. In addition to an exceptionally well-preserved human skeleton (anthropologically sexed as female), the Nordre Kjølen mound contained the remains of a horse as well as the following objects: a sword (originally in a wooden scabbard), an axehead, a shield boss, five arrowheads, a spearhead, a horse bit, a whetstone and several indeterminate fragments of iron.

The sword from Nordre Kjølen is heavily corroded and the lower part of its blade is broken off (Plate 4.4). When the present author had the opportunity to personally examine this find in January 2018, the weapon's surviving length was 86 cm. The straight cross-guard is 12.5 cm long and 1 cm high, whereas the 'pommel' is 7.5 cm long and ca. 1.5 cm high. The features of the sword's handle leave no doubt that it belongs to Jan Petersen's type M. In his monograph Petersen listed as many as 198 examples of such weapons, dating them to the period from the middle of the ninth century to the beginning of the tenth century.[73] According to a recent study of Viking Age swords by Fedir Androshchuk, new discoveries of analogous specimens show that M-type swords are characteristic of eastern Norway where they typically date from the first part of the tenth century.[74] Apart from Norway, swords resembling the one found at Nordre Kjølen are also known from the Czech Republic, Denmark, France, Germany, Great Britain, Iceland, Ireland, Poland and Sweden, which means that the type was fairly well-known in Viking Age Europe.

The iron spearhead from Nordre Kjølen, which belongs to Jan Petersen's type K,[75] is corroded and measures around 30 cm in length (Plate 4.4). It has a very narrow socket (7 mm in diameter) and a narrow blade (3 cm). Spears of this kind were very common in Viking Age Norway, but this particular example is unusual in that it had been intentionally bent in half before it was placed in the grave. The bending of weapons is a ritual practice typically performed in connection with cremations but it is very rarely observed in the case of inhumations – we will return to this issue further below.[76]

The axehead from Nordre Kjølen is 18 cm long and the length of its cutting edge is 8 cm (Plate 4.4). It represents Jan Petersen's type G and has numerous parallels in Norway.[77] Due to their simple shape and relatively small blades, axes of this specific kind could be used for a plethora of purposes. Although they could certainly serve as weapons, they would also prove very useful in the household, for example to chop wood or prepare food. In other words, axes of type G should not be regarded as typical battle axes but rather as multifunctional tools.

All five arrowheads from Nordre Kjølen are corroded and fragmentarily preserved; they seem to belong to different types and their length varies from 7 cm to 12.5 cm (Plate 4.4).[78]

Regrettably, the shield boss – which Mørck classified as belonging to Rygh's type R563[79] – did not survive the fire accident in 1912 and therefore it is impossible to say anything else about its particulars.

As mentioned above, the Nordre Kjølen grave also contained other items that cannot be classified as martial equipment *per se* although they might have been used in connection with it. The large whetstone (19.5 cm long and ca. 3 cm wide) found at Nordre Kjølen is split along its axis in two halves, one of which is additionally broken into two pieces (Plate 4.4). Among the finds belonging to the same assemblage is also a square-sectioned iron rod. Measuring 14.5 cm in length and tapering from around 1 cm to 5 mm, this item probably served as a file or perhaps as a tool handle. When all the artefacts from Nordre Kjølen are taken collectively, it is possible to date this grave and its assemblage to the mid-tenth century.[80]

As already noted earlier in this book, when the archaeologist Gustav Mørck came to personally examine the site and the grave contents, everything had already been removed from its original context, but the farmer and his son were able to explain to him how the objects had been positioned in relation to the skeletal remains.[81] Apparently, the boy had first found the horse, whose bones lay at the feet of the human skeleton. Then he came across the remains of the deceased person who lay oriented E–W in a supine position with the head to the east. Apparently, behind the head was a large stone. According to the grave discoverers, the weapons and other goods were positioned in the following way: the sword was by the left side of the human skeleton with the handle directed towards the feet and with the tip of the blade pointing towards the head; the spearhead lay on the right side at the head and the axehead was also somewhere nearby; the shield (together with the shield boss) was probably placed *under* the head. The rest of the grave goods lay in 'various places' in the grave, but other than saying that 'some' objects were found between the legs of the deceased no further particulars are known. It is possible that some of the items (perhaps the arrowheads and the whetstone) originally lay directly on the body, but there is no way to be certain (Fig. 4.7). It is worth highlighting that in describing the context and the structure of the mound, Mørck was confident that this was a single grave and that there was no trace of any other burial inside it.

After the finds had finally been donated to the museum in Kristiania (Oslo) and after the reports had been published, for a considerable time the grave from Nordre Kjølen did not draw any further academic attention. The story of the alleged 'shieldmaiden' continued to thrive in local memory, however, and in 1982 a *bauta* stone was raised in the place of the grave's discovery.[82] The inscription on the stone says:

> Gravhaug hvor det i 1 august 1900 ble funnet kvinneskelett med mannsutstyr fra 900 tallet e. Kr.

Grave mound in which on 1 August 1900 a woman's skeleton from 900 AD with male objects was found.

After over eighty years since the discovery of the Nordre Kjølen grave, two Norwegian scholars, archaeologist Per Hernæs[83] and physical anthropologist Per Holck,[84] took up the challenge to re-examine its contents in an attempt to verify previous claims as to the 'warrior identity' of its occupant. The results of their investigation were published in the popular science journal *Nicolay* and the ultimate conclusion was far less spectacular than what previous scholars had postulated: Per Hernæs completely dismissed the previous 'shieldmaiden' interpretation (proposed by Mørck), arguing that the woman would have been too small and too weak to wield weapons:

> Ikke nødvendigvis berserker på 1.90 som kløyvde hoder ned til haka og tygde lindetreskjold som knekkebrød, men bondegutter som var vant til å jobbe med trespade fra de var en neve stor. En pike på snaue 1,50 og 30–40 kg ville ikke være noen motstander å snake om, selv for en nåtidens kontorkrakksliter, og ihvertfall ikke i sverdkamp.[85]

Not really a berserker standing 1.90 m tall who chopped down heads and chewed linden shields like crackers, but a peasant girl who from her infancy was accustomed to working with a wooden spade. A girl of just 1.50 m and 30–40 kg would not be a serious opponent even in a competition for today's office job and she definitely would not stand a chance in a sword fight.[86]

In describing the particulars of the Nordre Kjølen sword, Hernæs argued that for the sword to be effectively used in an armed struggle (to parry the blows, for example) specialist skills would be necessary. Indeed, fighting with any kind of weapon requires some expertise, but this does not mean that such skills are unattainable for a woman, even if she is of gracile build. As we shall see in Chapter 7, authentic historical cases from around the world show unequivocally that women can be as effective in battle as men; this is not so much a matter of biology and body type, but rather a matter of training, technique, skill and determination. In his article Hernæs also argued that the handle of the sword would have been too large for the woman's hand, suggesting that the weapon could not have been hers. Again, this claim can be easily dismissed. The sword could have been her property, but perhaps it had not been originally made *for* her – it is possible to imagine that at some point in her life the woman received it as a gift or heirloom or that the sword was a war trophy, to name but two out of many possible scenarios. In this context, it is worthy of note that today many Viking Age re-enactors use swords with hilts of various sizes and this does not impede their ability to fight.

In investigating the identity of the individual from Nordre Kjølen and in trying to unravel the meaning of the grave goods this person was laid to rest with, it may also be valuable to consider the location of the weapons in relation to

Fig. 4.7. Artistic reconstruction of the Nordre Kjølen grave. Illustration by Mirosław Kuźma. Copyright Mirosław Kuźma and Leszek Gardeła.

the body. Mørck writes that the sword was positioned with its point directed towards the woman's head and that the weapon was additionally sheathed in a scabbard. This is a very unusual case indeed, but several close parallels are known from Viking Age Norway. For instance, in grave S400 from the cemetery at Gulli in Vestfold an adult man likewise had a sword laid by his left side and pointing towards the face. This grave also contained a spearhead, an axehead, a shield, a sickle, riding gear (so-called *rangle*) as well as several other high-status objects.[87] In another grave from Tønsberg in Vestfold, a man was interred with a sword positioned by his left side and pointing towards the face.[88] As in the case of Nordre Kjølen, the weapon was sheathed, but here the scabbard was additionally adorned with a copper alloy chape representing a type well-known from Birka and other localities around the Baltic Sea.[89] In addition to the sword, the Tønsberg grave contained a shield, a sickle and a bundle of arrowheads. Remarkably, the man's body appears to have been laid *over* the shield, in the same manner as in the case of the grave from Nordre Kjølen. At the feet the skeletal remains of a dog were found – perhaps the man's beloved companion or an animal whose role was to protect the grave or guide the deceased on his otherworld journey.[90]

The practice of burying the dead with swords directed towards the face is also known from other cultural milieus, including those of the Anglo-Saxons,[91] Western Slavs[92] and Hungarians/Magyars,[93] but overall it is fairly uncommon in Europe. One particularly curious example of this custom has also been noted in one of the ship graves at Salme on Saaremaa. Here around 40 swords were discovered lying on the bodies and some of them were pointing towards the head or under the chin. As Price notes, the Salme weapons had also been burnt and treated in other, ritualistic ways including folding or thrusting them into the grave.[94]

In view of all these parallels, and regardless of the fact that the grave from Nordre Kjølen was discovered by an amateur, there are good reasons to believe that what the farmer's son told Gustav Mørck about the grave's layout was correct; the specific deposition of the different objects flanking the body closely matches the alignment of goods in professionally excavated and well-documented graves from eastern Norway.

In interpreting the grave from Nordre Kjølen and in trying to understand the identity of the deceased person, it is also crucial to devote increased attention to the unusual and 'inverted' position of the sword. Regrettably, extant textual sources say nothing about the meaning of this peculiar custom in the Viking Age, but if we turn to medieval imagery (especially manuscripts and the Bayeux tapestry), we will notice that aristocrats and kings are sometimes depicted with swords held in this very particular way – i.e. by the handle and with the sheathed blade resting on the left shoulder (Fig. 4.8).[95] Instead of signalling a 'battle-ready pose', this gesture likely symbolised empowerment, serving as a clear signal of the sword wielder's authority and social rank. In this context, and given the fact that other Norwegian Viking Age graves with inverted swords contain opulent furnishings (implying a high social status of the dead), it feels justified to speculate that the mourners orchestrating the funeral at Nordre Kjølen wanted to 'encode' within this weapon a very special message about the deceased woman. Perhaps, by placing the sword by her side in this manner (regardless of whether this was actually *her* sword), they wanted to emphasise the woman's elevated function in society or to make a reference to some important episode from her life when she had wielded considerable power. It will never be possible to learn the truth about the matter, but it does seem like the unusual position of the weapon served a 'mnemonic function' as a potent reminder for those who gathered at the graveside and as a symbol that would have been clearly understood by the mourners.

The life course of the Nordre Kjølen woman is bound to forever remain veiled in mystery, but it feels that the academic trend of identifying her as a 'warrior' or denying her the possibility of having ever played such a role misses the real point and leads to a considerable simplification of the complex messages and meanings that those who orchestrated her funeral wanted to convey. As scholars like Martin Carver,[96] Howard Williams[97] and Neil Price[98] have argued, early medieval funerals were ritual dramas which – similarly to poetry – were endowed with multiple layers of meaning intended to evoke and/or (re)create memories about dead. The burial at Nordre Kjølen was certainly no different in this regard.

The Kaupang graves, Vestfold

Similar to Birka, the Viking Age town of Kaupang was an important place of trade, exchange and cross-cultural interaction.[99] The significance of this site is clearly indicated by the quality and quantity of objects that have been discovered in the settlement area, but also by the wealth of grave goods accompanying the people buried in the neighbouring cemeteries. The dead at Kaupang were either cremated or inhumed, and they were often provided with rich furnishings including military equipment, jewellery, various kinds of tools and utensils as well as whole animals and/or their body parts.[100] Several chamber graves have been identified on site and there is also a significant number of boat burials containing the remains of one or more individuals.

Three cremation graves at Kaupang (Ka. 3, Ka. 10 and Ka. 16) which include axeheads might have belonged to female individuals. According Frans-Arne Stylegar's recent reassessment of the local burial customs, grave Ka. 3 (Nicolaysen's barrow 113) contained the following objects: two oval brooches (Jan Petersen's type 51), two beads (one possibly made of carnelian), an iron saucepan, an iron frying pan, an iron spit(?), a spindle whorl, a looped hone, two

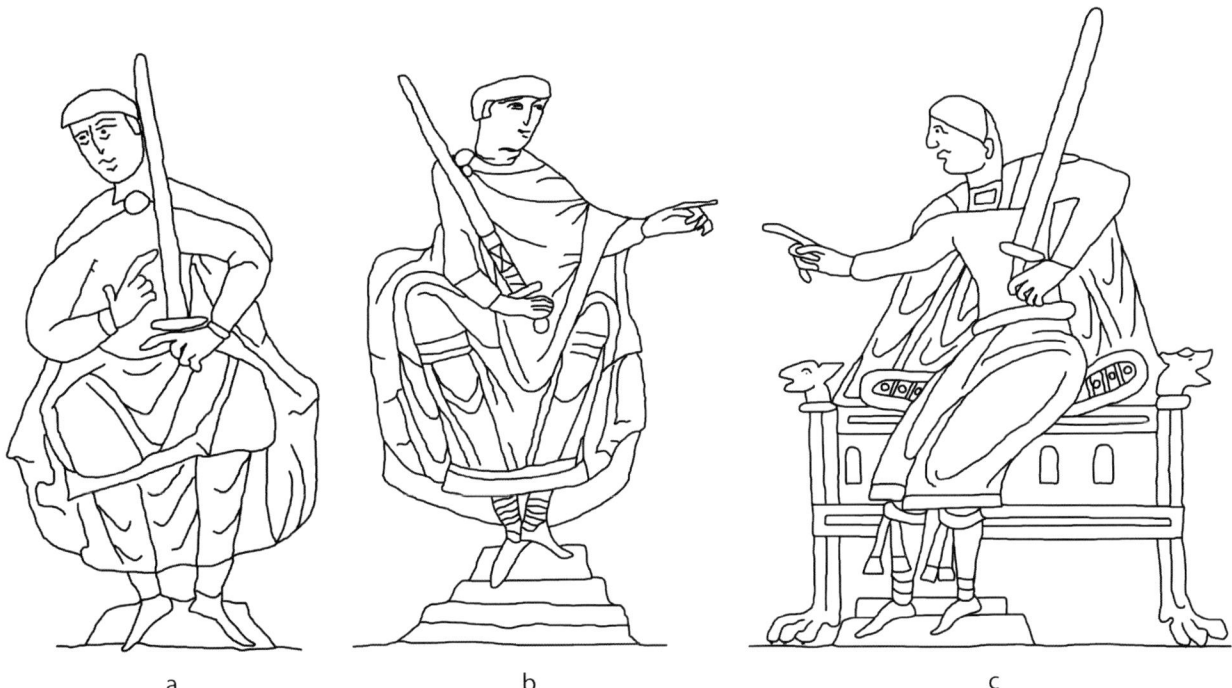

Fig. 4.8. Images from the Bayeux tapestry showing the ruler with an inverted sword, probably serving as a symbol of power and authority. Illustration by Leszek Gardeła.

sickles, an axehead (Jan Petersen's type H), a horse bit, a rivet, an iron rod, an iron cauldron(?) and an iron rattle.[101]

Grave Ka. 10 (Nicolaysen's barrow 85) included the following finds: two oval brooches, (Jan Petersen's type 51), two glass beads, a spindle whorl made of soapstone, an axehead (Jan Petersen's type K), a sickle, a soapstone vessel, an iron weaving sword, a horse bit, an iron hook, a casket handle, an iron rod, a rectangular iron mount, a hone and two–three rivets.[102]

The furnishings of grave Ka. 16 (Nicolaysen's barrow 77) were remarkably similar to the contents of the two graves mentioned above and comprised two oval brooches (Jan Petersen's type 51), textiles, an iron weaving sword, shears, a spindle whorl made of burnt clay, an axehead (Jan Petersen's type H), a sickle, a horse bit and a possible harness mount.[103]

The main stumbling block to interpreting the above-mentioned finds from Kaupang lies with the fact that the biological sex of the dead has been determined solely on the basis of the grave goods. The presence of glass beads, spindle whorls and weaving swords give strong reasons to assume that the deceased were female, but we cannot be absolutely sure of this. Furthermore, it is not unlikely – although impossible to prove – that some or all of the three graves from Kaupang held the remains of not one but two individuals. These uncertainties make it a challenge to determine the meaning of axeheads in these allegedly female graves. The fact that the axeheads represent types H and K, which are characterised by their multi-functionality, also means that we cannot unequivocally consider them as weapons.

Oseberg, Vestfold

The Oseberg grave is one of the most iconic finds from the Viking Age which has been attracting unparalleled scholarly attention since the moment of its discovery in 1903. Underneath an imposing burial mound constructed out of turf and clay rested an impressive and exceptionally well-preserved ship filled with a plethora of objects of exquisite quality (Fig. 4.9). Amidships stood a wooden tent or chamber with two beds upon which originally two women had been laid to rest (Fig. 4.10). According to the latest osteological analyses of the surviving skeletal material one of these individuals was aged around 50 and the other around 80 at the moment of death.[104]

The contents of the Oseberg grave have been extensively discussed in a five-volume monograph series dedicated specifically to this remarkable discovery,[105] but also in *literally* hundreds of other publications.[106] Even after over a century since its discovery, the research potential of Oseberg has not been exhausted and there are still many questions that await answers. Without delving too deep into the particular details of this remarkable grave, in light of the present discussion it is worthy of note that two axes were found inside the mound (Fig. 4.11).[107] However, given the grave's exceptionally elaborate contents, with dozens of objects and several different vehicles (*i.e.* sledges, wagon), it is challenging to interpret what these axes were actually supposed to represent. An additional obstacle is the fact that the grave was reopened and disturbed several times in the Viking Age,[108] which makes it difficult to determine if the axes were actually intended to serve the role of grave goods or if they were simply 'tools' left behind by the intruders who broke into the mound sometime after the funeral. As in the case of the Kaupang graves discussed above, the two Oseberg axes represent types that would have been equally effective in household chores as well as on the battlefield, which is something that additionally hinders their interpretation today.

In the most recent scholarly debates on the identity of the Oseberg women, there is a general consensus that at least one of the women was a ritual specialist.[109] This interpretation is substantiated by a number of finds from the grave, especially the elaborate textiles portraying a religious procession, as well as by the presence of other items that might have served as ritual accoutrements, for instance two wooden staffs. If the axes found at Oseberg actually belonged to the deceased women, then one may pose a tentative hypothesis that they were used as domestic tools and/or ritual implements. Further arguments for the use of axes in ritual contexts are provided in Chapter 5.

Frafjord, Gjesdal, Rogaland

In their thought-provoking article concerning women buried in boats and ships in Viking Age Norway, Hanne Lovise Aannestad and Zanette Glørstad have included a grave from Frafjord that allegedly held the remains of a female individual buried with weapons.[110] They do not specify the basis for their determination of the deceased person's sex, but it may be inferred that it relies on the grave's artefactual assemblage and on the fact that it mainly contained objects conventionally associated with women.

According to a report held at the Archaeological Museum in Stavanger the Frafjord grave was discovered by an amateur in 1955. It had the form of an earthen mound measuring around 8–10 m in diameter. The mound contained the remains of a clinker-built boat. Based on the overall number and measurements of the surviving iron rivets, the vessel's size has been reconstructed and it may be surmised that it was around 7 m long and 1.7 m wide. Regrettably, since the grave was discovered and excavated by a farmer who lacked experience in archaeological recording, no *in situ* documentation was made. The brief museum report only states that several objects had been found in one end of the boat, without specifying their exact position. Among these finds were two weapons (an iron shield boss and an axehead) as well as items associated with the manufacture of textiles (a weaving sword, shears and a weaving comb), a leaf shaped item with a hook (perhaps a horse bit or part of a bridle) and some indeterminate iron fragments (Plate 4.5). On the basis of the distinct typological features of these different artefacts, the Frafjord burial has been dated to AD 800–900, but overall this grave is difficult to interpret for exactly the same reasons as those pertaining to the graves from Kaupang – the sexing of the deceased person is based solely on the artefactual assemblage. The presence of as many as three different implements may be taken to suggest that the deceased was a woman, but it is not unlikely that the grave actually belonged to two people of opposite biological sex.

Sanddal, Sogn og Fjordane

Discovered in the visually dramatic county of Sogn og Fjordane in western Norway, the Sanddal grave is a remarkable testimony of a boat burial intended for a single individual.[111] The vessel was furnished with numerous high-status grave goods, the quality and quantity of which is impressive even by western Norwegian standards where many Viking Age graves are known to have been very elaborate. The deceased person had two oval brooches representing Rygh's type R657[112] (Plate 4.6) and a ca. 40 cm long chain made of silver wire (Plate 4.6). Aside from these exquisite adornments, the Sanddal grave contained an axehead representing Jan Petersen's type D (Plate 4.7) and an iron sickle. Furthermore, among the grave goods was an iron horse bit as well as the remains of two or three strap/rein distributors made of iron. Several different implements for textile production were also found, including a large weaving sword (82 cm in length), two woolcombs, four different spindle whorls made of blue-green stone, 10 loomweights (interestingly, one of them has the sign of the cross on its surface) and a fragmented whalebone plaque. Among the smaller objects discovered at Sanddal were a whetstone and a strike-a-light. The grave also contained various indeterminate fragments of iron, probably from chest fittings, as well as pieces of charcoal and a large number of boat rivets fused with small pieces of wood likely representing the remains of the boat in which the deceased person lay buried. Curiously, the grave was also furnished with 13 small stones (Plate 4.6):[113] except for one stone which looks like a ball, all the others are oval-shaped, a feature which implies that they did not serve as gaming pieces and had some other role to play. The fact that there are 13 of them is intriguing and could have had special significance, which regrettably remains obscure for us today.

The overall composition of the Sanddal grave, with objects mostly associated with women, as well as the fact that it contained two oval brooches and a silver necklace, permits the interpretation of this grave as that of a woman, regardless of the absence of well-preserved osteological material.

Terum, Aurland, Sogn og Fjordane

On several occasions in academic literature the grave from Terum in Aurland has been presented in the wider context of the debate on powerful women and/or Viking female warriors.[114] Regrettably, apart from the surviving artefacts,

Fig. 4.9. The Oseberg ship during excavations in 1904. From Brøgger, Falk, Shetelig 1917a: 76.

Fig. 4.10. The burial chamber onboard the Oseberg ship. From Brøgger, Falk, Shetelig 1917a: 32.

Fig. 4.11. Two axes from the Oseberg grave. After Grieg 1928: 162.

not much is known about the grave's external and internal structure. The Terum grave was fairly rich and contained several different pieces of jewellery: an oval brooch, a copper alloy bracelet and glass beads (Plate 4.8). It was also furnished with spinning and weaving implements, such as three different spindle whorls (one of which has a grooved ornament around the hole for the wooden spindle) and iron shears. Other tools discovered at Terum include a small iron file, an iron knife, an iron sickle and an iron hoe. Thirty-three round rivet heads made of iron were also found, as well as numerous small and large iron fragments, possibly representing the remains of a chest (one fragment has a clearly discernible rim, and there are also fragments that look like loops or hooks). A small piece of textile was also identified, as well as 10 pieces of flint.

The Terum grave is remarkable because in addition to all these different items it also contained two arrowheads (Plate 4.8). They are relatively poorly preserved, with their blades and tangs being broken and corroded. From what survives of these arrowheads, it seems that they were not identical in size: one blade is 8 cm while the other 7.3 cm long.

Similarly to other cremation graves found in Norway, in this case the sex of the deceased person has been determined solely on the basis of the accompanying goods. Although several cremated pieces of human bone have survived, they are too small to conduct specialist analyses of them (Plate 4.8). Regardless of this, and due to the fact that the Terum grave contained several different implements for spinning, as well as typically female jewellery, it is very likely that it belonged to a woman.

The presence of arrowheads in this grave does not, however, immediately justify its interpretation as the grave of a female warrior. Similarly to axes, arrows and arrowheads were multifunctional objects, which aside from having martial connotations could be used in hunting. It is also possible, although impossible to prove, that the arrowheads in the Terum grave did not represent actual grave goods but were the causes of the grave's occupant death – it is not inconceivable that the deceased person was cremated with the arrowheads stuck in the body.

In light of these different but all equally plausible interpretative scenarios, it would be risky to perceive the Terum grave as that of a potential warrior woman. Aurland, together with Vik, were some of the best agricultural areas in Sogn og Fjordane,[115] and this might explain the exceptionally elaborate nature of local funerary practices. These depositions of lavish goods in the Terum grave might thus have been intended to reflect the wealth of the buried individual or their community rather than manifesting this person's connotations with the martial sphere.

Aunvoll, Nord-Trøndelag

The grave from Aunvoll in Nord-Trøndelag, Norway was accidentally discovered in 1981 during construction work and – as a result of rapid professional intervention – partially excavated by the archaeologist Lars Stenvik from the NTNU (Norwegian University of Science and Technology). Available field reports and the online database Unimus indicate that the skeletal remains of a ca. 19–20-year-old woman were found around 40 cm beneath the surface (Plate 4.9). The deceased person lay supine with the head to the south and was accompanied by a wide range of goods including a double-edged sword, eight gaming pieces, a round white stone (perhaps serving as a gaming piece), a sickle, a whetstone, scissors, a file, a knife and a comb (Plate 4.10). A spearhead and a bead as well as numerous fragments of iron nails were found at the same site at a later date, but it is highly probable that they belong to the disturbed grave.

The sword from the grave at Aunvoll, which apparently lay by the woman's left side, is almost completely preserved but its pommel is broken off and missing (Plate 4.11). With a pattern-welded blade and a cross-guard decorated with tightly arranged parallel stripes of copper alloy, this would have been a fairly luxurious weapon. Despite its incomplete state of preservation, it can be surmised that the sword represents Jan Petersen's type H or I.[116] The blade measures 76.5 cm in length and the cross-guard is 10.7 cm long, 1.8 cm wide and 3 cm thick. There are some textile remains preserved on the handle, which together with pieces of birch wood and leather, likely represent the remains of a scabbard or fragments of the deceased person's garments.

It is not entirely clear how the other grave goods, surviving in various state of preservation, originally lay in relation to the deceased person's body. Judging by the numerous iron nails, however, there are reasons to believe that the woman was actually buried in a boat. In his brief discussion of this grave, Stenvik wrote:

> Vi står med andre ord ovenfor en nordtrøndersk amazone som rokker grundlig ved tradisjonell kjønnsrolleoppfatning. Sa langt står denne graven sørgelig alene, men det er i alle fall et varsku om at vi ikke uten videre skal overføre tradisjonell rollentekning på forhistoriske forhold.[117]

> In other words, we are looking at a north-Trøndelag Amazon who thoroughly challenges traditional gender roles. So far this grave is unique and serves as a warning that we should not project traditional divisions of roles onto prehistoric realities.[118]

The examples from Nordre Kjølen and Birka discussed in this chapter show that the grave from Aunvoll is actually not that unique after all. Perhaps the most striking aspect of all these three graves is that – except for the small bead from Aunvoll – they *do not* contain any diagnostically female jewellery. Even though the combs from Aunvoll and Birka represent the kinds of objects that are conventionally linked with women, we know that in some instances combs also appear in male graves, meaning that they cannot be considered as either 'female' or 'male' goods. In view of the above, the lack of oval brooches or other characteristically female jewellery in all three graves under scrutiny could suggest that these presumed women were dressed in an unusual way, perhaps in what would normally be regarded as 'male' clothing. Regrettably, due to the lack of well-preserved textile remains from these graves, which could shed more light on the type of garments the deceased were wearing, the idea that the dead were clad in manly costumes must remain speculation.

Another interesting aspect of the grave from Aunvoll is that among its furnishings were eight or nine gaming pieces (Plate 4.10). This feature brings to mind the gaming pieces discovered in grave Bj. 581 at Birka already discussed above. It is impossible to say if the number of gaming pieces that were found at Aunvoll represents the full set that had originally been buried with the deceased or just the remains of it; because the gaming pieces were made of organic material, some of them could have decomposed. But if what was found actually represents all the pieces that had been originally placed in the grave, then this should make us think about the significance of the number nine in this particular context. We know from multiple textual sources (and also from archaeological finds) that the number nine had special meanings for the Norse and was associated with ritual acts, for instance the nine-night ordeal during which the god Óðinn hung himself on the tree or the sacrifices at Gamla Uppsala that took place every nine years.[119] The presence of gaming pieces in Aunvoll might be seen as yet another example of using symbolically charged and multivalent objects to invoke particular reactions from the spectators of the funeral and/or to (re)create an image of the deceased person; in any case, we should be wary of reading them too literally. Furthermore, although our modern interpretations concerning the Aunvollen grave could be taken very far, the problematic circumstances of its discovery and the incompleteness of its surviving contents must always be borne in mind.

Mårem, Telemark

Grave 2 from the cemetery at Mårem in Telemark, Norway was professionally excavated in 2003 and – in contrast to many of the examples discussed above – its documentation is meticulous.[120] The skeletal remains were completely decomposed, but the repertoire of the accompanying grave goods allows us to make an educated guess that the deceased person was a woman (Plate 4.12 and Fig. 4.12).

The woman's body was laid in the grave in a supine position and dressed in an elaborate costume, many fragments of which have survived in very good condition (Plate 4.13). On her chest the woman had a pair of identical oval brooches made of copper alloy with a bead necklace suspended from them. Remarkably, she also had two additional strings of beads – one around the neck and the other around her right wrist, something that is very unusual in Viking Age female graves. At the neck there was a round brooch made of copper alloy and decorated in the Borre style. The woman also had a ring on one of the fingers of her right hand. In addition to these different pieces of jewellery, the deceased had a small copper alloy tube, probably suspended from one of the oval brooches. Similar tubes to this are conventionally interpreted as needle cases, but this particular example had small flakes of gold foil inside. An analogous item was found also in grave 3 from the same cemetery, which was a double grave probably belonging to a man and a woman (no bones have survived and therefore the sex of the deceased has been inferred only on the basis of objects that accompanied them). The goods associated with the presumed man included weapons (a sword, an axehead and a set of arrowheads) and tools (knife, strike-a-light), while the presumed woman was laid to rest with 14 colourful beads, a strike-a-light with a piece of flint and possibly a weaving comb. In contrast to grave 2, in the case of this particular grave, the copper alloy tube was actually found in connection with the man and lay somewhere at his pelvis. The tube contained felt or hair as well as small fragments of gold and silver foil. In her report on the Mårem cemetery, Ann-Kristin Engh argues that the two copper alloy tubes from graves 2 and 3 may have been used for magic purposes, as implied by the function of roughly similar items from different parts of the world.[121] It is not unlikely – as Engh believes – that they originate from the Black Sea area and that the foils contained some inscription, perhaps with apotropaic significance.[122] In any case, it is clear that the tubes did not serve as needle cases and instead were endowed with some very special meaning.

A further peculiarity of grave 2 – and of major interest in the context of the present discussion – is that it contained an axehead, which was placed by the left thigh of the deceased person. Somewhere at the feet lay an iron sickle. In addition to these objects, the same grave contained six nails, perhaps originally from a wooden chest, as well as some indeterminate fragments of iron, slag, burnt clay and quartz. A vertebrae was also discovered at the head-end of the grave pit and it has been interpreted as the bone of a sacrificed animal.[123] The assemblage of grave 2, including a rare type of object probably endowed with amuletic significance, an axehead and various kinds of beads used in an uncommon manner all provide very strong arguments to suggest that the deceased individual was someone extraordinary and that this person was engaged in the practice of magic. This idea will be further expanded later in this study.

Løve, Vestfold

The grave from Løve in Vestfold, Norway held the skeletal remains of a very young person, probably a woman, who, according to a tooth analysis, was less than 20 years old at the moment of death.[124] The deceased had a string of colourful beads around the neck, many of which date back

Fig. 4.12. Artistic reconstruction of the Mårem grave. Illustration by Mirosław Kuźma. Copyright Mirosław Kuźma and Leszek Gardeła.

to the Migration period (ca. 650–760), meaning they were already antiques at the time when the burial took place.[125] Among other puzzling items attached to the necklace was a copper alloy ring and two small pendants, all probably serving the role of amulets. By the woman's head lay an axehead (perhaps thrust into the ground, although this is unclear from the report) and at the foot-end rested the remains of a horse with a rattle or *rangle* lying over them. Although the horse's head was apparently missing from the grave (which could imply that it had been decapitated), an elaborately decorated bridle was found in its place. There were also three ice crampons on three of the animal's hooves (Plate 4.14 and Fig. 4.13).

Specialist analyses have revealed that the woman's clothing was adorned with gold thread. In addition, there were also some pieces of blue textile as well as a fragment interpreted as a veil. Intriguingly, all these costume details bear striking resemblance to the clothing of the so-called *völva* from grave 4 at the Viking Age cemetery at Fyrkat in Jylland, Denmark.[126]

The blue colour of the Løve woman's clothes is a feature that deserves further exposition. Not only were coloured clothes probably more costly and certainly more laborious to produce than undyed garments, but they also seem to have been perceived as indicators of status. The idea that coloured clothes served as a means to distinguish certain individuals from others is something we can observe in Old Norse literature, too. As Thor Ewing notes, in sagas and other texts the colours red and blue tend to indicate people of prominence.[127] Dark clothes, on the other hand, are usually worn by people of low social status, for example slaves.[128]

Interestingly, on several occasions in the sagas, the colour blue is associated with women who deal with magic (the most prominent examples include the *völva* Þorbjörg from *Eiríks saga rauða* and the malevolent sorceress Geirríðr from *Eyrbyggja saga*)[129] as well as with individuals who set out to kill another person (*e.g.* Hrafnkell in *Hrafnkels saga*).[130] The Old Norse term used to denote blue is *blár*, and while some scholars have suggested that *blár* referred to naturally pigmented black cloth, this idea seems problematic.[131] In light of more recent studies, it actually seems that *svartr* was the term used for a colour closest to what we today would consider as black. In textual sources the term *svartr* often appears as a byname, but it is also associated with people who are ugly and have unpleasant personalities.[132] Recent research on North European Viking Age textiles has shown that most dyed cloth was, in fact, blue and that woad was used in the production process, so the details conveyed by textual sources should be taken with a pinch of salt.[133]

In approaching the contents of the Løve grave holistically, there appear to be strong reasons to believe that the deceased person was a ritual specialist rather than someone who actively engaged in armed conflict. The expensive garments together with the numerous curated beads and amulets and the presence of a horse (an animal indicating status but also one which could be used to draw a wagon, for instance in a religious procession) imply that the local community held the woman in very high regard. The axe-head resting by her side might have been one of the tools she used in the household, but given the grave's special furnishings we should not rule out the possibility that – at least on some occasions – it was also used as one of her ritual accoutrements.

Other possibly female graves with weapons in Viking Age Norway

In addition to the examples reviewed above, there are several other Norwegian graves with weapons that might have held biologically female individuals. Regrettably, their comprehensive analysis and interpretation is hindered by the rudimentary nature of their *in-situ* documentation. Since these graves were discovered in the nineteenth and early twentieth centuries, a time when little effort was afforded to thoroughly examining and recording the external and internal form of burial and when the excavators' focus was largely centred on portable items alone, the documentation usually contains little else than just lists of grave goods. In the absence of specific information on the osteological remains, it is thus impossible to be certain if these graves belonged to just one person or if they held two or more individuals.

Regardless of these source-critical issues, a cremation grave from Hilde in Sogn og Fjordane is a very interesting case that deserves further exposition.[134] According to surviving records, inside this grave indeterminate human bone remains were found resting in a copper alloy bowl, while various objects lay scattered nearby. The artefactual assemblage comprised items typically associated with women's costume, such as a pair of oval brooches, different kinds of beads, as well as spindle whorls, a fragmented weaving sword and iron scissors, which altogether permit speculation that this was a woman's grave. A somewhat unexpected element of the artefactual assemblage is a tiny iron ring with nine Þórr's hammers, a type of item characteristic for the areas of Denmark and Sweden and one which doubtlessly had religious connotations, not least because it clearly referred to one of the major pre-Christian deities but also because of the symbolic significance of the number nine.[135] The Hilde grave also included other artefacts, such as a large cooking fork, an iron scoop, a roasting spit, an iron staff and various small metal implements. It is crucial to point out here that one of the objects discovered at Hilde resembles a shield boss, which is intriguing in view of the absence of other weapons in the grave. The fact that there was an iron staff in the assemblage (Fig. 4.14) – an item most likely serving as a distinctive attribute of a *seiðr* practitioner – may lead us to speculate that the shield boss had been used by the deceased person (or the mourners) in an unconventional way, perhaps as a ritual accoutrement.

Fig. 4.13. Artistic reconstruction of the Løve grave. Illustration by Mirosław Kuźma. Copyright Mirosław Kuźma and Leszek Gardeła.

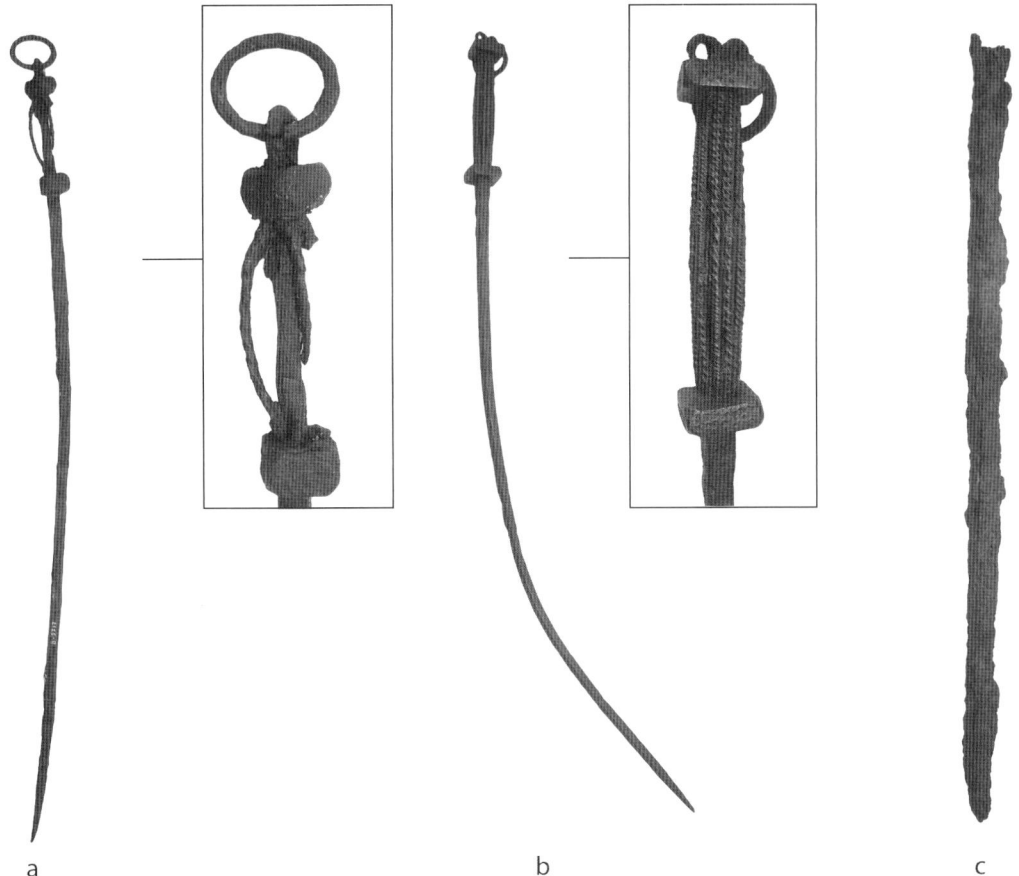

Fig. 4.14. Iron staffs from Hilde, Kvåle and Gausel in Norway, probably serving as ritual accoutrements in the practice of seiðr. All three staffs were found in burial contexts together with shield bosses and other goods. Photos by Leszek Gardeła.

Interestingly, weapons were also found in two other graves with iron staffs from Kvåle in Sogn og Fjordane and Gausel in Rogaland. At Kvåle the cremated remains, presumably belonging to a woman, had been placed inside an iron scoop. The grave goods were very rich and, among other things, included various tools for cooking and textile production as well as several brooches (oval, round and trefoil) and a shield boss.[136] The second grave, hailed by some scholars as the grave of the 'Gausel Queen', was likewise furnished with an impressive array of luxurious and imported goods including, *inter alia*, an elaborate horse bridle, a silver arm-ring, numerous beads and high-quality brooches as well as an item resembling a shield boss.[137] In looking at the graves from Hilde, Kvåle and Gausel collectively, it is interesting to note that although their contents are varied, they *all* contain iron staffs *and* shield bosses. Could it be that shield bosses (presumably attached to wooden boards) had been used by the occupants of these graves for some special, perhaps ritualistic purposes? We shall elaborate on this idea in Chapter 5.

Finally, in the present context it is also noteworthy that at Hopperstad in Sogn og Fjordane a possibly female individual was buried with rich jewellery, textile implements and a hoe (a kind of wood-working tool resembling an axe). Liv Helga Dommasnes has noted that the tool – likely used in boatbuilding – 'suggests responsibility for the building (and sailing?) of a ship'.[138]

Danish female graves with weapons

Gerdrup, Sjælland

The Gerdrup grave was discovered in 1981 on a beach ridge near an old tributary of the Roskilde fjord.[139] The burial pit was over a metre deep and held the remains of two adult individuals, a man and a woman (aged 35–40 and ca. 40 respectively), lying side by side in supine position with their heads to the north (Plate 4.15 and Fig. 4.15). This case is peculiar and very different from all the other examples discussed above not only due to the fact that we are certainly dealing with a double grave but also because at least one of the dead appears to have been violently executed.

Anthropological analysis of the skeletal remains of the man, together with the fact that his cervical vertebrae were found twisted, suggest that he might have died a violent death as a result of hanging.[140] According to surviving passages in medieval Scandinavian laws and literature, hanging was a penalty for treason, insolence, murder and offences

Fig. 4.15. Artistic reconstruction of the Gerdrup grave. Illustration by Mirosław Kuźma. Copyright Mirosław Kuźma and Leszek Gardeła.

of sexual nature such as seduction, abduction or adultery.[141] Upon excavation the man's legs were found spread open, implying that originally they might have been tied and/or that the man had been pushed into a grave pit that was too short for him. Only one object accompanied this individual – an iron knife resting on his chest. Nothing is known about the clothes he might have been dressed in.

The treatment of the woman's body also displays peculiar traits – her chest and right leg were found covered with two large boulders, indicating that in the course of the funeral the stones had been purposefully laid or thrown onto her. It is possible that this procedure imitated or alluded to a stoning execution and/or that these unconventional funerary acts were intended to practically and symbolically bind the woman to the grave to prevent her from undesired *post-mortem* activity. Old Norse sources preserve detailed descriptions of executions by stoning implying that it was one of the typical ways of dealing with malevolent *seiðr* practitioners; such acts were typically performed in isolated and marginal places, for instance beaches and mountain ridges.[142] Similarly to the man lying next to her, the woman was buried with a knife, but in her case it was placed on the waist together with a bone needle case containing an iron pin (Fig. 4.16). Remarkably, at the woman's feet lay a long spearhead representing Jan Petersen's type E (a type rarely encountered in Denmark) with the point directed towards the southern end of the grave, an unusual position the symbolic meaning of which shall be investigated in Chapter 5 (Fig. 4.17). It is also noteworthy that between the two deceased individuals fragments of sheep crania were found, perhaps representing the remains of food or animal sacrifice.

For a long time Viking specialists have been speculating about the relationship between the two individuals from Gerdrup, for instance suggesting that the man served as the woman's slave.[143] However, recent aDNA analyses have finally brought this aspect of the debate to an end, demonstrating unequivocally that the deceased were actually mother and son.[144] The familial relationship between the two Gerdrup individuals immediately brings to mind a passage recorded in the *Eyrbyggja saga* where a woman named Katla is stoned to death for performing malevolent magic and her son Oddr (who has been accused of cutting off a woman's arm) is killed by hanging.[145] Could the Gerdrup grave be a testimony to a ritual execution and could the two individuals have been accused of committing crimes similar to the crimes of the characters from the saga? We will never know the true answers to this question but the parallels are remarkably striking nonetheless.

Grave BB, Bogøvej, Langeland

Marked on the surface with a large stone, grave BB was one of the richest interments discovered within a small cemetery at Bogøvej in Langeland, Denmark comprising

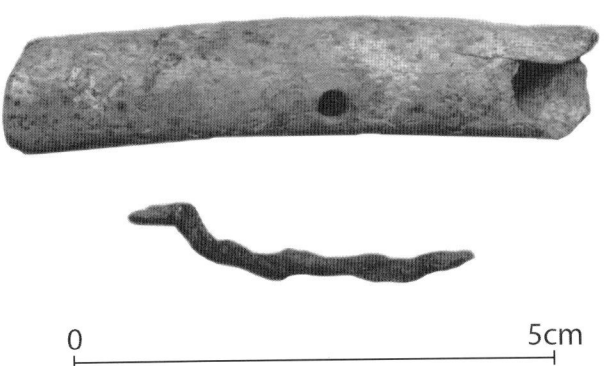

Fig. 4.16. Needle case and iron pin from Gerdrup. Photo by Leszek Gardeła.

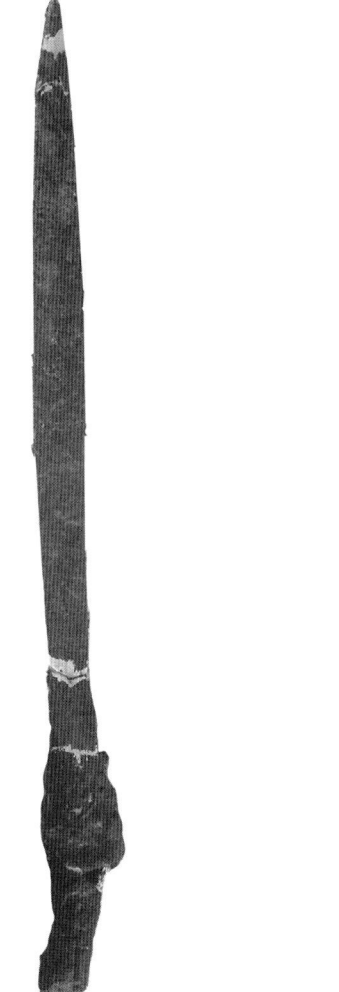

Fig. 4.17. Spearhead from Gerdrup. Photo by Leszek Gardeła.

a total of 49 inhumations.[146] Most of the graves in this site were rather modestly furnished with iron utensils such as knives as well as with glass beads and pottery fragments. Although the burial customs appear to have been fairly uniform, several graves displayed deviant characteristics; one man was buried in a prone position, one woman appears to have been decapitated (perhaps *post-mortem*), and a few of the deceased at Bogøvej had stones of various size lying directly over their bodies.[147]

According to an osteological analysis conducted by Pia Bennike, the person from grave BB was a 16–18-year-old woman. She lay in a supine position inside a coffin placed within a wooden chamber (Plate 4.16 and Fig. 4.18). Buried with this individual were a number of objects: an iron knife lay on the chest, a strike-a-light (Fig. 4.19) and a silver Arabic dirham of Nuh ibn Nasr (dated to AD 945) were placed on the pelvis, and an axehead rested by the right leg (Fig. 4.20). In addition, the grave contained two iron nails as well as 11 fragments of pottery and six pieces of flint.

Grave BB is remarkable because it is the only grave in the entire cemetery that contains a weapon. Another feature that adds to its peculiarity is its location in the south-western part of the site where it is spatially isolated from other interments. The chambered construction of the BB grave – one of just two examples of such funerary architecture at Bogøvej[148] – strongly indicates that it belonged to a person of prominent status or at least that this is how the mourners wanted to remember her.

In the original report detailing the excavations of the Bogøvej cemetery released in 1994, remarkably little attention was devoted to grave BB, but on a number of occasions the authors explicitly emphasised that the osteological sexing of the skeleton was certain,[149] something that is rarely seen in archaeological publications; the underpinning reason behind this may have been to show potential sceptics that the authors of the study were fully confident about the results of their analysis. Regardless of this, however, no attempts were made to explain why a woman had been buried with a weapon and what this could potentially say about her identity in life as well as in death. Instead, the presence of the axehead was explained away as potentially representing a 'symbolic cremation of a missing male',[150] who – for some unknown reason – could not be buried together with the woman.

There are several untapped aspects of this grave that deserve attention. We shall first consider the implications of chambered construction with an additional coffin inside. Although chamber graves are not uncommon in Viking Age Denmark, especially in the period spanning the tenth to eleventh centuries,[151] it appears that in the majority of instances the chambers did not include additional containers for the body – usually the dead were laid to rest directly on the floor of the chamber, in some cases perhaps on a bier or mat. Some Danish chamber graves (*e.g.* including one grave from Bogøvej and the grave from Oens discussed below),[152] however, contain detachable bodies of wagons on which the deceased lay buried, but it is evident that in the case of grave BB at Bogøvej an actual coffin was used. Although

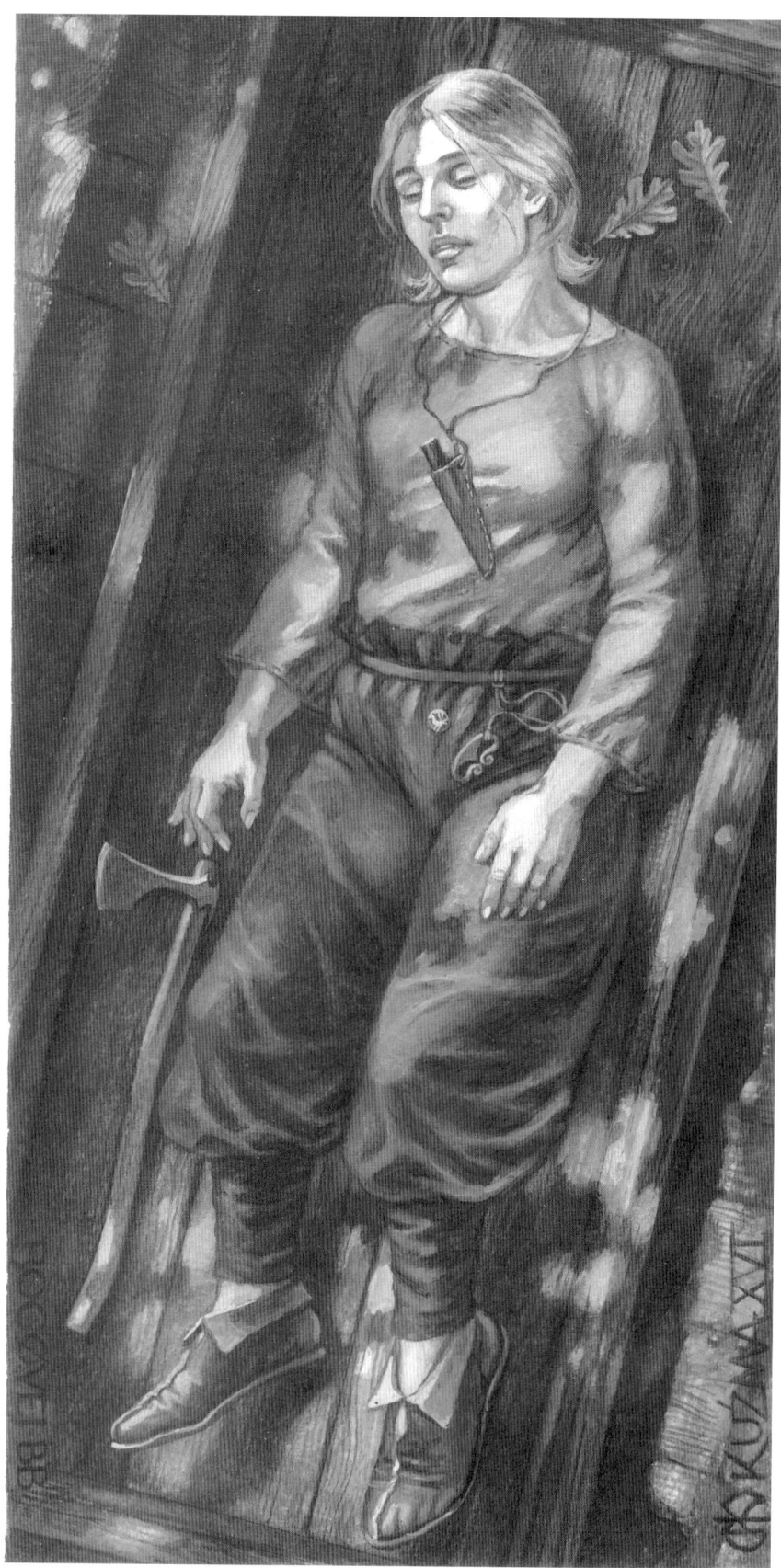

Fig. 4.18. Artistic reconstruction of grave BB from Bogøvej. Illustration by Mirosław Kuźma. Copyright Mirosław Kuźma and Leszek Gardeła.

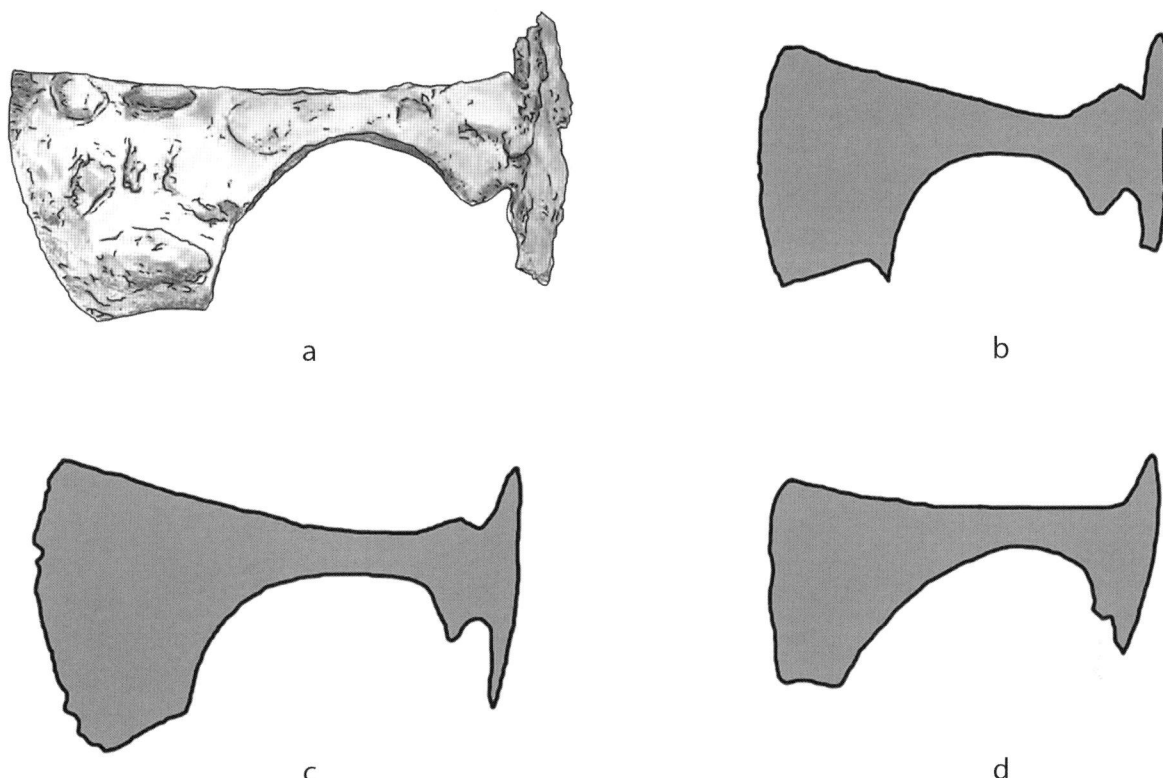

Fig. 4.20. Axehead from Bogøvej (a) and a selection of axeheads from Central Europe representing Nadolski's type Va: Czarna Wielka, Poland (b), Końskie, Poland (c), Końskie, Poland (d). Redrawn by Leszek Gardeła on the basis of Grøn, Hedeager Krag, Bennike 1994: 120 and Nadolski 1954: 257. Not to scale.

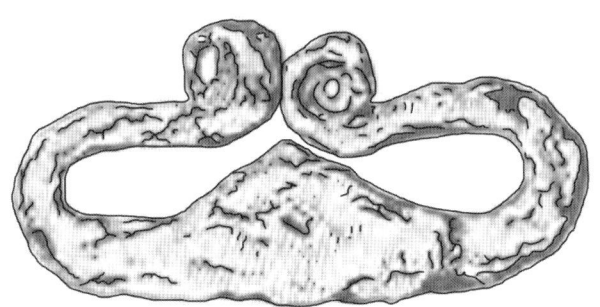

Fig. 4.19. Strike-a-light from Bogøvej. Redrawn by Leszek Gardeła on the basis of Grøn, Hedeager Krag, Bennike 1994: 121.

rarely encountered in Denmark, the custom of adding coffins to chamber graves was very commonly practiced in the Western Slavic territories of Poland and Pomerania in the late tenth and eleventh centuries, i.e. a period that coincides with the dating of grave BB. Examples of this custom are known from Viking Age cemeteries at Bodzia, Ciepłe, Dziekanowice and Kałdus.[153] New investigations of these graves, involving detailed morpho-metric and typological studies of their contents, additionally supported by isotope and aDNA analyses of the skeletal remains, have shown that the majority of the deceased were local, and thus probably Slavic.[154] In this light, there are reasons to believe that chamber graves with coffins were characteristic of the Western Slavic area which permits careful speculation that grave BB belonged to a foreigner. A further strand of evidence that can provide support for this view is the type of axehead the deceased person was buried with.

The axehead from Bogøvej has a beard, a slender neck and a cap in the butt-end. Axeheads of this particular kind are *extremely* rare in Viking Age Denmark and elsewhere in Scandinavia, but they are characteristic of Central and Eastern Europe. Very close parallels are known from the area of Poland, for example from Góra,[155] Końskie,[156] Korzybie,[157] Mazowsze Płockie,[158] Pień[159] and Radom.[160] In Andrzej Nadolski's classification, they represent type Va[161] and in the more recent classification system created by Piotr N. Kotowicz they belong to type V Variant IB.5.20 dated to the second half of the tenth century.[162] It is noteworthy that axes of this kind sometimes have a small hole in the blade, probably allowing the user to draw a string and attach a special protective sheath made of wood. In the Baltic area, similar axes tend to have an additional protrusion at the lower end of the beard and are occasionally inlaid with non-ferrous metals. In contrast to the Baltic examples, however, the axehead from Bogøvej is undecorated and does not have a hole in the blade. The lack of these features brings it closer to the variants from the area of today's Poland.

The strike-a-light found in grave BB at Bogøvej is yet another object that may suggest a potentially foreign identity of the grave's occupant (Fig. 4.19). It belongs to a type with spiral ends that is very unusual in Denmark but quite commonly found in Central Europe (especially Poland) and the Baltic countries. To the author's knowledge, the only parallels from Denmark discovered so far are known from the Viking Age fortress at Fyrkat. The presence of such items at this particular site is intriguing, especially in light of the fact that a number of other artefacts discovered there – both in funerary contexts and within the fortress – bear Central and/or Eastern European characteristics.[163] Among them are small pendants in the shape of duck feet discovered in grave 4 (interpreted as belonging to a sorceress) and probably originating from the area of Rus or Poland.[164]

The unusual construction (wooden chamber with a coffin), the presence of an evidently Central or Eastern European axehead and a strike-a-light likely of the same provenance, as well as the fact that other traces of interaction between Slavs and Scandinavians have been noted in the vicinity of Bogøvej all strongly imply that the person buried in grave BB was a foreigner. This should not come as a surprise, especially in view of the wider geographical setting of Bogøvej; the convenient location of Langeland between the Bay of Kiel and Storebelt would have made it a perfect meeting point and a melting pot for the representatives of different cultural milieus and social strata.

It is noteworthy that at Nørre Longelse, a site located at a relatively short distance from Bogøvej, another high-status grave of a person possibly originating from the Slavic area was found.[165] This individual, probably a man, was buried with a lavish set of spurs decorated with intricate knotwork motifs and with terminals resembling the head of a snake. Although the spurs from Nørre Longelse are one of a kind, analogies to some features of their decoration (especially the snake head terminals) can be seen very clearly on so-called 'zoomorphic spurs' discovered in the area of Poland in places like Cerkiewnik, Ciepłe, Lubniewice, Lutomiersk and Wrocław Ostrów Tumski. It has recently been argued that such spurs belonged to Western Slavic riders who may have been members of the elite retinue of the Piast rulers.[166] Several years ago, a goad of a spur of this kind was discovered at Skegrie in Skåne, Sweden not far away from Harald Bluetooth's fortress at Trelleborg, implying some kind of relationship and interaction between the representatives of the highest echelons of Western Slavic and the local Scandinavian society in the late tenth century.[167]

In this context, and knowing that Harald Bluetooth had close ties with Western Slavic aristocracy[168] – as is reflected in his marriage with princess Tova, the daughter of Polabian chieftain Mistivoj – it is not unlikely that the person buried in grave BB at Bogøvej also had some connections with the Danish ruler(s) and played a prominent role in the multi-ethnic population of Langeland. Whether this role necessitated taking active part in martial activities is difficult to gauge today but cannot be completely ruled out.

Grave A505, Trekroner-Grydehøj, Sjælland

Grave A505 from an early Viking Age cemetery at Trekroner-Grydehøj in Sjælland can be regarded as one of the most intriguing female inhumations discovered in Denmark in the course of the last two decades.[169] The funerary acts that led to its creation were both laborious and violent, and they would have surely been long remembered by those who gathered at the graveside. Since the grave was excavated to a very high standard, we can reconstruct the sequence of events that took place during the funeral – something that is often impossible in Viking archaeology due to matters of poor preservation (Plate 4.17 and Fig. 4.21).[170]

The initial stages of the burial involved digging a fairly long and wide pit and placing a female body inside it in a supine position with the head to the north. Then followed a range of violent acts, including the slaughter of a dog and an old stallion.[171] Remarkably, the dog was bisected, placed at the woman's feet and one part of its body was additionally pressed by a boulder. Then the horse was killed and its carcass was laid directly on the woman partly covering the left side of her body. Probably at around the same time a number of different grave goods were deposited around the woman's corpse – these included a wooden chest with an iron knife placed inside or over the chest's lid, a wooden bucket with an iron handle, as well as an iron chain (perhaps serving as a kind of dog leash), and a curious copper alloy item resembling an arrowhead or spearhead with an iron tip (Fig. 4.22). Two additional knives were placed by the chest and on the woman's waistline. The grave also included a couple of ordinary nails.

At some point during the later stages of the funeral the woman's body was covered with large stones: one was placed over her head and another over her chest. Stones were also laid or thrown on the horse carcass and the grave was then filled up with mid-sized stones and pebbles. The placing and throwing of stones may have been conceptualised by the people participating in the funeral as an act of *post-mortem* stoning, perhaps conducted with a similar intention as in the case of the Gerdrup grave.

Further ritual acts conducted at Trekroner-Grydehøj involved the deposition of bodies or body parts of two other human individuals, a man and a woman. In the course of the excavation, their remains were found in a pit located directly above the grave of the initially buried female individual. It is unclear whether the placement of these fragmented human remains had been part of the same funeral or whether this act took place sometime later and after the first grave was sealed. It is possible to speculate that the burial of the two individuals was an act of human sacrifice, but it may have had other meanings, not necessarily negative.

Fig. 4.21. Artistic reconstruction of grave A505 from Trekroner-Grydehøj. Illustration by Mirosław Kuźma. Copyright Mirosław Kuźma and Leszek Gardeła.

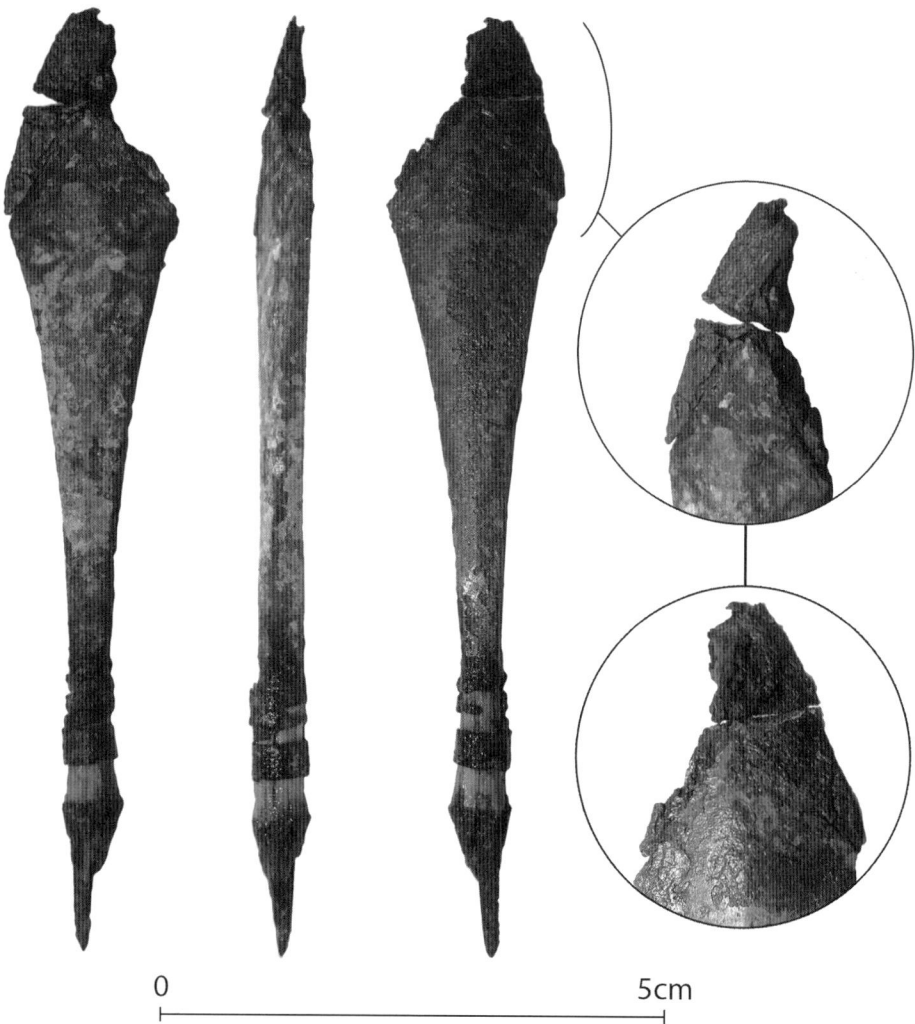

Fig. 4.22. Copper alloy arrowhead, spearhead or staff from grave A505 from Trekroner-Grydehøj. Photo by Leszek Gardeła.

The strange copper alloy item placed at the woman's side and resembling an arrowhead or a small spearhead is a one-of-a-kind artefact with no direct parallels anywhere in the Viking world. Its potential meanings and conceptual parallels will be investigated in detail in Chapter 5, but here we can already hint that it strongly suggests the deceased person was involved in the practice of magic.

Oens, Jylland

Professionally excavated in 2003 by Charlotta Lindblom and her team, the Oens grave is another recently discovered example of a possible female grave furnished with items possessing martial connotations.[172] The surviving traces of very characteristic architectural features leave no doubt that this was a chamber grave (measuring 3×2 m and oriented N–S) inside of which a body of a wagon had been placed. The chamber's construction comprised vertically standing wooden planks with several additional wooden logs used for additional support. Interestingly, nine large stones were found inside the grave fill[173] – originally, the stones had probably been laid over the chamber's lid or roof to serve as grave-markers, but when the lid/roof eventually decomposed, the stones fell inside the grave.

The body of the wooden wagon was found completely decomposed, but its construction and size could be inferred on the basis of the remains of rivets and various metal fragments. Like other wagons known from Viking Age sites across Scandinavia,[174] the one from Oens had a clinker construction. The remains found inside the wagon indicate that during the funeral the deceased person's body rested on pillows or some kind of duvet filled with down.

The deceased individual – whose skeletal remains decomposed completely thus making osteological analyses impossible – was accompanied by a range of goods, all located on the right hand side of the body: an iron knife was placed by the arm, a whetstone and a bone comb lay at the hips and an axehead (probably representing Jan Petersen's type H; Charlotta Lindblom pers. comm. 2021) rested at the feet (Plate 4.18). The remains of two iron spurs discovered at the foot-end of the wagon's body strongly imply that the deceased person had them on their feet. Outside of the wagon, in the eastern part of the chamber, lay further goods such as the remains of two wooden vessels (probably buckets) and a wooden chest as well as iron fragments potentially serving as decorative harness parts. Based on the overall form and assemblage of this grave, Lindblom has dated it to the tenth century. No other graves were found at Oens during the 2003 excavations, but it is noteworthy that the grave that concerns us here was somewhat unusually located *between* two Viking Age buildings.[175]

Overall, the Oens grave is a very peculiar case, and its contents do not provide unequivocal hints as regards the biological sex and socially constructed gender of the deceased individual. Items like combs, whetstones and chests occur in both male and female graves discovered across Viking Age Scandinavia, while axes are more characteristic of the graves of men, although – as we have seen above – they do occasionally occur in connection with female individuals. Wagon burial, on the other hand, is a mortuary tradition characteristic of Viking Age Denmark and one that is exclusively linked to high-status women. Due to the absence of human osteological remains, in speculating about the sex and gender of the deceased individual from Oens, all we can do is try and qualify if the grave's surviving features point more strongly towards a male or female identity of the deceased or if they blur or nuance these categories. Referring to comparative evidence, Charlotta Lindblom argues that the presence of the wagon's body permits a careful identification of the deceased as female. The other goods, such as the whetstone, comb and buckets do not contradict this and neither does the presence of the axehead. Only the spurs can pose some interpretational problems, since in funerary contexts they are conventionally associated with men and since they occur in female graves extremely rarely.[176] It is also worth highlighting in this context that even grave Bj. 581, which included two horses, weapons and various riding equipment, *did not* include spurs. Regardless of this, the effort invested in the construction of the Oens grave, as well as its relatively rich furnishings, give reasons to believe that the buried individual was a person of prominence and rank. In consequence, rather than serving as gender markers, the spurs may have been used in the burial ceremony to amplify this individual's elevated status and special role in society. The axehead may have had the same symbolic purpose, but we should not rule out the possibility that it additionally alluded to some specific activities the deceased had once engaged in, for instance the performance of magic. As we have seen in the discussions above, there are hints suggesting that axes were used by Viking Age sorceresses in divination practices. Wagons, too, are shown in extant textual sources as vehicles associated with people who had links with the supernatural and/or with women who engaged in martial activities. The best example of the relationship between powerful women and wagons – also highlighted in Lindblom's paper[177] – is that of the renowned *valkyrja* Brynhildr, the ill-fated lover of Sigurðr, who according to Old Norse texts, was cremated on a wagon.

***

Having now surveyed the archaeological evidence for the burial of women with weapons in Viking Age Scandinavia, we can see that the iconic grave Bj. 581 from Birka is not as unique as some people would like to think, although it is doubtlessly special in many regards. As this chapter has shown, a number of other presumed female graves with weapons are known from Northern Europe; the deceased are buried with axeheads, swords, spearheads, arrowheads and shield bosses (or complete shields) as well as with an array of luxurious jewellery and exotic goods.

The important preliminary takeaway from this investigation is that no two female graves with weapons are ever exactly the same – the disparate ways of burial may have reflected a whole plethora of ideas echoing real or imagined identities and worldviews of the deceased and the memories, beliefs and aspirations of the mourners. Following a detailed examination of the multifarious images of armed women in Old Norse literature (Chapter 3) and having acquired a thorough understanding of the funerary material, we are now armed with the necessary apparatus to commence a deeper exploration of the social and symbolic meanings of weapons in Viking Age female graves and other female-related contexts.

Notes

1 See, for example, Shetelig 1912; Petersen 1919; 1928; 1951.
2 See, for example, Brøndsted 1936; Arbman 1940; 1943; Ramskou 1950.
3 For examples of osteologically sexed weapon graves from the Viking Age, see Sellevold *et al.* 1984; Buko 2015; Pedersen 2014a; Janowski 2015; Błaszczyk 2017.
4 For previous overviews of presumably female graves with weapons in Viking Age Scandinavia, see Klos 2006; Gardeła 2013b; 2018b.
5 Gardeła & Odebäck 2018; Gardeła in press-a; in press-b; in press-c.
6 Gardeła & Toplak 2020.
7 For examples of osteologically sexed Viking Age female skeletons with jewellery, see Sellevold *et al.* 1984; Speed & Walton Rogers 2004.
8 Hedenstierna-Jonson *et al.* 2017; Price *et al.* 2019.
9 Hedenstierna-Jonson 2009.
10 Arbman 1940; 1943; Gräslund 1980; Price 2012a.
11 Hedenstierna-Jonson 2006a; 2006b; Holmquist & Kalmring 2019.
12 Arwidsson 1984; 1986; 1989b; Hedenstierna-Jonson 2012; Hedenstierna-Jonson & Kjellström 2014; Price 2012a.
13 Hedenstierna-Jonson *et al.* 2017.

14 For further details on the contents of these graves, see Arbman 1940; 1943: 142–144, 191–192.
15 On Viking Age chamber graves, see Eisenschmidt 1994; Ringstedt 1997; Mihajlov 2011; Price 2012a; Gardeła 2013c; Pedersen 2014a; Janowski 2015; Błaszczyk & Stępniewska 2016; Błaszczyk 2017.
16 Gardeła 2013c; 2016a.
17 Hofmann 2015; Klevnäs 2015; 2016; Gardeła 2016a.
18 Arbman 1943: 188.
19 Scans of these plans are shown and discussed in detail in Androshchuk 2018.
20 See Kjellström 2012: 71, 73.
21 Arwidsson 1989a: 144.
22 Hedenstierna-Jonson *et al.* 2017.
23 Androshchuk 2018: 54–58. For more details, see Kovalenko *et al.* 2012: 322–335; Kovalenko 2013: 280–286.
24 The (re)interpretation of the Birka grave as that of a 'warrior woman' was heavily criticised by Judith Jesch on her blog (www.norseandviking.blogspot.com). Howard Williams has also contributed to the debate on his blog (www.howardwilliamsblog.wordpress.com). So far, neither of the two scholars have released their opinions on Bj. 581 in a peer-reviewed academic publication.
25 Price *et al.* 2019.
26 Price *et al.* 2019: 192.
27 Price *et al.* 2019: 194.
28 Price *et al.* 2019: 194.
29 As mentioned earlier, the sword type is not entirely clear. Two different swords were drawn on Hjalmar Stolpe's grave plans – see Androshchuk 2018. The sword that is currently attributed to Bj. 581 has been illustrated in the work of Arbman 1940; 1943: 189; Price *et al.* 2019: 187.
30 For a new discussion on this and similar miniature items, see Gardeła in press-a.
31 Arbman 1943: 190.
32 Härke 2014. See also the discussion in Chapter 1.
33 Brunning 2019: 106.
34 Apart from Bj. 581, swords were found in the following inhumation graves at Birka: Bj. 496 (Arbman 1943: 143–144), Bj. 514 (Arbman 1943: 153–154), Bj. 524 (Arbman 1943: 160–161), Bj. 542 (Arbman 1943: 167–168), Bj. 544 (Arbman 1943: 170–171), Bj. 561 (Arbman 1943: 180–181), Bj. 624 (Arbman 1943: 205–207), Bj. 643 (Arbman 1943: 220–221), Bj. 644 (Arbman 1943: 221–226), Bj. 731 (Arbman 1943: 253–255), Bj. 735 (Arbman 1943: 256–259), Bj. 736 (Arbman 1943: 259–261), Bj. 750 (Arbman 1943: 267–272), Bj. 752 (Arbman 1943: 273–274), Bj. 832 (Arbman 1943: 303–304), Bj. 834 (Arbman 1943: 304–308), Bj. 842 (Arbman 1943: 314–316), Bj. 850 (Arbman 1943: 323–325), Bj. 855 (Arbman 1943: 330–332), Bj. 886 (Arbman 1943: 344–346), Bj. 942 (Arbman 1943: 364–366), Bj. 944 (Arbman 1943: 368–371), Bj. 957 (Arbman 1943: 381–382), Bj. 977 (Arbman 1943: 403–404), Bj. 1151 (Arbman 1943: 474–476). For a more detailed discussion on swords from Birka, see Thålin-Bergman 1986a and Androshchuk 2014; 2018: 55; Sayer *et al.* 2019. On weapon combinations in the Birka graves, see Thålin-Bergman 1986b.
35 For examples of Norwegian Viking Age graves with multiple shields and for discussions on their symbolic meanings, see Schetelig 1905; Oestigaard 2015; Gardeła 2019e.
36 For a recent discussion on this issue, see Gardeła & Odebäck 2018 with further references.
37 Nordberg 2002; 2003.
38 Price 2002: 148.
39 Hedenstierna-Jonson *et al.* 2017.
40 On gaming pieces and gaming boards in Viking Age graves, see Hall 2016. See also Arbman 1940; 1943; Owen & Dalland 1999; Rundkvist & Williams 2008; Gardeła 2019a: 167–169, 172, 174 for more detailed discussions on specific examples of these items stemming from funerary contexts.
41 Gardeła 2019b. For further remarks on games and pastimes in Viking Age Scandinavia, see Gardeła 2012a.
42 Jesch 2006.
43 Text and translation after Jesch 2006: 5.
44 van Hamel 1934.
45 Text and translation after Dronke 1997: 9.
46 Text and translation after Dronke 1997: 23.
47 Viking Age copper alloy bowls have been extensively discussed in the work of Poklewski 1961 and Trotzig 1991. For more recent studies on their various exemplars from Northern and Central Europe, see Janowski & Kurasiński 2002; Janowski 2003; 2015; Munch 2003; Stylegar 2007: 95–99.
48 It is vital to highlight here that not all graves with copper alloy bowls have been osteologically sexed and that the sex of some individuals has been determined only on the basis of grave goods that accompanied them. Gustav Trotzig lists several graves with bowls from Gotland which appear to have belonged to women (see Trotzig 1991: 189–192, 205–211, 214–220, 242–249, 262–263). A grave of a possible woman buried with a copper alloy bowl was also found in the cemetery at Wolin Młynówka, Poland (grave 252; for further details, see Wojtasik 1967: 67–68; Janowski 2003: 338–339); the deceased person had two copper alloy temple rings and a clay spindle whorl. Although the Wolin grave has not been osteologically sexed, its furnishings are characteristic of Western Slavic female graves.
49 Viking Age equestrian graves containing sets of spurs, stirrups and military equipment are discussed in Brøndsted 1936; Braathen 1989; Pedersen 2014a; Gardeła *et al.* 2019a; 2019b; Gardeła & Kajkowski 2021a; Toplak in press.
50 On the problems of identifying weapon graves as belonging to warriors (in various early medieval cultural milieus, including those of the Anglo-Saxons, the Scandinavians and the Western Slavs), see Chapter 1 and the work of Härke 2014; Williams 2006; Sikora 2014; Odebäck 2018.
51 The sequence of funerary procedures leading to the composition of grave 59:3 from Klinta in Öland has been reconstructed and extensively discussed in the work of previous scholars *e.g.* Petersson 1958; Schultze 1987: 55–62, 102–112; Price 2002: 142–149. The information provided in this chapter is mainly based on Price's analysis.
52 For a detailed analysis of the staff from Klinta, see Price 2002: 183–185; 2019: 139–141, 146–147; Gardeła 2016b.
53 On bird symbolism in the Viking Age and the presence of bird remains in funerary contexts, see Kulakov & Markovets 2004; Gräslund 2006; Bourns 2012; Carstens 2018; Karpińska 2018; Vretemark 2018.
54 On Þórr's hammer rings in the Viking Age, see Andersson 2005a; Jensen 2010: 65–72.

55 See, for example, Price 2002: 142–149; 2019; Andersson 2015; 2016: 34, 35; Gardeła 2016b.
56 Price 2002: 149.
57 Artelius 2003; 2005.
58 Artelius 2005: 264.
59 Artelius 2005.
60 Wickholm 2006.
61 Artelius 2005: 265. See also Hagberg 1937; Häggström 2003; 2005.
62 On the symbolic significance of knives in Western Slavic culture, see Wrzesiński 2000; Kurasiński 2008; Gardeła 2017b: 51–53, 59–61; Szczepanik 2017.
63 Artelius 2005: 273.
64 Svanberg 2003: 197.
65 Svanberg 2003: 253–254.
66 Thunmark-Nylén 2006: 249.
67 Thunmark-Nylén 2006: 63.
68 Thunmark-Nylén 2006: 393.
69 Thunmark-Nylén 2006: 400.
70 Thunmark-Nylén 2006: 427.
71 Thunmark-Nylén 2006: 434.
72 Mørck 1901: 70.
73 Petersen 1919: 117–121. On M-type swords in Norway, see also Hernæs 1985.
74 Androshchuk 2014: 69.
75 Petersen 1919: 31–33.
76 See, for example, Artelius 2005; Aannestad 2018 with further references.
77 Petersen 1919: 43.
78 On Viking Age arrowheads, see Sognnes 1988; Halpin 2008; Hjardar & Vike 2016.
79 Rygh 1885.
80 Hernæs 1984: 34.
81 Mørck 1901: 71.
82 Hernæs 1984: 34.
83 Hernæs 1984.
84 Holck 1984.
85 Hernæs 1984: 34.
86 Translation by Leszek Gardeła.
87 Gjerpe 2005b: 38–45.
88 Lie 2016.
89 On Scandinavian-style sword scabbard chapes, see Androshchuk 2014. On their exemplars discovered in Central and Eastern Europe, see also Janowski 2007 with references.
90 On the roles of dogs in Viking Age graves, see Gräslund 2004; Gardeła 2012b.
91 Brunning 2019.
92 Janowski 2014.
93 Révész 2014: 48–49.
94 Price 2016: 160.
95 Kyhlberg 2012: 79–87; Brunning 2019: 36–42.
96 Carver 1998.
97 Williams 2006.
98 Price 2010b.
99 The results of different excavation campaigns at Kaupang, together with specialist analyses of various categories of artefacts, have been extensively discussed in the following publications: Blindheim *et al.* 1981; Blindheim & Heyerdahl-Larsen 1995; Blindheim *et al.* 1999; Blindheim 2008; Skre 2007; 2008; 2011; Pedersen 2016.
100 For the latest analyses of the contents of Kaupang cemeteries, see Stylegar 2007; Moen 2019a; 2019c.
101 Stylegar 2007: 104–105; see also Blindheim *et al.* 1981: 200–201.
102 Stylegar 2007: 104–105; see also Blindheim *et al.* 1981: 204.
103 Stylegar 2007: 106–107; see also Blindheim *et al.* 1981: 205.
104 Holck 2006; 2009; Bill 2008.
105 Brøgger *et al.* 1917b; 1917a; Brøgger & Shetelig 1927; 1928; Christensen & Nockert 2006.
106 For some of the most recent discussions on the Oseberg grave, see Gansum 2002; 2004; Bill 2008; 2016a; 2016b; Bill & Daly 2012.
107 Christensen 1992: 88.
108 Bill & Daly 2012.
109 For further arguments suggesting that the Oseberg women were ritual specialists, see Price 2002; 2019; Gardeła 2016b.
110 Aannestad & Glørstad 2017: 162.
111 Aannestad & Glørstad 2017: 162–163.
112 Regrettably, only one of these brooches is now held in the collections of the University Museum of Bergen; the second brooch was stolen in 2017 and was not found among the objects recovered by the police in 2018.
113 One stone is blue-grey, two are grey-green and the rest are light grey or grey-white.
114 Dommasnes 1979: 110–111; Gardeła 2018b: 398.
115 Dommasnes 1987: 72.
116 Petersen 1919: 89–105.
117 Stenvik 2005: 151.
118 Translation by Leszek Gardeła.
119 On the significance of the number nine in Norse societies, see Sołtysiak 2003b; 2003a; Simek 2006: 232–233.
120 Engh 2009: 152–156.
121 Engh 2009: 158.
122 Engh 2009: 154.
123 Engh 2009: 155.
124 Resi 2013.
125 Resi 2013: 118–119.
126 On grave 4 from Fyrkat and the identity of its occupant, see Roesdahl 1977; Price 2002: 149–157; 2019; Pentz *et al.* 2009.
127 Ewing 2006: 224
128 Ewing 2006: 224.
129 Ewing 2006: 223.
130 Ewing 2006: 226 asserts that 'although the number of killers dressed in blue far exceeds the number dressed in other colours, we can see that blue is not the only colour chosen by killers'.
131 The meaning of the colour blue in Old Norse literature has been extensively investigated by Wolf 2006.
132 Wolf 2006: 1073–1074.
133 Ewing 2006: 224–225; see also Wolf 2006: 1076.
134 For further details on this grave's contents, see Gardeła 2016b: 298–299.
135 On small rings with Þórr's hammers, see Jensen 2010. On the discoveries of Þórr's hammers in Norway, see Nordeide 2006; 2011: 235–244.
136 For further details on this grave's contents, see Gardeła 2016b: 302–303.
137 For further details on this grave's contents, see Bakka 1993; Sørheim 2011; Gardeła 2016b: 292–293; Armstrong Oma 2018.
138 Dommasnes 1987: 74.

139 Christensen 1982; 1997; Lauritsen & Kastholm Hansen 2003; Gardeła 2013b: 280–282; 2016b: 82–84; 2017b: 180–183; Kastholm 2015; 2016; Hjardar & Vike 2016: 104; Lindblom 2016: 53.
140 Christensen 1982; 1997.
141 On hanging in Northern law and literature, see Gade 1985.
142 For further particulars on the act of stoning in Old Norse literature and the various connotations of this practice, see Ström 1942: 102–115; Gardeła 2016b: 78–82; 2017b: 177–180.
143 Christensen 1997.
144 Walsch et al. 2020.
145 Eyrbyggja saga, ch. 20. Einar Ólafur Sveinsson & Matthias Þórðarson 1935: 54.
146 Grøn et al. 1994: 34–35.
147 For a wider discussion on deviant/atypical burials from Bogøvej, see Gardeła 2013a; 2017b: 106–108, 150–151, 153–154.
148 Grøn et al. 1994: 30–34.
149 Grøn et al. 1994: 7–8. Allegedly, a more recent analysis suggests that the deceased from grave BB was biologically male (Otto Uldum pers. comm. 2019), but the details of this re-evaluation have never been released in a peer-reviewed publication. For this reason, and before a new and conclusive sex identification (ideally involving aDNA) is officially announced, it is assumed here that the person buried in grave BB is biologically female.
150 Grøn et al. 1994: 120.
151 On chamber graves in Viking Age Denmark, see Brøndsted 1936; Eisenschmidt 1994; Pedersen 2014a.
152 Grøn et al. 1994: 30–34.
153 On Viking Age chamber graves from Poland and Pomerania, see Buko 2015; Janowski 2015; Błaszczyk 2017; Wadyl 2019. See also the collection of papers edited by Błaszczyk & Stępniewska 2016.
154 The latest results of isotope analyses of chamber graves from Poland are discussed in the work of Błaszczyk 2017; 2018. See also Wadyl 2019.
155 MKP 1958.
156 Nadolski 1954: 257.
157 Nadolski 1954: 44.
158 Nadolski 1954: 257.
159 Drozd & Janowski 2007.
160 Kurasiński & Skóra 2016: 43–45, 59, 168.
161 Nadolski 1954.
162 Kotowicz 2018: 97–98.
163 Roesdahl 1975.
164 On grave 4 from Fyrkat, see Roesdahl 1977: 83–104; Price 2002: 149–157; Pentz et al. 2009.
165 Brøndsted 1936; Pedersen 2014a: 103.
166 For a detailed discussion on West Slavic zoomorphic spurs, see Gardeła et al. 2019a.
167 Söderberg 2014; Gardeła et al. 2019c; Gardeła & Kajkowski 2021a.
168 On Harald Bluetooth's connections with Western Slavs, see Dobat 2009; Price et al. 2011; Gardeła 2019d; Gardeła & Kajkowski 2021b.
169 Ulriksen 2011; 2018; Gardeła 2016b: 85–88.
170 For a stimulating discussion on time and motion in Viking Age funerals, including the mortuary acts conducted in the course of the burial at Trekroner-Grydehøj, see Price 2014.
171 According to Ulriksen (2018: 235), the stallion was at least 16–18 years old at the moment of death, meaning that it was no longer in its prime and was 'unlikely to have served as a splendid steed'.
172 Lindblom 2016; Lindblom & Balsgaard Juul 2019: 53–54.
173 The number nine is interesting in this context because – as already mentioned above – in Old Norse beliefs this was a number of great symbolic significance.
174 On Viking Age wagon burials, see Müller-Wille 1985. On the meaning of wagons in Old Norse religion and ritual practice, see Gunnell 2017.
175 Lindblom 2016: 96.
176 Cf. Lindblom 2016: 100–101
177 Lindblom 2016: 98.

Chapter 5

Interpreting the arsenal of armed women

After a review of different examples of Scandinavian Viking Age female graves with weapons, we are now familiar with the complete find corpus and can proceed to delve into the meanings of militaria in female hands. As we have seen, women were buried either with single weapons or with 'sets' consisting of two, three or more exemplars. In discussing these finds in the previous chapters of this study, and in speaking about the nature of burial data more broadly, it has already been noted that military equipment can possess deep symbolism and can be used for a plethora of purposes extending beyond the martial sphere. The goal of this chapter is to elaborate on this thought and comprehensively investigate the meaning-content of Viking Age weapons and their relationships with women using a constellation of sources, including archaeology, texts and folkloristic material.

Women and axes in the Viking Age

The survey conducted in Chapter 4 has demonstrated that axeheads feature prominently in female graves containing artefacts with martial connotations. In this section, we will take a more contextual and inquisitive look at these objects,[1] exploring their various applications and investigating their occurrences in other funerary and settlement contexts across the Viking world. Together with a review of relevant Old Norse textual sources and with an additional appraisal of folkloristic material, an attempt will thus be made to reveal the multivariate meanings of axes in the hands of Viking Age women.

Axes in the Viking Age

Axes were some of the most commonly used metal objects in Viking Age Scandinavia and served as essential tools inside and outside the household; without them it would have been impossible to build a house, to construct a boat or even to chop firewood. In the period spanning the ninth to eleventh centuries, axes were also used as essential kitchen tools, and they were employed at all stages of food preparation – from slaughtering animals to cutting joints of meat. Even though the economic situation of Viking Age societies varied from place to place, it is indeed difficult to imagine a farm without an axe. In addition to their practical applications as everyday tools, however, most axes could be employed as dangerous and deadly weapons.[2]

The omnipresence of axes in the Viking Age is confirmed by the results of archaeological excavations carried out all across Scandinavia, the British Isles, Ireland and Continental Europe: axes are found at settlement sites and strongholds[3] as well as in the so-called ports of trade.[4] They are also frequently discovered in funerary contexts where they accompany the dead buried in cremation and inhumation graves.[5]

Over the years, Viking Age axes have received substantial attention from scholars. Among the most crucial studies is Jan Petersen's monograph *De norske vikingesverd. En typologisk-kronologisk studie over vikingetidens vaaben* (*The Norwegian Viking Sword. A Typological-Chronological Study of Viking Age Weapons*) published in 1919.[6] In this seminal work, Petersen assembled a substantial corpus of Viking Age axes from Norway, predominantly from graves, and his close examination of their different shapes and sizes resulted in creating a typological and chronological system, which to this day is widely used by international academics and military history specialists.[7]

In the course of over eighty years since the release of Petersen's foundational work, scholars have investigated axes from all Scandinavian countries and other areas of Europe. In addition to conducting detailed analyses of their distribution patterns and establishing more precise chronologies of their various types,[8] attention has also been devoted to the symbolic role of these objects – a theme that is of particular interest here.[9]

Axes in Viking Age funerary contexts

Between the ninth and eleventh centuries, axes were buried in both cremation and inhumation graves.[10] They were usually not the only goods accompanying the dead, however, and many of the graves contained other furnishings, some of which were very costly and/or exotic. In the case of so-called 'weapon graves', typically containing several items of martial and/or equestrian equipment, axes are found either singly or in combination with swords, spears and shields.[11] On some occasions, they are also discovered alongside blacksmithing tools.[12]

The positioning of axes in cremation graves always depends on the manner in which the ashes have been handled after the burning process – *i.e.* on whether the remains have simply been scattered on the surface, placed loose in a pit or deposited in a special container. Because axes are relatively large objects, they are typically found outside of the vessels containing cremated bones. One illustrative example is the aforementioned grave 59:3 at Klinta in Öland (see Chapter 4) where an axe lay in the upper part of a burial pit which, among many other goods, also contained a clay pot with burnt human bones. This particular grave was excavated to a very high standard and the documentation – including field drawings and photographs gives a clear picture of its original appearance. In this light, there is no doubt that the axe was one of the last objects to be deposited in the course of the funeral ceremony.[13] It is also worthy of note that the axe was found with its blade directed downwards, as if it had been purposefully driven into the grave, perhaps with the intention to convey a very special message to those who participated in the funeral. Another intriguing example of a cremation with an axe thrust into the ground beside an urn is grave Bj 205 from Birka in Uppland, Sweden.[14] An equally interesting case was found at Myklebostad in Nordfjordeid, Sogn og Fjordane, Norway where an iron axe, together with other weapons, was placed stratigraphically *above* a copper alloy bowl containing the burnt remains of a man and as many as 12 shield bosses.[15] In contrast to the Klinta grave, which was furnished with a relatively small clay vessel for the bones, the copper alloy bowl from Myklebostad would have been large enough to hold both the human remains *and* the axe, but for reasons unknown to us today the people responsible for the burial decided to bury the weapon separately.

In the case of graves with cremated bones that have been scattered on the surface to form a flat layer, axes are usually found clustered together with other goods (sometimes piled-up), which makes it difficult to determine if their position in relation to the rest of the finds had special meaning. Another obstacle in attempts to examine and understand the role of axes in cremation graves of this particular type is the fact that many such graves – especially in Norway – were discovered in the nineteenth and early twentieth century by amateurs (*e.g.* farmers, estate owners) who had no experience in archaeological excavation and recording. Because of that, field drawings and photographs are usually unavailable.[16]

In contrast to cremations, inhumation graves can reveal much more information about the possible symbolic meanings axes had for the dead and for the mourners responsible for the burial ceremonies. Generally speaking, axes are placed to the left or right of the interred body and by the deceased person's waist or legs, with very occasional cases when they are located in the head area (thus making the grave from Løve, discussed in Chapter 4, quite exceptional).[17] The cutting edge of the axe can be directed towards the corpse or face away from it. While in most instances axes are laid flat, examples are known where they are found deliberately driven into the floor of the grave or into the wooden bier;[18] some scholars have interpreted this peculiar ritual practice as a means of 'dedicating' the dead to Óðinn, an act similar to the widespread custom of thrusting spears into graves.[19]

It is significant to note that axes found in Viking Age funerary contexts display a wide variety of forms and sizes, suggesting that while some of them were multifunctional objects, others served strictly as weapons. Large axes with very broad blades (*e.g.* Jan Petersen's type M) were predominantly intended for martial purposes, but in the case of other types of axes (*e.g.* Jan Petersen's types G, H and K), the difference between a working tool and a weapon is not always clearly defined.[20]

Miniature axes

In Chapter 4 and in the sections above we have focused our attention on graves with full-size axes, but it is noteworthy that on occasion Viking Age people were buried with axes in miniature form. In the tenth and eleventh centuries in Scandinavia and Continental Europe, miniature axes were conventionally made of copper alloy, silver and amber although examples fashioned from organic material are occasionally encountered as well. Today, objects of this kind are conventionally classified by scholars as amulets and/or pins and regarded as symbols of status and/or protection.[21] Together with small shields, spears and swords, they belong to a very broad category of 'miniature weapons', objects which probably played special roles in the Viking world.[22]

To date only one female grave with a completely preserved copper alloy miniature axe is known from the archaeological record in Norway. Discovered at Svingesæter in Sogn og Fjordane (B6483) and meticulously documented by Haakon Schetelig,[23] this grave has the capacity to shed important light on the diversity and meaning of Viking Age burial customs in Western Scandinavia (Plate 5.1 and Fig. 5.1). The mound that covered the Svingesæter grave consisted of soil and stones and was 8.8 m long, 2–3 m wide and 0.7 m high. Inside it was a stone cist around 1.5 m long and 0.4–0.5 m wide with the deceased person inhumed in supine position, head to the WNW. In addition to the aforementioned miniature axe, the grave goods included two oval brooches (similar to Rygh's type 649), 57 beads, two small needles made of copper alloy, a spindle whorl, an iron key, an iron knife, an indeterminate iron object (10.5 cm long), chest fittings and charcoal (Plate 5.2).

Quite remarkably for Western Norway, where bone preservation is usually very poor, several fragments of the human skeleton have survived in a decent condition. An

Fig. 5.1. Artistic reconstruction of the Svingesæter grave. Illustration by Mirosław Kuźma. Copyright Mirosław Kuźma and Leszek Gardeła.

osteological analysis has revealed that the remains belong to a woman who was over 20 years old when she died.[24] Interestingly, during the excavation Schetelig noticed that fragments of the woman's cranium lay *over* the oval brooches, implying that this person had been inhumed in a seated position. Seated burials are very uncommon in Viking Age Norway,[25] and they are more characteristic of elite chamber graves in Sweden and Rus.[26] In these areas, the dead were probably seated on small wooden chairs or stools, but in the case of Svingesæter the woman either rested against a small heap of soil or her body was propped up with cushions to keep it upright. In any case, the manner of handling, dressing and displaying the corpse at Svingesæter indicates unequivocally that this was a prominent individual.

The miniature axe placed at the woman's waist may have served as a symbol emphasising her social position (Plate 5.3), while at the same time perhaps having the properties of an amulet.[27] Its design to a remarkable extent resembles full-size axes from the Viking Age – one side of the blade has a ridge imitating the construction of axes made of several layers of iron. The miniature axe from Svingesæter also has a tapered shaft with a sharp point at the end, which was perhaps originally fitted into an organic handle that has now decayed.[28] Although the overall design of this object is unique, a few relatively close parallels (also with shafts integrated with the blades) are known from the Viking world; the best known examples include the miniature axes from Dublin, Ireland[29] and Avnsøgård in Zealand, Denmark.[30] It is difficult to say if, beyond its alleged role as a status symbol, the miniature axe had any practical application as a tool or utensil. It is too short to have served the role of a hair pin for example, but it may have potentially been used to remove dirt from underneath the nails or as a decorative clothing pin.

Small-size and fully functional axes are known from several sites in Scandinavia. In Norway, a grave from Torshaug (Gjedrum s. & p., Akershus) contained an axe made of iron, which was only 9 cm long;[31] regrettably, in this case the sex of the deceased person is unknown. A small iron axe was also found at Fyrkat in Jutland, Denmark in grave 24, which appears to be the grave of a child.[32]

It is noteworthy that in addition to miniature axes made of ferrous and non-ferrous metals, there are also examples produced from amber. One such find is known from the cemetery at Birka in Uppland, Sweden where it accompanied an individual (probably a woman) buried in a richly furnished grave Bj. 954.[33] Interestingly, the same grave also contained a miniature silver shield. Examples of amber axes have also been found in Truso/Janów Pomorski in Poland and on Gotland.[34] While it is not entirely clear if they should be associated with Scandinavian, Slavic or Baltic people, it is beyond doubt that these objects have an 'eastern orientation'.[35] Intriguingly, this also fits very well with the fact that the woman at Svingesæter was buried seated, a custom characteristic of the eastern parts of the Viking world. In light of the above, it is permissible to speculate that the woman was a foreigner.

Close analysis of the corpus of miniature axes reveals a pattern suggesting that they were associated with the representatives of the highest strata of society and that – at least in some instances – they were intended as symbols of rank.[36] Moreover, judging by the graves' assemblages, there are reasons to believe that some individuals buried with miniature axes and shields played the role of magic workers. The miniatures might have served as indicators of their position in society and might have had some special function in the performance of rituals. At the present moment, however, it remains unknown how exactly these items were used.

Interpreting axes in Viking Age female graves

Chapter 4 has demonstrated that the internal and external constructions of female graves with axes vary considerably and that there are even further divergences with regard to their furnishings. Nevertheless, when these graves are viewed collectively, a number of very intriguing confluences begin to emerge:

- Virtually all female graves with axes (cremations and inhumations) contain opulent grave goods, many of which are of exceptionally high quality.
- The axes from female graves represent several different types (Jan Petersen's types D, G, H, K, M and the Slavic type), but in most instances they are of relatively small size suggesting that they were not intended as weapons *par excellence*. Only two graves contain typical battle axes (Birka Bj. 581 and Bogøvej BB).
- With one exception, it is difficult to say much about the deliberate positioning of axes in female cremation graves. In grave 59:3 at Klinta, the cutting edge of the axe was directed downwards, implying that it had been purposefully thrust into the grave.[37] It has been argued that similar ritual acts (although typically involving spears) were intended to dedicate the dead to Óðinn.
- As regards inhumation graves, axes are usually placed in the waist area and by the right side of the deceased person (the grave from Mårem is the only example where the axe is located to the left). The placement of axes by the right side, often close to the hand (in some cases the women's hands may have actually rested on the axe handles), could refer to how these items were used in life and at the same time imply that the buried dead were right-handed. If this interpretation is correct (which, of course, relies on the somewhat problematic assumption that the objects deposited in graves *belonged* to the dead – see Chapter 1) then perhaps the woman from the Mårem grave, who had an axe by her left side, was left-handed?
- Three graves (Klinta 59:3, Løve and Mårem) contained objects likely serving as amulets.[38] Their presence in

these very specific funerary contexts implies that the women played some role in religious practices, perhaps as ritual specialists.
- At least two graves contained antiques or curated objects: the Løve grave was furnished with beads dating to the Migration period;[39] the bearded axe in the grave from Klinta may have been an heirloom dating from the Vendel period.[40]

It is noteworthy that the graves under scrutiny here also display other very unique features. Of particular interest is the grave from Løve with the axe placed by the woman's head. This is a rarely observed custom in Viking Age weapon graves and one that could imply that the axe had some special significance for the deceased woman or that it played some outstanding role in the burial ceremony. The same grave also contained a (possibly) decapitated horse, and although single female graves with horses (or horse body parts) are not uncommon in the Viking world,[41] this is the only known example where the horse's head is completely missing from the burial pit. Another peculiarity worth emphasising is that the Løve grave was located in close proximity to a Bronze Age stone circle, suggesting that the mourners wanted to link the woman's burial with an ancient and potentially numinous site.

Grave BB from Bogøvej is likewise peculiar, not only due to its marginal location in the southern part of the site and in isolation from other interments but also because it is the only weapon grave in the entire cemetery. As highlighted in Chapter 4, the axe from this grave represents a type that was very uncommon in Denmark[42] but characteristic of the southern Baltic, especially the area of today's Poland.[43] Furthermore, the way the woman was buried – inside a chamber grave and within an additional coffin – closely reflects elite burial traditions of the Piast state and Pomerania.[44] Taken collectively, all these traits suggest that the person buried in grave BB at Bogøvej might have originated from a non-Norse cultural milieu. Without specialist genetic and isotope analyses, however, the Slavic origin of this individual must only remain a tentative hypothesis.

Women and axes in textual sources and folklore

Statistically speaking, in Old Norse literature spears and swords are the most common weapons used by women, while axes in female hands are mentioned very occasionally in extant texts.

As seen in Chapter 3, one instance when a woman reaches for an axe is recorded in *Grœnlendinga saga* where Freydís Eiríksdóttir, the sister of the saga's main protagonist, uses it to kill five other women.[45] This situation is both unusual and violent, but the axe is employed more as a tool rather than as a weapon in the strict sense. The *Íslendingasögur* do not portray women who use axes in strictly military endeavours in battles or in duels.

The case of the sorceress Þórhildr from *Ljósvetninga saga* – who employs an axe in a violent prophetic ritual – can be particularly enlightening in our attempts to unravel the symbolic meaning of axes in the Norse world. Regardless of the relatively late date of the saga, the abundance of archaeological sources reviewed above compels us to consider the possibility that at least some of its details might reflect actual ritual practices from the Viking Age. Let us recall the fact that the female graves from Løve and Mårem were both furnished with an array of goods with religious connotations. The curated beads at Løve and the decapitated horse at the woman's feet, as well as the curious copper alloy tube from Mårem with flakes of gold foil inside, permit the interpretation that these individuals were regarded as ritual specialists who perhaps used axes as important paraphernalia in their ritual toolkit. While it is impossible to know exactly what they did with them and whether or not the axes were employed in prophetic rituals similar to the one from *Ljósvetninga saga*, their sheer presence in the burial context compels us to consider them as things of *some* importance. Of all the different goods that could have been selected for burial, someone decided these women should be interred with axes, and they did so for a reason. Moreover, we should also draw attention to the fact that axes are the only 'weapons' in these graves, and the assemblages do not contain any other goods exclusively associated with men.[46]

The prominence of axes as ritual tools is also attested in European folklore. In Scandinavia, Germany and Finland, there are records of using axes in healing practices, for instance to metaphorically cut off a sickness that has stuck to a person (Fig. 5.2).[47] A medieval text known as *Summa*

Fig. 5.2. An example of using an axe in a magic ritual in Finland in 1910. From Holck 1996.

de confessionis discretion found in a Cistercian monastery in Rudy in Silesia, Poland describes a curious ritual which involves hitting (or perhaps rather tapping) a woman who has given birth to a child with an axe to keep her in good health.[48] Also in much later Slavic folklore we may encounter examples of people using Stone Age axes for healing; they would sometimes knap them and throw their broken pieces to the water in which they would then bathe their children in the hope this would bring well-being. All these examples, stemming from different and often very distant cultural milieus, show explicitly that axes played significant roles in folk imagination – it is highly probable that these customs dated back to the Viking Age or even to more archaic times.

Women and axes in the Viking Age: conclusions

As we have seen above, Viking Age axes were likely regarded as multifunctional and multivalent objects that, depending on the circumstances, could be used as tools, deadly weapons and magic accoutrements. By thoroughly analysing the contexts of the axes' discovery and by using a wide array of sources (archaeological, textual and folkloristic), it has been argued that the presence of these objects in female graves might suggest that the women had played important roles in pre-Christian religious practice. Although it will forever remain obscure how exactly the axes had been used, Old Norse texts and folkloristic material give good reasons to believe that at least in some instances they had been employed in prophetic and/or healing rituals. This interpretation of axes as ritual tools, rather than as weapons or mundane objects *per se*, is additionally supported by the occurrence of other ritual paraphernalia in the graves under scrutiny (amulets, curated items, etc.). Even though the archaeological finds, Old Norse textual accounts and folklore discussed above are chronologically removed from each other, this survey has demonstrated compelling case studies suggesting that in some instances these different stands of source material can be used collectively to inform and illuminate our understanding of the Viking past. Future studies and re-evaluations of archival finds, as well as new archaeological discoveries have the potential to nuance or alter the tentative hypotheses proposed here.

Women and swords in the Viking Age

Only three presumably female Viking Age graves from Scandinavia contain swords. In the case of grave Bj. 581 from Birka, the deceased person was interred in a wooden chamber, whereas in Aunvollen the body was laid in a boat. The Nordre Kjølen grave, on the other hand, was covered by a mound of substantial size. The diverse manner in which these three individuals were buried, as well as the graves' opulent furnishings, give strong reasons to believe that the deceased belonged to the elite. The following sections will investigate the social significance of Viking Age swords in an attempt to provide a wider perspective on these three remarkable interments.

Swords in the Viking Age

The sword is one of the most iconic weapons of the Viking Age. Archaeological finds of swords, as well as references to them in Old Norse literature and other medieval textual sources from Continental Europe and beyond, demonstrate unequivocally that they were highly prized, symbolically charged and deadly tools of war. The sword could be used when fighting on foot, but it was also effective from horseback, making it a very practical and multifunctional weapon.

Sword production was a time-consuming and technologically difficult process which required mastering specialist skills. Iron was the material typically used to manufacture blades and other essential components of these weapons, such as the pommel and the cross-guard. Occasionally, however, parts of the hilt were cast from copper alloys or carved in bone, antler or ivory.[49] Some of the most elaborate swords have intricate inlays in silver and copper on their pommels and cross-guards as well as additional inscriptions on the blades.[50]

Viking Age swords are usually found in graves. Occasionally, they can also be encountered as part of sacrificial deposits, especially in rivers and lakes.[51] In some instances sword components, such as pommels and cross-guards, are discovered as stray finds or in special workshop areas within settlement sites, ports-of-trade, and emporia.[52]

In contrast to other weapons like axes and spears, most swords were probably carried at the belt in a scabbard made of wood and leather.[53] In some parts of the Viking world, scabbards were additionally decorated and had copper alloy or silver chapes at the lower end, perhaps serving as religious symbols, indicators of status and/or as material markers of very particular group affiliation of their owners.[54]

Medievalists have been fascinated with swords for a long time, and over the last two centuries numerous publications focusing on this type of weapon have been released around the globe. As regards Viking Age swords specifically, Jan Petersen's seminal study *De norske vikingesverd. En typologisk-kronologisk studie over vikingetidens vaaben* still remains a widely-cited classic, regardless of its various shortcomings and a largely outdated corpus of material.[55] Petersen developed his own sword typology by focusing mainly on the shapes and sizes of pommels and crossguards. His classification system is still used today (albeit sometimes with alterations), but it is worthy of note that over the years since the release of his monograph other sword typologies have been created.[56] While early studies of swords only focused on macroscopic analyses of these bladed weapons, today swords are examined using a wide plethora of specialist equipment allowing more insight into the multifaceted techniques of their production and use.[57] Swords also continue to draw attention from researchers interested in ideology, iconography, religion and symbolism.[58] Recent phenomenological approaches to swords, together with more advanced studies of their material aspects, offer exciting opportunities to nuance our understanding of the symbolic and practical dimensions of military equipment in the Middle Ages.[59]

Swords in Viking Age funerary contexts

In the Viking Age, swords formed part of the assemblages of cremation and inhumation graves[60] either as the only weapon accompanying the dead or together with axes, spears, battle knives, shields and arrows. Interestingly, in some graves swords were buried in combination with blacksmithing tools.[61]

The manner in which swords were treated in cremation burials varies considerably across space and time. In many funerary contexts, especially in Norway, swords have been found purposefully bent or coiled, a laborious practice which (at least on some occasions) might have required re-forging the blades before burial.[62] Purposeful damage to the weapons has been variously interpreted – one idea is that the intention was to 'kill' their spiritual essence and to thereby make them harmless, another is that the purpose behind damaging swords was to render them useless for potential robbers. Recently, it has also been observed that purposefully coiled swords formally resemble coiled snakes, and that perhaps this expression of 'material citation' – to use Howard Williams' terminology[63] – was intended to display intricate metaphorical links between swords and snakes.[64] In addition to the coiled examples, some Viking Age swords have been found vertically thrust into graves, a custom that tends to be interpreted in the context of Óðinnic rituals. A thrust sword was found in grave 59:2 at Klinta, and it is worth recalling here that the second 'part' of this grave (59:3), separate from 59:2 and located a short distance away, belonged to a woman buried with a vertically thrust axehead (see Chapter 4).

In inhumation graves swords are usually laid by the right-hand side of the deceased person, although divergences from this pattern do occur sometimes.[65] The placement of swords on the left might suggest that the buried individual was left-handed, but this is difficult to prove without specialist pathological analyses and when bone preservation is poor.[66] In some instances it seems as if the deceased were buried with the swords cradled in their arms – this may have been the case with some of the seated burials at Birka but also in Bodzia, Poland.[67] In Viking Age graves swords are rarely placed away from the body, for example standing against the wall of the burial chamber,[68] and it seems that more often than not the mourners wanted to place the prized military equipment as close to the deceased person as possible. The proximity of the weapon to the interred probably emphasised its importance for the dead, and at the same time amplified the idea that swords were considered as animated objects with their own agency and personhood, something that would have made them actual 'companions' of warriors. As Sue Brunning has convincingly argued:

> The connection between warriors and their 'person-like' swords may indeed have been similar to comradeship, involving the type of reliance and mutual understanding that exists between two human warriors.[69]

The strong bonds that existed between medieval warriors and their weapons are also echoed among today's professional soldiers as well as in the thriving historical re-enactment milieu. The best example of this is the 'Rifleman's Creed', known by every US Marine Corps recruit:

> This is my rifle. There are many like it, but this one is mine. My rifle is my best friend. It is my life. I must master it as I master my life … My rifle is human, even as I, because it is my life. Thus, I will learn it as a brother. I will learn its weakness, its strengths, its parts, its accessories … we will become part of each other.[70]

Since swords were very difficult to produce and since they were among the most costly commodities available to the people of the Viking Age, it is highly probable that at least some examples from funerary contexts represent actual possessions of the deceased, which were used and cherished by them. However, it should also be borne in mind that some Viking Age swords discovered in graves are made from poor quality steel which would have significantly impeded their performance in combat. It is not unlikely, therefore, that at least some of those bad quality swords were regarded not as weapons *per se* but as 'theatrical props' with special roles to play in funerary ceremonies.

In discussing the significance of weapons in Viking Age mortuary contexts, it is vital to be critically aware of the fact that military equipment is not found exclusively with adults, and that on some occasions swords, axes, spears and other tools of war are also discovered in children's graves. One of the most remarkable cases is a grave from Birka which held the remains of a young child (possibly a boy, although a firm determination of the biological sex of this individual is impossible) buried with a full set of weapons, including a sword.[71] Another child's grave containing military equipment (a sword and two spears) and two animals (a horse and a dog), was found at Ire on Gotland.[72] Also elsewhere in the Viking world and in various cultural milieus children were occasionally interred with military equipment,[73] including both real and fully functional weapons as well as their miniatures, for example in the form of small axes. In Western and Eastern Slavic contexts miniature axes have often been interpreted as symbols of group affiliation, status and/or religion and as items related to the cult of the sky god Perun.[74]

Overall, in the majority of cases swords seem to have been buried with men. As we have seen above, only three possible female graves with swords have been recorded in Scandinavia (Aunvoll, Birka Bj. 581, Nordre Kjølen). However, we should bear in mind that a substantial number of 'male' graves with swords have been sexed only on the basis of the accompanying grave goods, meaning that in the future – as a result of specialist osteological and genetic analyses – more graves of women with swords might be identified and re-interpreted.

Women and weaving swords

Aside from the (possible) female graves with actual swords, there are also a number of cases where women are accompanied by large weaving swords made of iron (Fig. 5.3). This funerary custom was characteristic of Norway[75] and was relatively rarely practiced elsewhere in the Viking world.[76] In Sogn og Fjordane, for instance, inhumation and cremation graves with weaving swords often contain other objects such as jewellery, tools and various domestic implements.[77] The fact that the dead tend to be buried on ships or boats implies that they belonged to the elite.[78]

Weaving swords differ considerably in form and function from actual Viking Age swords, but some confluences can be observed nonetheless. Similar to swords, most weaving swords are made of iron and have very long blades (ranging from ca. 60 to 80 cm), but their edges are blunt and their points are rounded.[79] Instead of having a handle, the lower end typically has a socket for a wooden shaft, a feature that makes weaving swords appear like very large spears. It is noteworthy that in some parts of the Viking world weaving swords were made of whalebone and they could be more than 1 m long.[80]

Weaving swords were certainly not meant to be employed as weapons, but if a necessity arose they could be used for this purpose. It is noteworthy that in various cultural contexts, when human life is under threat, people tend to use all kinds of domestic items to defend themselves, which sometimes leads to creating 'hybrid weapons'. In eighteenth- and nineteenth-century Poland, for example, a special military formation known as *kosynierzy* comprised peasants armed with 'melee weapons' in the form of modified scythes, axes and spears. The fact that the *kosynierzy* typically used agricultural tools rather than actual military equipment did not diminish their fighting skills, and they are still remembered today for their prowess in some of the most turbulent battles in Polish history.

While Viking Age weaving swords cannot be regarded as weapons *per se*, there are hints in Old Norse literature that in some instances they could be associated with martial activities, albeit in a symbolic sense. The most explicit example of this idea is seen in the poem *Darraðarljóð*, interpolated in *Brennu-Njáls saga*,[81] where twelve supernatural women weave battle on a macabre loom.[82] In this 'wholly heathen' poem,[83] the act of producing cloth and using actual weapons instead of weaving implements exemplifies yet another curious connection between women, swords and sword-like objects in the Viking Age. The relevant stanzas of *Darraðarljóð* are worth citing here in full:

Mannahöfuð váru fyrir kljána, en þarmar ór mönnum fyrir viptu ok garn, sverð var fyrir skeið, en ör fyrir hræl. Þær kváðu þá vísur nökkurar:

> Vítt er orpit
> fyrir valfalli
> rifs reiðský:
> rignir blóði.
> Nú er fyrir geirum
> grár upp kominn
> vefr verþjóðar,
> er vinur fylla
> rauðum vepti
> Randvés bana.
> Sjá er orpinn vefr
> ýta þörmum
> ok harðkljáðr
> höfðum manna;
> eru dreyrrekin
> dörr at sköptum,
> járnvarðr yllir
> en örum hrælaðr.
> Skulum slá sverðum
> sigrvef þenna.[84]

Men's heads served as loomweights, and intestines from men as weft and warp, a sword as the beater, and an arrow as the pin beater. Then they spoke some verses:

> Far and wide
> with the fall of the dead
> a warp is set up:
> blood rains down.
> Now, with the spears,
> a grey woven fabric
> of warriors is formed,
> which women friends
> of Randvér's killer [Óðinn]
> complete with red weft.
> The fabric is warped
> with men's intestines
> and firmly weighted
> with men's heads;
> blood-stained spears serve
> as heddle-rods,
> the shed rod an iron-bound axe
> and arrows are pin beaters.
> With our swords we must beat
> This fabric of victory.[85]

The twelve women engaged in creating 'the fabric of victory' are identified as *valkyrjur*, supernatural beings closely associated with Óðinn. As noted in Chapter 3, in other literary expressions of Old Norse thought the *valkyrjur* are often attributed with martial characteristics, and some of their names allude to weapons and the physical violence of battle. *Darraðarljóð* likewise portrays the *valkyrjur* as dangerous creatures capable of bearing arms and influencing human fate. Towards the end of the poem, the women tear the cloth apart and ride away on unsaddled horses armed with swords.

There is no evidence to suggest that women actually (in a physical sense) took part in the violent clash described in the poem, but the men who engaged in it may have shared a belief in the presence or even assistance of supernatural women on the battlefield and in their role in watching over the fight and 'choosing' the dead. The poem *Darraðarljóð* is the only product of Old Norse literature that mentions women using (weaving) swords in a ritualistic context which involves looking into the future and shaping the outcome of a battle. In a way, however, the unconventional use of weapons in *Darraðarljóð* could be conceptually linked to the event described in the aforementioned *Ljósvetninga saga* where a cross-dressing sorceress uses an axe as an essential accoutrement in a prophetic ritual. Both *Darraðarljóð* and *Ljósvetninga saga* indicate that it may have indeed been possible for some women to transgress gender boundaries and invert meanings typically ascribed to weapons.

Women and swords in iconography

Intricate relationships between women and swords can also be witnessed in Viking Age iconography, especially within the corpus of small anthropomorphic female figures made of non-ferrous metals (Fig. 5.4).[86] The identification of these miniatures' sex is, of course, open to discussion, but what supports the idea that they are female is that they are often depicted with long hair and trailing dresses. For many years these finds were typically regarded in Viking scholarship as representations of the *valkyrjur*, but as a result of a series of recent studies by Rudolf Simek,[87] Neil Price,[88] Leszek Gardeła[89] and other researchers this somewhat one-sided interpretation has been contested. The specific details of so-called 'valkyrie figurines' are discussed in further detail in Chapter 6, so here they will be only mentioned in passing.

In discussing iconography and the peculiar associations between women and swords, it is worth pointing out that apparently female characters holding such weapons are also portrayed on the Oseberg tapestry.[90] This outstanding masterpiece of medieval textile work depicts a procession of anthropomorphic figures (probably humans, although this is not entirely certain), several of which are clad in trailing dresses and bear arms (Fig. 5.4). They are accompanied by horses, some of which are shown pulling wagons.

Long hair suggests that some of the weapon-carrying figures on the Oseberg tapestry could be female. This

Fig. 5.3. Viking Age weaving sword from Sanddal. Photo by Leszek Gardeła.

pertains especially to the long-haired figure shown on Fragment 4, which is also wearing a long dress.[91] Intriguingly, the figure is facing left and holding the sword in an unconventional way – *i.e.* not by the handle (as one would normally use the weapon in combat) but by the bare blade with the point directed towards the ground; this detail gives the figure a somewhat passive appearance, and it does not immediately bring to mind armed warriors getting ready for battle; instead, one may get the impression that the figure is carrying the sword with the intention to deposit it somewhere or to pass it on to somebody. Another curious feature of this image is that the sword's blade is additionally decorated with an interlace motif, perhaps alluding to pattern welding.

The motif of the inverted sword is probably symbolically charged, and might imply some kind of 'inversion of meanings', suggesting that in this particular case the sword should not be taken literally as a weapon and that the individual carrying it should not be seen as an actual warrior. As will be discussed further below, similar ideas could pertain to metal figurines depicting women holding shields in an unusual manner under their arm and with the shield bosses towards the body. The inversion of weapons – as seen on the Oseberg textile and the metal figurines – might be conceptually linked to the unconventional position of the sword in the aforementioned Nordre Kjølen grave – the sword's point was directed towards the woman's head. To the spectators of the burial ceremony, the special position of the sword might have been symbolic of something extraordinary the woman had done in her life and/or emphasised a very particular role she had once played.[92] A more detailed investigation of the meaning of different positions of weapons in Viking Age burials is provided further below in a section devoted to spears.

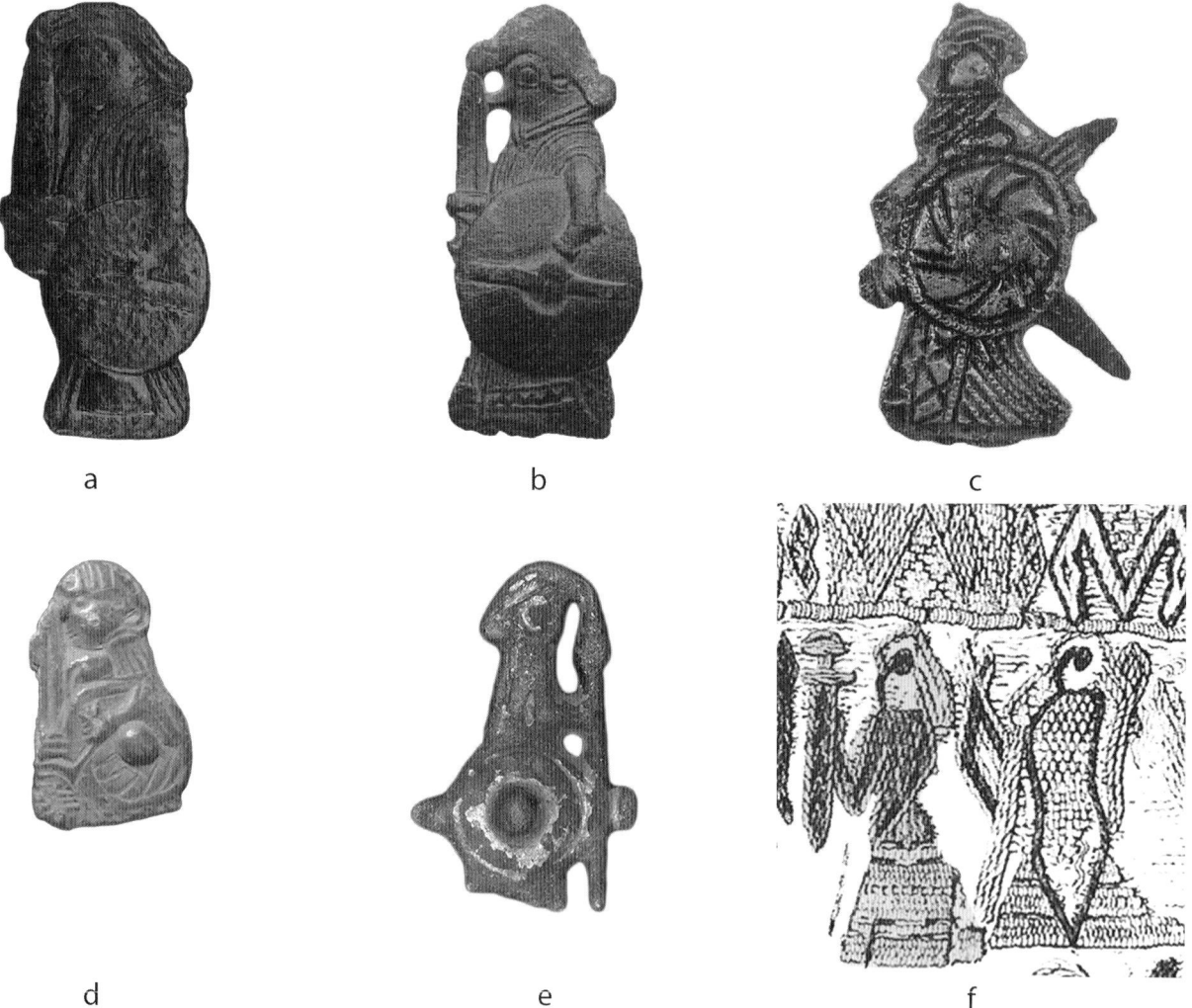

Fig. 5.4. Selection of anthropomorphic female(?) figurines carrying swords from Gammeltoften, Denmark (a), Skodsebølle, Denmark (b), Rostock-Dierkow (c), Unknown location in Jutland, Denmark (d), Rutland, England (e) and a fragment of the Oseberg tapestry portraying a sword-carrying female (f). Photos (a), (b) and (d) by the National Museum of Denmark. Photo (c) courtesy of Sebastian Messal. Photo (e) from the Portable Antiquities Scheme Database. Drawing (f) based on an illustration by Sofie Krafft and edited by Leszek Gardeła.

It is noteworthy that the abovementioned sword-bearer is not the only anthropomorphic figure on the Oseberg tapestry that wields the weapon in an unusual way. Another fragment of the tapestry shows a tall character wearing a horned helmet who appears to be holding two sticks (staffs or spears, perhaps?) in the right hand and a sword in the left.[93] Again, the sword is held not by the handle but by the blade. This individual's identity remains obscure, but this is doubtlessly someone significant, perhaps a religious specialist. Three figures holding swords with the blades directed towards the ground are also depicted on the Tängelgårda I picture stone from Gotland; they appear to be participating in a procession or perhaps in an act of sacrifice (Fig. 5.5).[94]

Miniature swords

In considering the relationship between women and swords, it feels appropriate to also devote some attention to miniature swords from the Viking Age (Fig. 5.6).[95] Often resembling full-size swords, to the extent that it is possible to ascribe them to particular sword types from Jan Petersen's classification system, miniature swords have been discovered in several different parts of the Viking world, predominantly in Denmark and Sweden, but also in Norway and present-day Germany and Russia.[96] Most of the miniature swords known to date have been found stray – largely as a result of amateur metal detecting – but some stem from more 'secure contexts' such as settlement sites and graves. Based on the diagnostic features of the miniature sword's pommels and cross-guards (often resembling Jan Petersen's swords of the K and O type), it is possible to date this artefact group between the late ninth and tenth centuries.[97] Regardless of the fact that only a few miniature swords have been found in graves, there are fairly strong reasons to presume that – similar to other miniature weapons like shields and spears – they were used predominantly (or exclusively) by women.[98] Similar to other small-size weapons, the function of miniature swords was probably manifold – they could be worn on the body as pendants or appliques or carried in a pouch. When their find corpus is viewed holistically, it seems that they served as amulets and/or as ritual deposits, perhaps substituting for the deposits of full-size weapons. In light of current research – and contrary to the views of previous scholars who have argued for the miniature swords' connection with Óðinn, Þórr or Freyr[99] – it does not feel justified to associate these tiny items with any particular Norse deity or supernatural entity. Rather, it is safer to assume that their meaning-content and function were fluid and largely depended on the decisions of the individuals using them.

Interpreting swords in Viking Age female graves

Burial evidence and iconographic material surveyed above strongly indicates the existence of a very special relationship between women and swords in the Viking Age. However, in dealing with the three allegedly female graves containing

Fig. 5.5. Sword-carrying figures on a picture stone from Tängelgårda on Gotland. Based on Nylén and Lamm 2003: 67 and edited by Leszek Gardeła.

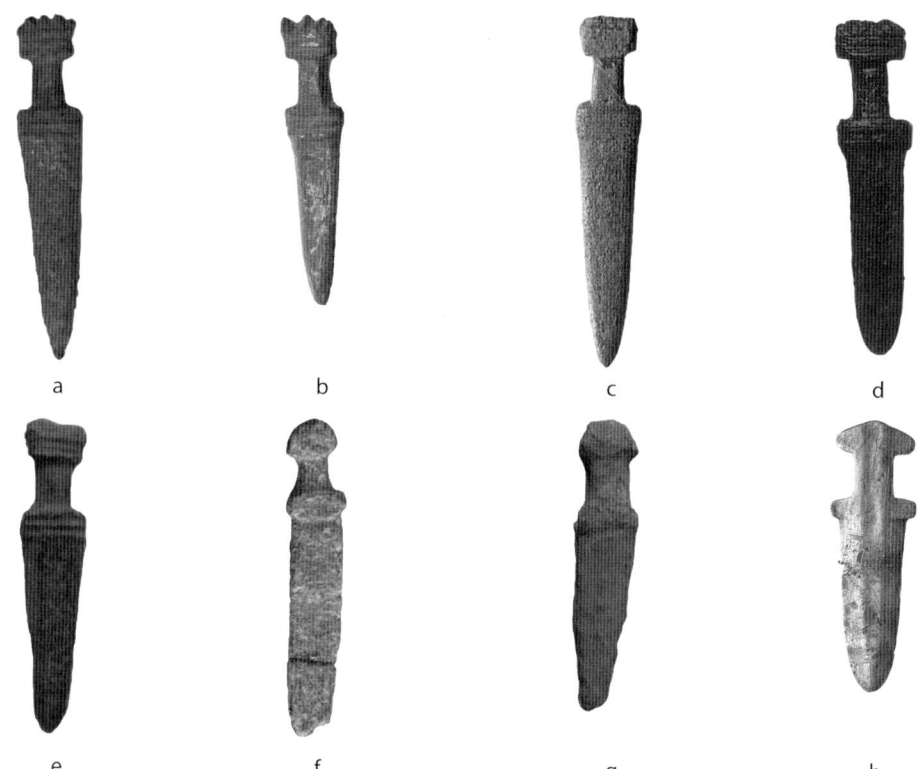

Fig. 5.6. Selection of Viking Age miniature swords: Dragedyssegård, Denmark (a), Kalmergården, Denmark (b), Nørholm, Denmark (c), Gamborg Vest, Denmark (d), Voel II, Denmark (e), Hoby, Denmark (f), Engsiggård, Hodde, Denmark (g), Stavnsager, Denmark (h). Photos by the National Museum of Denmark, edited by Leszek Gardeła.

swords, we must not forget about the controversial circumstances of their discovery and/or their insufficient and in some regards questionable documentation. In view of these concerns, it is difficult to make definite claims about them, and whatever interpretation of them we choose to follow, we must always remain critical and open to alternative readings. Even if we take the available reports for granted and decide to see the discoveries from Nordre Kjølen, Birka and Aunvoll as 'single female graves furnished with weapons', this should not immediately lead to the one and only conclusion that the deceased were warriors in life. This interpretation – although not completely unlikely – is significantly weakened by the fact that osteological analyses have not provided any unequivocal evidence of bone trauma inflicted in combat and also by the fact that the assemblages of the graves in question contain items deposited in a manner suggesting that they were intended to convey unconventional and metaphorical meanings. As already discussed in Chapter 1, many recent studies emphasise the ambiguity of burial data and the difficulties in determining the professions and identities of the dead based on the items that accompanied them in their graves.[100] It has also been demonstrated through extensive empirical surveys that weapon burials in early medieval societies were much more than merely designators of warrior identity; this is seen most explicitly whenever military equipment is found in connection with very young children and elderly people.[101]

Knowing that the Viking Age dead did not bury themselves and that funerals were orchestrated by the living who had different agendas and aspirations, we should be open to the idea that the placement of swords in *both* male and female graves might have signalled a plethora of meanings, in some instances probably much more sophisticated that we can fathom today. While many of these meanings will probably continue to remain obscure, it feels justified to perceive the presence of swords in burial contexts as an expression of some form of literal or metaphorical *empowerment* of the dead and/or those responsible for the mortuary acts. On the most general level, this is probably how the swords from Aunvoll, Birka and Nordre Kjølen ought to be seen. Regardless of whether the deceased were male or female (in terms of their sex and/or gender) and regardless of whether they actually participated in armed conflict, the swords laid by the side of these individuals served as evocative statements of power.

Women and swords in Old Norse sources

As discussed in Chapter 3, sword-bearing female characters appear in different genres of Old Norse sources including, among others, the *Íslendingasögur*, the *fornaldarsögur* and the eddic poetry. The aforementioned *Gísla saga Súrssonar* tells a story of a woman named Þórdís who decides to take revenge upon the man who has killed her brother.[102] One day, when an opportunity arises, she reaches for a sword and thrusts it out at him. Unfortunately for Þórdís, the sword gets caught against the table, and as a result the woman is only able to inflict a thigh wound. Another memorable account portraying a weapon-wielding woman is recounted in *Eiríks saga rauða*[103] when one of the story's protagonists, Freydís Eiríksdóttir,[104] picks up a sword to defend her camp from the Skrælingar. In order to frighten the attackers, she bears her breast and slaps the sword's blade with it.[105] Another saga known as *Laxdæla saga*[106] recounts the remarkable story of Bróka-Auðr[107] whose husband divorces her on the grounds that she tends to behave and dress like a man. Not before long, Bróka-Auðr decides to teach her former husband a lesson. Under the cover of night, she rides to his home where she finds him sound asleep in bed. She then draws her short sword and inflicts a shameful wound which cuts the man across the nipples. Although certainly driven by strong emotions, it seems that Bróka-Auðr's intention is not to kill him but to demonstrate her utter discontent.

As noted in Chapter 3, in a thought-provoking analysis of the episodes from *Eiríks saga rauða*, *Laxdæla saga* and *Ljósvetninga saga*, Kirsten Wolf has made an interesting observation that they portray women who are either widows (Þórhildr), divorced (Auðr) or contemplating divorce (Freydís). As Wolf notes, 'without a husband, the woman can no longer be labelled as a wife, with all the subordinating baggage that attends the designation'. Therefore, through the adoption of male dress and/or objects usually associated with men (*e.g.* weapons) these individuals are free to act in ways that challenge social conventions: they can appropriate the power of the 'dominant stratum' and at the same time display their own sexual identity. In other words, as Kirsten claims, the absence of the husband 'removes the limitations imposed by male control and thus permits the reassignment of female identity'.[108]

In all these different episodes from the *Íslendingasögur* women take hold of weapons under very special circumstances and they never engage in actual hand-to-hand combat. In the *fornaldarsögur*, however, women with weapons are portrayed rather differently, and – as we have seen in Chapter 3 – this corpus of texts abounds with examples of female warriors who actively engage in armed conflict and sometimes even lead armies to battle.

The remarkable female heroine Hervör[109] whose deeds are recorded in *Hervarar saga ok Heiðreks* is worthy of particular attention.[110] In the course of her various exploits and adventures, she uses a wide variety of weapons including a bow, a shield and a sword. On one memorable occasion she visits her father Angantýr's burial mound to claim his famous sword Tyrfingr, a weapon considered by Carol Clover as 'the emblematic representation of the larger patrimony'.[111] In this way, Hervör becomes what Clover has called a 'functional son'. Hervör's extraordinary story can give us an idea of why and under what circumstances some women would have stepped into a male role. In this context, it is not unlikely that for similar reasons the real women, whose graves we have examined above and who were buried with weapons (including swords), at some point in their life had to take on masculine roles.

In conclusion, we can see that there are several very clear patterns that emerge from Old Norse accounts featuring the motif of the sword in female hands:

- Women typically reach for swords in critical moments when it is necessary to make a strong non-verbal statement and/or exercise revenge (*e.g. Gísla saga Súrssonar, Laxdæla saga*)
- Swords are used spontaneously and in dramatic circumstances when women are compelled to defend their property. In such cases, women not only reach for weapons but also resort to other 'provocative' and performative acts, for instance involving slapping the sword's blade with the breast (*Eiríks saga rauða*) or putting on breeches, the latter probably with the intention to appear more masculine or to instil a sense of confusion in the minds of the enemies (*Þorgils saga ok Hafliða*).
- In legendary sagas (*fornaldarsögur*) and eddic poetry, sword-wielding women often engage in actual physical combat and other martial endeavours. Whether these stories had any basis in reality or merely serve as examples of vivid literary fiction is difficult to ascertain, however.

For archaeologists, philologists, historians of religion and other scholars seeking to investigate and understand the idea of women and weapons in the Viking Age and other historical periods, the different examples surveyed above should serve both as sources of inspiration and as warnings against offering simplistic and literal readings. The diversity and ambiguity of these textual accounts clearly illustrate that there are many ways to interpret the sword in female hands. This is certainly something to bear in mind when approaching women's graves furnished with military equipment but also when dealing with iconography portraying human and/or supernatural females wielding weapons.

Women and swords in the Viking Age: conclusions

As a result of thorough analyses of archaeological finds, including a critical assessment of burial evidence and iconography, intricate connections between women and swords in the Viking Age begin to emerge. When all available sources are taken collectively, however, it appears that, as of yet, it is rather difficult to identify the remains of a sword-wielding woman warrior in the archaeological record. Even though three (possibly) female graves with swords are known from Viking Age Scandinavia, the presence of these weapons can be interpreted in a variety of ways. Contextual analyses give reasons to believe that the swords should not be perceived in a literal sense as clear indicators of the deceased person's status as an active warrior. The different features of these female graves rather imply that we should view their contents as complex and multi-layered poetic metaphors, which may or may not have referred to actual, imagined or even mythological events. As demonstrated above, in Old Norse literature (and especially in the more 'realistic' *Íslendingasögur*) women tend to reach for swords only in very exceptional circumstances: when they are left with no other choice and when they want to fulfil greater ambitions. The most reasonable conclusion, therefore, is that in those texts swords in female hands ought to be understood predominantly as tools of empowerment. Careful analyses of the contexts and contents of female graves with swords give very strong reasons to follow the same line of thought.

Women and spears in the Viking Age

Four Viking Age female graves known to date have been furnished with spears: Aunvollen, Birka Bj. 581, Gerdrup and Nordre Kjølen. In Chapter 4, we have examined the material and typological aspects of these weapons as well as their specific position within these funerary contexts. The following discussion takes the argument further and seeks to outline the broader significance of spears in the Viking world as well as to investigate the specific meanings they acquired when they were used by women.

Spears in the Viking Age

Together with shields and axes, spears were probably the most frequently encountered offensive weapons on the Viking Age battlefield. The reason for their outstanding popularity was the fact that the production of spears (at least as regards their undecorated and fairly simple examples) was a relatively cheap, fast and uncomplicated process.[112] Spearheads were typically made of iron, but some of their more elaborate variants had decorations in silver, copper and copper alloy.[113] In rare instances, spearhead sockets were gilded, and such beautifully adorned pieces of military equipment – commissioned by or for prominent individuals – likely served as outstanding symbols of status and rank. Depending on their overall shape, weight and length, spears could be used when fighting on foot or from horseback. These deadly shafted weapons could also be thrown, however, and several Old Norse sources mention that during battles the casting of spears was commonplace before the violent hand-to-hand combat commenced.[114] Extant texts imply that the act of casting of the first spear had both practical and symbolic meanings.[115] As Kim Hjardar and Vegard Vike have argued:

> The suitability of the spear as a throwing weapon gave it a poetic identity alongside the arrow, as the airborne raptor of the battlefield, the falcon which spots its pray from afar and swoops down with beak and claw. The metaphor is particularly powerful if you imagine a hunting falcon cast up into the air from the hand of the hunter.[116]

Viking Age spears are found in virtually all archaeological contexts, ranging from cemeteries to settlement sites and sacrificial deposits. Most spears, however, are known from graves where they occur either as the only weapon accompanying the deceased or in combination with swords, axes, battle knives and shields.

The first typology of Viking Age spears was created by Norwegian archaeologist Jan Petersen in 1919[117] and it is still widely used today, even though researchers such as Andrzej Nadolski[118] and Bergljót Solberg[119] have created their own, more sophisticated classification systems. Since Petersen's time, Viking Age spears have been discussed in countless publications, focusing on their different types, distribution, practical usage in combat and role in mortuary contexts. A substantial body of work has also been done on the symbolism of spears, investigating the meaning-content of their archaeological exemplars, their decoration and their find contexts.[120] The multifarious roles of spears in medieval literature,[121] including Old Norse sagas and poetry,[122] have also been the subject of academic scrutiny.

Spears in Viking Age funerary contexts

Similar to other types of Viking Age weapons, spears are found in both cremations and inhumations.[123] In the vast majority of cases, only one spear accompanies the deceased buried in single graves, but occasional exceptions to this rule have been encountered in the archaeological record.[124]

In cremation graves spears tend to be clustered together with other goods and sometimes they are additionally twisted, bent or thrust into the ground, as in the case of the grave discovered on the shore of Lake Dalstorp in Västergötland, Sweden discussed in Chapter 4.[125] The custom of purposefully damaging spears resembles the ritual bending of swords, and the intentions behind it were likely similar. The thrusting of spears, however, is a practice that can be more firmly related to 'dedicatory rituals' associated with Óðinn, which are recorded in Old Norse accounts.

In the case of inhumation graves, spears are usually placed in close proximity to the body, often with the blade positioned by the head and with the wooden shaft lying parallel to or over one of the arms. Spears are typically located by the right-hand side of the deceased person, perhaps imitating the way they would have been held in life by the majority of the population (*i.e.* in the right hand).[126] The position of spears in the chamber graves at Birka is somewhat unusual compared to their usage in burial customs elsewhere across the Viking world – here spears are found in various parts of the chamber, sometimes at a considerable distance from the body.[127] Moreover, it appears that while some spears were placed in the Birka graves together with their wooden shafts, others were buried without them and even with their sockets thrust into the ground and with the tip of the blade pointing up.[128] As mentioned previously, in some of the Birka graves spears appear to have been thrown into the chambers, perhaps as part of a special ritual intended to dedicate the dead to Óðinn. An interesting case worth highlighting here is the grave from Ballateare from the Isle of Man where as many as three spears have been found, one of which lay inside the coffin together with the body (Fig. 5.7). The spear shaft had probably been broken to ensure the weapon fits inside the grave. It appears that at Ballateare the intentional destruction of the spear had both practical and symbolic significance.[129] Another intriguing detail is that the spearhead was directed towards the foot end of the coffin, a funerary motif that has a parallel in the aforementioned Gerdrup grave and one that we will investigate more closely below.

Although across the Viking world spears tend to be found predominantly in the graves of men, they represent the kind of weapon that could be effectively used by people of any gender. In fact, women with a more tender frame would have probably found it much easier to fight armed with a spear than to use short-range and relatively heavy weapons like swords, axes and shields.[130] This might perhaps explain why – at least in extant textual sources – weapon wielding women are often portrayed with spears.

Women and spears in iconography

Iconographic representations of women holding spears are fairly rare in the Viking world, at least compared to images of women armed with swords and shields.

Fragment 13 B2 of the Oseberg tapestry depicts five weapon-wielding and female-looking figures.[131] Interestingly, they are grouped together, almost as if they were forming a tight fighting unit. Apart from holding spears, they are armed with round shields with identical decorative motifs. Among the characteristic features that permit us to identify these figures as females is not only their long hair, but also their trailing dresses. In his study of the iconography of the Oseberg tapestry, Bjørn Hougen has boldly but probably wrongly interpreted this particular scene as depicting the famous battle at Brávellir/Bråvalla,[132] the details of which have already been discussed in Chapter 3, and he also perceives the armed women as 'shieldmaidens'.[133] Although it is probably safer to avoid linking the armed figures from the Oseberg tapestry with specific historic or legendary personae and events, it is worth drawing attention to the fact that spear imagery is remarkably prominent on the surviving textile fragments. Aside from spear-bearing females, several apparently male figures are also armed with spears – they have short hair, tunics and either baggy or skinny trousers.[134]

Aside from the Oseberg tapestry, evocative images of spear-bearing characters – presumably women – are also known from Viking Age metalwork. One well-preserved example is a figurine from Cawthorpe,[135] England, holding a long spear and a shield as well as having a sheathed sword at the side. Presently, only two close analogies to this find are known from Fæsted in Denmark and Rutland in England.

Miniature spears

In contrast to miniature axes and shields, miniature spears are rarely found in Viking Age archaeological sites (Fig. 5.8).[136] In his catalogue of Viking Age amulets, Bo Jensen has included 27 exemplars of miniature spears: three from Germany, three from Denmark, five from Gotland and 16 from Sweden.[137] As many as 16 miniature spears are made of copper alloy, but silver and iron examples also known. One miniature spear made of wood (not included in Jensen's catalogue) has been found in the Viking Age town of Wolin, Poland.[138] As a result of a recent extensive survey conducted by the present author, several further examples have been identified in Scandinavia and Russia and the current corpus includes over 30 specimens.[139]

Miniature spears closely resemble their full-size counterparts, and some of them can even be ascribed to a specific type from Jan Petersen's classification system. In his monograph, Jensen has identified some of the miniature spears as representing Petersen's types B, C, D, G, H, M and the winged type, implying that the miniatures were used throughout the entire Viking Age.[140] Considerably broad chronology is something that differentiates these items from miniature shields, which were only used in the period spanning the tenth and eleventh/twelfth centuries.

The fact that the majority of miniature spears have been discovered in settlement sites significantly hampers their interpretation, clouding our knowledge of how exactly they were used and by whom. Nevertheless, knowing that in Viking Age funerary contexts miniature weapons are predominantly associated with women, we can surmise that small spears were also considered as mainly female adornments and amulets. The idea that they were associated with women can be even further supported by the fact that one miniature spear was found in the upper layers of grave Bj. 581 at Birka.[141] What exactly these miniatures meant to their owners, and whether they were symbols of protection, status, devotion to Óðinn – as some scholars have previously argued – or material expressions of other ideas is difficult to comprehend today. Any or all of these interpretations are plausible, but neither can be confirmed with certainty.

Interpreting spears in Viking Age female graves

Interpreting spears in Viking Age female graves is an arduous task. We may recall that the famous grave from Gerdrup, discussed in Chapter 4, had a large spear placed by the woman's right side. While it may have been her special attribute, perhaps symbolic of her status or religious authority (*e.g.* a kind of magic staff), it is not completely

Fig. 5.7. Artistic reconstruction of the Ballateare grave. Illustration by Mirosław Kuźma. Copyright Mirosław Kuźma and Leszek Gardeła.

unlikely that the woman actively employed the spear as a weapon. Alternatively, the spear could only have been used by the mourners on the occasion of the funeral (perhaps as part of some ritual performance linked to Óðinnic beliefs) to be later deposited in the grave.

One significant detail that draws attention is the positioning of the Gerdrup spear with its tip pointing towards the foot-end of the grave. This manner of depositing spears is rare in Viking Age graves in Scandinavia and was thus likely endowed with special significance. Unconventional ways of positioning spears in early medieval funerary contexts have recently been investigated by Tomasz Kurasiński in a highly erudite and thought-provoking article.[142] Kurasiński observes that although in most inhumation graves spears are placed in the head area and with the tip directed toward the head-end of the grave, a number of instances are known where the spearhead is located by the feet and pointing towards the foot-end; examples of this custom have been noted in early medieval cemeteries in Estonia, Finland, Iceland,[143] Latvia, Norway,[144] Poland,[145] Russia,[146] Slovakia[147] and Sweden.[148] In Kurasiński's opinion, while the position of spears in graves with the blade pointing 'up' likely referred to the manner these weapons were used in life (for instance when marching), it is rather improbable that spears would have been carried around with the tip pointing down; therefore, the spears' 'inverted' position (*i.e.* with the blade pointing 'down') likely communicated special meanings. Based on his cross-cultural survey of early medieval burial evidence, Kurasiński has arrived at the conclusion that the custom of burying 'inverted' spears occurred most frequently in the areas surrounding the Baltic Sea, including the territories of present-day Estonia, Russia, Latvia, eastern Sweden and southern Finland, which leads to the presumption that the original idea stemmed from these parts of Europe.[149]

Kristina Creutz[150] and Tomasz Kurasiński[151] have both observed that medieval iconography might also provide hints as to the meaning of the peculiar position of spears in graves. Portrayals of warriors holding spears pointing towards the ground are known from a number of sites in Scandinavia and England, including Vendel, Valsgärde and Sutton Hoo, and they are also present on a copper alloy patrice from Torslunda in Öland (Fig. 5.9). These images were used to adorn high-status helmets from the sixth–eighth centuries, and contemporary scholars tend to interpret the characters depicted on them as Wotan/Óðinn worshippers and/or representations of semi-legendary rulers.[152] Interestingly, some

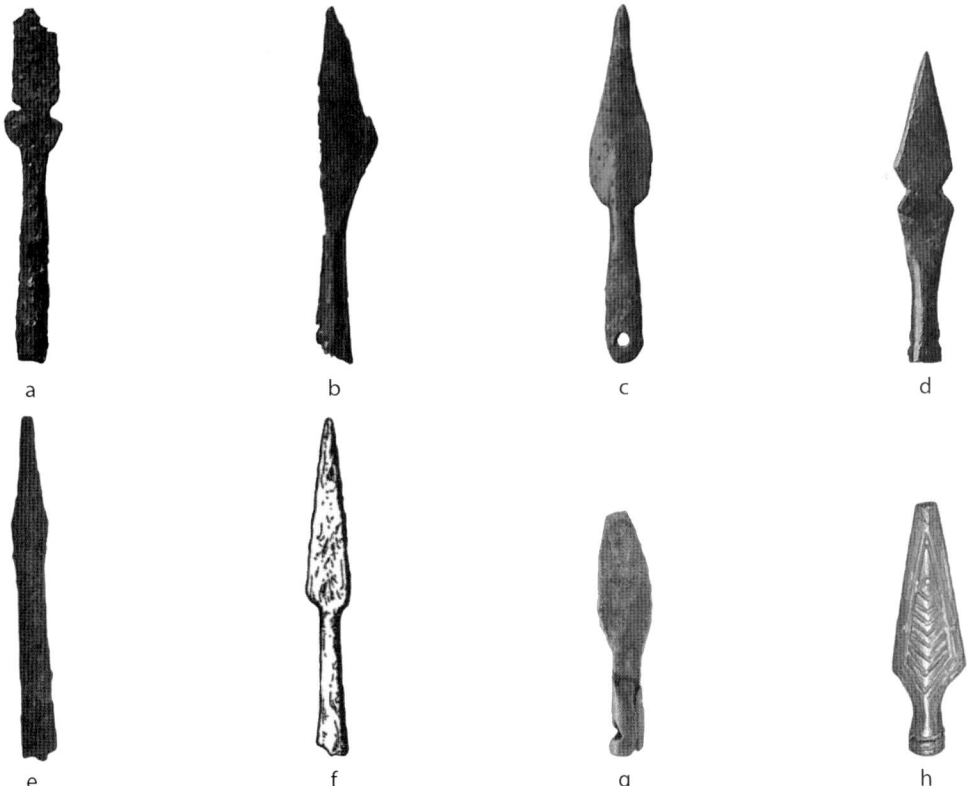

Fig. 5.8. Selection of Viking Age miniature spears: Helgö, Sweden (a), Västerljungs, Sweden (b), Bruzelius collection, Sweden (c), Birka Svarta Jorden, Sweden (d), Birka grave Bj 581, Sweden (e), Birka grave Bj. 944, Sweden (f), Tissø, Denmark (g), Trelleborg, Denmark (h). Photos (a–d) after Arrhenius 1961: 148, 148, photo (e) from the Statens Historiska Museum Online Database, drawing (f) from Arbman 1943: 370, photos (g–h) by Leszek Gardeła.

of the 'warriors' with spears are portrayed in 'dancing' poses, which leads to the supposition that the imagery referred to some kind of ritual practice, perhaps a 'war dance'. One enigmatic figure shown on the ninth-century Oseberg tapestry, dressed in what looks like animal skin (perhaps that of a bear), also carries a spear pointing towards the ground (Fig. 5.10).[153] The costume of this figure, together with the spear's unusual position, indicates that this was someone out of the ordinary – indeed, the 'otherness' of this individual has led a number of scholars, for instance Bjørn Hougen,[154] to interpret them as a berserker, a fearless warrior deeply devoted to Óðinn who knew no fear and in battle behaved like a wild animal.

Kurasiński argues that pre-Christian cosmology may also illuminate the possible meanings attributed to inverted spears in early medieval graves.[155] Textual and archaeological sources confirm that Scandinavians, Slavs and Balts shared a belief in the tree of life, which is commonly defined as a symbolic representation of the centre of the world and as an axis that connects three (or more) tiers of the universe: heaven, earth and the underworld.[156] Each world set upon the world axis has its own unique characteristics, but the general pattern – in Kurasiński's view – is that heaven or the sky is viewed in positive terms while the underworld tends to have negative connotations. In Kurasiński's opinion, the horizontal space inside the grave might have mimicked or referred to the ideas associated with the different vertical tiers of the universe. Seen in this way, the head area would be endowed with generally positive characteristics, while the foot-end would refer to the potentially dangerous chthonic sphere.

Other expressions of this symbolically loaded perception of space can be encountered in medieval iconography, both from the Viking Age and from chronologically younger periods. For instance, a carved stone from the Isle of Man portrays an anthropomorphic figure holding a winged spear (Ger. *Flügellanze*) with its blade pointing down and fighting a wolf-like beast which is attempting to bite the figure's leg (Fig. 5.11). This scene has been quite reasonably interpreted as a depiction of Ragnarök, with the spear-holding figure representing Óðinn engaged in a deadly struggle with the monstrous wolf Fenrir.[157] In religious art of the High Middle Ages, saints like St George as well as various heroes are often portrayed in a very similar fashion, mounted on horseback and striking a dragon (a symbol of evil and chthonic forces) with their spear pointing down.[158] We also can notice analogous motifs on medieval coinage where the ruler is portrayed attacking a dragon with a spear typically pointing down.

The basic conclusion arising from detailed analyses of different medieval iconographic motifs showing a struggle between a warrior armed with a spear (often mounted on horseback) and an evil beast is that they were intended to portray a mythical conflict between the forces of good and evil, a conflict which in some cultural milieus might have referred to the archetypal cosmogonic myth involving two antagonists fighting for world domination.[159] In light of these comparative sources, Kurasiński eventually arrives at the conclusion that early medieval people buried with spears at the foot end of the grave and with the tip pointing down might have conducted some valiant deeds in their lives[160] – for instance, they might have been warriors who won great military victories or individuals who were particularly praised for 'protecting' (in a practical and symbolic sense) their communities. In Kurasiński's view, with which the present author partly agrees, people dealing with magic, metalworking or hunting may have also been among such 'protectors'.[161]

As regards the symbolism of the spears from grave Bj. 581, it has already been observed in Chapter 4 that at least one of these weapons could have played a part in a ritual linked to Óðinn. This interpretation is certainly plausible, but it relies on the assumption that the deceased person *and* those responsible for the burial stemmed from the Nordic cultural sphere or at least that they shared a belief in the Norse god(s). In view of the peculiar contents of Bj. 581, including a characteristic silver hat cap and decorative tassels doubtlessly originating from Eastern Europe (which in the Viking Age was inhabited by Slavs, Scandinavians and various multi-ethnic nomadic peoples) as well as by the fact that the isotopic signature of the deceased has shown non-local origin, the religious beliefs of this person's and their cultural background remain obscure. The potential foreign ethic identity of the occupant of Bj. 581 does not rule out the possibility that at some point in life this person 'converted' to Norse pre-Christian religion or the likelihood that the mourners wanted to bury them in a 'Viking way'.

Fig. 5.9. Spear-carrying figure on a matrix from Torslunda. Creative Commons. CC-BY.

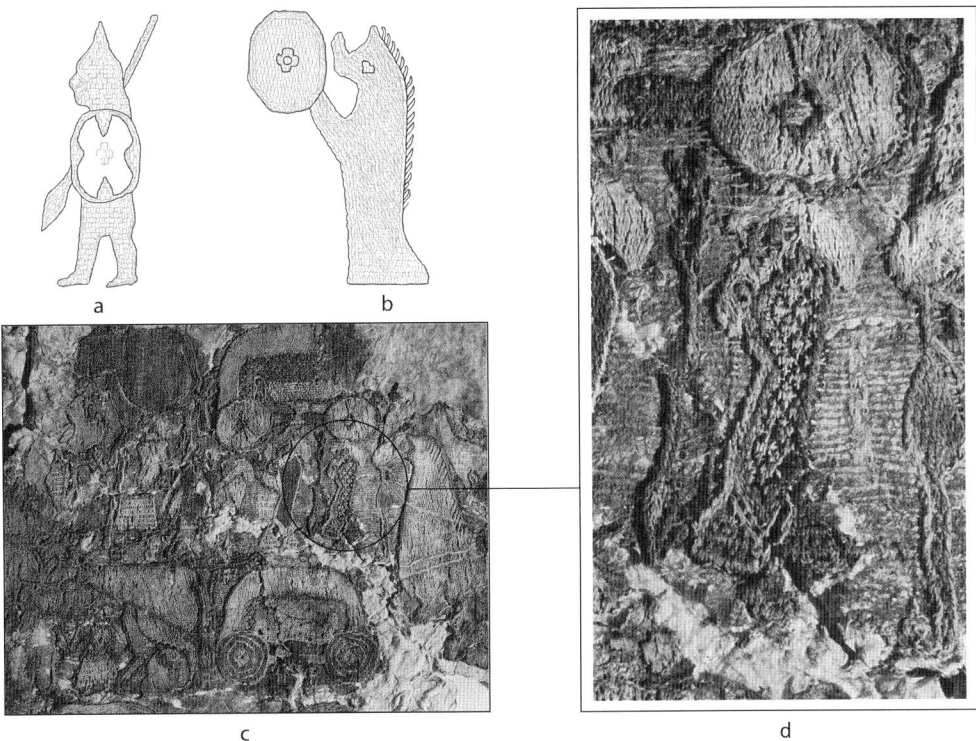

Fig. 5.10. Armed figures in animal costumes from the Oseberg tapestry: figure (a) has a shield and a spear, and figure (b), possibly a woman (as indicated by the trailing garment), is equipped with a shield. The photos (c–d) depict a scene with a female figure holding an unusual spear or staff. Images (a–b) based on Hougen 1940: 104 and redrawn by Leszek Gardeła. Photos (c–d) by E.I. Johnsen, MCH. Used by kind permission.

Fig. 5.11. Carved stone from the Isle of Man probably portraying Óðinn and the wolf Fenrir. Notice the winged spear held by the god. Photos by Leszek Gardeła.

The spears in the graves from Nordre Kjølen and Dalstorp, although treated in a similar way (bent), probably communicated quite different meanings. In the former case, the bending of the spear might have reflected a desire to render it useless for potential robbers, while at Dalstorp the bent and thrust spears probably served an apotropaic purpose, ensuring the dead person would forever remain in the grave. At the present moment, it seems that the best explanation for the spear- or arrow-like object from Trekroner-Grydehøj is that it served as a status symbol, probably being an attribute of a sorceress. There is nothing peculiar about the spear from the Aunvoll grave, and we can only speculate that it either represented the deceased person's personal possession or that the mourners felt it was appropriate to bury it as a potent symbol of, for instance, warrior status, power, prominence, etc.

Women and spears in Old Norse sources

Among all the women who appear in Old Norse literature it is the *valkyrjur* who are most closely associated with spears. In Chapter 3 and above, we have already discussed how these supernatural beings wove battle on a macabre loom made of spears and axes, but the strong link between spears and the *valkyrjur* is also visible in their very names.

In his seminal monograph, Neil Price has assembled a corpus of *valkyrja* names. Those of them that refer specifically to spears include: Geirahöd (Spear-Battle), Geiravör (Spear-Goddess), Geirdríful (Spear-Flinger), Geir-Róta (Spear-Disorder), Geirskögul (Spear-Shaker, Spear-Battle), Geirvífa (Spear-Wife), Geirölul (Spear-Waver, Spear-*Alu*), Geir[r]önul (Spear Charger).[162] It is interesting to note that the names not only associate the *valkyrjur* with spears as weapons *per se*, but they also signal battle-related agency and movement, involving 'shaking', 'flinging', causing 'disorder' or 'charging'.

Apart from *Darraðarljóð*, spear-wielding women are mentioned in the eddic poem *Grottasöngr*, which speaks of two enslaved female giantesses, Fenja and Menja, whom king Frodi forces to grind prosperity using a magic grindstone. In doing their work, the giantesses recall their great feats and fights against 'bearlike warriors'[163] and they reminisce how they once 'sliced with sharp spears blood from wounds'.[164]

The reason why spears were so closely associated with the *valkyrjur* are not easy to gauge, but it may have something to do with these beings' special relationship with Óðinn (who also had a spear known as Gungnir as one of his main attributes) as well as with the swiftness and effectiveness of the spear when fighting on foot and from horseback.

Women and spears in the Viking Age: conclusions

The spear is one of the most archaic weapons known to man, and one of the easiest to make. Although it is typically employed in hand-to-hand combat, the spear's length allows the enemy to be kept at a far greater distance than when using a sword or axe, making it an effective and deadly weapon when handled by a skilled warrior. Furthermore, spears tend to be much lighter than swords and axes, which also makes them ideal for individuals with relatively low body mass and a tender frame. When necessary, spears can also be thrown, meaning that they are actually some of the most multifunctional weapons of the Viking Age.

The above investigations have shown intricate associations human and supernatural women had with spears. The meanings attributed to spears that emerge from extant sources allow us to perceive them as symbols of status, religious function and – when they come in miniature form – as potent amulets and apotropaics. The analysis of the occurrence of spears in female graves has also demonstrated that each case is different and that they all have to be interpreted individually and with close attention to their wider context.

Women and shields in the Viking Age

Aside from the problematic grave from Frafjord in Rogaland, Norway and the finds from Gausel, Hilde and Kvåle (which must be taken with caution due to their poor recording and/or preservation – see Chapter 4), only two female graves discovered so far in Scandinavia contain shields: Bj. 581 from Birka and Nordre Kjølen. Although the funerary evidence pertaining to the motif of women and full-size shields is relatively scarce, the associations between women and shields, both in textual sources and iconographic material from the Viking Age, are very strong, which necessitates a more thorough investigation. The following sections will thus seek to paint a wider panorama of the significance of shields in the Viking world in an attempt to nuance our understanding of their links with women.

Shields in the Viking Age

The round shield with a diameter of ca. 80–95 cm was the most basic defensive weapon of the Viking Age, and was commonly used in single combat as well as in battles involving dozens of warriors. However, since the boards of Viking Age shields were made predominantly out of wood like pine and spruce,[165] today usually very little of them survives in the archaeological record – the iron boss, placed in the centre of the shield, is often the only thing that archaeologists find during excavations. In some cases, shields were additionally reinforced with iron rivets and had special metal rims and decorative copper alloy fittings for their handles; due to the persistent nature of ferrous and non-ferrous metals, the remains of these constructional features have survived at a number of sites, for example at Birka in Sweden, Myklebostad in Norway and Świelubie in Poland.[166]

Viking Age shields and their remains (typically in the form of iron shield bosses) are usually discovered in graves, but sometimes also at settlement sites and as part of special deposits. The best preserved and most complete exemplars of shields come from the Norwegian ship grave at Gokstad in Vestfold, Norway[167] and from the fortress of Trelleborg in Sjælland, Denmark (Fig. 5.12).[168] Studies of Viking Age iconography (*e.g.* figurines, shield-shaped amulets and textiles), together with specialist analyses of surviving shield boards (for example from Ballateare, Gokstad, and Grimstrup), show that shields could be painted in various vivid colours.[169] The meaning of shield decoration remains obscure, however – it may have been a way to distinguish warriors on the battlefield, to signal group affiliation, rank and status, to convey religious meanings or all or none of the above.

Shields and shield bosses continue to remain largely under-studied in Viking Age scholarship. The first Scandinavian scholars who drew attention to archaeological finds of shields were Oluf Rygh in his classic study *Norske oldsager*[170] published in 1885 and Jan Petersen in his monograph *De norske vikingesverd* from 1919.[171] It is noteworthy, however, that each of the two researchers devoted less than *one* page of text to this category of finds, meaning that their work can be regarded as cursory at best. Still today the typology developed by Rygh is commonly used in Viking studies, regardless of its many imperfections and inaccuracies. It can be expected that new research by archaeologists like Kerstin Odebäck[172] and Rolf Fabricius Warming[173] will help nuance our current understanding of these essential defensive weapons. Beyond a shadow of a doubt shields were of crucial importance in Viking Age warfare, as evidenced not only by archaeology but also by the intricate symbolic meanings ascribed to them in Old Norse poetry and religious practice.[174] It is worth highlighting the fact that, according to Kim Hjardar and Vegard Vike, more than 300 kennings have been associated with shields, making them the weapon with the largest number of poetic metaphors.[175]

Shields in Viking Age funerary contexts

Shields are found in both cremation and inhumation graves[176] where they tend to occur in combination with other types of weapons such as swords, spearheads, axeheads, arrowheads and battle knives.[177] Both types of graves typically contain only one shield, although a number of instances from Sweden and Norway have been recorded where several exemplars of shields have been found buried together with a single individual.[178]

In cremation graves shields and their fragments tend to be heaped or bundled up with other metal grave goods. One exceptional case is the aforementioned grave from Myklebostad in Nordfjordeid, Norway where as many as 12 shield bosses were placed inside a copper alloy bowl to cover and/or protect the burnt remains of a deceased man.[179] The number 12 in this case may have been symbolic and

Fig. 5.12. Authentic reconstruction of a Viking Age round shield. The shield is built as part of a project led by Rolf Warming (Society for Combat Archaeology) in collaboration with Trelleborg Viking Fortress (National Museum of Denmark) based on new research data (Warming, Larsen, Sommer, Ørsted Brand, Pauli Jensen 2020). Photographer: Tom Jersø/The Viking Shield Project. Used by kind permission.

potentially referred to the idea of 12 elite warriors some chieftains allegedly had in their retinues.[180]

As a result of poor preservation and often imprecise recording, it is challenging to determine the most common patterns in the way shields were deposited in cremation graves, and it is also difficult to gauge if they were typically laid flat with the boss pointing up or the other way round. Interestingly, archaeological excavations have shown that in some graves inverted shield bosses were used as 'containers' and filled with various other objects.[181]

In contrast to cremations, much more is known about the specific ways of using shields in Viking Age inhumation graves. The shield could be placed over the body (essentially on the deceased person's chest or head), but in some exceptional instances it was the body that was laid on top of the shield (*e.g.* Nordre Kjølen, Tønsberg).[182] In the chamber graves at Birka, shields were either placed over the deceased or stood leaning against one of the walls.[183] The aforementioned chamber-like grave from Ballaterare in the Isle of Man diverges from the rest because in this case the shield was placed outside the coffin, probably leaning against it.[184] It is also worthy of note that the iron boss of the Ballateare shield appears to have been deliberately damaged (perhaps during the funeral), as indicated by deep parallel cuts on its surface. Another peculiarity pertaining to the use of shields in the Viking Age is that in some Norwegian funerary contexts shield bosses bear traces of damage inflicted by the same weapons (*e.g.* spears) that belong to the burial assemblage.

As already mentioned above, although most single inhumation graves from the Viking world tend to include just a single shield, archaeological excavations have revealed a number of instances with two or more exemplars. The meaning of this custom is obscure, and it is unknown if all or any of the shields actually belonged to the deceased person or if they represented the people who gathered at the graveside. If the latter was the case, the shields could be viewed as symbols of allegiance or protection, expressions of mourning or objects that communicated other profound ideas.

Several Old Norse textual sources refer to the use of shields in connection with funerals and apotropaic practices. *Göngu-Hrólfs saga* (ch. 33), for example, mentions a shield being placed over the face of a dying sorcerer, likely with the intention to ensure protection from the undesired effect of his 'evil eye'.[185] It remains unknown whether this was the intention behind the aforementioned cases of placing shields over the bodies of the deceased in Viking Age cemeteries.

Women and shields in iconography

The archaeological record of Viking Age Scandinavia preserves a fairly substantial corpus of iconographic representations of shield-carrying characters presumably representing women. In the sections above, we have already discussed the Oseberg tapestry, which depicts several such characters armed with shields and spears. Small two-dimensional metal figurines usually called 'valkyrie brooches' which portray an armed rider (occasionally with a shield attached to the back of the horse) facing a standing figure in a trailing dress and holding a shield are also very similar to the Oseberg motifs. A detailed analysis of these artefacts will be presented in Chapter 6. Small stand-alone figurines plausibly interpreted as representations of females (usually on the grounds that they have long hair and trailing dresses) are also occasionally shown carrying shields. These items, together with the curious three-dimensional figurine discovered at Hårby in Fyn, Denmark are also discussed in Chapter 6.

Miniature shields

Regardless of their diminutive size (ca. 2–3 cm in diameter), miniature shields look almost exactly like their full-size counterparts; they are round and have a pronounced boss in the centre, and some exemplars also have a small handle riveted to their reverse, imitating the wooden handles of full-size shields (Fig. 5.13). The main material used for the manufacture of miniature shields was silver, copper alloy, and lead. Similar to their full-size counterparts, the boards of the miniatures tend to be decorated with swirling patterns (also known as the 'running wheel motif') usually consisting of punched dots or circles, but in some cases they have other kinds of ornamentation, for example in the form of punched triangles with pellets inside.[186] Recent studies have shown that miniature shields form the largest group among all types of small-size weapons recovered from Viking Age graves, settlements and hoards. To date at least 79 examples are known from Western Europe, Scandinavia and Poland, and there are at least another 60 from the territory of present-day Russia.[187]

Miniature shields have been drawing attention from scholars since the nineteenth century, a time when their first examples were discovered in Scandinavia and Eastern Europe. However, the first detailed studies of these artefacts started to appear only in the second half of the twentieth century.[188] The most thorough and multidisciplinary analysis of miniature shields was published in 2018 by Leszek Gardeła and Kerstin Odebäck,[189] who conclude that miniature shields from funerary contexts appear to be exclusively connected with women, implying that this was probably a typically female ornament. Based on careful analyses of female inhumation graves and the positions in which miniature shields have been found within them, Gardeła's and Odebäck's study has also demonstrated that miniature shields were used in various ways: suspended around the neck (as part of a necklace), sewn on to clothing or carried in a pouch. In view of the fact that a number of miniature shields are devoid of handles on the reverse and that they have no loops for suspension, it is possible that some of their exemplars were not meant to be worn on the body at all.

Analyses of Viking Age graves with miniature shields discovered at Birka have also shown that some specimens were buried together with other types of objects with possible amuletic significance, such as Þórr's hammers and figurines in anthropo- and zoomorphic form.[190] In this light, it is not unlikely that the women interred with such elaborate sets of amulets had special roles to play in their society, perhaps as ritual specialists. Interestingly, however, none of the graves with miniature shields were furnished with full-size weapons or large ritual paraphernalia like iron staffs.

In the context of the present discussion, it is worthy of note that, in addition to having a miniature shield, the person buried in an opulent grave at Flakstad in Norway also had a trefoil brooch.[191] Brooches of this kind, often called 'the third brooch',[192] were typically worn by Norse women, and served as fastenings for a cloak or shawl. They were particularly popular in eastern Scandinavia, but their different exemplars are also known from other parts of the Viking world. One thing that often skips the attention of scholars is that these pieces of jewellery were actually modelled on Carolingian sword strap distributors (Fig. 5.14),[193] a detail that adds further nuance to the debate on the various associations between women and weapons in the Viking Age. Thus, even though the Flakstad grave had no functional and full-size weapons, the deceased person was actually laid to rest with as many as two pieces of jewellery with martial connotations.

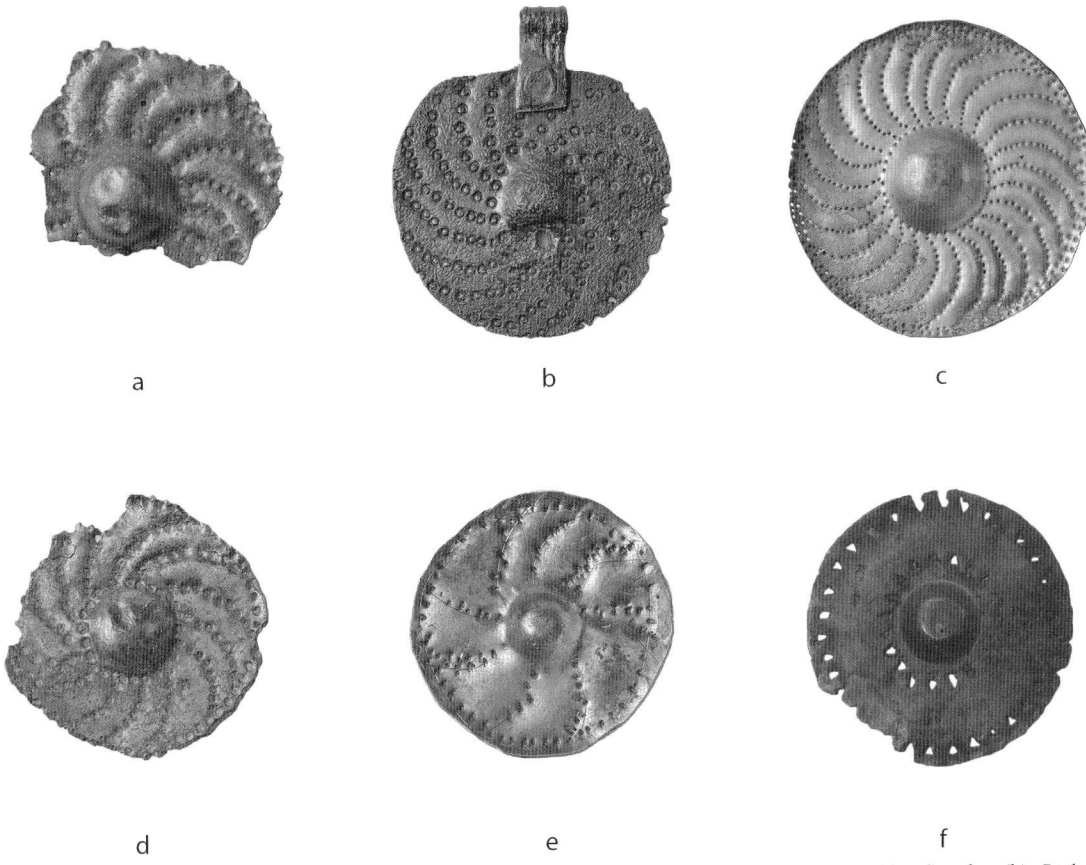

Fig. 5.13. Selection of Viking Age miniature shields: Birka grave Bj. 533, Sweden (a), Birka grave Bj. 825, Sweden (b), Birka grave Bj. 835, Sweden (c), Birka grave Bj. 963, Sweden (d), Birka grave Bj. 987, Sweden (e), Truso/Janów Pomorski, Poland (f). Photos (a–e) by Gabriel Hildebrand (Collections of the Statens Historiska Museum), photo (f) by Leszek Gardeła.

Two graves from Birka (Bj. 954 and 968) also included trefoil brooches in addition to being furnished with miniature shields. Interestingly, grave Bj. 954 contained two Þórr's hammers and a poorly preserved amber pendant, which may have originally had the form of an amber axe. Grave Bj. 968, on the other hand, contained a small anthropomorphic figurine (sometimes referred to as a 'valkyrie' pendant), an amulet in the form of a miniature chair (*kubbstol*),[194] as well as a range of other small objects with possible amuletic properties. Based on its assemblage, some scholars have interpreted this particular grave as potentially belonging to a sorceress.[195] The observation that in addition to the multiple amulets this grave also had two objects with martial connotations (miniature shield and trefoil brooch) adds nuance to our perception of this woman's presumed role in society.

Interpreting shields in Viking Age female graves

Two shields accompanied the deceased person in the Birka grave Bj. 581, something that is rarely observed in Viking Age Sweden where single graves are conventionally furnished with just one shield. In Bj. 581 the first shield was probably placed leaning against the western wall of the chamber, while the second shield stood against the raised platform with the two horses. It is interesting to note that the two shields were positioned in such a way that their bosses would point away from the body (which is seated between them), as if they were actually intended to flank and protect the deceased person. Whether such an arrangement of the shields was devised purely for practical and aesthetic reasons or whether it had some deeper symbolic significance is difficult to gauge.

In the case of Nordre Kjølen, according to what Gustav Mørck heard from the farmer who had found and personally excavated the grave, the deceased individual had apparently been laid *over* a shield, with the shield boss located somewhere in the head area. This is also an example of an unusual mortuary practice, since – as we have seen above – in the Viking Age most shields are either placed flanking the body or over it.

Regrettably, the wooden boards of the shields from Birka and Nordre Kjølen have completely deteriorated as a result of post-depositional processes, so it is impossible to say anything about the decorations they potentially had. If the shields had been ornamented, the imagery might have held important meanings and played some role in the burial

Fig. 5.14. Viking Age trefoil brooches are modelled on Carolingian strap distributors. The photo shows a replica of one such item from Östra Påboda in Söderakra socken in Småland, Sweden. Replica by Mikołaj Organek (Organek Arts and Crafts). Photo by Jacek Gajak. Used by kind permission.

ceremony, but this will forever remain unknown. Another problem with Nordre Kjølen is that the shield boss no longer survives, because it was destroyed in a fire in 1912. All we know about this object is that it belonged to Rygh's type R563. As regards the two shield bosses from grave Bj. 581 at Birka, it is unclear if they had ever been used prior to their deposition in the grave; in any case they do not appear to have any evident traces of damage.

Women and shields in Old Norse sources

As noted in Chapter 3, Old Norse literature portrays several women who use shields in their exploits. It is said in *Hervarar saga ok Heiðreks* that Hervör trained with sword and shield already as a child and so did Þornbjörg of *Hrólfs saga Gautrekssonar*. Later in her life, Þornbjörg uses her shield on a number of occasions, two of which are worthy of exposition as they appear to be loaded with symbolic meanings: when Hrólfr visits Þornbjörg to ask for her hand, she beats her shield to silence his words, but after she is defeated by Hrólfr in battle, she returns to her father's court and ceremoniously lays the shield in front of him, succumbing to his will and thus agreeing to become his wife. The first instance can be interpreted as an evocative display of power and independence, while the latter can be seen as something quite the contrary and as an act of submission. Another woman named Ólöf, who rules over Saxaland and whose deeds are mentioned in *Hrólfs saga kráka*, also carries a sword and shield but does not actively participate in battle; her weapons, therefore, ought to be seen as royal attributes and symbols manifesting her social prominence and authority.

Supernatural women were also no strangers to shields and other weapons. In Chapter 3, we have investigated the *valkyrjur* whose names often refer to military equipment, including shields. Randgníðr (Shield-Scraper) and Randgríðr (Shield-Truce, Shield-Destroyer, Shield-Violence) immediately bring forth connotations with fierce warfare and invoke the disturbing sounds that accompany armed conflict. All of the above-mentioned cases illuminate the symbolic nature of shields in female hands and are worth bearing in mind, especially when analysing the imagery of small metal figurines, a group of artefacts that we shall thoroughly explore in Chapter 6.

Women and shields in the Viking Age: conclusions

Iconographic finds, Old Norse textual sources and archaeological discoveries of full-size shields in female graves all imply the existence of a special relationship between these weapons and Viking Age women. The term 'shield-maiden', commonly used today in popular culture and in the work of professional scholars, was coined already in the Middle Ages, and probably not without a reason. The image of a woman wielding a shield, whether supernatural or human, must have resonated strongly in the minds of the Viking Age Scandinavians. At the present moment it is difficult to judge, however, whether and how often such individuals were actually witnessed on the battlefield or in other martial or ritualistic contexts. The remarkable Oseberg tapestry, which portrays several shield-bearing women, and which is some of the best surviving iconographic sources we have from the Viking Age, can be variously interpreted and seen as portraying either real or imagined events. The armed women on the tapestry could represent actual female fighters, but they could also depict women only carrying shields in some kind of procession, perhaps linked to a funeral. Alternatively, the whole scene could portray a story or myth the contents of which are lost in the mists of time. Regardless of how we choose to interpret the imagery of the Oseberg tapestry, other archaeological discoveries, especially in the form of small two- and three-dimensional figurines, as well as female graves furnished with full-size shields or their miniature equivalents, all imply that the idea of the shield-bearing woman was widely known among Norse societies. While the shields buried with the women at Nordre Kjølen and Birka may not have belonged to the deceased, the abundance of miniature shields in Sweden and other parts of the Viking world lead to the assumption that at least some of these small amulets were actually used in life by the women they were buried with. Because some women wore miniature shields around the neck, we could perhaps consider them as 'shieldmaidens' of sorts, but it is impossible to take this interpretation any further and determine if they had ever used real weapons on the battlefield. We might, however, dare to speculate that their 'battles' were fought on a different, metaphysical level, especially if we permit the interpretation that some of these women held the role of ritual specialists. The idea that some of the women buried with miniature shields (and perhaps also those buried with other types of miniature weapons) were sorceresses may be further supported by the fact that as many as three presumably female graves with iron staffs (*i.e.* items likely used the practice of *seiðr*) contained full-size shield bosses (Gausel, Hilde, Kvåle – see Chapter 4). Could these women have dressed up as shieldmaidens in the course of their rituals, in this way transforming themselves into human embodiments of the mythical *valkyrjur*?

Women, bows and arrows in the Viking Age

Arrowheads have been discovered in several Viking Age female graves, including the inhumations at Birka (Bj. 581) and Nordre Kjølen and the cremations at Barshalder, Ire, Laxare, Terum and Nennesmo, but their presence and purpose in these funerary contexts is not easy to understand. Determining the role of arrowheads in cremation graves (especially those that lack any other military equipment) is even further complicated due to the uncertainty of whether the arrowheads had been intended as grave goods or if their occurrence among the cremains is simply the result of them having been stuck in the body of the person burnt on the pyre. The main goal of the sections below is to provide contextual information on bows and arrows in the Viking Age and to outline the different ways in which they were employed in mortuary practices. This will allow us to situate the finds of arrowheads in female graves into a wider perspective and to broaden the spectrum of their possible interpretations.

Bows and arrows in the Viking Age

Since bows were typically carved out of wood like yew and elm, and only occasionally had additional features made from other material (*e.g.* bone or antler), they very rarely survive in the archaeological record.[196] Based on existing evidence, it appears that the longbow was the most typical bow in Scandinavia.[197] Some of the best preserved examples of Viking Age longbows are known from Hedeby where one such weapon was discovered complete and measured 191 cm in length. Well-preserved Viking Age bows and bow fragments are also known from Ballindery, Co. Westmeath,[198] Dublin (Kilmainham/Islandbridge)[199] and Waterford in Ireland. Textual sources suggest that bows were commonly used during armed conflicts on land, but there are also records demonstrating their effectiveness in naval warfare.[200] Visual representations of archers and their equipment are generally rare in medieval iconography, but they can be encountered on runestones and stone crosses.[201]

In contrast to bows, Viking Age arrowheads were made of iron, and it is due to the persistent character of this metal that so many of them have survived to the present times even though their wooden shafts have deteriorated. In fact, as Andrew Halpin rightly observes, the arrowhead is the real weapon, while the bow is practically an accessory.[202]

The shape, size and weight of arrowheads differed considerably across medieval Europe (*e.g.* some exemplars had a socket and others were tanged), and while some were strictly destined to be used in combat others would serve multiple functions, for instance in hunting.[203] In his study of Viking Age arrowheads from Dublin, Halpin has made a noteworthy observation that 'some arrowhead types are, in effect, miniature versions of spearheads. In such cases the distinction between large arrowheads and small spearheads is often far from obvious'[204] – as will be shown below, this remark is also relevant in regards to the ambiguous find from Trekroner-Grydehøj.

Viking Age arrowheads are often encountered in settlement contexts and strongholds where they are sometimes embedded into wooden parts of ramparts or stuck into the remains of houses. Excavations at Birka have provided numerous examples of arrowheads; their large concentrations in certain areas of the island suggest that a fierce battle had taken place there. Aside from strongholds and settlements, all across the Viking world arrowheads are also found in graves, either singly or in bundles. Regrettably, due to issues of poor preservation, in most cases it is difficult to say if they were originally buried with quivers or without them (the bundled arrowheads from Bj. 581 were probably in a quiver, however).

Over the course of the nineteenth and early twentieth centuries, a number studies on Viking Age bows and arrows were released, beginning with the seminal publications of Oluf Rygh[205] and Jan Petersen[206] both of whom created the first classification systems. In more recent years a number of other scholars have examined arrowheads from various European cultural milieus and proposed their own typologies.[207] For example, well-preserved arrowheads from Oppdal in Central Norway discovered together with wooden shafts were scrutinised in the work of Oddmunn Farbregd in 1972.[208] Another significant contribution to the study of Viking Age arrowheads from Norway is the work of Kalle Sognnes entitled *Iron Age Arrow-Heads from Hordaland, Norway: Testing a Classification System*, published in 1988.[209] Andrew Halpin's recent study on *Weapons and Warfare in Medieval Dublin* is also a highly erudite work, providing a wealth of contextual information on bows and arrows in the Viking Age and later periods.[210]

Bows and arrows in Viking Age funerary contexts

Arrowheads, like all other types of Viking Age weapons, are found in both cremation and inhumation graves.[211] The number of arrowheads in cremations can vary from just one to several examples, and similar tendencies can be observed in the case of inhumations. Poor preservation often makes it challenging to assert if people buried complete arrows (together with their organic shafts) or arrowheads alone, and whether the procedure of committing them to the ground involved special ritual acts similar to the aforementioned practice of thrusting, bending or breaking other elements of martial equipment – the surviving metal arrowheads are often too small to make any firm conclusions about their original position and to determine whether or not they were shot or thrust vertically into the grave or simply laid flat on the ground.[212] As regards inhumations, arrowheads are located in different places in relation to the deceased person's body – they can be on the left or the right side, but sometimes they are placed in the head- or foot-end of the grave. In the case of graves containing several arrowheads, the weapons often represent the same or very similar typological variants, meaning that people were typically buried with whole sets rather than with different arrowheads intended for various purposes (*e.g.* arrows for piercing armour, stunning, hunting, etc.). Opulent graves furnished with several arrowheads probably also included wooden bows, which, regrettably, rarely survive in the archaeological record.

Interpreting bows and arrows in Viking Age female graves

It is impossible to determine if all female inhumation graves with arrowheads also contained bows. However, given the fact that grave Bj. 581 and the grave from Nordre Kjølen included several different types of military equipment (swords, axeheads, spearheads, arrowheads), it is highly probable that bows were also part of their assemblages. Presuming that this was indeed the case, we may speculate that the bows either represented the possessions of the deceased or that they were added to the grave by the mourners with some deliberate intention in mind.

Unravelling the purpose of arrowheads in the cremation graves from mainland Sweden and Gotland poses more interpretational and source-critical challenges than in the case of the inhumations discussed above. The features of the specimens from Terum, Nennesmo and several Gotlandic graves hamper a firm determination whether the arrows or arrowheads accompanied the deceased on the funeral pyre or whether they were added to the graves unburnt. As argued above, we also cannot rule out the possibility that instead of representing 'inalienable possessions of the deceased' or 'grave goods' added by the mourners, the arrowheads were the actual causes of death of the individuals from these graves – it is not totally inconceivable that they had been stuck in their bodies and that after the cremation process they were gathered together with the burnt bones and buried.

In discussing the symbolic meaning of weapons in Viking Age female graves, it is crucial to pay closer attention to the item discovered in grave A505 at Trekroner-Grydehøj, already discussed in Chapter 4. The body of the object is cast in copper alloy and has an additional inserted blade made of iron (Fig. 5.15). The artefact's angular rhomboid body with a distinct midrib is 2 cm in its widest part and ca. 5 mm in its narrowest part.[213] The long tang of this item was originally fitted into a wooden shaft and additionally wound with a copper alloy wire to hold it firmly in place. Lacking close parallels in the corpus of Scandinavian arrowheads from Sweden, Norway and Denmark, as well as among weapons typically used in Viking Age Ireland, the design of this artefact is absolutely unique. However, upon closer inspection it can be argued that – in terms of shape and size – it resembles rhomboid arrowheads commonly employed by nomadic people, for example Hungarians/Magyars. These parallels are striking and thus worthy of further investigation.

Since Eurasian nomads lived a dynamic and peripatetic lifestyle, constantly remaining on the move, it is often challenging to trace their physical presence in the archaeological record, especially outside the areas of their main activity. Therefore, aside from occasional discoveries of burials containing very distinctive sets of goods (*e.g.* sabretaches, arrowheads, stirrups, horse remains),[214] the physical presence of mobile and militarised nomad groups beyond their homelands and in different parts of Europe is actually usually indicated by the finds of tanged arrowheads, which are the most characteristic traces of their material culture.[215] These tanged arrowheads differ considerably from the 'socketed' arrowheads commonly used by warriors in Viking Age Scandinavia and Central Europe, allowing a firm cultural identification.

In an excellent study concerning the presence of nomadic warriors in Central Europe, especially in the basin of the Oder and the Vistula rivers, Witold Świętosławski has distinguished seven characteristic types of nomadic arrowheads: they are all tanged, but the appearance of their body ranges from rhomboid to leaf-shaped (Fig. 5.15).[216] While the constructional design of the composite item from Trekroner-Grydehøj is unparalleled (as it consists of parts made in copper alloy and iron), its overall form is, in fact, very similar to so-called 'flat rhomboid arrowheads with the greatest width above the middle of the blade'.[217] According to Świętosławski, the earliest exemplars of such arrowheads, dating to the sixth century, come from the vicinity of Lake Baikal in southern Siberia, but they continued to be used in Eastern Europe between the eighth and thirteenth centuries AD. In Hungary and Slovakia, for example, arrowheads of this particular type are commonly found in graves dated from the ninth to the tenth centuries, which perfectly dovetails with the dating of Trekroner-Grydehøj. In light of these analogies, it is not unlikely that the puzzling arrow/spear/staff from the Danish grave was either imported from distant lands or based on 'exotic' nomadic arrowheads perhaps with the intention to emphasise its alleged special powers and/or to manifest the prominence and/or peculiarity of its owner. In view of its unique design and fragility (the iron part would easily break off, if used in battle), it is unlikely that it would have been employed as an actual piece of martial equipment, but it might have served the role of a symbolic weapon instead.

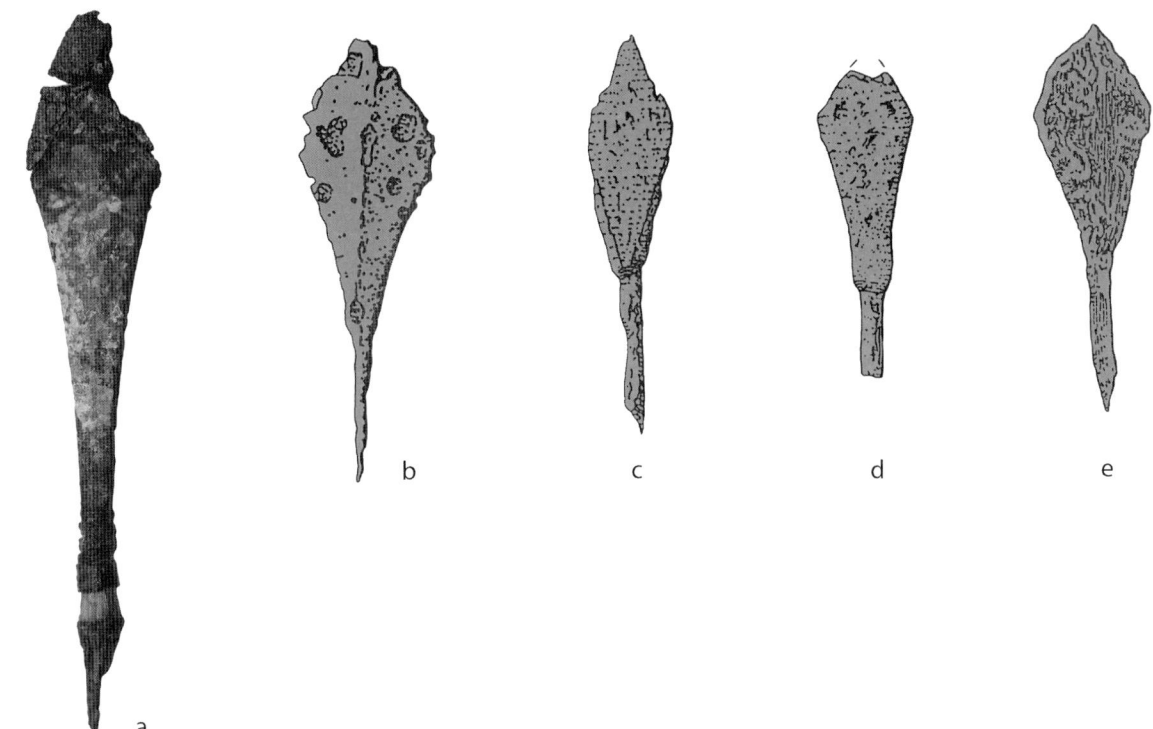

Fig. 5.15. The curious arrowhead, spear or staff from grave A505 in Trekroner-Grydehøj (a) and similar arrowheads from the nomadic world: Bruszczewo, Poland (b), Trepcza, Poland (c), Trepcza, Poland (d), Łazy, Poland (e). Photo (a) by Leszek Gardeła. Drawings (b–e) based on Świętosławski 2006: 92 and edited by Leszek Gardeła.

Women, bows and arrows in Old Norse sources

Old Norse literature preserves relatively scarce information about the use of bows and arrows by women. The best known case is that of the Giantess Skaði – discussed more thoroughly in Chapter 3 – who arms herself with a bow and ventures to Ásgarðr to avenge the death of her father. Although she never actually employs these weapons in combat (or at least we know nothing about it from extant texts), she apparently enjoys hunting, an activity where bow and arrows are handy if not essential. Another Giantess, Þorgerðr Hölgabruðr, however, uses arrows on an actual battlefield but in a very unusual way – she shoots them from her fingers. The *valkyrjur* are occasionally associated with arrows, too, for example in the poem *Darraðarljóð* where they employ them in the process of 'weaving battle' on a macabre loom.

Finally, it is worth pointing to an interesting episode preserved in *Brennu-Njáls saga*, partly related to the broader theme of 'women and weapons', in which a woman named Hallgerður refuses to give strands of her hair to Gunnarr so that he could restring his bow. Her behaviour is obviously driven by revenge, and she does not shy away from reminding him of a slap he once gave her.

Women, bows and arrows in the Viking Age: conclusions

As demonstrated above, women are rarely buried with bows and arrows, and the relationship between female characters (human and supernatural) and these weapons are also scarcely mentioned in extant medieval accounts. Since the bow is a long-distance weapon, the use of which does not require considerable physical strength, it is not unlikely – although difficult to prove based on the material that we have at hand – that some women used bows in hunting as well as in combat. At the present moment, however, it is impossible to determine how common this might have been.

Generally speaking, in contrast to actual weapons like swords and spears, arrowheads and bows should be seen as multifunctional objects, and their occurrence in funerary contexts – especially when other military equipment is absent – should not be taken as a clear indication of a warrior identity of the deceased. In the case of Bj. 581 and Nordre Kjølen, however, the arrowheads can be regarded as weapons that complement the rest of the elaborate grave goods with martial connotations; their design would have made them effective in both hunting and on the battlefield.

Women, riding equipment and horses in the Viking Age

A number of female weapon graves from Viking Age Scandinavia surveyed in the preceding chapter contained riding equipment and/or horse remains and/or wagons. The list below serves as a reminder of the specific types of horse-related objects found in these particular funerary contexts:

- Birka Bj. 581: horse bits, four horse crampons, as well as iron rings and an iron hook which may have been part of horse tack
- Kaupang Ka. 3: horse bits
- Kaupang Ka. 10: horse bits
- Kaupang Ka 16: horse bits
- Løve: horse bridle, three crampons, *rangle*
- Nordre Kjølen: horse bit
- Oens: spurs, wagon and perhaps a bridle
- Oseberg: wagon
- Sanddal: horse bit
- Trekroner-Grydehøj: possible iron parts of a saddle

It is also noteworthy to mention that although grave 22 from Nennesmo did not contain any riding equipment, it held the remains of a horse. Uncremated horses were also discovered in Birka Bj. 581, Nordre Kjølen, Løve and Trekroner-Grydehøj.

The following sections will seek to provide an overview of riding equipment in the Viking Age, as well as offering additional information about its occurrence in funerary contexts. The goal of this survey is to nuance the interpretations of horses and horse-related equipment in female weapon graves.

Riding equipment in the Viking Age

Riding equipment, including spurs, stirrups, saddles, bits and bridles was typically used by the most mobile members of Viking Age society: namely, the armed equestrian warriors, often at the service of powerful chieftains and kings. Surviving examples of spurs, stirrups, bridles and bits are typologically varied and often adjusted to the physique of a particular animal or to the requirements and abilities of the rider. While most elements of horse tack are made of iron, some items are occasionally additionally decorated with silver, copper or copper alloy inlays, serving as visually spectacular manifestations of *inter alia* wealth, rank, status, group affiliation and, in some cases, religious belief.

In Viking Age Scandinavia and elsewhere in the wider Viking world riding equipment tends to be found in richly furnished graves, often containing weapons, but it is also encountered in other contexts such as settlement sites and strongholds. In recent years, many new examples of Viking Age equestrian equipment have been recovered as a result of intensive metal detecting campaigns in Denmark, Sweden[218] and England,[219] a process which has not only led to an exponential growth of the find corpus, but also to a more nuanced understanding of past people's mobility and cross-cultural interaction.[220]

Viking Age riding equipment has been studied by many different scholars, resulting in the development of a range of classification systems. Current research shows that in the period spanning the ninth to eleventh centuries there seems to have been quite a variety in the forms of spurs, stirrups and bridles, on the one hand reflecting personal preferences of their users and on the other hand bearing witness to local technological and stylistic traditions. Norwegian archaeologist Oluf Rygh was among the first authors to cover these aspects of Viking Age material culture in Scandinavia, and his work was further developed in more detailed studies by scholars like Helge Braathen,[221] Anne Pedersen[222] and others.[223]

Riding equipment and horses in Viking Age funerary contexts

Viking Age riding equipment is found in both cremation and inhumation graves.[224] Some graves contain only selected elements, such as spurs, bridles or horse bits, while others include the complete set comprising spurs, bridles, bits and stirrups together with the remains of horses. There seem to be no strict rules dictating the placement of riding gear in cremation graves, but in the case of inhumations the equipment is usually deposited at the feet of the deceased person. In some instances the dead are even buried wearing spurs, as if they were dressed for a horseback journey.[225] Usually, graves with full sets of riding equipment also contain weapons, such as spears, swords and axes, and these come either singly or in sets. It is often argued that such graves belonged to prominent personae, perhaps even rulers, or that the dead were members of elite retinues. Richly furnished graves with equestrian equipment had their heyday in the late tenth and early eleventh centuries, a turbulent time when Northern and Central Europe underwent the dynamic process of political and religious transformation associated with the founding of early states.[226]

Interpreting riding equipment and horses in Viking Age female graves

Riding equipment in female graves can signal many different meanings and refer to a wide plethora of ideas. Aside from being symbolic of wealth, power and social prominence of the deceased and/or those who buried them, the presence of riding equipment and horses in graves might be also related to religious ideas concerning the afterlife and the (potentially long, arduous and dangerous) journey that led there. It is not unlikely that in order to reach the desired destination in the otherworld women were in need of animal companions. The idea of horses as supernatural guides or carriers of souls (*psychopompoi*) is widespread among Indo-European societies,[227] and it was probably not uncommon among Viking Age Scandinavians, too.[228] In Old Norse literature we can find references to horses being used for forays to the otherworld, with Oðinn's eight-legged stallion Sleipnir serving as the best example.[229] In Snorri Sturluson's *Gylfaginning* (48), Sleipnir even jumps over the fence surrounding Hel, the realm of the dead.

In discussing the significance of horses in mortuary contexts one has to pay very close attention to the specific ways these animals were treated during the funeral and one also has to consider the manner in which they were later deliberately positioned in the grave. Based on the surviving material remains from female inhumation graves, it appears that there were actually several different ways of interring horses in these specific contexts in the Viking world. In Bj. 581, the two horses (interestingly, a mare and a stallion) were laid on a raised clay platform at the foot-end of the burial chamber. The deposition of animal carcasses in this part of the grave is something we can also observe at Nordre Kjølen, (here, however, the animal was simply laid on the ground, on the same 'level' as the human remains). In terms of their general layout, Bj. 581 and Nordre Kjølen closely resemble some of the male graves with equestrian equipment and horse remains found at Birka[230] as well as those from other localities in Scandinavia and Iceland.[231] As we have seen, however, they also differ from these graves in certain ways, especially with regard to the peculiar placement of the weapons in relation to the body.

Against this background, the position of the horse remains in grave A505 at Trekroner-Grydehøj is outstanding: the animal's carcass is laid parallel to the deceased woman and with its head at her feet. The placement of animals (*e.g.* horses, dogs) side by side humans is rarely observed in Viking Age graves, especially in Denmark,[232] but it is encountered among nomadic peoples, for example the Hungarians/Magyars. These parallels deserve further exploration, especially in light of what has earlier been said about the possible nomadic inspirations behind the design of the 'arrowhead' from Trekroner-Grydehøj.

In Hungarian/Magyar inhumation graves from the tenth century the dead are typically laid out in supine position and the animals are placed by their side or at the feet (Fig. 5.16). The same graves also tend to include riding equipment such as stirrups and bits as well as weapons (axes, arrows/arrowheads) and other personal items (*e.g.* sabretaches).[233] Horses are rarely placed in the graves whole, however, and usually only selected parts of their bodies are chosen for burial: the head/skull and the shinbones.[234] The reason lies in the fact that in the course of the funeral, after the horse is ritually slaughtered, its skin tends to be removed. Sometimes the skin of the animal is placed inside the grave, either folded at the feet of the deceased person or spread out nearby.[235]

In the absence of genetic and isotopic analyses of the remains of the individual buried in grave A505 at

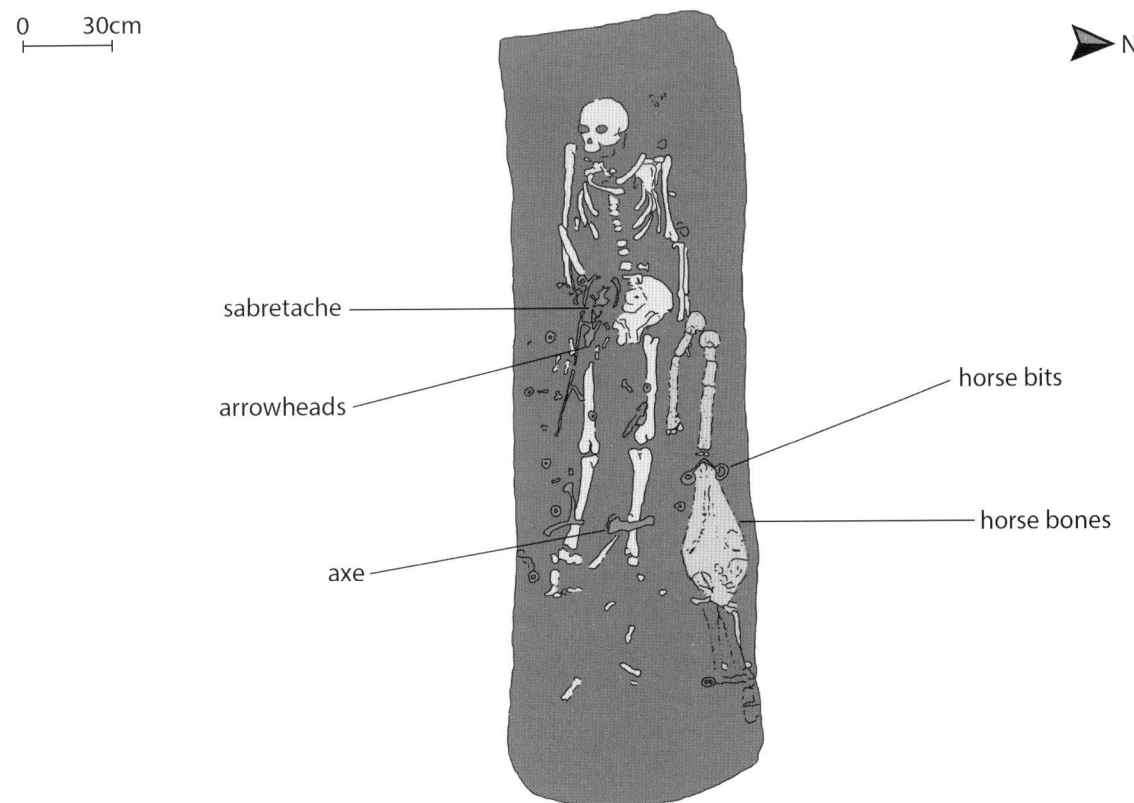

Fig. 5.16. Magyar grave from Przemyśl, Poland. Redrawn by Leszek Gardeła after Koperski 2004: 91.

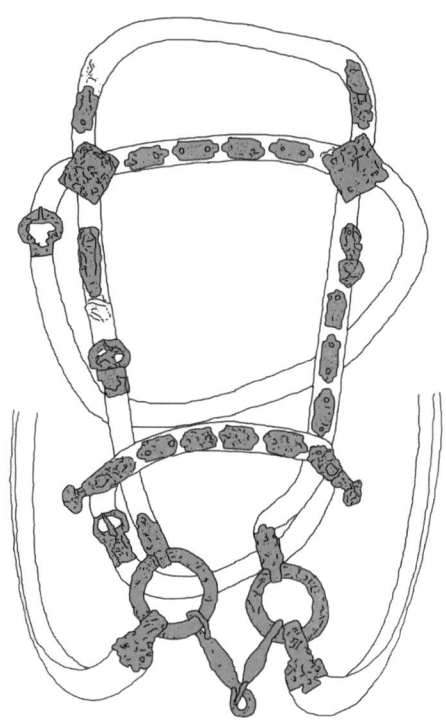

Fig. 5.17. Reconstruction of the horse bridle from Løve. Redrawn by Leszek Gardeła after Resi 2013: 119.

Trekroner-Grydehøj, it is currently impossible to say unequivocally where the woman originated from. The overall composition of her burial, as well as the fact that the peculiar arrowhead/spear that accompanied her is typologically similar to the arrowheads used by Eurasian nomads (Hungarians/Magyars), permit a careful suggestion that she was a foreigner. Further specialist studies might perhaps shed more light on her cultural background and identity.

Also at Løve the horse appears to have been buried parallel to the body of the deceased woman. Regrettably, both the human and the animal bones are rather poorly preserved, which hampers a more precise reconstruction of their position in the grave. Since so far the grave has only been cursorily published, many further details of its composition remain unknown. Nevertheless, both in terms of its contents and with regard to its overall layout, the grave appears very unique. The presence of a *rangle* – an object characteristic of Norwegian Viking Age graves – indicates that the buried person might have been of Norse provenance, but this cannot be proven in the absence of specialist analyses of the skeletal remains. The foreign origin of many of the beads found in this grave also does not provide any clear hints that would help determine the cultural identity of the deceased person. One interesting aspect of Løve is that the grave contained a very elaborate horse bridle, which has no direct parallels anywhere in the Viking world (Fig. 5.17). Its exquisite nature certainly emphasised the prominence of the rider, and the bridle was probably a prized possession. Elaborate bridles with decorative mounts are very rarely found in Viking Age female graves in Norway; one well-known example is a bridle discovered in a grave from Gausel in Rogaland.[236] In this case, the mounts on the bridle are decorated in insular style and have been refashioned from book fittings. The graves from Gausel and Løve differ considerably, since the latter only contained the cut off head of the horse with the rest of the carcass missing. Both graves, however, were furnished with items strongly implying that the deceased were involved in the practice of magic.

We cannot know for sure if the people buried with horses actually rode those animals in life and whether they shared some special bond with them. However, the close proximity of human and animal bodies in some of the graves discussed here (especially in Trekroner-Grydehøj and Løve, where in the former case the horse was actually laid over the deceased) indicates that this may have indeed been the case.

Women and horses in Old Norse sources

Old Norse literature mentions male and female riders on a number of occasions. This should not come as a surprise, especially when the texts concern Scandinavian lifeways in Iceland where horses were commonly used for travel and transport.[237] The special significance of these animals in this part of the Norse world is further amplified by the fact that horse burials are often found in cemeteries, implying that the animals were treated with care and respect in life as well as in death.[238]

In Old Norse mythology horses seem to have a very particular link to the Vanir gods, something that we see explicitly in the name of the horse Freyfaxi which belonged to Hrafnkell from *Hrafnkels saga*. Furthermore, according to *Ólafs saga Tryggvasonar en mesta*, a herd of stallions was apparently kept near Freyr's temple in Þrandarheimr.[239]

While horses are valued mounts of male gods like Óðinn and Freyr, only one female character from the Norse pantheon appears to own a horse. Known as Gná, she belongs to some of the more enigmatic deities and is only mentioned in *Gylfaginning* (34) where she is listed as the fourteenth Æsir goddess.[240] Snorri Sturluson writes that Gná is a servant of Frigg who sends her with messages all around the world. According to Snorri, Gná's horse was called Hófvarfnir (Hoof-thrower) and was begotten by the stallion Hamskerpir and the mare Garðrofa.[241] Interestingly, the horse appears to have been endowed with supernatural skills and could run through the air and over water.

Margaret Clunies Ross has recently observed that a significant number of horses known from Old Norse literature have names. This implies that even though these creatures were:

primarily classified as animals, they were also considered to have human-like traits and to have been thought of as individuals. Their identity as individuals was intimately bound up with that of their human owners, who, importantly, were usually also their riders.²⁴²

Clunies Ross also remarks that in Old Norse literature almost all named horses are male and are ridden by men, whereas mares rarely have names and lack free will and intelligence. Using structuralist theory, she arrives at the conclusion that:

> Mares thus belong on the natural side of the binary divide, as one would expect from the general nature of Old Norse myths, in which females are equated with nature and males with culture.²⁴³

In light of the above, it is interesting to highlight the fact that the horse from the grave at Løve had an elaborate and probably custom-made bridle. The effort invested into designing and manufacturing this precious item suggests that it was not only intended to manifest the prominence of the rider, but perhaps to demonstrate the close emotional ties the owner had with the animal, or even to highlight the horse's unique identity.

One aspect of Norse culture where associations between women and horses are particularly prominent is the use of wagons in ritual practices. Several independent textual sources (*e.g.* Tacitus' *Germania*) that refer to the Germanic cultural zone speak of wagons being employed in cultic processions,²⁴⁴ likely leading from wild and uninhabited places in the open landscape to the halls of the social elite. The same sources also emphasise the performative nature of Germanic and later Norse religious practice, and the crucial importance of movement, sometimes over long distances, and thus conceptually 'between the worlds'. In a recent enlightening study, Terry Gunnell has argued that these ritual acts could attest to the special physical connection between the Vanir gods and the landscape 'and the subsequent transference or spreading of the "goodness" of a god (or goddess) to other places permanently or temporarily'.²⁴⁵

The custom of wagon burial is characteristic of elite graves from the area of Denmark (*e.g.* Fyrkat 4), but wagons or wagon parts have also been found in funerary contexts in Norway (*e.g.* Oseberg).²⁴⁶ In Viking archaeology female wagon burials are conventionally interpreted as belonging to women of the highest social strata, sometimes endowed with additional prerogatives in the sphere of ritual practice. The famous grave 4 from Fyrkat has long been regarded as the grave of someone special, potentially a magic worker, an idea further substantiated as a result of ground-breaking analyses by scholars like Neil Price,²⁴⁷ Peter Pentz and others.²⁴⁸ In terms of its contents, Fyrkat 4 is very unique, and most of the other female graves with wagons do not come anywhere close to it in terms of the quantity, quality and symbolic undertones of their furnishings. One puzzling item in Fyrkat 4 is a long iron spit that terminates in a blade reminiscent of a spear blade – could this object have been a special kind of staff, and one that is linked with elaborate ideas surrounding armed women in the Norse world?

Women, horses and riding equipment in the Viking Age: conclusions

In light of the interdisciplinary evidence discussed above, it appears that the presence of riding equipment and/or the remains of horses in Viking Age female graves might have held a broad range of meanings. While in some cases such grave goods likely represented personal possessions of the deceased and might have been essential equipment enabling them to successfully perform their social duties (*e.g.* activities requiring increased mobility), in other instances they might have served other purposes. In the course of the funeral ceremony the deposition of riding equipment and horses might have been intended to invoke allusions and/or aspirations to the lifestyle of the elite or served as equipment necessary for an afterlife journey. As in the case of all the other types of grave goods discussed above, there is no fixed way of interpreting them – in each case they appear to tell a different story.

At the current state of research, it remains difficult to gauge if the women buried with horses actually rode those animals in life and if the animals belonged to them. However, given the fact that many of the graves discussed in this chapter contained opulent furnishings, and that in some instances the animals were buried very close to the bodies of the deceased (Trekroner-Grydehøj and Løve), the existence of intimate bonds between these people and horses seems highly probable. As argued above, there are good reasons to believe that the women from Trekroner-Grydehøj and Løve played the role of ritual specialists, which also lends credence to the idea that the horses they were buried with had been used in rituals they themselves performed. The presence of these animals in graves, as trusted companions and former 'assistants' in life, is therefore understandable: they lived together and died together.

Whether the individuals interred in graves with a more 'martial feel', such as those from Birka (Bj. 581) and Nordre Kjølen, rode the horses they were buried with is impossible to determine, but not unlikely. In the case of Bj. 581, the deceased woman was buried with stirrups, a piece of equipment that would have made riding much easier, especially if one wanted to use weapons at the same time (*e.g.* bow and spear). As mentioned in Chapter 4, one interesting aspect of Bj. 581 is that although horses and horse-riding equipment were present among its contents, the grave lacked spurs. In richly furnished equestrian graves in Viking Age Scandinavia, and Bj. 581 certainly belongs to this category, it is customary to find stirrups together with spurs, and so their absence is somewhat puzzling. However, it should be pointed out that spurs were only a characteristic piece of equipment among Western and Central European equestrian warriors, and they were hardly ever used by Eurasian nomads (*e.g.* Maygars/Hungarians and others).²⁴⁹ Together with the fact that the Birka grave contains an Eastern European hat, as well as possible remains of a caftan, this gives a further indication that the deceased might have originated from the East or at least that at some point in life this person decided to adopt an Eastern or nomadic style of clothing, fighting and riding.

***

The 'eastern connections' that many of the graves discussed herewith display are a theme that deserves further attention and contextualisation, and thus – after a brief chapter dedicated to armed women in Viking Age iconography – in Chapter 7 we shall immerse ourselves in the stories of armed women from Eastern Europe and Asia. This endeavour will give the topic of 'Amazons of the North' a much needed cross-cultural angle and will help broaden and sophisticate the final interpretations.

Notes

1. For preliminary ideas on the meaning of axes in Viking Age female graves, see Grøn *et al.* 1994; Gardeła 2013b: 298–299; 2017c; 2018b; Sigurðsson 2017: 112–113.
2. On the use of axes in Viking Age combat, see Griffith 2009: 176–178; Short 2014: 71–85; Hjardar & Vike 2016.
3. *E.g.* Roesdahl 1977; Skov 2005: 37; Halpin 2008: 163–165; Eriksen *et al.* 2009: 88–89; see also Sankiewicz & Wyrwa 2013; Kotowicz 2014; 2018.
4. Stylegar 2007; Jagodziński 2010: 57; Maixner 2010: 65.
5. *E.g.* Shetelig 1912; Petersen 1919; Paulsen 1939; 1956; Arbman 1940; 1943; Grieg 1947; Skaarup 1976; Roesdahl 1977; Braathen 1989; Christensen 1992; Sørheim 1997; Hedenstierna-Jonson 2006b; Stylegar 2007; Wrzesiński 2011; Pedersen 2014a; Barndon & Olsen 2018.
6. Petersen 1919.
7. For alternative axe typologies, see Wheeler 1927; Kotowicz 2014; 2018.
8. *E.g.* Nadolski 1954; Heindel 1992; Kazakevičius 1996; Kurasiński 2005; Kotowicz 2014; 2018; Pedersen 2014a; Hjardar & Vike 2016.
9. *E.g.* Trotzig 1985; Mäntylä 2005; Kotowicz 2011; 2018. On the symbolism of miniature axes, see Zeiten 1997: 15–17; Jensen 2010; Kucypera *et al.* 2011; Gardeła 2014a: 100–102; in press-c.
10. On Danish Viking Age graves with axes, see Brøndsted 1936; Skaarup 1976: 110–111, 119–120, 177; Nielsen 1991; Grøn *et al.* 1994: 34–35, 120–121, 136; Jeppesen 2005: 72–73; Eriksen *et al.* 2009: 272–273, 275–277, 291–292; Stoumann 2009: 75, 196–199, 563, 586; Arents & Eisenschmidt 2010a: 79–80; Pedersen 2014a. On Norwegian Viking Age graves with axes, see Petersen 1919; Braathen 1989: 51–52, 54, 56–57, 59, 68, 70–73, 75, 77–79, 83, 86–89, 92; Sørheim 1997; Stylegar 2007; Engh 2009; Nordeide 2011; Barndon & Olsen 2018. On Swedish Viking Age graves with axes, see Arbman 1940; 1943; Svanberg 2003; Thunmark-Nylén 1998–2006. On English, Scottish and Irish Viking Age graves with axes, see Graham-Campbell & Batey 1998: 122–127, 133–134, 150; Paterson *et al.* 2014: 90–100, 139, 159, 162–163, 165, 167–169; Harrison & Ó'Floinn 2015. On Polish Viking Age graves with axes, see Drozd & Janowski 2007; Wrzesiński 2011; Kotowicz 2014; Kotowicz 2018.
11. *E.g.* Thålin-Bergman 1986b; Braathen 1989; Pedersen 2014a.
12. *E.g.* Barndon & Olsen 2018.
13. For various interpretations of this grave, see Petersson 1958; Schultze 1987: 55–62, 102–112; Price 2002: 142–149, 183–185; Gardeła 2013b: 292–293; 2016b; Toplak 2016: 64, 199–200.
14. Gräslund 1980: 76.
15. Rygh 1885: 727; Oestigaard 2015.
16. But see the new study by Barndon & Olsen 2018.
17. *E.g.* Resi 2013.
18. *E.g.* Paterson *et al.* 2014: 139.
19. See Nordberg 2002.
20. On the problems of distinguishing between axes as weapons and axes as tools, see Kotowicz 2014; 2018.
21. *E.g.* Zeiten 1997; Jensen 2010; Kucypera *et al.* 2011; Gardeła 2014a: 100–102; Edberg & Söderberg 2018; Gardeła & Toplak 2020.
22. *E.g.* Gardeła & Odebäck 2018.
23. Schetelig 1911; 1912: 31–32.
24. Schetelig 1911: 6.
25. Mokkelbost 2007.
26. *E.g.* Gräslund 1980; Price 2002; Robbins 2004; Mihajlov 2011; Janowski 2015.
27. Zeiten 1997: 16.
28. The wooden handle that now forms part of the artefact is a modern addition. It does not necessarily reflect the original appearance this object had in the Viking Age.
29. Schetelig 1911: 10.
30. Zeiten 1997: 15; Pedersen 2014a: 239.
31. Braathen 1989: 57.
32. Roesdahl 1977: 141–142; Zeiten 1997: 16.
33. Arbman 1943: 377–379; Gardeła & Odebäck 2018: 116–117.
34. *E.g.* Fuglesang 1999: 307; Gardeła 2014a.
35. Zeiten 1997: 15.
36. Zeiten 1997: 16.
37. Price 2002: 148
38. On Viking Age amulets and their possible meanings in female graves, see Price 2002: 203–207; Gräslund 2005; Jensen 2010; Gardeła 2014a; 2020a.
39. Resi 2013.
40. Price 2002: 148.
41. *E.g.* Price 2010b; Ulriksen 2011; 2018; Armstrong Oma 2018.
42. Pedersen 2014a.
43. For parallels, see Nadolski 1954; MKP 1958; Kotowicz 2014; 2018.
44. *E.g.* Janowski 2015; Błaszczyk & Stępniewska 2016; Błaszczyk 2017.
45. Jesch 1991: 184; Jochens 1996: 109.
46. As regards the Klinta grave, Price (2002: 149) considers wood-working tools as typically male objects. Indeed such tools are usually discovered in connection with men, but it must be borne in mind that occasionally they are also found in female graves (*e.g.* Hopperstad).
47. *E.g.* Reichborn-Kjennerud 1928: 159; Holck 1996: 98–99; Zeiten 1997: 17.
48. Karwot 1955: 21; Matczak & Chudziak 2018.
49. On sword parts made of organic material, see Androshchuk 2014: 87–88. For a thorough analysis of an ivory Viking Age sword pommel from Gniezno, Poland, see Sawicki 1990. The

well-known antler cross-guard from Sigtuna is discussed in detail in O'Meadhra 2018.
50 Głosek 1973; Oakeshott 1999: 143–147; Marek 2004; 2005: 47–57; Hjardar & Vike 2016: 171–173.
51 On the discoveries of swords and other weapons in watery locations, see Wrzesiński 2007; Wyrwa et al. 2011; Braunmüller 2013; Raffield 2014.
52 Jagodziński 2010; 2015; Biborski et al. 2010.
53 On Viking Age sword scabbards, see Nadolski 1955; Bersu & Wilson 1966; Ellis Davidson 1998: 88–103; Janowski & Kurasiński 2009; Androshchuk 2014: 107–127; Hjardar & Vike 2016: 174.
54 On sword scabbard chapes, see Strömberg 1951; Paulsen 1953; Kazakevičius 1992; Sikora 2001; Hedenstierna-Jonson 2002; 2006a; 2015; Janowski 2006; 2007; Liwoch 2008; Androshchuk 2014.
55 Petersen 1919.
56 See, for example, Geibig 1991; Oakeshott 1991. See also Androshchuk 2014 for recent modifications to Petersen's typology.
57 See, for example, Biborski et al. 2010; Wyrwa et al. 2011; Brunning 2019.
58 See, for example, Ellis Davidson 1998; Raffield 2014; Brunning 2015; 2019; Mayburd 2020; Gardeła in press-b.
59 Brunning 2019.
60 On Danish Viking Age graves with swords, see: Brøndsted 1936; Arents & Eisenschmidt 2010a; 2010b; Pedersen 2014a. On Norwegian Viking Age graves with swords, see Rygh 1885; Shetelig 1912; Petersen 1919; Braathen 1989; Stalsberg & Farbregd 2011. On Swedish Viking Age graves with swords, see Arbman 1940; 1943; Androshchuk 2014. On Central European Viking Age graves with swords, see Sarnowska 1955; Głosek & Nadolski 1970; Głosek 1984; Wrzesiński 1998; Marek 2004; 2005; Janowski 2014.
61 E.g. Barndon & Olsen 2018.
62 Aannestad 2018.
63 Williams 2016.
64 E.g. Brunning 2015; 2019; Gardeła 2020a.
65 For examples of Viking Age graves with swords buried on the left-hand side of the deceased, see Thålin-Bergman 1986b.
66 In her recent study of early medieval swords, Brunning (2019: 59–110) has identified a number of swords which bear characteristic traces of wear indicating their use by left- or right-handed people. These traces are particularly clear on sword pommels and handles, which would have rubbed against the body on either the left or right side.
67 Robbins 2004; Buko 2015.
68 For examples of Viking Age graves with swords placed away from the body, see Arbman 1943; Thålin-Bergman 1986b.
69 Brunning 2019: 155.
70 Cited after Brunning 2019: 155–156.
71 Gräslund 1998; Raffield 2019: 825.
72 Toplak 2019b: 57.
73 On Icelandic Viking Age children's graves with weapons, see Callow 2006; Gardeła 2012a. For examples and interpretations of children's burials with arrowheads, see Kurasiński 2004.
74 On miniature axes from children's graves, see Kucypera et al. 2011.
75 For examples of Norwegian Viking Age female graves with weaving swords, see Rygh 1885; Shetelig 1912.
76 On weaving swords in Anglo-Saxon burial contexts, see Harrington 2007.
77 For examples of those graves, see Shetelig 1912.
78 Aannestad & Glørstad 2017.
79 Rygh 1885: 440; Solberg 2003: 235–236.
80 Rygh 1885: 439; Poole 1991: 136.
81 Einar Ólafur Sveinsson 1954.
82 For detailed discussions on and analyses of this poem, see Poole 1991; Price 2002: 331–337.
83 Poole 1991: 122.
84 Text after Poole 1991.
85 Translation after Price 2002: 333.
86 Helmbrecht 2011.
87 Simek 2002.
88 Price 2006.
89 Gardeła 2015a; 2018b.
90 Hougen 1940; Price 2002: 173, 337, 374; Christensen & Nockert 2006.
91 Hougen 2006: 33.
92 Inverted swords are also known from several graves in Finland. For further details, see Moilanen 2020: 232.
93 Hougen 1940: 93.
94 Hougen 1940: Plate VI; Nylén & Lamm 2003: 67.
95 For more thorough surveys and interpretations of this particular artefact category, see Zeiten 1997; Jensen 2010; Rosengren 2010; Gardeła in press-b.
96 Gardeła in press-b.
97 Jensen 2010: 47.
98 Gardeła & Odebäck 2018; Gardeła in press-a.
99 E.g. Christensen 2015: 192–193, 516–517; Seiler & Magnell 2017: 205; Hjardar & Vike 2016: 158; Wamers 2017: 67.
100 See Härke 2014 with further references.
101 See, for example, Gräslund 1998; Kurasiński 2004; Callow 2006; Gardeła 2012a; Raffield 2019.
102 Björn K. Þórólfsson & Guðni Jónsson 1943.
103 Einar Ólafur Sveinsson & Matthias Þórðarson 1935.
104 On Þórdís Eiríksdóttir, see Wolf 1997: 669–670.
105 It is noteworthy that a group of women who reach for swords with the intention to scare their foes is also mentioned in Þorgils saga ok Hafliða (ch. 9). Interestingly, in this case the women also had breeches pulled over their dresses. It seems that this act of cross-dressing was intended to serve an additional role, making the women appear more powerful.
106 Einar Ólafur Sveinsson 1943
107 On Bróka-Auðr, see Wolf 1997: 667–670; Straubhaar 2002: 265–267.
108 Wolf 1997: 680.
109 On Hervör, see Clover 1986; Mayburd 2014.
110 Tolkien 1960.
111 Clover 1986: 38.
112 Hjardar & Vike 2016: 175.
113 For examples of elaborately decorated Viking Age spearheads, see Rygh 1885; Arbman 1940; 1943; Górecki 2001; Chudziak 2006; Hjardar & Vike 2016: 161, 176–179; Sankiewicz & Wyrwa 2018; Gardeła 2019a: 225–228.
114 Foote & Wilson 1970: 275.

115 For a wider discussion of this motif, see Banaszkiewicz 1987a; Nordberg 2002; 2003; Price 2002: 132–139, 148; Gardeła 2010.
116 Hjardar & Vike 2016: 45.
117 Petersen 1919.
118 Nadolski 1954.
119 Solberg 1984.
120 See, for example, Solberg 1984; Creutz 2003; Artelius 2005; Wickholm 2006; Gardeła 2010; 2019g; Gardeła & Ciesielski 2012; Kurasiński 2014; Short 2014: 86–96.
121 See, for example, Banaszkiewicz 1987a; 1987b; Kuczkowski 2008.
122 Price 2002; Gardeła 2010; 2019g.
123 For examples of Danish Viking Age graves with spears, see: Brøndsted 1936; Ramskou 1950; Sellevold *et al.* 1984; Pedersen 2014a. For examples of Norwegian Viking Age graves with spears, see Rygh 1885; Shetelig 1912; Petersen 1919; Braathen 1989; Stylegar 2007; Nordeide 2011. For examples of Swedish Viking Age graves with spears, see Arbman 1940; 1943; Svanberg 2003; Artelius 2005; Thunmark-Nylén 1998–2006.
124 For example the aforementioned grave Bj. 581 from Birka and the Ballateare grave from the Isle of Man – see Bersu & Wilson 1966; Wilson 2008; Gardeła 2014b.
125 Artelius 2005.
126 Kurasiński 2014: 160.
127 Arbman 1940; 1943.
128 See the discussion on this peculiar practice in Gräslund 1980; Gardeła & Ciesielski 2012.
129 Bersu & Wilson 1966; Wilson 2008; Gardeła 2014b.
130 Price 2013a.
131 Hougen 1940: 115; 2006: 39.
132 Hougen 1940: 115–116.
133 Hougen 2006: 38, 41.
134 Hougen 1940: 104–105
135 Leahy & Paterson 2001: 192; Hall 2007: 107; Helmbrecht 2011: 128; Gardeła 2012c: 147–148.
136 For previous discussions on miniature spears, see Zeiten 1997; Jensen 2010: 45–47; Gardeła 2014a: 102–104; Pedersen 2014a: 239–240.
137 Jensen 2010: 46.
138 Gardeła 2014a: 102–104.
139 Gardeła in press-a.
140 Jensen 2010: 47.
141 Arbman 1943.
142 Kurasiński 2014; see also the previous work on this motif by Creutz 2003: 267–268.
143 In Iceland, a spear pointing towards the foot-end is known from an unnumbered grave at Grásiða – see Kristján Eldjárn & Adolf Friðriksson 2000; Kurasiński 2014: 168–169.
144 In Norway, a grave with a spear pointing towards the foot-end is known from Gulli (grave S400) – see Gjerpe 2005a; Kurasiński 2014: 166.
145 In Poland, graves with spears at the feet and pointing towards the foot-end are known from Lubień (graves 5, 21 and 103), Pokrzywnica Wielka (graves 19 and 28), and Radom (grave 41) – see Kurasiński 2014: 163, 165.
146 In Russia, graves with spears at the feet and pointing towards the foot-end are known from Gnëzdovo (mound 61) and Pskov (Lenin Street) – see Kurasiński 2014: 166–167.

147 In Slovakia, graves with spears pointing towards the foot-end are known from Michal and Žitavou (grave 24/56), Tvarožná (grave 9) – see Kurasiński 2014: 166.
148 In Sweden, graves with spears pointing towards the foot-end are known from Birka (graves Bj. 581, Bj. 735, Bj. 842, Bj. 850, Bj. 985) – see Kurasiński 2014: 166.
149 Kurasiński 2014: 171.
150 Creutz 2003.
151 Kurasiński 2014: 172.
152 For various interpretations of the imagery presented on helmet plaques, see Holmqvist 1960; Price 2002; 2019; Gräslund 2020: 233–234.
153 Hougen 1940.
154 Hougen 1940: 104; see also Hjardar & Vike 2016: 97.
155 Kurasiński 2014.
156 Simek 2006: 375–376.
157 Wilson 2008: 79.
158 See, for example, Deptuła 2003 and Kurasiński 2014: 179–184 with references.
159 See, for example, Tomiccy 1975; Tomicki 1976.
160 Kurasiński 2014: 184–187.
161 Kurasiński 2014: 185.
162 Price 2002: 338.
163 *Grottasöngr* (15). Translation after Larrington 1999: 261.
164 *Grottasöngr* (15). Translation after Larrington 1999: 262.
165 Hjardar & Vike 2016: 185. For a recent excellent exploration of Germanic shields of the Iron Age and Viking Age, see Warming *et al.* 2020.
166 Arbman 1940; 1943. For examples of ornamented shield handles, see Schetelig 1905; Gardeła 2019a: 175–176; Hedenstierna-Jonson 2006a.
167 Nicolaysen 1882.
168 Dobat 2013.
169 On painted shields from Viking Age contexts, see Bersu & Wilson 1966; Hjardar & Vike 2016: 187.
170 Rygh 1885.
171 Petersen 1919.
172 Odebäck 2018: 71–74.
173 Warming *et al.* 2020.
174 Falk 1914.
175 Hjardar & Vike 2016: 184.
176 For examples of Danish Viking Age graves with shields, see Brøndsted 1936; Pedersen 2014a. For examples of Norwegian Viking Age graves with shields, see Nicolaysen 1882; Rygh 1885; Mørck 1901; Schetelig 1905; 1912; Petersen 1919; Braathen 1989; Blindheim & Heyerdahl-Larsen 1995; Blindheim *et al.* 1999; Gjerpe 2005a; Stylegar 2007; Nordeide 2011. For examples of Swedish Viking Age graves with shields, see Arbman 1940; 1943; Svanberg 2003; Thunmark-Nylén 1998–2006. For examples of Irish Viking Age graves with shields, see Harrison & Ó'Floinn 2015. For examples of Viking Age graves with shields from the British Isles, see Graham-Campbell & Batey 1998.
177 Thålin-Bergman 1986b.
178 For examples of Viking Age graves with multiple shields, see Schetelig 1905; Arbman 1943; Price 2010b.
179 Schetelig 1905.
180 Gardeła 2019e.
181 Odebäck 2018: 73–74.
182 Mørck 1901; Lie 2016.

183 Arbman 1943.
184 Bersu & Wilson 1966; Gardeła 2014b.
185 Gardeła & Odebäck 2018: 101–103. On the motif of the 'evil eye' in the Old Norse world and other cultural contexts, see Dundes 1992; Lassen 2003; Gardeła 2013a.
186 Gardeła 2014a.
187 Gardeła & Odebäck 2018; Gardeła in press-c.
188 Duczko 1989; Zeiten 1997, see also the work of Jensen 2010.
189 Gardeła & Odebäck 2018.
190 Miniature shields have been found in the following inhumation graves at Birka: Bj. 531 (Arbman 1943: 163); Bj. 800 (Arbman 1943: 290–291); Bj. 825 (Arbman 1943: 298–300); Bj. 835 (Arbman 1943: 308–309); Bj. 844 (Arbman 1943: 318–319); Bj. 849 (Arbman 1943: 322–323); Bj. 946 (Arbman 1943: 372–373); Bj. 954 (Arbman 1943: 377–379); Bj. 963 (Arbman 1943: 386–388); Bj. 966 (Arbman 1943: 392–393); Bj. 968 (Arbman 1943: 394–396); Bj. 973 (Arbman 1943: 398–400); Bj. 980 (Arbman 1943: 406–408); Bj. 983 (Arbman 1943: 409–411); Bj. 987 (Arbman 1943: 413–415).
191 Petersen 1928; Gardeła & Odebäck 2018.
192 Solberg 2003: 231–234.
193 Gardeła & Toplak 2020.
194 On the symbolic meaning of miniature chairs, see Price 2002: 163–167; Vierck 2002; Pesch 2018; Kalmring 2019.
195 Gräslund 2005; Gardeła & Odebäck 2018.
196 Halpin 2008: 40–41; Hjardar & Vike 2016: 181–183.
197 Hjardar & Vike 2016: 182.
198 Halpin 2008: 37–39, 42, 50.
199 Halpin 2008: 50–62.
200 Halpin 2008: 36.
201 Halpin 2008: 36 mentions images of archers on high crosses from Monasterboice, Kells and Durrow.
202 Halpin 2008: 45.
203 On the challenges of distinguishing military arrowheads from hunting arrowheads, see Halpin 2008: 79–80. Some scholars argue that hunting arrowheads ought to be wider and heavier than military arrowheads so as to inflict more damage to the animal tissue. Military arrowheads, on the contrary, ought to be more compact and streamlined, as this design is more effective in causing damage to warriors wearing defensive body armour. In reality, however, the distinction between military and hunting arrowheads is not so clear cut.
204 Halpin 2008: 75.
205 Rygh 1885.
206 Petersen 1919.
207 Nadolski 1954; Halpin 2008: 80–81.
208 Farbregd 1972.
209 Sognnes 1988.
210 Halpin 2008: 35–130.
211 For examples of Danish Viking Age graves with arrowheads, see: Brøndsted 1936; Pedersen 2014a. For examples of Norwegian Viking Age graves with arrowheads, see Schetelig 1905; 1912; Petersen 1919; Braathen 1989; Nordeide 2011. For examples of Swedish Viking Age graves with arrowheads, see Arbman 1940; 1943; Svanberg 2003.
212 Arrowheads thrust vertically into the ground in tenth-century Hungarian/Magyar graves are sometimes interpreted as traces of apotropaic practices intended to 'prevent evil spirits from burrowing into the grave'. In Hungary, axes struck in the floor of the grave allegedly served the same purpose. See Révész 2014: 49.
213 Gardeła 2016b: 278–279.
214 See, for example, Koperski 2004.
215 Świętosławski 2006: 66, 79; Révész 2014: 24–25, 41, 95.
216 Świętosławski 2006: 66–100.
217 Świętosławski 2006: 89–94.
218 See, for example, Gardeła et al. 2019c.
219 See, for example, Williams 1997.
220 See, for example, Gardeła 2019d; Gardeła et al. 2019a; 2019c; Gardeła & Kajkowski in press.
221 Braathen 1989.
222 Pedersen 1997; 2014a.
223 On Viking Age riding equipment from England, see Williams 1997. On Viking Age riding equipment from Poland as well as its typology, decoration and symbolism, see Hilczerówna 1956; Świętosławski 1990; Gardeła 2018c; Gardeła et al. 2019a; 2019b; Gardeła & Kajkowski 2021a.
224 For examples of Danish Viking Age graves with riding equipment, see Brøndsted 1936; Pedersen 1997; 2014a; Stoumann 2009; Bagge 2015. For examples of Norwegian Viking Age graves with riding equipment, see Rygh 1885; Schetelig 1905; 1912; Petersen 1919; Braathen 1989; Gjerpe 2005a; Stylegar 2007; Resi 2013; Armstrong Oma 2018. For examples of Swedish Viking Age graves with riding equipment, see Arbman 1940; 1943; Svanberg 2003; Thunmark-Nylén 1998–2006; Toplak in press. For examples of Polish Viking Age graves with riding equipment, see Kostrzewski 1921; Rajewski 1937; Jażdżewski 1951; Hilczerówna 1956; Nadolski et al. 1959; Świętosławski 1990; Malinowski 2005; Ratajczyk 2013; 2016; Gardeła 2019a.
225 For examples of Viking Age inhumations with spurs worn on the feet of the deceased, see Ratajczyk 2013; Pedersen 2014a; Lindblom 2016; Gardeła et al. 2019b.
226 Braathen 1989; Dobat 2009; Pedersen 2014a; Gardeła & Kajkowski 2021a.
227 On the symbolic meanings attributed to horses in various Indo-European societies, see Rajewski 1975; Gapski 2014; Kajkowski 2016; 2018; Szymczak 2018.
228 On horses ensuring the transition from one world to the next, see Clunies Ross 2014: 52. On the symbolism of horses in Scandinavia and elsewhere in the Viking diaspora, see also Sikora 2003–2004; Armstrong Oma 2018.
229 Simek 2006: 293.
230 Arbman 1943.
231 Kristján Eldjárn & Adolf Friðriksson 2000: 181–184.
232 One peculiar example of an adult individual buried side by side with a dog is known from grave CA at Kaagården in Langeland, Denmark. The animal was laid on the proper right side of the deceased. For further details, see Grøn et al. 1994: 74–75.
233 See, for example, Koperski 2004; Świętosławski 2006: 67–78; Révész 2014: 44–49, 52–53, 68, 80–81.
234 Révész 2014: 47.
235 Révész 2014: 49.
236 On the Gausel find, see Price 2002; 2019; Armstrong Oma 2018.
237 *Laxdœla saga* describes a female rider dressed in trousers. As discussed in detail in Chapter 3, the same woman, known as Auðr, also uses a sword to wound her former husband and in this way punishes him for his unfaithfulness.

238 Adolf Friðriksson 2000; Þóra Petursdóttir 2007.
239 Gunnell 2017: 117.
240 Simek 2006: 113.
241 Clunies Ross 2014: 54.
242 Clunies Ross 2014: 54.
243 Clunies Ross 2014: 60.
244 On processions in the Viking Age, see Nygaard & Murphy 2017.
245 Gunnell 2017: 125.
246 On wagons and wagon burials in Viking Age Scandinavia, see Roesdahl 1977; Müller-Wille 1985; Gunnell 2017.
247 Price 2002; 2019.
248 Pentz *et al.* 2009.
249 Świętosławski 2001.

Chapter 6

Women and weapons in Viking Age iconography

The material culture of the Viking Age abounds with miniature objects made of ferrous and non-ferrous metals. These relatively light and tiny items, rarely more than 10 cm in length, come in many forms: anthropomorphic, zoomorphic and resembling full-size weapons (swords, spears, axes, shields, helmets), tools and furniture (chairs). Since the nineteenth century, numerous archaeologists have been researching the origins, distribution, materiality and meaning of this curious group of artefacts, and today there seems to be a general agreement about the objects' inherent amuletic nature and religious significance.[1] Anthropomorphic and zoomorphic miniatures in particular have been commonly – although not necessarily correctly – perceived as representations of or allusions to well-known mythological figures, especially gods and goddesses like Óðinn, Þórr and Freyja and various supernatural beings. This chapter focuses on specific variants of anthropomorphic miniature figures that depict armed females. It discusses their imagery and seeks to unravel their potential links with motifs and ideas from Old Norse literature and mythology.

The so-called 'valkyrie brooches': distribution and materiality

Over the last few decades archaeological excavations and amateur metal detecting have brought to light a substantial group of miniature finds depicting a figure clad in a trailing garment, carrying a shield and standing next to a mounted horse (Fig. 6.1). Since the 1990s these items have been typically hailed in Viking scholarship as 'valkyrie brooches' (in German *Walkürenfibeln* and in Danish *Valkyrie-fibulær*, in Polish *walkirie*).[2] At the present moment over 40 examples are known from different locations in Denmark (*e.g.* Ribe, Stentinget, Sønder Tranders, Tissø),[3] Germany (*e.g.* Ellingstedt, Hedeby),[4] England (*e.g.* Bylaugh, Peterborough, Winterton)[5] and Poland (Truso).[6] Since most of them have been found in Denmark, it is highly probable that this is where they were originally designed.

The majority of the finds that make up the corpus are made of copper alloy, sometimes with niello inlay and gilding,[7] but a few silver examples are also known. This implies that some of them were expensive and perhaps produced for a very select group of people. A comprehensive analysis of the materiality of these artefacts, including a catalogue all their examples, will be provided in a forthcoming study written by this author in collaboration with Neil Price and Peter Pentz. This chapter focuses mainly on their most distinctive features, their possible symbolic significance and their relationship to the broader theme of armed women in the Viking world.

The miniatures from Tissø (Fig. 6.1) – showing an armed standing figure and a rider – are exceptionally well preserved compared to other exemplars from the corpus, which means that they can be used as a 'reference collection'. At first glance, the long trailing dress of the standing figure and the knotted ponytail of the rider might suggest that *both* individuals are female: in conventional explanations of Viking Age iconography, these features are usually regarded as identifiers of women. In the case of the figurines that concern us here, however, this interpretation is complicated by the fact that the allegedly female rider has baggy trousers instead of a dress. Perhaps this anomaly could be explained in purely practical terms – sitting on a horse in a typically feminine garment would not be very comfortable, especially when one is to engage in martial activities. Alternatively, this could be interpreted as a deliberate attempt to portray the masculine nature of warrior women. We shall return to this problem further below.

In the examples from Tissø and other locations around Denmark, we also can clearly see that the rider is holding a sword in the right hand and has a winged spear beneath the right leg.[8] The standing figure appears to be holding a shield with a swirling pattern and an elongated object, which some scholars have interpreted as a horn or beaker.[9]

Another intriguing detail, which is visible on virtually all of the completely preserved miniatures depicting a standing figure and a mounted horse, is a chequered 'board' with nine fields located directly beneath the horse's belly. This motif has been previously interpreted as a 'web of destiny' (in reference to the Old Norse poem *Darraðarljóð*), or as a 'border' between the land of the living and the land of

Fig. 6.1. Selection of miniatures depicting a rider and an armed figure: Tissø, Denmark (a), Hedeby, Germany (b), Ribe, Denmark (c), Stentinget, Denmark (d), Bylaugh, England (e), Truso/Janów Pomorski, Poland (f). Photos (a) and (d) by the National Museum of Denmark, photos (b), (c) and (f) by Leszek Gardeła, photo (e) by Norwich Castle Museum & Arts Gallery, used by permission.

the dead (*Helgrind*).[10] In a different study, I have suggested the alternative possibility that it could represent a gaming board.[11] Interestingly, an unmistakable depiction of a gaming board, similarly shaped and also with nine fields, appears on a runestone from Ockelbo in Gästrikland, Sweden[12] (Fig. 6.2), which lends support to the above interpretation. As noted in Chapter 4, in Norse worldviews, playing board games could indeed be seen as a symbolically charged act, since it relates to the idea of fate.[13] How the alleged gaming board might relate to the horse and rider depicted on the miniature find is difficult to understand, however.

(Re)interpreting the so-called 'valkyrie brooches'

Most studies concerning representations of a standing figure and rider consider these miniatures as 'brooches' or 'fibulas'. This interpretation is called into question once the reverse of these artefacts is examined more closely. On the well-preserved finds (*i.e.* those whose reverse side is not damaged) there is *never* a fastening mechanism that would be characteristic for Viking Age brooches (*i.e.* a needle and catch plate). Instead, the artefacts have two closed loops (Fig. 6.3), implying that they were intended to be worn as pendants or perhaps as clothing appliques. The first scholar to observe this detail was Michaela Helmbrecht, who writes:[14]

> Diese Funde werden in der Regel als 'Walkürenfibeln' bezeichnet. Die parallelen Ösen auf die Rückseite und das Fehlen jeglicher Nadelkonstruktion sprechen jedoch eher für eine Verwendung als Anhänger oder Kleiderbesatz.

As a rule, these finds have been interpreted as 'valkyrie brooches'. However, the parallel loops on the reverse and the lack of any needle construction suggest that they were used as pendants or appliques.

Given these observations, I agree with Michaela Helmbrecht that we ought to abandon the interpretation of such artefacts as 'brooches', and instead only call them 'pendants' or 'appliques'. What still remains unclear, however, is how exactly they were worn. Since they all come as stray finds, we cannot know for certain if they were hung around the neck on a string, sewn onto clothing or perhaps riveted to some other piece of equipment, for instance made of leather.

Having discussed the miniatures' functional aspects, we may now attempt to investigate their symbolic content. The label 'valkyrie brooches', was first introduced by Peter Vang Petersen in 1992, who interpreted the figurines' iconography in light of Old Norse texts describing the *valkyrjur*,[15] drawing especially on the aforementioned *Darraðarljóð*.[16] Although for nearly twenty years this interpretation has been enthusiastically repeated in dozens of academic publications and museum exhibitions, it now requires a careful verification in light of new discoveries and in view of the fact that the find corpus has expanded exponentially.[17]

Close reading of different academic studies mentioning 'valkyrie brooches' leads to the inevitable conclusion that their interpretations actually tend to be very laconic, impressionistic and often limited to just a couple of sentences. Below is a selection of citations from a range of publications released since the late 1990s, which clearly illustrate the urgent need for a new analysis:

- In 1997, Sue Margeson described a find from Bylaugh saying that 'it shows a horseman being greeted by a woman with a shield, with the end of her trailing dress broken off. This scene can be interpreted as a valkyrie, in pagan belief one of Odin's followers, welcoming a Viking warrior to Valhall, Odin's kingdom'.[18]
- In discussing the imagery of Gotlandic picture stones and a miniature find from Hedeby, in 2002 Neil Price argued that 'there is support for a *valkyrja* interpretation in the find of a bronze brooch from Hedeby, depicting a rider being welcomed by such a woman in the same composition as on the picture-stones. Unusually, however, the woman is not just carrying a drinking horn but also a shield – a clear indication that she has a martial aspect'.[19]
- With regard to one of the finds from Tissø, in 2013 James Graham-Campbell wrote: 'Another version of a "valkyrie" scene is known in metalwork from both Viking Age Denmark and England. A shield-bearing woman faces a female rider, with braided hair, armed with sword and spear'.[20] Later, Graham-Campbell also added that the standing figure is offering a horn to her 'superior' sister.
- In describing a miniature from Peterborough, Jayne Carroll, Stephen H. Harrison and Gareth Williams offered the following interpretation: 'This may well be an image of a Valkyrie welcoming a hero to Valhalla, the hall of the slain and presided over by Odin'.[21]

The citations above demonstrate that the tendency to classify these small metal objects as representations of the *valkyrjur* relies predominantly on Old Norse mythological texts or on seeking parallels in the imagery of Gotlandic picture-stones, such as Tjängvide I and Stenkyrka Lillbjärs, which portray a standing figure facing a rider (Fig. 6.4).[22] These picture-stones have been conventionally interpreted as depicting a *valkyrja* welcoming a fallen equestrian warrior to Valhalla (Old Norse *Valhǫll*). While there is little doubt that the rider on the stones is male, in the case of the metal figures most scholars actually presume the rider is female, mainly on the grounds of the distinctive hairstyle.[23] This view is highly problematic and gives rise to the question of *why* and *where* would a (standing) female '*valkyrja*' welcome another woman (rider). Another major obstacle in accepting this interpretation is the fact that extant textual accounts *never* mention women entering *Valhǫll* and becoming *einherjar* (slain warriors living there).[24] Is it possible, therefore, to offer alternative readings of the scene depicted by the miniatures? Some potential avenues will be outlined below.

Freyja and a warrior woman?

Although surviving records of Old Norse beliefs present *Valhǫll* as a hall reserved exclusively for men, one should take

Fig. 6.2. Detail of the runestone from Ockelbo in Gästrikland, Sweden showing two figures playing a board game. Drawing by Leszek Gardeła.

Fig. 6.3. The obverse and reverse of the double miniature from Tissø. The reverse has two well-preserved closed loops; this constructional feature implies such artefacts were probably used as pendants and/ or appliques. Photo courtesy of Mads Dengsø Jessen (National Museum of Denmark). Edited by Leszek Gardeła.

Fig. 6.4. The 'welcoming scene' on a Gotlandic picture stone from Tjängvide I. Notice the rider in baggy trousers and the standing figure holding a horn. In some regards the imagery resembles the double figurines from Denmark. Photo by Leszek Gardeła.

note that it is apparently not the only otherworldly place the deceased warriors would inhabit. This observation gives rise to the question of whether there existed a special otherworld for women who in the course of their lives had engaged in martial activities and whether such a place (or the journey that led there) could be depicted in Viking Age iconography?

Two Old Norse accounts mention an intriguing place called *Fólkvangr*, which was ruled over by the goddess Freyja – a deity with links to the martial sphere and one who, just like Óðinn, was skilled in magic.[25] As we read in *Grímnismál* (14):

> Fólkvangr er inn níundi,
> en þar Freyia ræðr
> sessa kostom í sal.
> Hálfan val
> hon kýss hverian dag,
> en hálfan Óðinn á.

> Field of Battle is the ninth,
> and there Freyja determines
> the right rank of seating in the hall.
> Half of the slain
> she selects every day,
> and half Óðinn has.[26]

Roughly the same information is repeated by Snorri Sturluson in his *Gylfaginning*:

> Annat barn hans er Freyja. Hon er ágætust af ásynjum. Hon á þann bø á himnum er Fól<k>vang<r> heitir, ok hvar sem hon ríðr til vígs á hon hálfan vl allan en hálfan Óðinn.

> His [Njǫrðr's] other child is Freyja. She is the most glorious of the Ásynjur. She has a dwelling in the heavens that is called Fólkvangr, and wherever she rides to battle she gets half of all the slain, and Óðinn gets the other half.[27]

The name *Fólkvangr* (Folkvang) is translated as 'field of the host',[28] 'people's field' or 'army field'[29], and clearly has martial overtones. As Lindow writes in his guide to Norse mythology:

> If we understand Fólk- as 'army', Fólkvang begins to look like some kind of alternative to Valhöll, where the einherjar dwell until Ragnarök. Freyja too has an association with warriors who, like the einherjar, fight each day and feast each night, in that she presides over Hjadingavíg (an eternal combat of warriors). In that case the end comes not with Ragnarök but with the intervention of a Christian.[30]

If warrior women really existed in the Viking Age, we might speculate that, instead of going to *Valhǫll*, they were believed to depart to *Fólkvangr*, a place which would seem quite appropriate for women engaged in warfare. This idea may be further supported by the fact that, in some accounts, Freyja (who like Oðinn, Hel and Rán is also a goddess of death) is attributed with martial characteristics and in *Gylfaginning* is said to 'ride to battle'. Although the available textual evidence is admittedly scant, it may perhaps point towards some conceptual link between Freyja and potential real-life warrior women.[31]

In this light, it is not wholly inconceivable that the scene on the miniatures from Denmark, England, Germany and Poland represents a goddess and a deceased warrior woman entering *Fólkvangr*. What remains difficult to determine, however, is which of the two figures could be Freyja. Is she the standing figure (who is sometimes depicted with an object resembling a horn or beaker) or the one on the horse? At this stage of research, it is still too early to provide unambiguous answers.

Sigurðr and Brynhildr/Sigrdrífa?

Another plausible interpretation of the standing figure and rider scene is that it represents a memorable event in the famous story of Sigurðr Fáfnisbani, namely the moment when the hero rides on his horse Grani to claim the hand of a beautiful (shield)maiden named Brynhildr.[32] This story has a number of variants from eddic poetry and the sagas. Some of its scenes are also represented in Viking Age art and can be encountered on stone carvings in Scandinavia and the Isle of Man, but also on a wooden door from Hylestad, Norway.

Vǫlsunga saga (27) preserves a passage particularly relevant for the present discussion, which speaks of Sigurðr's journey to Brynhildr:

> Siðan ríðr Sigurðr ok hefir Gram í hendi ok bindr gullspora á fætr sér. Grani hleypr fram at eldinum, er hann kenndi sporans.

> Then Sigurðr rode with Gram in his hand and on his feet he bound golden spurs. When he felt the spurs, Grani leapt forward toward the fire.[33]

Apart from describing Sigurðr riding a horse and carrying a sword named Gram, it is also said in *Vǫlsunga saga* that Brynhildr wore a coat of mail and a helmet, and – like the male hero – held a sword. The military equipment of the story's protagonists closely resembles that of the figures depicted in the scene on the metal miniatures, whereby the mounted rider holds a sword and the standing figure wears a helmet. Perhaps the puzzling 'square' underneath the horse's belly is not a 'web of destiny' or a 'gaming board', as some scholars have previously suggested, but rather a representation of the fire that Sigurðr has to cross? When the miniatures are interpreted in this light, we could plausibly identify the rider as Sigurðr and the standing figure as Brynhildr.

It must be emphasised, however, that although several attributes of the figures fairly closely correspond with those mentioned in *Vǫlsunga saga*, there are also some discrepancies between the metal miniatures and the text of the story. For example, unlike in the story, the rider in the miniatures sometimes has a shield (attached to the back of the horse) and a spear (curiously positioned under the right thigh), while the standing figure holds a round shield and what may be interpreted as a horn or beaker. Some of these details might be better understood in the context of yet another variant of the Sigurðr story preserved in the prose introduction to the eddic poem *Sigrdrífumál*:

> Sigurðr reið up á Hindarfiall oc stefndi suðr til Fraclanz. Á fiallino sá hann liós mikit, svá sem eldr brynni, oc liómaði af til himins. Enn er hann kom at, þá stóð þar scialdborg oc up ór merki. Sigurðr gecc í scialdborgina oc sá, at þar lá maðr oc svaf með ǫllom hervápnom. Hann tóc fyrst hiálminn af hǫfði hánom. Þá sá hann, at þat var kona. Brynian var fǫst, sem hon væri holdgróin. Þá reist hann með Gram frá hǫfuðsmátt bryniona í gognom niðr, oc svá út í gognom báðar ermar.

> Sigurðr rode up onto Hindarfell and headed south towards the land of the Franks. On the mountain he saw a great light, as if fire were burning, and gleaming up against the sky. And when he came there, there stood a shield-wall with a banner flying over it. Sigurðr went into the shield-wall and saw someone lying there asleep and fully armed. First he took off the helmet, then he saw that it was a woman. Her corslet was tight, as if it had grown into her flesh. So with his sword Gram he cut from the neck of the corslet downwards, and so along both the sleeves.[34]

In light of this eddic account, the standing figure's horn or beaker could potentially refer to the drinking horn that Sigrdrífa (another name for Brynhildr) offers Sigurðr after he wakes her from her sleep.

Other details of the miniatures, such as the rider's spear and the standing figure's shield, are slightly more difficult to interpret. It is perhaps possible that the spear underneath the rider's thigh is a reference to the banner that marked Sigrdrífa's location. It is noteworthy that the spear seems to be of a winged type: these were exactly the kinds of spears that were used for banners in the Viking Age. The standing figure's shield, if not related to the shield wall behind which Sigrdrífa lay asleep, might instead serve as an indicator of her temperament and fierce nature. Although these interpretations and ideas require a considerable stretch of the imagination, not to mention the available evidence, it is nonetheless clear that all elements of the scene depicted in the miniatures were there for a reason and to convey meanings. The significance of these details – extending beyond their serving an ornamental role – is emphasised by the fact that they are consistently repeated on numerous examples that make up the find corpus.

We may tentatively conclude that, while it is possible that the scene on the miniatures represents Brynhildr/Sigrdrífa welcoming Sigurðr, it is also conceivable that the military equipment (sword, spear, shields, helmet) carried by the two figures has some other significance (for example, alluding to warrior women, Freyja and *Fólkvangr*, as suggested above). It is also possible that, despite their formal similarities, the miniatures discussed herewith were never meant to refer to just one fixed concept, story or myth; Viking Age people in Denmark, England, Germany and Poland might have attributed different and very fluid meanings to them.

Other iconographic representations of armed females in Viking Age Scandinavia and England

The 'double' miniatures discussed above are not the only Viking Age metal objects that seem to depict armed women. Due to intensified metal-detecting activities in Scandinavia and the UK, as well as the fairly liberal laws pertaining to this popular pastime, the corpus of pendants or clothing appliques depicting stand-alone and apparently female figures with weapons is constantly growing (Fig. 6.5). The best-known and best-preserved examples include copper alloy figurines from Cawthorpe[35] and Wickham Market[36] in England and a silver figure from Galgebakken/Vrejlev in Jutland, Denmark.[37]

The interpretation that these and similar artefacts represent (human and/or supernatural) females usually rests on the fact that they all wear trailing dresses and have elaborate hairdos which seem more characteristic of women rather than men. It is noteworthy that although some of the details of the figurines are varied, they are all portrayed with shields, often with decorative patterns: the figure from Rostock-Dierkow (Fig. 5.4) has a shield with a swirling design and the figure from Galgebakken/Vrejlev (Fig. 6.5) has a shield with convex concentric lines. The figure from Wickham Market (Fig. 6.5) is particularly exceptional because it carries the shield *beneath* the arm with the shield boss towards the body, so that the back side of the shield is showing (including a handgrip and, interestingly, decoration in the form of swirling patterns). The figure from Cawthorpe (Fig. 6.5) is the 'best equipped' of all the finds listed here, since it has a spear, a sheathed sword and a shield. Another important find (though not belonging to the same typological group as the objects above) is a three-dimensional figure discovered in 2012 at Hårby, Denmark (Fig. 6.5), which shows an apparently female character (with a knotted ponytail) carrying a sword and a shield with the running wheel motif.[38]

Fig. 6.5. Selection of standalone armed miniature figures: Hårby, Denmark (a), Galgebakken/Vrejlev, Denmark (b), Wickham Market, England (c), Cawthorpe, England (d), Søllested, Denmark (e). Photos (a) and (e) by the National Museum of Denmark, photo (c) from the Portable Antiquities Scheme Database, photo (d) from Hall 2007 and photo (b) by Leszek Gardeła.

As Helmbrecht[39] has recently observed, single and armed female figures have only been found in Denmark and England; such artefacts do not occur in the archaeological material from other parts of the Viking world and there are no analogies in Norway, Sweden, Poland, Russia and Iceland. Like the miniatures representing a standing figure and rider, these artefacts have been conventionally regarded as depicting the *valkyrjur*, although this may not be the only plausible interpretation.[40] As highlighted in Chapter 3, in Old Norse mythology, weapons are not only carried by the *valkyrjur*, but also by other mythical female characters, such as Giantesses, not to mention the cases of 'real' human women of the sagas and poems who occasionally reach for arms. The stand-alone figurines could thus represent some or none of these individuals. As in the case of the 'double figures', our ability to interpret them is significantly hampered because they all are stray finds from settlements or other sites. Discovering such a miniature in a female grave could potentially provide new pieces to the puzzle and open up new interpretational avenues.

As noted in Chapter 5 weapon-wielding women are also shown in other iconographic materials from the Viking Age. The most evocative among them is probably the Oseberg textile, which represents an elaborate (funeral?) procession.[41] Among the depicted characters are females carrying swords and holding spears. The anthropomorphic figure clad in animal skin (possibly boar skin) and holding a shield might also be female, as suggested by the trailing costume.[42] The same textile also shows a standing figure with what looks like a horned helmet;[43] in each hand the figure is holding two stick-shaped items, perhaps staffs or short spears. Judging by the long, trailing garment, this figure also could be viewed as a woman. If this interpretation is proved true, then it might call into question the general assumption that all 'horned figures' (both those made as stand-alone metal figurines and those that form part of two-dimensional scenes) represent men. Perhaps some of them actually depict (armed) females? This line of thought will not be pursued here, but it is certainly worthy of discussion.

***

This chapter has investigated various images of human and supernatural women wielding weapons and has shown that the common assumption that they all represent the *valkyrjur* must be re-evaluated. In view of the evidence examined herewith, it is possible that some of the artefacts depict other supernatural beings (for example, the goddess Freyja), heroes (Sigurðr and Brynhild/Sigrdrífa) or perhaps even real women of the Viking Age. This interdisciplinary endeavour has shown that, similarly to funerary evidence, Viking Age iconography cannot be studied in isolation – it is critically important to be aware of the complete find corpus and to draw on other comparative sources. We should also be careful to not cling on to just one reading of the archaeological material established by scholarly tradition – very much like today, past people may have viewed the same things differently.

Notes

1. On Viking Age miniature objects, see, for example, Schetelig 1911; Arrhenius 1961; Fuglesang 1989; Zeiten 1997; Price 2002; Gräslund 2005; 2007; Jensen 2010; Helmbrecht 2011; Gardeła 2014a; 2020a; in press-a; in press-c; Gardeła & Odebäck 2018; Croix *et al.* 2020; Wicker 2020.
2. Jagodziński 2010: 106; Helmbrecht 2011: 68.
3. Nilsson 1992: 7; Petersen 1992b: 41–46; 2005: 77; 2010: 76–78, 136; Jørgensen 2005: 137–138; Pedersen 2009: 296; 2014a: 247–248; Helmbrecht 2011: 69; Feveile 2013: 35, 58; Graham-Campbell 2013: 163; Price 2013a: 116; Williams 2013: 79; Pentz 2018: 18.
4. Price 2002: 337; Vierck 2002: 20, 28; Maixner 2010: 109; Helmbrecht 2011: 68–69; Majchczack 2016: 96–97.
5. Margeson 1997: 12; Price 2002: 337; Helmbrecht 2011: 70–71; Pestell 2013: 243; Carroll *et al.* 2014: 76.
6. Trupinda 2004: 97; Jagodziński 2010: 106; 2015: 93; Helmbrecht 2011: 71; Gardeła 2014a: 78–81.
7. Helmbrecht 2011: 105, 441, 443, 446–447; Graham-Campbell 2013: 163; Carroll *et al.* 2014: 76.
8. The winged spear is a very characteristic type of weapon originating from the Carolingian milieu, but not very common in Viking Age Scandinavia. See, for example, Pedersen 2014a: 91–93.
9. Helmbrecht 2011: 70; Graham-Campbell 2013: 163.
10. Helmbrecht 2011: 70.
11. Gardeła 2014a: 81.
12. Orrling 2008: 28.
13. See, for example, van Hamel 1934.
14. Helmbrecht 2011: 68. Translation by Leszek Gardeła.
15. Petersen 1992a; 1992b.
16. See, for example, Capelle 1968: 89; Elsner 1992: 78; Zeiten 1997; see also comments in Helmbrecht 2011: 68.
17. But see some early attempts by Vierck 2002; Helmbrecht 2011: 68–71; Gardeła 2015a; 2018a; 2019g.
18. Margeson 1997: 17.
19. Price 2002: 337.
20. Graham-Campbell 2013: 163.
21. Carroll *et al.* 2014: 76.
22. See, for example, Margeson 1997: 17; Helmbrecht 2011: 69; Graham-Campbell 2013: 161–163.
23. Although this may not necessarily apply to the finds from Hedeby – see Helmbrecht 2011: 68, who interprets the riders as male due to the lack of a distinctive hairstyle.
24. On *Valhǫll* and *einherjar*, see Ellis 1943: 66. Old Norse sources generally provide very little information about the afterlife of Viking Age women.
25. Ellis 1943: 66, 75; Näsström 1995; Lindow 2001: 118; Orchard 2002: 114; Simek 2006: 87.
26. *Grímnismál* (14). Text and translation after Dronke 2011: 115 with my amendments.
27. *Gylfaginning* (19). Text and translation after Heimir Pálsson & Faulkes 2012: 42–43.

28 Orchard 2002: 114.
29 Lindow 2001: 118; similarly Simek 2006: 87.
30 Lindow 2001: 118.
31 On Freyja see, for example, Lindow 2001: 126–128; Orchard 2002: 119–120; Simek 2006: 90–91.
32 I wish to thank Professor Jörn Staecker who first suggested this interpretation during our meeting at the Viking World Conference in Nottingham in 2016.
33 *Vǫlsunga saga* (27). Text after Guðni Jónsson 1950: 175–176. Translation after Byock 1990: 80 with my amendments.
34 *Sigrdrífumál* (introduction). Text after Kuhn & Neckel 1983: 189. Translation after Larrington 2014: 163 with my amendments.
35 Leahy & Paterson 2001: 192; Hall 2007: 107; Helmbrecht 2011: 128; Gardeła 2012c: 147–148.
36 Helmbrecht 2011: 127–128; Williams 2013: 79; Pedersen 2014a: 248.
37 Pedersen 2009: 296; Helmbrecht 2011: 127–128; Varberg 2011: 82; Williams 2013: 79.
38 Henriksen & Petersen 2013; Murphy 2013; Gardeła 2013b: 304; Price 2013b: 165; 2015: 5–7.
39 Helmbrecht 2011: 128.
40 Williams 2013: 79. See also discussion in Helmbrecht 2011: 127–128.
41 Hougen 1940.
42 Hougen 1940: 104.
43 Helmbrecht 2011: 97.

Chapter 7

Women with weapons: a cross-cultural phenomenon

The idea of the armed woman is not at all unique to Viking Age Scandinavia. World history has witnessed numerous women who reached for weapons as a result of various circumstances, sometimes of their own volition and sometimes because they were left without a choice. While it is highly probable that *some* of the surviving written accounts that speak vividly about Amazons or other fierce female heroines from Antiquity and the Middle Ages merely reflect the imagination of early historians and compilers, it is beyond a shadow of a doubt that female warriors were real and existed not only on parchment.

The topic of women warriors in history is too broad to embrace and comprehend in its totality, but by bringing together selected case studies from different time periods and cultural milieus, it is nonetheless possible to trace some recurring patterns. The purpose of this chapter is therefore to draw attention to these sometimes overlooked histories of armed women and to the ongoing international research pertaining to them. We will begin with a discussion of women warriors in prehistory, drawing mostly on the work of scholars dealing with the archaeology of the Eurasian steppes. After an overview of the lifeways and worldviews of several different nomadic tribes, among whom it was not uncommon to find weapon-wielding women, further sections of this chapter will be devoted to armed women in sixteenth- to eighteenth-century Netherlands, followed by discussions on the female warrior troops of Dahomey and the manifold roles of women in the most terrifying conflicts of the modern era – the First and Second World Wars.

Warrior women in prehistoric times

In 2000, Jeannine Davis-Kimball published a stimulating book entitled *Warrior Women: An Archaeologist's Search for History's Hidden Heroines*, a study which describes its author's journey to remote parts of Kazakhstan in a quest to find the truth behind the stories of female warriors.[1] Combining archaeology, iconography, textual sources, first-hand ethnographic experiences and memoirs, Davis-Kimball's book is remarkably broad in scope and explores not only the involvement of women in warfare but also the sophisticated lifeways and shamanic worldviews of Eurasian nomads, as well as providing thought-provoking cross-cultural excursions into the deeds of female heroines beyond the steppes and in different parts of Iron Age Europe.

Substantial attention in *Warrior Women* is afforded to opulent Early Sarmatian graves discovered at Pokrovka in Kazakhstan,[2] a site excavated by Davis-Kimball herself. The cemetery at Pokrovka comprised mid-sized mounds (so-called *kurgans*) built of soil and sod and richly equipped with military equipment (*e.g.* arrowheads) as well as different kinds of utensils and objects of amuletic and religious significance (*e.g.* small altars).[3] The dead were typically buried supine with the top of the head pointing towards the east and the rising sun; this consistently observed custom was dictated by the very specific beliefs of the nomads. Research conducted by Davis-Kimball and her colleagues shows that the impressive funerary architecture at Pokrovka was reused multiple times after the initial interment; old graves served as places of burial for subsequent individuals, but the nomads also used the *kurgans* for different (perhaps non-funerary) celebrations, as evidenced by the presence of animal bones at the edges of some of the mounds.

Archaeological excavations at Pokrovka have led to many groundbreaking discoveries, but perhaps the most remarkable of all is the grave of a teenage Early Sarmatian woman buried with around 40 arrowheads, an iron dagger and oyster shells.[4] This person also had a curious copper alloy arrowhead suspended around her neck in a leather pouch[5] as well as an amulet in the form of a six-inch-long boar's tusk.[6] The characteristic types of grave goods imply that she lived around 300 BC. Davis-Kimball has argued that the woman was a 'warrior-priestess' and that 'her training as a warrior within her tribe had been taken seriously'.[7]

Based on research on other nomadic female graves, it appears that the majority of alleged female warriors died in their teens, leading Davis-Kimball to conclude that 'riding would have been the first skill they mastered'.[8] Ethnographic studies provide further support for this assumption, since among the Mongols and Kazakhs even one-year-old toddlers are seated on horseback (supported by adults) and by the time they are three years old or so, they already become skilled riders.⁹ As Davis-Kimball adds:

> When it came to military instruction among the ancient nomads, boys and girls most likely were trained together by skilled mentors. Girls who demonstrated exceptional ability would have been designated as warriors and slated to receive more extensive instruction, while others would be selected for hearth-woman or priestess roles and concentrate on the skills needed for those vocations. The style of warfare practiced by the ancient steppe nomads was particularly well suited to women.[10]

As a matter of fact, the nomadic style of horseback fighting would have made women, even those who were gracile, as effective and deadly as men; in such remote parts of the world, success in combat relied not only on physical strength but first and foremost on training, dexterity and speed.[11] Projectile weapons, such as the bow, as well as occasionally the spear, were the most important military equipment among these people and they could be used by women without difficulty. We should be cautious, however, in considering every nomad woman buried with a bow and/or arrows as a warrior. While it is highly probable that at least some of them took active part in warfare, the presence of arrowheads could also hold different meanings. Knowing that in nomadic societies men and women tend to share many of the same duties,[12] and that hunting is a crucial part of their subsistence strategies, it is not inconceivable that rather than indicating warriors, arrowheads in some female graves should be seen as reflecting the women's elevated social position and/or their active engagement in hunting. It is also not unlikely that arrowheads, as well as many other goods in Iron Age *kurgans*, were intended to convey particular messages about the mourners (*e.g.* reflect their identities, agendas and/or aspirations) rather than exclusively signaling the status and profession of the dead. As in the case of the finds from the Viking Age, considerable caution is thus advised in approaching this material.

Expanding on some of the themes previously discussed by Davis-Kimball, in 2008 Katheryn M. Linduff and Karen S. Rubinson edited a stimulating volume provocatively entitled *Are All Warriors Male? Gender Roles on the Ancient Eurasian Steppe*.[13] The book contains nine chapters written by archaeologists, historians and cultural anthropologists whose contributions mainly, although not exclusively, concern the nomadic cultures of the eastern steppes. This timely collection explores various examples of female graves with weapons, but – in contrast to some of their predecessors – they approach them in a careful and nuanced way, often acknowledging and addressing the issue of multivalence of funerary assemblages, while at the same time remaining open to the possibility that some of the women may have actually engaged in martial activities.

For instance, Natalia Berseneva's chapter investigates the lives and roles of women and children in Western Siberian Iron Age Sargat culture, a highly hierarchical society of 'settled herders, hunters and pastoral nomads' who lived between the Ural Mountains and the Ural-Siberian forest-steppe zone.[14] The people of the Sargat culture practiced inhumation, and research shows that some 20% of the female graves contained arrowheads and parts of the bow, but never swords and armour.[15] Interestingly, women's graves were occasionally furnished with equestrian equipment (bits, buckles, cheek pieces, harnesses and metal belt plaques), something that has also been encountered in several of the Viking Age female graves discussed in Chapters 4 and 5. Berseneva's analyses of the funerary remains have led her to the conclusion that:

> It is difficult to comment on the existence of 'women-warriors' even though females were quite often buried with weapons, since the overwhelming majority of these artefacts are arrowheads, sometimes only one or two. One may suggest more confidently that these women belonged to warrior (elite) clans, and arrowheads may well have been a marker (or sign) of this.[16]

In a sense, therefore, Berseneva's views on the meaning of weapons in women's graves in Sargat culture can be seen to correspond with the conclusions arising from the analysis of Viking Age female graves with arrowheads discussed earlier in this book – the bottom line is that they do not necessarily have to indicate a warrior status of the deceased.

Another chapter in *Are All Warriors Male?*, written by Karen S. Rubinson, explores aspects of gender and identity in the cemetery at Tillya Tepe in Northern Afghanistan near the town of Shibargan.[17] The site belonged to a group of people considered (not necessarily correctly) by some modern scholars as 'proto-Kushans'[18] who lived around the middle of the first century AD.[19] All of the graves excavated at Tillya Tepe were remarkably rich, with the bodies of the deceased covered with golden ornaments, but one of them caused particular amazement: this was a grave of a woman accompanied by a battle axe, two Siberian-style daggers, two anklets and two Chinese mirrors.[20] Unsurprisingly, shortly after the discovery, this unique individual was hailed a 'woman warrior' or a 'warrior priestess', mainly on account of the military equipment she was interred with.[21] In her thought-provoking re-assessment of this find, Rubinson challenges these ideas by arguing that this person could have had multiple identities and that the funerary assemblage should not be read in a simplistic and straightforward way. In her view, the objects buried with the dead may have reflected 'idealised roles' the mourners wanted to emphasise during the funeral or, in the particular case of the Tillya Tepe population, they may have mirrored the attitudes of a complex society during a time of historical transition. Cultural transformation within the society could have spurred the people orchestrating the funerals to devise innovative ways to 'express change' through special and sometimes unconventional types of objects.[22] Rubinson concludes her discussion on the identity of the woman from Tillya Tepe in these words:

> It is possible that the weapons mark her as a warrior, since the military role is certainly a possibility within the sociohistorical steppe context, but perhaps these weapons designate her position as a senior female, and perhaps, as with the mirrors, they represent identity, or some mixture of explanations.[23]

Of crucial importance to the debate on women warriors is also the aforementioned ground-breaking study by Adrianne Mayor entitled *The Amazons: Lives and Legends of Warrior Women Across the Ancient World* released in 2014.[24] Its author, a leading American historian, has brought together a vast array of sources including texts, archaeology and iconography to paint a compelling picture of women who were actively engaged in ancient warfare. Mayor's monograph has deservedly received international acclaim and is now regarded as one of the most significant contributions not only to the studies of warrior women *per se* but also to the much wider field of research on gender in the past.

Recently, also Pamela D. Toler published an engaging monograph entitled *Women Warriors: An Unexpected History*, a study which provides a compelling overview of different female warriors across time and space, covering a vast territory spanning from China, through the European continent and all the way to America.[25] Aimed at a popular rather than strictly academic audience, the book nonetheless includes a fair amount of useful footnotes and references as well as a section dedicated to the roles of women in the Viking world including stimulating remarks on the discussions surrounding the famous grave Bj. 581 from Birka.[26]

One somewhat unexpected but noteworthy example of how warrior women have been conceptualised in human history is linked with Aztec ritual practices surrounding birth. According to Barbara Tedlock, author of a compelling study entitled *The Woman in the Shaman's Body*, 'a pregnant woman facing childbirth was described as a warrior going to fight'.[27] As Tedlock notes, when contractions began, the midwife would give the woman in labour a toy shield, weapons and weaving battens and she would encourage her by uttering war cries.[28] The verses of the following Aztec song vividly illustrate the idea of a woman in labour as a female warrior:

> My daughter, the battle is yours
> What are we to do for you? Here are your mothers.
> Yours alone is the task.
> Take up the buckler, daughter, my little one.
> You are a woman warrior, be like one!
> This means put forth all your strength.
> Emulate the warrior woman, the valiant woman.[29]

Although chronologically and culturally removed from the main body of the archaeological and textual material discussed in the present study, the use of small weapons in childbirth is particularly interesting in the context of miniature militaria found in female graves in Viking Age Scandinavia (see Chapters 4 and 5). It is not unlikely – although impossible to prove – that at least some of these items were conceptually linked with another kind of battle, a battle that took place at home and within the woman's body rather than on the typical battlefield.

Female cross-dressers in early modern Europe

In 1989, two Dutch authors, Rudolf M. Dekker and Lotte C. van de Pol, released a ground-breaking and thought-provoking study on the *Tradition of Female Transvestism in Early Modern Europe*, revealing the experiences of real women who dressed up and lived as men. The geographical scope of their book is centred on the Netherlands in the period spanning the late sixteenth to eighteenth centuries, during which time the Dutch Republic was one of Europe's leading sea powers. At that point in history many people sought their fortune by engaging in long-distance trade, especially with India,[30] and the Dutch Republic had 'the largest standing army, proportionate to the number of inhabitants, in Europe'.[31] The prospect of serving in the military on land or sea was therefore an attractive and profitable career for men, but women had much fewer options, especially if they stemmed from poor families. In the words of Dekker and van de Pol:

> For a great many of our women, the combination of pure necessity and the knowledge that other women had been successful as cross-dressers before, must have been the primary reason – or at least the inducement – to decide to dress in men's clothing and enter service as a soldier or sailor. The suggestion to pursue this particular means of escape from hunger and poverty also came frequently from others.[32]

Dekker's and van de Pol's study draws on 93 case studies of women who had their professions as men. Remarkably, as many as 83 of them were working as soldiers or sailors who served with the East or West India Company.[33] The majority of the data presented in their book is drawn from court trial records, which attests to its authenticity. Thorough investigation of the lives of cross-dressing women in the Netherlands has led Dekker and van de Pol to some interesting conclusions regarding the reasons why some women decided to become men; these conclusions are worth summarising here, due to their remarkable relevance to our main debate on armed women in the Viking world.

As Dekker and van de Pol demonstrate, for a woman to don men's clothing and to follow a typically male profession was 'a very radical decision'.[34] In the case of the Dutch Republic, we are fortunate to have records from courts of law as well as occasional autobiographical accounts that precisely explain why women made such choices. According to Dekker and van de Pol, from this body of evidence, four general motives arise: 1. romantic, 2. patriotic, 3. economic and 4. criminal,[35] but it is evident that for many women the decision to become men resulted from a mixture of these motives and other circumstances.

As regards romantic motives, Dekker and van de Pol have investigated cases of women who attempted to join the crews of ships sailing to India because their husbands and lovers were among the seamen.[36] In order to be able to take part in the journey, however, the women obviously had to dress up in men's clothing. Although some of them succeeded in transforming themselves and reaching their goal, others, like a certain Maeyken Blomme, were discovered and taken from the ship. Apparently, parting from her husband, who had stayed onboard, was a traumatic experience for Blomme – the woman lost her sanity and ended up in prison in Middelburg.

In the context of our previous discussion on female warriors and sailors in Scandinavia (see Chapter 3), it is interesting to note that romantic motives led some Dutch women not only to dress up as men but also to change other aspects of their appearance so as to look even more masculine. For instance, in 1839, in order to be able to join her lover in the military, a certain Jaantje Martens not only put on men's clothing but also cut off her hair.[37] Back in the day this kind of transformation would have required much more courage than today, and in some instances it might have even been a profoundly traumatic experience.

It is worthy of note that in the course of their research Dekker and van de Pol have also discovered that not only love but also hatred motivated some women to temporarily 'become men'.[38] Surviving records show that this occasionally happened when women wanted to leave their husbands and take up work in another town or return to their homelands.

Love of one's own country could also be the reason why some women decided to take on a male role and don men's clothing. Historical accounts mention Dutch women who actively engaged in armed conflicts including the Dutch Revolt against Spain and the First Dutch–English War. As Dekker and van de Pol argue:

> War, or the threat of war, was of course a favourable opportunity for, a suitable inducement to, or a last push toward, the transformation into a man. The social and economic dislocation, the streams of refugees, and, of course, the great demand for sailors and soldiers often reinforced the decision to resort to cross-dressing. These women could certainly have been caught up in the excitement of war, and in their patriotism itself have seen a justification for breaking through the barrier of sex.[39]

We have seen in Chapter 3 that Norse and other medieval women also took up arms in the face of danger, not necessarily because they wanted to but because they had to. Similar events also occurred during the course of the First and Second World Wars and we shall discuss the activities of women in these armed conflicts in more detail further below.

As mentioned earlier, in the Netherlands the perspective of raising one's own economic status was also one of the motivations for women to don men's clothing and to become a soldier or sailor. Poverty was a serious issue for many women of the seventeenth and eighteenth centuries, and the possibilities to improve one's financial situation were especially limited if one stemmed from a poor family. Moreover, women who performed exactly the same jobs as men often received lower wages.[40] Therefore, in acts of desperation, some women had no other choice but to resort to prostitution, a profession which carried a considerable stigma. In fact, according to Dekker and van de Pol 'prostitution was as marginal as begging and vagrancy, and was defined and persecuted as a crime in the Dutch Republic'.[41]

Because in the seventeenth and eighteenth centuries the Dutch maintained strong trade links with the Indies, sailors returning home were able to sell goods they had acquired during their journeys; this prospect may have been tempting for women as well and may have spurred some of them to try and become seamen. It is not difficult to imagine that similar reasons might have inspired some Viking Age women to join overseas expeditions, for example to Rus territories which abounded in exotic goods unavailable in their Scandinavian homelands.[42] For the Dutch women, on the other hand, the chance to join the crew of a long-distance ship opened up exciting prospects to find a better life in the East: it was commonly believed that this part of the world was literally 'a paradise for European women' and a place where they could easily find wealthy partners. Seventeenth-century records mention women who succeeded in achieving this goal and who apparently lived ostentatiously luxurious lifestyles in the Indies.[43]

In the Dutch Republic female cross-dressing was also a means to facilitate certain types of crime. In the course of their research Dekker and van de Pol have found cases of eighteenth-century women who became members of bands of thieves and who, dressed as men, eagerly and actively participated in raids.[44] Some of these women were extremely violent and brutally tortured their victims. Aside from women who made raiding their main profession, there are also accounts describing women who only temporarily donned men's clothing either to evade the law (*e.g.* after having committed a murder) or to conduct acts of crime. Again, all this evidence is not very far removed from some of the Old Norse texts we have discussed in Chapter 3 concerning female warriors.

Surviving records demonstrate that in the Dutch Republic female cross-dressing was generally considered a criminal offence. The price women had to pay was very high and the punishment for contravening social norms could involve whipping, imprisonment and, in the most severe cases, banishment or death sentence, for instance by strangulation.[45] However, as the studies of Dekker and van de Pol show explicitly, this did not discourage female individuals from pursuing this alternative lifestyle and effectively 'becoming men'.

Around the time when Dutch women donned male clothing to become soldiers and sailors, similar events also occurred in Eastern Europe. One of the most interesting cases is that of Nadezhda Durova (1783–1866), daughter of a hussar captain who from her earliest childhood had a thirst for adventure and a desire to follow the path of a soldier.[46] In her youth, having cut off her hair and dressed in male clothing (a behaviour similar to that of her counterparts from Old Norse literature), Durova joined a regiment of Cossacks and soon began a career in the Russian army. Her deeds on the battlefield are variously and sometimes contradictorily evaluated in the surviving records (including her own autobiography), but she was actually the first woman to be awarded the Cross of St George – a prestigious reward for undaunted courage.[47] Over the course of her 10-year military career, Durova (also known under male names like Alexander Durov, Alexander Sokolov and Alexander Andreevich Alexandrov) fought with the Russian army in the Prussian campaign of 1813 and she also took part in military operations in the area of today's Poland and on Russia's western border.[48] Interestingly, after she ended her career in the army and – with Alexander Pushkin's encouragement – became a successful writer, she apparently still continued to wear male clothing.[49]

The Amazons of Dahomey

In discussing the lives and deeds of female warriors across space and time, it is crucial to devote attention to the captivating history of eighteenth- and nineteenth-century women from the kingdom of Dahomey in Western Africa (the area of today's Benin). Known as *gbeto*, *abosi* or *minos* in their native language and dubbed 'Amazons of Black Sparta' by Stanley B. Alpern (author of the most important monograph concerning their lives), these armed women were initially elephant hunters who supplied ivory to the king of Dahomey.[50] Later on they served as palace guards to eventually develop into a fully-fledged military troop (Figs 7.1–7.2).

Stories of the Dahomey Amazons survive in oral traditions and eye-witness accounts written down predominantly by Western Europeans who either lived permanently or temporarily stayed in West Africa in the eighteenth and nineteenth centuries.[51] The abundance of sources pertaining to these women confirm Alpern's claim that they are the 'only thoroughly documented amazons in world history'.[52] In addition to these various texts, however, there is also a substantial body of pictorial data in the form of drawings and etchings, portraying different aspects of the life of the Dahomey women (Fig. 7.3). From these images (some of which, admittedly, may have been stylised and exaggerated to instil a sense of curiosity) we can learn more about their physique, clothing and military equipment.

In looking at the above-mentioned imagery and in reading surviving accounts, it is striking that some women warriors are portrayed in very elaborate or even flamboyant costumes, which probably were not very comfortable during combat. For instance, British entomologist J. Alfred Skertchly, who witnessed them during his eight-month stay in Dahomey, watched the women parading in front of the king 'dressed in dull-brown petticoats, and indigo-dyed tunics, with black sashes, profusely ornamented with magic relics'.[53] The women carried muskets and wore their hair loose 'save a circular patch on the top of the poll, where it was combed out like a brush'.[54] The different 'regiments' of Amazons also employed special marks of distinction worn on cotton skullcaps and resembling animals like the crocodile, shark and tortoise as well as symbols such as a cross or crown. In some cases, however, the costumes of Dahomey Amazons were designed in such a way as to conceal the fact that their wearers were women – for instance, the breasts were flattened and the headgear had side flaps to cover the holes in the women's earlobes. This technique of concealment apparently worked, since in the battle of Abeokuta in 1851 their opponents had no idea they were fighting against female warriors until they captured one of them (something that echoes certain episodes from Old Norse literature involving warrior women – see Chapter 3).[55]

In some respects the women of Dahomey resemble other female warriors from around the globe, but they also differ from them in significant ways. For instance, in contrast to the nomadic women, they did not ride horses,[56] and weapons like bows, axes[57] and shields were very rarely employed in their military endeavours.[58] A significant difference between these women and those from Old Norse accounts is that they generally did not produce offspring and remained in celibacy.[59] Most importantly, as Alpern observes, although they had their own officers, the fierce female warriors of Dahomey were completely devoted to their king, meaning that they were, in fact, governed by men.[60]

Before becoming members of the troop, the women of Dahomey had to complete rigorous training and learn to use a variety of weapons including traditional ones like machetes and clubs as well as more modern muskets. They also received training in other activities, such as hunting, dancing and playing music. However, as Alpern graphically puts it:

> Their basic purpose in life was to make war. They lusted for battle, rushed into it with blood-curdling cries, reveled in it, and fought with fury and valor, seemingly immune to fear. In victory they were pitiless. They terrified their neighbors. Men regarded them as worthy, implacable adversaries.[61]

Unsurprisingly, the training of Dahomey warrior women had ritualistic undertones and can be considered as a form of

Fig. 7.1. The Mino around 1890. Public domain.

Fig. 7.2. Group photograph of 'Amazons of Dahomey' taken during their stay in Paris. Public domain.

Fig. 7.3. Seh-Dong-Hong-Beh, a leader of the Dahomey warrior women. Public domain.

an initiation rite – surviving records say that some women were sent to the forest for five to nine days and had to devise their own strategies of survival.

In view of the staggering evidence outlined above, one may wonder why Dahomey was the place where such a remarkable female troop emerged. Some specialists think that the explanation lies in the abnormal and 'masculine' physique of local women who were tall and muscular.[62] Another (and perhaps more probable) reason could lie in the fact that Dahomey was particularly involved in warfare and slave trade,[63] activities that together with the kingdom's totalitarian regime could have led to a 'higher male attrition rate'[64] and the development of a militarised society where the female sex of the warriors was not seen as an obstacle.

Surviving accounts demonstrate that the warrior women of Dahomey were involved in various clashes between local rulers and took part in annual wars to capture slaves (the first record of their presence in battle is from 1729),[65] but they are particularly remembered for their fierce participation in armed conflict with the French in the late nineteenth century.

The Franco-Dahomean wars were the result of European encroachment into West Africa, and although the Amazons fought with admirable courage and ruthlessness (surviving accounts mention a woman who tore a man's throat with her teeth),[66] they were doomed to be defeated by Western Europeans who had far more superior firepower, including repeating rifles and gunboats.

In concluding this section it is noteworthy to mention that in Dahomey women who were not actual warriors were occasionally witnessed carrying weapons. This was the case of the favourite wives of the king of Dahomey, whose role during public ceremonies was not only to serve food and drink but also to display the king's weapons (muskets, pistols, sabre, etc.). Although they apparently had no martial role whatsoever, Alpern notes that some early observers may have arrived at the wrong conclusion that they were the king's personal bodyguards.[67]

The custom of carrying and displaying weapons of a ruler by his wives is interesting also in the context of Viking Age Scandinavia. In Chapters 4 and 5 we have discussed the richly decorated tapestry from Oseberg showing women seemingly passively carrying weapons (*e.g.* by holding swords and spears with the point directed towards the ground) and participating in some kind of procession. In light of this comparative evidence from Dahomey, it is thus not completely improbable that – if the scene on the Oseberg tapestry depicts actual events – the women with weapons were not warriors *per se* but someone's loyal companions, wives or even servants. We can never be certain, of course, but this scenario deserves further consideration. In connection with the above, it is also worth pointing out the case of British explorers, who in the 1820s:

> saw royal females carrying spears in two towns northeast of Dahomey. When the king of Kaiama, in the country of Borgu, approached the British visitors on horseback, he was accompanied by six naked girl-wives (or slaves) who danced around his horse singing their husband's (or master's) praises and brandishing their weapons. When they followed the king into the visitors' lodgings, they left their spears outside.[68]

The everyday reality for most women in Dahomey was far less spectacular and glamorous than the life of those who took up arms and joined the army. A typical woman had to engage in cleaning and cooking, she took care of children, tended livestock and collected firewood and plants. Furthermore, women were also involved in all stages of textile production, a particularly complicated and time-consuming activity.[69] Despite a significant chronological and geographical distance from their Norse counterparts in the Viking world, women's lives in Dahomey were therefore not that different. One opportunity for change was to become a warrior – this was a ticket not only to a more interesting and prosperous life, but also a chance to climb up the social ladder. With the change in status also came another kind of transformation: the idea that women who fight effectively *become* men,[70] something that is well illustrated in one of the songs that survives in Dahomey oral tradition:

> We are men, not women...
> Whatever town we attack
> We must conquer
> Or bury ourselves in its ruins.[71]

The adjectives by which the Dahomey Amazons have been described over the years, including 'brave, courageous, valorous, valiant, fearless', etc. show that many of them were not only successful on the war path but that in living the life of warriors these women were in no way lesser than men. In fact, one observer noted that 'the women's army is accounted much more warlike than the men's'.[72]

Women in the First and Second World Wars

Women warriors were active not only on ancient, medieval and early modern battlefields, but also participated in the more advanced and sophisticated type of warfare that developed in the course of the First and Second World Wars. As Pamela D. Toler rightly observes, however, the transformation from woman to man was now much more complicated because 'extensive medical examinations made it difficult for women to avoid disclosure before they enlisted'.[73] Still, this did not deter some women from joining the army and engaging in martial activities. American women, for instance, could legally participate in the First World War in the role of navy yeomen. After some time, however, their opportunities for a career in the military grew and they could perform other tasks as 'radio operators, supervisors for naval shipments, telegraph operators, commissary stewards, fingerprint experts, and camouflage designers'.[74]

The case of a Serbian woman named Milunka Savić (1892–1973) is particularly worth recalling here since she had a remarkably long career as an active soldier and took part in some of the most challenging armed conflicts of the twentieth century (Fig. 7.4).[75] Her bravery in the Second Balkan War at the battle of Bergalnica – in which she fought disguised as a man – earned her a medal. Savić continued her service during the First World War and then she received numerous rewards for her outstanding deeds. In the course of the Second World War the brave Serbian woman ran a hospital for people wounded in combat, an endeavour that led to dire consequences as she was eventually arrested and sent to a concentration camp. When she died in 1973, Savić was buried with full military honours.

When it comes to the presence of women in the military, Russia during the First World War was doubtlessly the world leader. Initially, women were not allowed to fight, but as time went by and when the army suffered shortages, some commanders turned a blind eye to the law.[76] After a series of incidents that significantly weakened the Russian army and its fighting spirit, in May 1917 an official decision was made to create an all-female battalion.[77] According to Pamela D. Toler, at one point in 1917 'roughly four thousand Russian women served in combat'.[78] The battalion, known as the First Women's Battalion of Death, was led by Maria Bochkareva (1889–1920), who stemmed from a poor peasant family from Siberia. Her difficult childhood, an alcoholic father and later a husband who likewise did not shy away from excessive drinking, all must have had a strong influence on the life choices she eventually made.[79] In light of her difficult past, it seems that to Bochkareva war was an opportunity to escape a hopeless existence, and we can see clearly that her story does not differ much from those of her early modern counterparts in the Dutch Republic. Surviving records concerning the Russian army during the First World War demonstrate, however, that not only barely literate women felt the need to serve the Tzar in the trenches and on the open battlefield – among them were also individuals with secondary and higher education as well as members of the social elite.[80] It is evident that these women had various motivations to fight, including love for their country and patriotic obligation.

In the course of the Second World War (1939–1945) women engaged in warfare in many different roles, either

Fig. 7.4. Milunka Savić (1892–1973). Public domain.

directly taking part in armed combat as actual soldiers or partisans or serving as messengers, telephone operators, spies, nurses and doctors to name but a few of the many activities they were involved in.

It appears that the Soviet Union used women in the most extensive manner in the course of the Second World War – according to Pamela D. Toler, as many as 8% of all Soviet combatants were actually female.[81] In the Red Army women worked not only in auxiliary positions, but also effectively used sniper rifles and machine guns, drove tanks and served as anti-aircraft personnel. With 'three regiments of bombers, fighter pilots, navigators and airplane mechanics',[82] Soviet women were certainly a force to reckon with.

In contrast to the Russian army, it appears that German women did not – at least officially – engage in actual combat. Some of them, however, worked behind-the-scenes of the ongoing horror of the battlefields of the Second World War, for example as secretaries in offices responsible for devising military plans,[83] but also as school teachers indoctrinating the youth into the Nazi ideology. In those cases, instead of guns, the actual weapons of these individuals were pens, typewriters and syringes.[84] According to Pamela D. Toler, in Germany 'some 450.000 women joined female auxiliary units' and thus 'they filled 85 percent of the German army's support posts'.[85]

On another side of the spectrum were women who took part in armed conflicts of the Second War with the sole intention to defend themselves, their loved ones and/or their property, as well as women who were driven by purely patriotic concerns. In August 1944, when the Warsaw Uprising broke out, many women took active part in armed combat in the Nazi-occupied city, but they also acted as paramedics, messengers and sentries.[86] It is estimated that there were around 7000 women among the insurgents.[87] Their efforts are remarkably well documented and survive in the form of photographs, original video recordings and published memoirs (Fig. 7.5–7.7).

Anna Jakubowska, also known as 'Paulinka' to her fellow combatants, recalls that despite all kinds of difficulties associated with guerrilla warfare in a Nazi-occupied city, both she and her female companions made efforts to take care of hygiene and stay as clean as possible.[88] Her involvement in the activities of the Home Army (in Polish *Armia Krajowa*) before the Warsaw Uprising necessitated a slight change of her appearance, however, as she had to cut off her long braids. 'Paulinka' also remembers that until the outbreak of the Uprising (on 1 August 1944) women would refrain from wearing trousers as this could have attracted too much attention from the enemy. During the Uprising, however, some of them were given so-called 'trouserskirts' (in Polish *spódnicospodnie*) made of stiff and poor quality material that irritated the skin, but which were actually quite comfortable when moving through difficult terrain.[89] As 'Paulinka' recalls, shortly before the Uprising women were also provided with pure white shirts made of a special kind of material that did not require ironing; only later they found out that the shirts were, in fact, made out of parachutes belonging to the Cichociemni – Polish special operations paratroopers trained in Great Britain who fought in Nazi-occupied Poland during the Second World War. In surviving memoirs from the Warsaw Uprising the women wearing these shirts were called 'angels in white shirts' (in Polish *anioły w białych bluzkach*).[90] An immediate thought that springs to mind in the context of our main discussion on Viking female warriors is that these female insurgents, aiding the wounded and removing the dead from the battlefield, were very much like the Norse *valkyrjur*.

Emerging patterns and conclusions

This chapter has shown that since deep prehistory women have taken active and important part in warfare. In their different roles as warriors fighting in the forefront of the army, as nurses tending the sick and wounded, and as messengers and military secretaries (to name but a few of their many professions and activities) they did not in any significant way differ from their male counterparts and were capable of the same acts of courage. As we have seen, regardless of the fact that in some societies female participation in warfare was forbidden by law, women found ways to overcome these restrictions; in order to become soldiers they would resort to changing their names, cross-dressing or wearing costumes that would conceal their biological sex, as well as (fairly mild) bodily modifications usually involving the cutting of hair. Surviving records from the Dutch Republic also inform us that in order to avoid disclosure and to be able to successfully conceal their identity, some women, especially those serving in the navy, even used special 'urination aids', which allowed them to urinate while standing upright.[91]

It appears that as time went by European countries became more liberal in allowing women to join the military, first in auxiliary roles and later on as active combatants. The struggle for gender equality still continues to this day, however, and women soldiers tend to face ostracism or various forms of verbal or physical abuse from other fellow combatants and their high commanders.

In concluding this chapter it is worthy of note that female warriors of the modern era can also be found in non-military contexts, for example in boxing rings and in Mixed Martial Arts (MMA) arenas.[92] Their motivations to take up this type of lifestyle are extremely varied – some women engage in these activities purely for sport, others are driven by economic reasons and others yet feel the need to prove something to themselves or their families, friends, colleagues and the wider public. Through all the different case studies surveyed in this chapter, we can clearly see that biological sex is not at all a barrier to perform well on the ancient, medieval or modern battlefield. The only barriers

Fig. 7.5. Female paramedics at Moniuszki Street during the Warsaw Uprising in 1944. Public domain.

Fig. 7.6. Tunnel guides near Malczewskiego Street during the Warsaw Uprising in 1944. Public domain.

Fig. 7.7. Participants of the Warsaw Uprising on a tank near Okopowa Street. Public domain.

that exist are in the human mind and in the form of social conventions. The histories of warrior women presented here have shown that all those barriers can be overcome regardless of biological sex.

Notes

1. Davis-Kimball 2002. Prior to the release of her monograph, Davis-Kimball published a series of articles concerning women warriors in the Eurasian steppes. See, for example, Davis-Kimball 1997a; 1997b; 1997–1998; 2001.
2. Davis-Kimball (1998: 142–143) has argued that 15% of female graves at Pokrovka were furnished with weapons. On Scythian, Sauromatian and Sarmatian burial customs, see also Petrenko 1995; Petrenko *et al.* 2004; Berseneva 2008: 132. According to Smirnov (1989: 169; cited in Berseneva 2008: 139), as many as 20% of female graves contain arrowheads and occasionally other weapons like daggers, spearheads and swords. Bunyatyan (1985: 91–92; cited in Berseneva 2008: 139), on the other hand, asserts that 50% of Scythian female graves included military equipment, but because his study relies on traditional artefact-based sexing methods this estimation is probably too high and should be approached with caution.
3. Davis-Kimball 2002: 24.
4. As Davis-Kimball (2002: 59) observes, in funerary contexts fossilised oyster shells (which would have made good containers) are often found together with bronze mirrors, suggesting that they may have served as religious paraphernalia of priestesses. For alternative views on the role of mirrors in burial contexts, see Rubinson 2008: 60.
5. Davis-Kimball 2002: 56–57.
6. Davis-Kimball 2002: 58.
7. Davis-Kimball 2002: 58.
8. Davis-Kimball 2002: 61.
9. Davis-Kimball 2002: 61.
10. Davis-Kimball 2002: 62.
11. Davis-Kimball 2002: 62.
12. Davis-Kimball 2002: 36–39. On the position of women in steppe societies in the late second and early first centuries BC in today's China, see also Shelach 2008. Shelach notes that weapons were predominantly buried in male graves, with only occasional instances where they accompanied women. He concludes that 'what they [*i.e.* the weapons] symbolize, probably warrior identity, was not an attribute strictly governed by biological association – many males were buried without them as well – but was socially gendered, so that a few females could also attain this masculine identity' (Shelach 2008: 105).
13. Linduff & Rubinson 2008.
14. Berseneva 2008: 132–133, 141.
15. Berseneva 2008: 141–142, 149.
16. Berseneva 2008: 150.
17. Rubinson 2008. On Tillya Tepe, see also Davis-Kimball 2000.
18. Rubinson 2008: 51.
19. Rubinson 2008: 55.
20. Rubinson 2008: 56.
21. Rubinson 2008: 51.
22. Rubinson 2008: 54–55.
23. Rubinson 2008: 61.
24. Mayor 2014.

25 Toler 2019.
26 Toler 2019: 200–204.
27 Tedlock 2005: 257.
28 Tedlock 2005: 257.
29 Tedlock 2005: 258.
30 Dekker & van de Pol 1989: 9.
31 Dekker & van de Pol 1989: 32.
32 Dekker & van de Pol 1989: 32.
33 Dekker & van de Pol 1989: 9.
34 Dekker & van de Pol 1989: 25.
35 Dekker & van de Pol 1989: 25–39.
36 Dekker & van de Pol 1989: 28.
37 Dekker & van de Pol 1989: 29.
38 Dekker & van de Pol 1989: 29–30.
39 Dekker & van de Pol 1989: 31.
40 Dekker & van de Pol 1989: 33.
41 Dekker & van de Pol 1989: 32.
42 On female traders in Rus, see Stalsberg 1991; 2001.
43 Dekker & van de Pol 1989: 34.
44 Dekker & van de Pol 1989: 35.
45 Dekker & van de Pol 1989: 36–37.
46 Durova 1988; Toler 2019: 44–51.
47 Toler 2019: 49.
48 Toler 2019: 50.
49 Toler 2019: 173.
50 Alpern 2011: 20. Much ink has been spilled on the lives of the Dahomey Amazons since the first release of Alpern's monograph, and their deeds feature prominently in the work of various international scholars who deal with the phenomenon of armed women – see, for example, Tedlock 2005: 260–261; Toler 2019: 184–190; Bochnak 2020.
51 Alpern 2011: 12.
52 Alpern 2011: 11.
53 J. Alfred Skertchly cited in Alpern 2011: 20.
54 J. Alfred Skertchly cited in Alpern 2011: 20.
55 Alpern 2011: 54.
56 Alpern 2011: 11.
57 Although axes may not have been the most deadly weapons of the Dahomey Amazons, there are records suggesting that they were used by some of the Dahomey 'war-chiefs'. Interestingly, some axes were apparently decorated with skulls. For further details, see Alpern 2011: 67.
58 Alpern 2011: 70.
59 Alpern 2011: 11. As Alpern (2011: 40) notes: 'Some amazons [in Dahomey] were daughters of amazons, which proves that not all soldieresses were virgins, as is sometimes claimed … But as sacrosanct wives of a divine king, the amazons were sworn to celibacy under pain of death'.
60 Alpern 2011: 12.
61 Alpern 2011: 11.
62 Alpern 2011: 36
63 Alpern 2011: 37.
64 Alpern 2011: 37.
65 Toler 2019: 187.
66 Alpern 2011: 194.
67 Alpern 2011: 26–27.
68 Alpern 2011: 27.
69 Alpern 2011: 48.
70 Toler 2019: 184.
71 Alpern 2011: 117.
72 Alpern 2011: 162.
73 Toler 2019: 173.
74 Toler 2019: 176.
75 Toler 2019: 169–170.
76 Toler 2019: 190.
77 Toler 2019: 192.
78 Toler 2019: 177.
79 Toler 2019: 192.
80 Toler 2019: 193.
81 Toler 2019: 197.
82 Toler 2019: 198.
83 Lower 2015: 119, 171.
84 Lower 2015: 108.
85 Toler 2019: 198.
86 On the roles of women in the Warsaw Uprising, see Bukalska 2013; Sulej 2014; Cubała 2019.
87 Bukalska 2013.
88 Sulej 2014: 186.
89 Sulej 2014: 183.
90 Sulej 2014: 185.
91 Dekker & van de Pol 1989. On female urination aids, see also Toler 2019: 174.
92 Chutnik 2017.

Chapter 8

Amazons of the North? Women and weapons in the Viking world

The wooden chamber is now complete and the mourners slowly gather at the graveside. The wind blows their hair as they stand thoughtful and focused. Some weep, others are holding back their tears, and some show no emotion at all. There is tension in the air, and the neighing and groaning of the two horses, a mare and a stallion, make some people tremble. The mourners know that more lives will be taken today in accordance with the old custom and that the black soil of Birka will once again be reddened with blood. Now, they place precious goods inside the chamber: weapons, riding gear, vessels and exotic garments. Powerful words are being uttered, recalling memories of times long since past. As soon as the chamber is properly sealed, the construction of the mound commences. Eventually, a large stone is erected to mark the grave's location – this silent and cold guardian will stand undisturbed for a thousand years until someone decides to reveal the secrets of the grave's female occupant.

A bone needle passes swiftly through the thick cloth and a lavish procession of humans and animals begins to appear. The participants are variously dressed but many of them carry weapons. Their hair is long and tied into a knot.

Red hot metal hisses as it fills the intricate designs carved in clay. Small sparks fall onto the ground. When the bronze eventually cools down, the craftsworker cracks the mould and reveals his new creation. The obverse portrays an armed and long-haired rider facing a standing figure with a horn and shield.

A helmeted sorceress wades into an Icelandic fjord with an axe in her hand. As part of her prophetic ritual, she strikes the surface with her weapon and the water turns red. The woman looks into the future and knows there will be no peace.

These four images echo a selection of funerary, iconographic and textual sources that have been thoroughly examined in the preceding chapters of this book. The first three are based on actual archaeological material originating from ninth- and tenth-century Scandinavia. The fourth refers to a unique account preserved in *Ljósvetninga saga*, a text put to parchment several centuries after the events it claims to describe. Comprehensive analysis of these and other sources has shown unequivocally that the associations between women and weapons in the Viking Age took a plethora of forms. All these sources can be variously interpreted, and the conclusions will vary depending on the methodological and theoretical stance we choose to adopt. The present study has aimed for an interdisciplinary approach, critically assessing a broad range of archaeological finds, written accounts, folklore and comparative evidence from past and present times. Although much has already been said here about the possible meanings of weapons in female hands, many readers would probably want to know the answer to the burning question of whether 'Norse Amazons' were merely imaginary creations of medieval authors or actually existed in the Viking Age. This chapter will thus seek to bring all the different strands of source material together in an attempt to weave some plausible answers.

Women and weapons in Viking archaeology

Careful analysis of mortuary practices in Scandinavia and the wider Viking world has revealed that in the period spanning the ninth to the late tenth centuries less than 1% of all known female graves contained weapons. Notwithstanding the fact that in Scandinavian Viking archaeology the sex and gender of the deceased is typically estimated on the basis of grave goods alone, it is doubtful that this ratio would rise substantially if the analyses had been aided by more sophisticated osteological and genetic studies. Archaeological research in other areas of Europe – where bone preservation is usually decent and allows all kinds of analyses to be made – demonstrates unequivocally that in early medieval funerary contexts weapons are almost exclusively associated with the (biologically) male part of the society. It thus feels justified to surmise that also in the North biological women were buried with weapons far less frequently than biological men, and that the 'female weapon burial' was a rarely practiced funerary custom.

As demonstrated in Chapter 4, in mainland Sweden only four possibly female graves were furnished with weapons. They include grave Bj. 581 (where the female biological sex of the deceased has been confirmed by genomics), a grave found in mound A24 at Lake Dalstorp and graves 4 and 22 from Nennesmo. In the case of the finds from Lake Dalstorp and Nennesmo, the female sex determination is uncertain and relies solely on the accompanying goods.

On Öland only one weapon grave belonged to a woman. Found at Klinta, this grave was created as a result of an elaborate funeral involving the cremation of two individuals of opposite biological sex on a boat or ship. When the fire died, their remains were separated and buried in different locations within the same cemetery. Intriguingly, alongside a number of paraphernalia probably used in the practice of magic, the woman's grave contained an axehead.

In Norway, the occupants of two weapon graves from Nordre Kjølen and Aunvollen have been osteologically sexed as female, but since the analyses were conducted many years ago, their results cannot be taken for granted; modern genetic investigations are necessary to confirm or dismiss the original sex estimation. Aside from Nordre Kjølen and Aunvoll, three possibly female inhumation graves from Løve, Mårem and Sanddal contained axeheads. Although the osteological remains were extremely poorly preserved, the layout of these graves as well as the goods they held (*e.g.* jewellery, spinning and weaving tools) strongly suggest that the deceased were women. Axeheads and arrowheads are also known from several cremation graves from Kaupang (*e.g.* Ka. 3, Ka. 10 and Ka. 16), which likely held the remains of women as suggested by the accompanying grave goods. It is also possible that the individual buried at Terum was female, although this must remain in the sphere of speculation due to the extremely poor condition of the bone material. Interestingly, three graves from Gausel, Hilde and Kvåle, convincingly interpreted as belonging to Norse ritual specialists, contained shield bosses.

In Denmark, two certain and two possible female graves were furnished with weapons or objects with martial connotations. The double inhumation grave from Gerdrup, containing the skeletal remains of mother and son contained a spearhead placed by the woman's side. Grave A505 from Trekroner-Grydehøj was furnished with a shafted copper alloy object resembling an arrowhead or small spearhead. In grave BB from Bogøvej, possibly belonging to a woman (as suggested by an osteological analysis), lay an axehead most likely originating from Slavic or Baltic territories. Also the remarkable Oens grave, which held a probable female individual buried on the body of a wagon, contained an axehead.

It is beyond doubt that the swords, spears and shields buried in the graves discussed in the present study *were* weapons and that they could be effectively used in combat. The purpose of axes or axeheads is more difficult to gauge, since most of them have ambiguous morpho-metric features: they usually represent Jan Petersen's types D, G, H and K, which means that they were multifunctional objects which might have been used as tools and/or as weapons. Also, arrowheads found in several presumably female graves could have had various applications – for instance as hunting implements or military equipment. It is not unlikely that in some cases (especially in cremation graves), arrowheads should not be seen as grave goods *per se*, but as weapons by means of which the buried person had been killed.

Although the evidence for burials of biological females with full-size weapons is relatively scarce in the Viking world, it is noteworthy that a substantial number of possibly female graves include militaria in miniature form. Shields are the most popular category of miniature weapons accompanying women in their graves, but occasionally small swords, axes and spears are also found in the burial record. These tiny items, often intricately decorated and made from expensive materials (silver, copper alloy), can be variously perceived, but in light of their specific form and contexts of their discovery, it feels justified to consider them as amulets and/or indicators of the special status and role the deceased person held in their society. Extant sources certainly do not allow us to view these miniatures as 'material markers' of warrior women.

Overall, apart from the exceptional grave Bj. 581 from Birka, we can see that there are no solid grounds to suggest that the aforementioned individuals buried with martial equipment had lived their lives as active warriors. While it is not unlikely that some of them had occasionally used weapons, before proposing any far-reaching conclusions we should first seriously consider the following facts:

- Apart from Bj. 581 and Gerdrup, *all* other graves from Viking Age Scandinavia discussed above have been labelled as belonging to women *only* on the basis of osteological investigations and/or the goods that accompanied them. Therefore, in the absence of genetic analyses, the biological sex of the deceased remains uncertain.
- Surviving skeletal material from Viking Age 'female weapon graves' (including Bj. 581) does not display any traces of trauma and there is no indication that the deceased had been actively involved in combat or any other activities related to the martial sphere (*e.g.* horseback riding, rowing, archery, etc.).
- A number of 'female weapon graves' contain items with amuletic or ritualistic connotations, for instance different kinds of metal pendants, curated or exotic beads and other imported goods (*e.g.* Klinta, Løve, Mårem). Several graves also include iron staffs (Gausel, Hilde, Klinta, Kvåle) – objects that were most likely used in connection with the practice of *seiðr* magic. It is therefore probable that the different militaria in these very specific burial contexts represent elements of the sorcerer's toolkit rather

than signalling a warrior identity of the deceased.
- In several cases, the position of weapons in female graves diverged from the commonly practiced mortuary customs. The swords from Aunvollen, Birka and Nordre Kjølen were all positioned on the left-hand side of the body, while the general norm in the Viking Age was to bury swords on the right. Moreover, the sword from Nordre Kjølen was inverted, bearing witness to a very unusual custom only known from several burial sites in Norway (*e.g.* Gulli, Tønsberg) and a few localities elsewhere in Europe. The spearhead buried with the Gerdrup woman was also inverted and pointed towards the foot-end of the grave – this, again, is very rarely seen in Viking Age funerary contexts. The point of the enigmatic copper alloy item from Trekroner-Grydehøj was likewise positioned towards the foot-end. All these cases imply that the unconventional placement of weapons alongside female bodies was intended to convey special messages. Their meaning was probably different than the meaning associated with weapons in other and more normative burial contexts – the mourners' intention might have been to highlight the deceased person's social role and status (real, imagined or deliberately constructed during the funeral), for instance as Clover's 'functional son', and/or to serve as a reminder of their past achievements. Alternatively, instead of relating directly to the deceased, the swords could potentially communicate something very particular about the people participating in the funeral. Each case is doubtlessly special and thus each might, in fact, be loaded with different symbolism.

Although Viking Age funerary archaeology provides scarce evidence for the actual existence of female warriors, a substantial and diverse group of small portable items with rich iconographic details is proof that the *idea* of the warrior woman indeed existed in the minds of ninth- and tenth-century Scandinavians. These small two-dimensional anthropomorphic figurines carry shields, swords and spears (objects conventionally associated with men), but their long hair and trailing garments – strikingly resembling the characteristic features of presumably female images on runestones and on the famous Oseberg tapestry – strongly suggest that they are, in fact, depictions of human and/or supernatural women. The corpus of these curious finds (which is likely to expand as a result of ongoing metal detecting endeavours in Scandinavia) currently encompasses over 60 examples from Denmark, England, Germany and Poland, attesting to the wide spread of the idea of the armed woman both in the Norse homelands and the Viking diaspora.

Since the 1990s, armed female figures have been typically viewed as representations of the mythical *valkyrjur*. New analyses of these items' iconography, wider contexts and geographical distribution have cast a shadow of doubt on these views, indicating that the figurines are not homogenous in terms of their overall appearance and that they can be variously interpreted, for instance as portrayals of prominent characters from Old Norse myths, heroic poetry and legendary sagas (*e.g.* Freyja, Sigurðr and Brynhildr/Sigrdrífa). It is particularly noteworthy that some of the figurines carry weapons in unconventional ways: the shields are held with the bosses facing the body, which is not how one would normally wield them in combat. This peculiar manner of portraying shields echoes the unusual placement of military equipment in some of the female graves discussed above (*e.g.* on the left-hand side of the body, inverted, etc.), but it remains obscure if this is just a coincidence or if these motifs were conceptually linked and referred to the same idea.

Regrettably, so far all of the armed female figurines have been found in settlement sites or as a result of metal detecting, which hampers our interpretations of them. However, knowing that in funerary contexts different kinds of amulets (found either as single pieces or as part of elaborate necklaces) tend to be associated with women, it is highly probable that the armed figurines were also part of the female attire (similar to miniature shields which are exclusively found in women's graves). At the present moment, it remains unknown who exactly their owners were, what professions they had and whether or not they ever used weapons or actively engaged in armed conflict.

In order to broaden the spectrum of interpretations of 'female weapon graves' and armed figurines, a substantial part of the present study has been devoted to the exploration of weapon-bearing women in medieval textual sources. Although the majority of surviving accounts are considerably younger than the Viking Age they claim to describe, usually dating from the thirteenth century, they can offer interesting hints and – in some instances – inform our understanding of the archaeological material.

Women and weapons in medieval texts

Old Norse literature depicts an impressive variety of armed female characters. It is noteworthy, however, that in the *Íslendingasögur*, commonly regarded as the most 'realistic' saga genre, women are never portrayed as actual warriors – they reach for weapons only in times of tension and social crisis. As argued in Chapter 3, in the memorable episodes from *Laxdæla saga* and *Gísla saga Súrssonar*, swords in female hands ought to be seen principally as tools of empowerment, signalling the women's ability to act and step outside of the feminine sphere, as well as emphasising their capacity to take matters into their own hands when no other options are available. The unique and memorable episode from *Ljósvetninga saga*, on the other hand, shows that occasionally weapons could be used in unconventional ways – here, a cross-dressing sorceress employs an axe in a prophetic ritual. Although this is a one-off account, it has been argued that it might actually depict a genuine practice from the Viking Age and provide stimulating clues as to the identity of the aforementioned women buried with axes and magic accoutrements.

Although completely absent in the *Íslendingasögur*, warrior women who eagerly participate in overseas expeditions and leap fearlessly into the fray play prominent roles in the *fornaldarsögur* and eddic poems. While the eddic sources are fairly laconic (*e.g. Atlamál in grænlenzko*), legendary sagas provide a wealth of information about the circumstances that spur certain female individuals to enter the warpath (*e.g. Hervarar saga ok Heiðreks konungs, Hrólfs saga Gautrekssonar*). From the early days of their childhood these female heroines prefer combat training and hunting to mundane domestic chores. Their tomboyish nature is unsurprising in view of their often aristocratic origin; in the elite social environments from which these individuals typically stem, warrior ideals are highly praised, and preparing for war or waging it on a regular basis is an essential component of life. The main problem with the *fornaldarsögur* is that these sources intertwine historical personae, locations and facts with outbursts of saga-writers' imagination, meaning that the task of isolating authentic references to the Viking Age from a plethora of literary and fantastic embellishments is extremely challenging and in some cases simply impossible.

Apart from the varied portrayals of armed human female figures, Old Norse literature is saturated with images of supernatural women who share strong ties with the broadly understood martial sphere. The most iconic of these are, of course, the *valkyrjur* who choose the dead on the battlefield, fall tragically in love with great heroes and serve mead to the *einherjar* in Óðinn's hall. Their names often allude to weapons, invoking the disturbing sights and sounds of armed conflict. Giantesses, too, have the capacity to wield arms, and some of them – like the famous Þorgerðr Hölgabrúðr – wreak real havoc on the battlefield by raising devastating hailstorms and firing arrows from their fingertips.

When the surviving Old Norse accounts of armed women are compared to other medieval texts depicting female warriors, we can often trace common patterns and motifs. For instance, Saxo Grammaticus' portrayal of warrior women is remarkably similar to what can be found in the *fornaldarsögur* – the heroines are beautiful, courageous and often reluctant to marry unless the suitor proves himself worthy and overcomes a series of deadly challenges. Like the anonymous creators of the *fornaldarsögur*, Saxo praises the warrior women's exceptional fighting abilities, but at the same time we get the impression that he considers their unconventional lifestyles odd or even inappropriate.

Other medieval sources pertaining to non-Norse cultural milieus that seem more historically credible than Old Norse poetry, sagas and Saxo's writings, rarely speak of women involved in martial activities, and when they do, these individuals hardly ever engage in actual physical combat. In their role as queens, the women are typically responsible for devising cunning military strategies and orchestrating the building of defensive architecture. They are certainly powerful and respected political players and in no way lesser than their male counterparts, but whether we can consider them as warriors is open to discussion and relies on the definitions we choose to adopt.

The way of the warrior: past and present

Our modern understanding of past identities, and what we can infer about them from graves and their contents, is admittedly blurry. Nevertheless, based on the results of the work of scholars like Henrich Härke, Howard Williams and others (discussed in detail in Chapter 1), we can say with considerable confidence that not every grave with weapons belonged to an active warrior, regardless of the biological sex of the deceased. Weapons could represent a wide range of ideas and meanings – not all of them positive – and/or serve as statements of prestige and power or as mnemonic devices intended to invoke particular memories and emotions among the participants of the funeral. One thing that will forever remain elusive to today's scholars is how the dead saw themselves and whether they actually considered themselves as warriors. As we shall see further below, even in modern times the people who personally participate in martial activities tend to perceive warriorhood in different ways. The opening chapter of this monograph illustrated the challenges scholars tend to face when attempting to define what it meant to be a warrior in the Viking Age. A fine line of distinction was drawn between those people who actively engaged in armed conflict and those who – through various actions – aspired to or embodied the warrior ideal.

The population of Viking Age Scandinavia and the wider Viking world lived at a time of profound social transformations when armed conflicts would probably be witnessed, or at least heard of, regularly. As predominantly oral societies, the Norse lived in what Neil Price has called 'an intensely storied world'.[1] Everything that survives of these stories today, in the form of sagas, poetry, visual imagery and so on, is likewise saturated with references to warriors and weapons, creating an image of a martial society constantly ready for war.

Individuals who stemmed from the elite probably had the most profound understanding of what waging war and engaging in armed conflict really entailed, both on a practical and symbolic level. Children who grew up in such aristocratic families would probably witness warriors on a regular basis: they would hear their tales and would look up to them in the same way modern teenagers admire rock stars and supermodels. Although the *fornaldarsögur* (which are admittedly the most detailed Old Norse sources on warrior women available today) are generally deemed biased and unrealistic, they do seem to convey at least some truth in showing that boys and girls who grew up in elite environments had the capacity to witness and learn the art of war from their infancy. The best examples of this are the cases of Hervör and Þornbjörg. The insatiable thirst for an adventurous lifestyle among Viking Age children was inspired even further by the very particular material culture that surrounded them – not only real-size weapons and warships but also their various miniatures made of wood and metal.[2] In the Norse cultural environment, even innocent games involving wooden swords would have likely been one of the first steps leading towards one day wielding a real bladed weapon in actual combat. Running in the woods and hunting, on the other hand, would have developed stealth skills and improved strategic thinking. Playing board games, might have been useful, too, if not to devise actual battlefield strategies then at least to learn how to handle defeat and rise again as a mentally stronger person.

In view of the above, looking back at Bj. 581 and its opulent furnishings, which include practically everything one would associate with the luxurious lifestyle of the Viking Age warrior elite, we can speculate that this individual was also born in or accepted into a wealthy group of people among whom it was not uncommon to engage in armed conflict. Perhaps this person, regardless of their gender, at one point in life consciously decided to pursue an unconventional lifestyle and become a warrior, but it is not unlikely that someone or something else compelled them to follow this path. These are, of course, just two of many possible scenarios explaining why weapons and so many other precious goods were laid in the now famous Birka grave.

In Chapter 7, dedicated to women from various cultural milieus who took part in warlike activities, we have seen that a significant proportion of real-life female warriors – like their counterparts from Old Norse literature – stemmed from privileged backgrounds. Interestingly, a number of these women decided to pursue the warrior's path because this was part of their family's tradition. Such was probably the case with many of the prehistoric nomads who lived in the vast territories of today's Ukraine and Russia. A more recent case is that of Nadezhda Durova (1783–1866), a female soldier in the Russian army who was a daughter of a hussar captain. Further expressions of the same pattern can be found in many other cultures around the globe.

If we turn to the most recent and well-documented stories of female warriors who serve in modern armed forces, we can also see that in choosing their career path some of them decided to continue a firmly established family tradition. Amber Smith, for instance, a female US Army officer who flew a Kiowa combat helicopter during numerous military operations in Iraq and Afghanistan boldly says in her book that she was born to fly and that flying is in her blood.[3] Her family's aviation legacy dates back three generations, with her grandfather taking part in the First World War in the battle of Verdun and her father being a paratrooper in the Army 82nd Airborne Division in the 1960s. Remarkably, Smith's mother also had a successful career as an aviator and served as a civilian pilot instructor.[4] In her thought-provoking book, recounting her life as a soldier, Smith recalls that when she was a child listening to her dad's stories about his wartime experiences kept her and her sister hanging from their seats:

> It sounded exciting to jump out of airplanes, talk all the way the Army guys talked ('pass the fucking salt, please'), and be an overall badass paratrooper. He jumped out of airplanes, shot machine guns, and 'camped' in the woods. It all sounded like an incredible adventure. I was awestruck by my dad's experiences and told myself that someday I'd join the Army just like he had.[5]

If we substitute 'airplanes' for 'ships', 'paratroopers' for 'sailors' and 'machine guns' for 'swords', we will get an impression how Viking Age children might have felt when they heard stories of accomplished warriors boasting in the fire-lit halls of Northern Europe about their exploits and adventures.

An earth-shattering event that ultimately triggered Smith's decision to become a soldier was the 2001 attack on the World Trade Center. In that very moment, as Smith recalls, 'everything changed in an instant. Instead of the military being something I had always thought about doing, now I wanted to join'.[6] In view of Smith's particular family background and upbringing, it should not come as a great surprise that after a while her sister also decided to enlist in the Army.

As Amber Smith observes, although much has improved in terms of social equality, being a woman in the military still means having to tackle all kinds of prejudices maintained by some of their male colleagues:

> The first thing I learned was to shut my mouth, to never say something without thinking first, and to always consider my audience. The less I talked, the less unwanted attention I'd receive. For a woman in the Army, any type of attention drawn to you – good or bad – was bad. The less I stood out, the better.[7]

Today, as an accomplished military officer, Smith still continues her quest to challenge intolerance and hurtful stereotypes, and she pointedly notes that 'wearing lip gloss and shooting enemies are not mutually exclusive'.[8] It is striking that in reading the extant saga accounts pertaining to warrior women, we can encounter very similar patterns – in the *fornaldarsögur* men enjoy mocking or even humiliating the shieldmaidens, until they eventually realise that they are playing with fire. While many of these stories are probably literary constructs, it is nonetheless intriguing how closely they reflect actual human behaviour in completely different and culturally and historically removed environments.

Returning to the difficult issue of how weapon-bearing women perceive themselves in times of conflict, and whether we can consider each one of them as a warrior, it is stimulating to refer to the real-life stories of female insurgents who took part in the Warsaw Uprising in 1944. As already noted in Chapter 7, these women had numerous roles to play, acting as paramedics, messengers, sentries and in some instances also as active combatants. In a book entitled *Sierpniowe dziewczęta '44* (*August Girls '44*), Patrycja Bukalska has assembled interviews with these female heroines, and it is interesting to discover how today they reflect back on their actions and identities during the difficult time of the Second World War.[9] As Anna Jakubowska or 'Paulinka' says:

> Obraziłabym się, gdyby ktoś wtedy powiedział, że nie jestem żołnierzem. Nigdy jednak nie chciałam strzelać, zabijać. Moim zadaniem było być i pomagać, ale to chłopcy o wszystkim decydowali. Znałam swoje miejsce w szeregu, ale nie traktowałam tego jako czegoś niewłaściwego. Jednocześnie chłopcy bardzo nas szanowali.
>
> I would be offended if someone told me then that I am not a soldier. Nevertheless, I never wanted to shoot, to kill. My task was to be there and help, but it was the boys who decided about everything. I knew where my place was and it did not feel inappropriate. At the same time, the boys had great respect for us.[10]

Many of the women who took part in the Warsaw Uprising never actually held a real weapon – not only because of the specific roles assigned to them by their military superiors, but also because the insurgents' supplies of arms were extremely limited. As the paramedic Halina Jędrzejewska notes:

> Uważa się, że sanitariuszka nie ma broni, więc to nie żołnierz, ale ja czułam się żołnierzem. Tak też byłam traktowana przez wszystkich dowódców.
>
> It is said that because the paramedic has no weapon she is not a soldier, but I felt I was a soldier. This is also how I was treated by all my superiors.[11]

Other young women did not think of themselves as soldiers but considered their participation in the Uprising as a (patriotic) duty. As Krystyna Zachwatowicz-Wajda 'Czyżyk' recalls:

> Byłam smarkata i dosyć dziecinna. Nie miałam świadomości, że służę w wojsku. Myślę, że harcerstwo wpłynęło na to, że to wszystko wydawało mi się naturalne, było po prostu obowiązkiem.
>
> I was young and very childish. I was not aware I was serving in the army. I think the fact that I had been a scout before influenced me deeply, and it was all simply my duty.[12]

These selected stories of female insurgents demonstrate with great clarity how fluid the understanding of what it means to be a soldier/warrior can be. Although culturally and chronologically distant from the Viking Age that occupies us here, they can help sophisticate our attempts to comprehend what it meant to be a warrior over one thousand years ago. More than anything else, however, these accounts illustrate perfectly the complexities of human nature, the motivations that spur people to engage in war, and how varied their perceptions of themselves can be even if they happen to perform exactly the same functions in society.

***

Returning to the Viking Age, but keeping in mind everything that has been said above, we must acknowledge that a person is always more than their job and more than the deeds they commit in life or the objects they are eventually laid to rest with. The archaeological, iconographic and textual sources thoroughly assessed in this book show unequivocally that the idea of the armed woman was not at all foreign to the population of the Viking world, and that such women warriors *may have* really existed. Some perhaps died during their first encounter with the enemy, others might have lived to see more than just one battle, while others yet might have engaged in armed conflict in indirect or symbolic ways, devising strategies, orchestrating the construction of defensive architecture, performing magic spells intended to influence the outcome of the fight and so on. Regardless of the different scenarios of their lives, this does not make such women in any way lesser than their male Viking counterparts. What is remarkable about them, however, is that these same women probably engaged in a whole plethora of other activities, which ranged from performing various domestic chores, raising children and taking care of animals to craftsworking, trading and travelling. In trying to reconstruct their lives, let us therefore abstain from seeing the armed women of the past merely as 'warriors', 'sorceresses' or 'functional sons', but let us embrace them as humans with all their wonderful complexities and contradictions. This feels like an appropriate way to honour their memory today.

Notes

1. Price 2010b: 145.
2. Gardeła 2012a; Raffield 2019.
3. Smith 2016: 7.
4. Smith 2016: 7.
5. Smith 2016: 8.
6. Smith 2016: 13.
7. Smith 2016: 71.
8. Smith 2016: 36.
9. Bukalska 2013.
10. Bukalska 2013: 9. Translation by Leszek Gardeła.
11. Bukalska 2013: 13. Translation by Leszek Gardeła.
12. Bukalska 2013: 12. Translation by Leszek Gardeła.

Appendix

Table 1. List of (possible) female inhumation graves from Viking Age Norway furnished with swords, spearheads, axeheads and arrowheads

	Location	Grave goods	Basis for biological sex determination	Museum number	References
1.	Aunvoll, Nord Trøndelag, Norway	Sword (Petersen's type H or I; the pommel is missing), comb, sickle, shears, ca. 120 iron fragments (nails and rivets), whetstone, eight gaming pieces made of bone, round white stone (possibly a gaming piece), bone fragments of an adult dog similar to the Norwegian *buhund*.	Osteological analysis	T20248	Stenvik 2005; Norderval 2006: 52, 144; Lindblom & Balsgaard Juul 2019: 55; Jóhanna Katrín Friðriksdóttir 2020: 63; Gardeła 2021: 87
		A spearhead (similar to Rygh's type R474) and a red/brown glass bead were found in the spoil heap after the excavation. These items probably belong to the grave.			
2.	Gausel, Hetland, Rogaland, Norway (grave S-1883)	Shield boss or lamp fragment, iron staff, two copper alloy oval brooches with gold gilding and animal ornamentation, silver equal-armed brooch, silver arm-ring made of thick wire, silver arm-ring, jet ring, 13 copper alloy bridle fittings, five mosaic beads, one glass bead, one stone bead, two iron knives, iron horse bit, fittings for three drinking horns, iron frying pan, rivets and a wooden chest handle, two copper alloy fittings originally serving as parts of a reliquary of insular provenance, fragments of a copper alloy vessel, pin from a penannular brooch, iron weaving sword, iron shears, fragment of a copper alloy chain.	Grave goods	B4233	Petersen 1951: 426; Bøgh-Andersen 1999: 47; Price 2002: 192; 2010b: 143–144; Gardeła 2016b: 292–293; Armstrong Oma 2018; Moen 2019: 105
3.	Løve, Vestfold, Norway	Axehead (Petersen's type H), knife, at least 20 beads of various material (several of which date to the Merovingian Period), copper alloy ring, three horse crampons, horse bridle, *rangle*/rattle, textile remains (wool) with gold thread.	Osteological analysis	C52536	Resi 2013; Gardeła 2013b: 286–287; 2021: 87

(Continued)

Table 1. List of (possible) female inhumation graves from Viking Age Norway furnished with swords, spearheads, axeheads and arrowheads (Continued)

	Location	Grave goods	Basis for biological sex determination	Museum number	References
4.	Mårem, Telemark, Norway	Axehead (Petersen's type H), oval brooches (similar to Rygh's type R655), round brooch decorated in the Borre style (similar to Rygh's type R666), copper alloy tube with flakes of gold foil inside, copper alloy ring, silver wire ring (probably worn on one of the fingers of the right hand), well-preserved textile fragments (wool), sickle, knife, six nails, iron ferrule, pieces of quartz, pieces of burnt clay, nine slag fragments, indeterminate fragments of wood, animal vertebrae. The grave also included three strings of glass beads (1. around the neck of the deceased; 2. suspended from the oval brooches; 3. around the right wrist). The beads (61 in total) were made of glass, mosaic glass, rock crystal, faiense, stone and lead. Some of the beads could originate from very distant locations, including south-east Europe, the Middle East and Egypt.	Grave goods	C53630	Engh 2009: 152–156, 162–164; Gardeła 2013b: 287–288; 2017a: 42–43; Gardeła & Toplak 2019: 141–143
5.	Nordre Kjølen, Åsnes, Solør, Hedmark, Norway	Sword (Petersen's type M), axehead (Petersen's type G), spearhead (Petersen's type K), arrowheads (tanged type), file, whetstone, shield boss (similar to Rygh's type R563; completely destroyed in a fire at the Nordre Kjølen farm), horse bit.	Osteological analysis	C22541	Guldberg 1901; Mørck 1901; Hernæs 1984; Holck 1984; Jochens 1996: 108; Lia 2004: 308–309; Klos 2006: 32; Gardeła 2017c: 9–10; 2018b: 393, 398–399; 2021: 85–86; Gardeła & Toplak 2019: 141; Lindblom & Balsgaard Juul 2019: 55; Moen 2019: 105; Jóhanna Katrín Friðriksdóttir 2020: 63
6.	Oseberg, Vestfold, Norway	Two axes with wooden shafts and dozens of other artefacts.	aDNA analysis	–	General references: Brøgger et al. 1917a; 1917b; Brøgger & Shetelig 1927; 1928; Christensen & Nockert 2006 Specific information on the axes: Christensen 1992: 88; Gardeła 2013b: 290–292; Gardeła & Toplak 2019: 141
7.	Sanddal, Alhus s., Jølster p., Sogn og Fjordane, Norway	Axehead (Petersen's type D), sickle, large weaving sword, oval brooches (similar to Rygh's type R657), silver wire chain, four spindle whorls, 10 loomweights, fragmented whalebone plaque, whetstone, strike-a-light, indeterminate iron fragments (parts of a chest?), 13 small stones (gaming pieces?), horse bit, rein distributors.	Grave goods	B11413	Aannestad & Glørstad 2017: 162–163

Table 2. List of (possible) female cremation graves from Viking Age Norway furnished with arrowheads and shield bosses

	Location	Grave goods	Basis for biological sex determination	Museum number	References
1.	Hilde, Innvik, Sogn og Fjordane, Norway	Possible shield boss, iron staff, large iron cooking fork, iron scoop, iron roasting spit, iron scissors, small iron sickle, small iron knife, iron key, fragment of an iron chest lock, fragments of iron (probably used as chest fittings), iron ring attached to an iron spike (probably part of a chest), two thin iron rods, two iron rings, fragment of an iron foil, two copper alloy oval brooches (type P51), decorated silver bead, two red beads, one small rock crystal bead, one mosaic bead, two spindle whorls (one made of clay and one made of steatite), burnt fragments of a bone weaving sword, fragments of a small whetstone with an iron ring. In the same location, one year after the original excavation, fragments of a copper alloy bowl were found as well as a small iron ring with nine Þórr's hammers. These artefacts were probably also part of the grave's assemblage.	Grave goods	B5717	Petersen 1951: 426; Bøgh-Andersen 1999: 47; Price 2002: 192; Gardeła 2016b: 298–299
2.	Kaupang, Vestfold, Norway (grave Ka. 3/Nicolaysen's barrow 113)	Axehead (Petersen's type H), two oval brooches (Petersen's type 51), two beads (one of which is possibly made of carnelian), iron saucepan, iron frying pan, iron spit(?), spindle whorl, looped hone, two sickles, horse bit, rivet, iron rod, iron cauldron(?), iron rattle.	Grave goods	–	Blindheim *et al.* 1981: 200–201; Stylegar 2007: 104–105; Gardeła 2013b: 288–289
3.	Kaupang, Vestfold, Norway (grave Ka. 10/Nicolaysen's barrow 85)	Axehead (Petersen's type K), two oval brooches (Petersen's type 51), two glass beads, spindle whorl made of soapstone, sickle, soapstone vessel, iron weaving sword, horse bit, iron hook, casket handle, iron rod, rectangular iron mount, hone, two–three rivets.	Grave goods	–	Blindheim *et al.* 1981: 204; Stylegar 2007: 104–105; Gardeła 2013b: 288–289
4.	Kaupang, Vestfold, Norway (grave Ka. 16/Nicoloaysen's barrow 77)	Axehead (Petersen's type H), two oval brooches (Petersen's type 51), textiles, iron weaving sword, shears, spindle whorl made of burnt clay, sickle, horse bit, possible harness mount.	Grave goods	–	Stylegar 2007: 106–107; see also Blindheim *et al.* 1981: 205; Gardeła 2013b: 288–289
5.	Kvåle, Stedje, Sogndal, Sogn og Fjordane, Norway	Shield boss, iron staff, copper alloy vessel, iron scoop, large iron pan, iron weaving sword, iron lamp (consisting of three twisted rods on which originally lay an iron bowl), large copper alloy bowl, two copper alloy oval brooches, trefoil brooch, round brooch, copper alloy needle, stone spindle whorl, iron shears, four small iron keys, fragment of a knife blade, two small sickles, iron rivets, horse bit, numerous iron rings, numerous iron rivets, iron fittings of a chest, fragments of a chest-lock, small bowl (probably part of a scales set), handle of an iron vessel, fragments of a weaving comb.	Grave goods	B3456	Petersen 1951: 426; Bøgh-Andersen 1999: 47; Price 2002: 192; Gardeła 2016b: 302–303
6.	Terum, Aurland, Sogn og Fjordane, Norway	Two arrowheads, iron hoe, oval brooch, copper alloy bracelet, glass beads, three spindle whorls, iron shears, small iron file, knife, sickle, three round iron rivet heads, numerous fragments of iron (probably the remains of a chest), small piece of textile, 10 pieces of flint.	Grave goods	–	Dommasnes 1979: 110–111; 1982: 77; Gardeła 2018b: 398; Moen 2019a: 105

Table 3. List of (possible) female inhumation graves from Viking Age Denmark furnished with spearheads and axeheads

	Location	Grave goods	Basis for biological sex determination	Museum number	References
1.	Bogøvej, Langeland, Denmark	Axehead (Nadolski's type Va, Kotowicz type V Variant IB.5.20), strike-a-light, Arabic dirham of Nuh ibn Nasr dated to AD 945.	Osteological analysis	–	Grøn et al. 1994: 34–35; Gardeła 2013b: 277–279; 2017c: 13–14; Kastholm 2015: 77; Lindblom 2016: 101–102; Lindblom & Balsgaard Juul 2019: 53–55; Moen 2019: 105
2.	Gerdrup, Sjælland, Denmark	Double grave of a man and a woman. Artefacts associated with the woman: spearhead (Petersen's type E), knife, bone needle case with an iron pin/needle. Artefacts associated with the man: iron knife. Between the two individuals lay fragments of sheep crania.	aDNA analysis, osteological analysis	–	Christensen 1982; 1997; Christensen & Bennike 1983; Lauritsen & Kastholm Hansen 2003; Gardeła 2013b: 280–282; 2016b: 82–84; 2017b: 180–183; 2017c: 10–13; Kastholm 2015; 2016; Hjardar & Vike 2016: 104; Lindblom 2016: 53; Moen 2019: 105
3.	Oens, Jylland, Denmark	Axehead, whetstone, comb, spurs, iron fittings possibly from a bridle.	Grave goods	–	Lindblom 2016; Lindblom & Balsgaard Juul 2019: 53–54
4.	Trekroner-Grydehøj, Sjælland, Denmark (grave A505)	Copper alloy spearhead/arrowhead/staff, iron handle of a bucket, fragments of a wooden chest (iron 'closing device'), two knives, copper alloy rivet, large iron ring with wood attached, iron nail, small iron rods, two massive rings with pins (possibly parts of a saddle). The grave contained the remains of two complete animals (horse and dog) and sheep bones.	Osteological analysis	–	Ulriksen 2011; 2018; Gardeła 2013b: 282–284; 2016b: 85–88; 2017b: 183–185; 2017c: 11–13; Price 2014

Table 4. List of female inhumation graves from Viking Age Sweden furnished with martial equipment

	Location	Grave goods	Basis for biological sex determination	Museum number	References
1.	Birka, Björkö, Uppland, Sweden (Bj. 581)	Sword decorated with copper alloy (Petersen's type E), battle knife (sax) in a scabbard with copper alloy fittings, iron spearhead with a socket ornamented with copper alloy, another spearhead with silver and copper decorations, axehead (Petersen's type M), 25 arrowheads (Wegraeus type D1), two shield bosses, iron fittings, two stirrups, iron knife, whetstone, 28 gaming pieces made of antler, three dice made of antler, three weights, quarter of an Arabic silver coin (Samanid dirham of Nasr ibn Ahmad dated to AD 913–933), ringed pin, silver fittings for a hat, copper alloy bowl, iron ring, large iron buckle and an antler comb. In addition to these artefacts, grave Bj 581 was furnished with riding equipment: horse bits, iron rings, four horse crampons made of iron and an iron hook. Iron fittings (probably from a chest) were also found as well as iron fittings of a gaming board. Among the items associated with this grave were a copper alloy buckle, ca. 40 fragments of a glass mirror, a miniature spear made of iron as well as three small pins made of tin	aDNA analysis, osteological analysis	–	Arbman 1943: 188–190; Kjellström 2012: 75–76; Lindblom 2016: 102; Hedenstierna-Jonson 2018; Hedenstierna-Jonson et al. 2017; Androshchuk 2018; Price et al. 2019; Moen 2019a: 108–109; Jóhanna Katrín Friðriksdóttir 2020: 58–60; Gardeła 2021: 84; Gardeła & Toplak 2019: 143–145

Table 5. List of (possible) female cremation graves from Viking Age Sweden furnished with spearheads, axeheads and arrowheads

	Location	Grave goods	Basis for biological sex determination	Museum number	References
1.	Dalstorp, Västergötland, Sweden	Five intentionally twisted and bent spearheads, 10 knives, comb fragments, brooches, beads.	Grave goods	–	Artelius 2005; Gardeła 2013b: 295–296
2.	Barshalder Roes, Grötlingbo sn., Gotland (grave 1:31/1952)	One arrowhead, fish-head shaped pendant (type 1), bead, glass bead, various iron fittings (probably from a chest) and rivets, burnt and unburnt bones.	Grave goods	GF C 10177	Thunmark-Nylén 2006: 249
3.	Klinta, Köpings sn., Öland	Axehead, iron staff, silver pendant (probably an Eastern European or Asian import), copper alloy jug, copper alloy basin, two copper alloy brooches (Petersen's type 51), two copper alloy cruciform mounts, two copper alloy rings, two copper alloy strap ends, copper alloy trapezoidal mount, two copper sheets with runic inscriptions, two pairs of iron shears, two iron knives, iron wood-working cramp, axehead (bearded, slim-bladed and driven vertically into the pit), L-shaped key, 25 fragments of an iron chain, two fragments of iron hook-eyes, 151 beads (carnelian, rock crystal, glass and glass paste), iron Þórr's hammer ring with four Þórr's hammers, over 30 fragments of iron mounts (probably from a bucket), brooch or reins-distributor made of copper alloy, fragments and melted droplets of copper alloy, over 40 fragments of iron mounts, two rowan berries. The grave pit also contained the remains of a bird, probably a chicken.	Grave goods	–	Petersson 1958; Schultze 1987: 55–62, 102–112; Price 2002: 142–149, 183–185; Gardeła 2013b: 292–293; 2016b; Gardeła & Toplak 2019: 140–141; Toplak 2016: 64, 199–200

(Continued)

Table 5. List of (possible) female cremation graves from Viking Age Sweden furnished with spearheads, axeheads and arrowheads (Continued)

	Location	Grave goods	Basis for biological sex determination	Museum number	References
4.	Ire, Hellvi sn., Gotland (grave 173A)	Two arrowheads, tweezers (type 1), knife, comb, iron nail, iron band, iron rod, charcoal, burnt bone.	Grave goods	GF C 9322	Thunmark-Nylén 2006: 393
5.	Ire, Hellvi sn., Gotland (grave 196)	One arrowhead in the grave fill, animal head brooches (types 7a and 7d), disc-on-bow brooch (type 2a2), copper alloy clothing pin (type 3b), burnt bone.	Grave goods	GF C 9322	Thunmark-Nylén 2006: 400
6.	Ire, Hellvi sn., Gotland (grave 374)	One fragmented arrowhead, fragmented disc-on-bow brooch (Vendel type or type 1), copper alloy bracteate (type E), fragmented copper alloy fish-head shaped pendants (type 1), knife with fragments of copper alloy scabbard fittings, rivet, fragments of iron, five glass beads (green and multicoloured), fossil (Astylospongia), bones.	Grave goods	SHM 20826	Thunmark-Nylén 2006: 427
7.	Ire, Hellvi sn., Gotland (grave 498)	Two arrowheads, animal head brooch (type 4c), tongue-shaped pendant, knife, comb, iron handle of a bucket, two iron crampons, iron fittings, rivets and nails, charcoal, burnt bone.	Grave goods	GF C 9322	Thunmark-Nylén 2006: 434
8.	Laxare, Boge sn., Gotland (grave 9)	One arrowhead, fish-head shaped pendant (type 1), comb, fossil, various iron fittings, iron ring, iron rivets and nails, five pottery shards, charcoal, burnt bone.	Grave goods	GF C 10038	Thunmark-Nylén 2006: 63
9.	Nennesmo, Västbo hundred, Reftele sn., Finnveden, Sweden (grave 4)	Two arrowheads, casket handle, four indeterminate iron fragments. The grave also included the cremated remains of a dog and pig.	Grave goods	–	Svanberg 2003: 197
10.	Nennesmo, Västbo hundred, Reftele sn., Finnveden, Sweden (grave 22)	At least three arrowheads, knife, eight copper alloy fragments, nail, four mounts with rivets, fragmented clasp, copper alloy needle, fire steel(?), 121 indeterminate iron fragments, pottery shard.	Grave goods	–	Svanberg 2003: 253–254

References

Primary sources

Andersson, T.M. & W.I. Miller 1997. The Saga of the People of Ljosavatn. In Viðar Hreinsson (ed.) *The Complete Sagas of Icelanders Including 49 Tales. Volume IV.* Leif Eiríksson Publishing, Reykjavík: 193–255.

Björn K. Þórólfsson & Guðni Jónsson (eds) 1943. *Vestfirðinga sögur. Gísla saga Súrssonar. Fóstbræðra saga. Þáttr Þormóðar. Hávarðar saga Ísfirðings. Auðunar þáttr Vestfirzka. Þorvarðar þáttr Krákunefs.* Hið íslenzka fornritafélag, Reykjavík.

Björn Sigfússon (ed.) 1940. *Ljósvetninga saga með þáttum, Reykdæla saga ok Víga-Skútu, Hreiðars þáttr.* Hið íslenzka fornritafélag, Reykjavík.

Blake, N.F. 1962. *Jómsvikinga Saga. The Saga of the Jomsvikings.* Thomas Nelson and Sons Ltd, London-Edinburgh-Paris-Melbourne-Johannesburg-Toronto and New York.

Byock, J. (ed.) 1990. *The Saga of the Volsungs.* Penguin, London.

Dronke, U. (ed.) 1997. *The Poetic Edda. Volume II. Mythological Poems.* Clarendon Press, Oxford.

Dronke, U. (ed.) 2011. *The Poetic Edda. Volume III. Mythological Poems II.* Clarendon Press, Oxford.

Einar Ólafur Sveinsson (ed.) 1943. *Laxdæla saga. Halldórs þættir Snorrasonar. Stúfs þáttr.* Hið íslenzka fornritafélag, Reykjavík.

Einar Ólafur Sveinsson (ed.) 1954. *Brennu-Njáls saga.* Hið íslenzka fornritafélag, Reykjavík.

Einar Ólafur Sveinsson & Matthías Þórðarson (eds) 1935. *Eyrbyggja saga. Brands þáttr örva. Eiríks saga rauða. Grænlendinga saga. Grænlendinga þáttr.* Hið íslenzka fornritafélag, Reykjavík.

Ellis Davidson, H.R. & P. Fisher (eds) 2008. *Saxo Grammaticus. The History of the Danes. Books I–IX.* D.S. Brewer, Woodbridge.

Finlay, A. 2010. The Saga of Ásmund, Killer of Champions. In M. Arnold & A. Finlay (eds) *Making History: Essays on the Fornaldarsögur.* Viking Society for Northern Research/University College London, London: 119–139.

Finlay, A. & Þórdís Edda Jóhannesdóttir (eds) 2018. *The Saga of the Jómsvikings. A Translation with Full Introduction.* Medieval Institute Publications, Western Michigan University, Kalamazoo.

Friis-Jensen, K. & P. Fisher (eds) 2015. *Saxo Grammaticus. Gesta Danorum. The History of the Danes. Volume I.* Clarendon Press, Oxford.

Guðni Jónsson (ed.) 1950. *Fornaldar sögur Norðurlanda I.* Forni, Reykjavík.

Heimir Pálsson & A. Faulkes (eds) 2012. *Snorri Sturluson. The Uppsala Edda. DG 11 5to.* Viking Society for Northern Research, London.

Hermann Pálsson & P. Edwards (eds) 1972. *Hrolf Gautreksson: A Viking Romance.* Southside, Edinburgh.

Hermann Pálsson & P. Edwards 1985. *Seven Viking Romances.* Penguin, London.

Hollander, L.M. (ed.) 2000. *The Saga of the Jómsvikings.* University of Texas Press, Austin.

Karwot, E. 1955. *Katalog Magii Rudolfa.* Zakład im. Ossolińskich, Wrocław.

Kunz, K. 1997a. The Saga of the People of Laxardal. In Viðar Hreinsson (ed.) *The Complete Sagas of Icelanders Including 49 Tales. Volume V.* Leifur Eiríkson Publishing, Reykjavík: 1–120.

Kunz, K. 1997b. The Saga of the Greenlanders. In Viðar Hreinsson (ed.) *The Complete Sagas of the Icelanders Including 49 Tales. Volume I.* Leifur Eiríkson Publishing, Reykjavík: 19–32.

Larrington, C. (ed.) 1999. *The Poetic Edda.* Oxford University Press, Oxford.

Larrington, C. (ed.) 2014. *The Poetic Edda. Revised Edition.* Oxford University Press, Oxford.

Mackintosh-Smith, T. & J.E. Montgomery (eds) 2014. *Two Arabic Travel Books. Accounts of China and India. Abū Zayd al-Sīrāfī. Mission to the Volga. Aḥmad ibn Faḍlān.* New York University Press, New York and London.

Regal, M.S. 1997. Gisli Sursson's Saga. In Viðar Hreinsson (ed.) *The Complete Sagas of Icelanders Including 49 Tales. Volume II.* Leifur Eiríkson Publishing, Reykjavík: 1–48.

Tolkien, C. (ed.) 1960. *Saga Heiðreks konungs ins vitra/The Saga of King Heidrek the Wise.* Thomas Nelson & Sons, London.

Turville-Petre, E.O.G. & C. Tolkien (eds) 1956. *Hervarar saga ok Heiðreks*. Viking Society for Northern Research/University College London, London.

Waterfield, R. (ed.) 1998. *Herodotus. The Histories*. Oxford University Press, Oxford.

Wortley, J. (ed.) 2010. *John Skylitzes: A Synopsis of Byzantine History 811–1057*. Cambridge University Press, Cambridge.

Secondary sources

Aannestad, H.L. 2018. Charisma, Violence and Weapons: The Broken Swords of the Vikings. In M. Vedeler, I.M. Røstad, E.S. Kristoffersen & Z.T. Glørstad (eds) *Charismatic Objects: From Roman Times to the Middle Ages*. Cappelen Damm AS, Oslo: 147–166.

Aannestad, H.L. & Z.T. Glørstad 2017. Kvinner og båtbegravelser i vikingtiden. In K. Kjesrud & N. Løkka (eds) *Dronningen i vikingtid og middelalder*. Scandinavian Academic Press, Oslo: 155–183.

Adolf Friðriksson 2000. Viking Burial Practices in Iceland. In Adolf Friðriksson (ed.) *Kristján Eldjárn's Kuml og haugfé. Ur heiðnum sið á Íslandi, 2 utgafa*. Fornleifastofnun Íslands/ Mál og Menning/Þjóðminjasafn Íslands, Reykjavík: 549–610.

Ahlström Arcini, C. 2018. *The Viking Age: A Time of Many Faces*. Oxbow Books, Oxford and Philadelphia.

Alpern, S.B. 2011. *Amazons of Black Sparta: The Women Warriors of Dahomey*. Hurst & Company, London.

Andersen, R., L.H. Dommasnes, Magnús Stefánsson & I. Øye (eds) 1985. *Kvinnearbeid i Norden fra vikingtiden til reformasjonen. Foredrag fra et nordisk kvinnehistorisk seminar i Bergen 3–7 august 1983*. Universitetet i Bergen, Bergen.

Anderson, S.M. 2002. Introduction: 'og eru köld kvenna ráð'. In S.M. Anderson & K. Swenson (eds) *Cold Counsel. Women in Old Norse Literature and Mythology. A Collection of Essays*. Routledge, New York and London: xi–xvi.

Anderson, S.M. & K. Swenson (eds) 2002. *Cold Counsel: Women in Old Norse Literature and Mythology: A Collection of Essays*. Routledge, New York and London.

Andersson, G. 2005a. With Thor on Our Side: The Symbolism of the Thor Hammer-Ring in Viking Age Burial Ritual. In T. Artelius & F. Svanberg (eds) *Dealing with the Dead. Archaeological Perspectives on Prehistoric Scandinavian Burial*. National Heritage Board, Stockholm: 45–62.

Andersson, G. 2005b. *Gravspråk som religiös strategi. Valsta och Skälby i Attundaland under vikingatid och tidig medeltid*. Riksantikvarieämbetet, Stockholm.

Andersson, G. 2015. The völva – a Woman of Prophecy. In M. Jansén (ed.) *Just One More Thing. 12 Experts Tell Fascinating Tales About 32 Fabulous Objects in the Swedish History Museum*. Statens Historiska Museum, Stockholm: 92–95.

Andersson, G. 2016. Women in the Viking Age: Many Different Roles. In G. Andersson (ed.) *We Call Them Vikings*. The Swedish History Museum, Stockholm: 30–35.

Andersson, G., K. Näversköld & E. Vedin 2015. *Arkeologisk efterundersökning av grav Bj 750 och intilliggande ytor, RAÄ 118, Adelsö sn. Uppland*. Statens historiska museer, Stockholm.

Androshchuk, F. 2014. *Viking Swords. Swords and Social Aspects of Weaponry in Viking Age Societies*. The Swedish History Museum, Stockholm.

Androshchuk, F. 2018. Female Viking Revisited. *Viking and Medieval Scandinavia* 14: 41–49.

Arbman, H. 1940. *Birka I: Die Gräber. Tafeln*. Kungl. Vitterhets Historie och Antikvitets Akademien, Stockholm.

Arbman, H. 1943. *Birka I: Die Gräber. Text*. Kungl. Vitterhets Historie och Antikvitets Akademien, Stockholm.

Arents, U. & S. Eisenschmidt 2010a. *Die Gräber von Haithabu. Band 1: Text, Literatur*. Wachholtz, Neumünster.

Arents, U. & S. Eisenschmidt 2010b. *Die Gräber von Haithabu. Band 2: Katalog, Listen, Tafeln, Beilagen*. Wachholtz, Neumünster.

Arman, J. 2018. *The Warrior Queen: The Life and Legend of Æthelflæd, Daughter of Alfred the Great*. Amberley, Stroud.

Ármann Jakobsson, A. Lassen & A. Ney (eds) 2003. *Fornaldarsagornas struktur och ideologi. Handlingar från ett symposium i Uppsala 31.8–2.9.2001*. Uppsala Universitetet Institutionen för nordiska språk, Uppsala.

Armstrong Oma, K. 2018. Transformative Theft of Past and Present: The Human-Horse Bond Reflected in the Biography of the Viking Period Gausel Bridle. In M. Vedeler, I.M. Røstad, E.S. Kristoffersen & Z.T. Glørstad (eds) *Charismatic Objects: From Roman Times to the Middle Ages*. Cappelen Damm Akademisk, Oslo: 125–145.

Arnold, B. & N. Wicker (eds) 2001. *Gender and the Archaeology of Death*. Altamira Press, Walnut Creek.

Arnold, M. & A. Finlay (eds) 2010. *Making History: Essays on the Fornaldarsögur*. Viking Society for Northern Research/ University College London, London.

Arrhenius, B. 1961. Vikingatida miniatyrer. *Tor* 7: 139–164.

Artelius, T. 2003. *Begravningsplatsen från järnaldern vid skolan Dalstorp*. Institutioner för Arkeologi, Göteborgs Universitet, Göteborg.

Artelius, T. 2005. The Revenant by the Lake. Spear Symbolism in Scandinavian Late Viking Age Burial Ritual. In T. Artelius & F. Svanberg (eds) *Dealing with the Dead. Archaeological Perspectives on Prehistoric Scandinavian Burial Ritual*. National Heritage Board, Stockholm: 261–276.

Arwidsson, G. (ed.) 1984. *Birka II:1: Systematische Analysen der Gräberfunde*. Almqvist & Wiksell International, Stockholm.

Arwidsson, G. (ed.) 1986. *Birka II:2: Systematische Analysen der Gräberfunde*. Almqvist & Wiksell International, Stockholm.

Arwidsson, G. 1989a. Kommentar zu den Knochenfunden aus den Gräbern, mit einem Appendix. In G. Arwidsson (ed.) *Birka II:3. Systematische Analysen der Gräberfunde*. Kungl. Vitterhets Historie och Antikvitets Akademien, Stockholm: 143–149.

Arwidsson, G. (ed.) 1989b. *Birka II:3: Systematische Analysen der Gräberfunde*. Almqvist & Wiksell International, Stockholm.

Arwill-Nordbladh, E. 1991. The Swedish Image of Viking Age Women: Stereotype, Generalisation and Beyond. In R. Samson (ed.) *Social Approaches to Viking Studies*. Cruithne Press, Glasgow: 53–64.

Ashman Rowe, E. 2010. Sögubrot af fornkonungum: Mythologised History for Late Thirteenth-Century Iceland. In M. Arnold & A. Finlay (eds) *Making History: Essays on the Fornaldarsögur*. Viking Society for Northern Research/University College London, London: 1–16.

Ashman Rowe, E. 2012. *Vikings in the West: The Legend of Ragnarr Loðbrók and His Sons*. Fassbaender, Wien.

Auður Magnúsdóttir 2014. Kvinnor i sagorna. In N. Coleman & N. Løkka (eds) *Kvinner i vikingtid. Vikingatidens kvinnor*. Scandinavian Academic Press, Oslo: 58–87.

Back Danielsson, I.-M. 2007. *Masking Moments. The Transitions of Bodies and Beings in Late Iron Age Scandinavia*. Stockholm University, Stockholm.

Bagge, M.S. 2015. Ryttergraven fra Fregerslev. *Museum Skanderborg Årbog* 2015: 3–11.

Bakka, E. 1993. *Gauselfunnet og bakgrunnen for det*. Universitetet i Bergen, Bergen.

Banaszkiewicz, J. 1987a. Włócznia i chorągiew. O rycie otwarcia bitwy w związku z cudem kampanii nakielskiej Bolesława Krzywoustego (Kadłubek III, 14). *Kwartalnik Historyczny* 4(94): 2–24.

Banaszkiewicz, J. 1987b. Kolorowe włócznie Wizygotów Euryka. *Kwartalnik Historyczny* 2(94): 3–16.

Barndon, R. & A.B. Olsen 2018. En grav med smedverktøy fra tidlig vikingtid på Nordheim i Sogndal. En analyse av gravgods, handlingsrekker og symbolikk. *Viking* 81: 63–88.

Beck, H. 1978. Haugbrott im Altnordischen. In H. Jankuhn, H. Nehlsen & H. Roth (eds) *Zum Grabfrevel in Vor- und Frühgeschichtlicher Zeit. Untersuchungen zu Grabraub und 'haugbrot' in Mittel- und Nordeuropa. Bericht über ein Kolloquium der Kommision für die Altertumskunde Mittel- und Nordeuropas von 14. bis 16. Februar 1977*. Vandenhoek & Ruprecht, Göttingen: 211–228.

Bek-Pedersen, K. 2007. Are the Spinning Nornir just a Yarn? *Viking and Medieval Scandinavia* 3: 1–10.

Bek-Pedersen, K. 2008. Weaving Swords and Rolling Heads. A Peculiar Space in Old Norse Tradition. In M. Mencej (ed.) *Space and Time in Europe: East and West, Past and Present*. Univerze v Ljubljana, Filozofska Fakulteta, Ljubljana: 173–187.

Bek-Pedersen, K. 2011. *The Norns in Old Norse Mythology*. Dunedin, Edinburgh.

Berseneva, N. 2008. Women and Children in the Sargat Culture. In K.M. Linduff & K.S. Rubinson (eds) *Are All Warriors Male? Gender Roles on the Ancient Eurasian Steppe*. AltaMira Press, Langham-New York-Toronto-Plymouth, UK: 131–151.

Bersu, G. & D.M. Wilson 1966. *Three Viking Graves in the Isle of Man*. The Society for Medieval Archaeology, London.

Biborski, M., M.F. Jagodziński, P. Pudło, J. Stępiński & G. Żabiński 2010. Sword Parts from a Viking Age Emporium of Truso in Prussia. *Waffen und Kostümkunde* 52(1): 19–70.

Bill, J. (ed.) 2008. *Levd liv. En utstilling om skjelettene fra Oseberg og Gokstad*. Kulturhistorisk Museum Universitetet i Oslo/ Vestfold Fylkeskommune, Oslo, Borre.

Bill, J. 2016a. Protecting Against the Dead? On the Possible Use of Apotropaic Magic in the Oseberg Burial. *Cambridge Archaeological Journal* 26(1): 141–155.

Bill, J. 2016b. Ambiguous Mobility in the Viking Age Ship Burial from Oseberg. In P. Bjerregaard, A.E. Rasmussen & T.F. Sørensen (eds) *Materialities of Passing: Explorations in Transformation, Transition and Transcience*. Routledge, London and New York: 207–220.

Bill, J. & A. Daly 2012. The Plundering of the Ship Graves from Oseberg and Gokstad: An Example of Power Politics? *Antiquity* 86: 808–824.

Blain, J. & R. Wallis 2000. The 'Ergi' Seidman: Contestations of Gender, Shamanism and Sexuality in Northern Religion Past and Present. *Journal of Contemporary Religion* 15(3): 395–411.

Błaszczyk, D. 2017. *Między ziemią a niebem. Groby komorowe na obszarze państwa pierwszych Piastów*. Instytut Archeologii Uniwersytetu Warszawskiego, Warszawa.

Błaszczyk, D. 2018. Pochodzenie i dieta mężczyzny pochowanego w grobie D162 z cmentarzyska w Bodzi w świetle badań izotopowych. *Światowit* 13–14(54–55)A/B 2015–2016: 133–157.

Błaszczyk, D. & D. Stępniewska (eds) 2016. *Pochówki w grobach komorowych na ziemiach polskich w okresie wczesnego średniowiecza*. Instytut Archeologii Uniwersytetu Warszawskiego, Warszawa.

Blindheim, C. 2008. *Kaupang-funnene. Bind IIc. Whetstones and Grindstones in the Settlement Area: The 1956–1974 Excavations*. Universitetets Oldsaksamling/Universitetet i Oslo, Oslo.

Blindheim, C. & B. Heyerdahl-Larsen 1995. *Kaupang-funnene. Bind IIa. Gravplassene i Bikjholbergene/Lamøya. Undersøkelsene 1950–57. Del A. Gravskikk*. Universitetets Oldsaksamling/Universitetet i Oslo, Oslo.

Blindheim, C., B. Heyerdahl-Larsen & A.S. Ingstad 1999. *Kaupang-funnene. Bind IIb. Gravplassene i Bikjholbergene/ Lamøya. Undersøkelsene 1950–57. Del B. Oldsaksformer. Del C. Tekstilene*. Universitetets Oldsaksamling/Universitetet i Oslo, Oslo.

Blindheim, C., B. Heyerdahl-Larsen & R.L. Tollsnes 1981. *Kaupang-funnene. Bind I*. Universitetets Oldsaksamling/Universitetet i Oslo, Oslo.

Bochnak, T. 2020. The Phenomenon of Burying Women with Weapons in Iron Age Poland: Tactical, Social and Funerary Considerations. *IDO Movement for Culture. Journal of Martial Arts Anthropology* 20(1): 1–13.

Bogacki, M. 2007. *Przemiany w wojskowości polskiej od połowy X wieku do 1138 roku. Kształt i organizacja armii*. Wydawnictwo Adam Marszałek, Toruń.

Bøgh-Andersen, S. 1999. *Vendel- och vikingatida stekspett: ej blott för köket, ett redskap med anor från Homeros' tid*. University of Lund, Lund.

Bourns, T.J.S. 2012. *The Language of Birds in Old Norse Tradition*. Háskóli Íslands (Unpublished MA Thesis), Reykjavík.

Boyer, R. 2014. *Les Valkyries*. Les belles lettres, Paris.

Braathen, H. 1989. *Ryttergraver: Politiske strukturer i eldre rikssamlingstid*. Universitetet i Oslo, Oslo.

Braunmüller, B. 2013. *Ritual, Tradition und Konvention – Wikingerzeitliche Opferfunde in Altdänemark. Volume I–II*. Habelt, Bonn.

Brøgger, A.W., H. Falk & H. Shetelig 1917a. *Osebergfundet I*. Universitetets Oldsaksamling, Kristiania.

Brøgger, A.W., H. Falk & H. Shetelig 1917b. *Osebergfundet III*. Universitetets Oldsaksamling, Kristiania.

Brøgger, A.W. & H. Shetelig 1927. *Osebergfundet V*. Universitetets Oldsaksamling, Oslo.

Brøgger, A.W. & H. Shetelig 1928. *Osebergfundet II*. Universitetets Oldsaksamling, Oslo.

Brøndsted, J. 1936. Danish Inhumation Graves of the Viking Age. A Survey. *Acta Archaeologica* 7: 81–228.

Bruder, R. 1974. *Die germanische Frau im Lichte der Runeninschriften und antiken Historiographie*. de Gruyter, Berlin.

Brunning, S. 2015. '(Swinger of) the Serpent of Wounds': Swords and Snakes in the Viking Mind. In M.D.J. Bintley & T.J.T. Williams (eds) *Representing Beasts in Early Medieval England and Scandinavia*. The Boydell Press, Woodbridge: 53–72.

Brunning, S. 2019. *The Sword in Early Medieval Northern Europe: Experience, Identity, Representation*. The Boydell Press, Woodbridge.

Buchholtz, P. 1968. *Schamanistische Züge in der altisländischen Überlieferung*. Bamberg-Münster.

Bukalska, P. 2013. *Sierpniowe dziewczęta '44*. Wydawnictwo Trio, Warszawa.

Buko, A. (ed.) 2015. *Bodzia. A Late Viking-Age Elite Cemetery in Central Poland*. Brill, Leiden-Boston.

Bunyatyan, E.P. 1985. *Metodika soztialnykh rekonstruktii v arkheologii. Na materiale Skifskikh mogilnikov IV–III vv. do n.e.* Naukova Duka Press, Kiev.

Callow, C. 2006. First Steps Towards an Archaeology of Children in Iceland. *Archaeologia Islandica* 5: 55–96.

Capelle, T. 1968. *Die Metallschmuck von Haithabu. Studien zur wikingischen Metallkunst*. Wachholtz, Neumünster.

Carlsson, D. 1999. *'Ridanäs'. Vikingahamnen i Fröjel*. Visby.

Carroll, J., S.H. Harrison & G. Williams 2014. *The Vikings in Britain and Ireland*. The British Museum, London.

Carstens, L. 2018. Land of the Hawk: Old Norse Literary Sources about the Knowledge and Practice of Falconry. In K.-H. Gersmann & O. Grimm (eds) *Raptor and Human – Falconry and Bird Symbolism throughout the Millennia on a Global Scale*. Wachholtz Murmann, Kiel-Hamburg: 799–826.

Carver, M. 1998. *Sutton Hoo. Burial Ground of Kings?* British Museum Press, London.

Cerezo-Román, J.I., A. Wessman & H. Williams (eds) 2017. *Cremation and the Archaeology of Death*. Oxford University Press, Oxford.

Chadwick, N.K. 1950. Þorgerðr Hölgabrúðr and the trolla þing: A Note on Sources. In C. Fox & B. Dickins (eds) *The Early Cultures of North-West Europe. H.M. Chadwick Memorial Studies*. Cambridge University Press, Cambridge: 395–417.

Christensen, A.E. 1992. Kongsgårdens handverkere. In A.E. Christensen, A.S. Ingstad & B. Myhre (eds) *Osebergdronningens grav. Vår arkeologiske nasjonalskatt i nytt lys*. Schibsted, Oslo: 85–137.

Christensen, A.E., A.S. Ingstad & B. Myhre 1992. *Osebergdronningens grav. Vår arkeologiske nasjonalskatt i nytt lys*. Schibsted, Oslo.

Christensen, A.E. & M. Nockert (eds) 2006. *Osebergfunnet IV. Tekstilene*. Kulturhistorisk Museum, Universitetet i Oslo, Oslo.

Christensen, T. 1982. Gerdrup graven. *Romu: årsskrift fra Roskilde Museum* 2: 19–28.

Christensen, T. 1997. The Armed Woman and the Hanged Thrall. In F. Birkebæk (ed.) *The Ages Collected from Roskilde Museum*. Roskilde Museum, Roskilde: 34–35.

Christensen, T. 2015. *Lejre bag myten. De arkæologiske udgravninger*. ROMU/Jysk Arkæologisk Selskab, Aarhus.

Christensen, T. & P. Bennike 1983. Kvinder for fred? *Skalk* 3: 9–11.

Chudziak, W. 2006. Wczesnośredniowieczny grot włóczni z Nętna – przyczynek do studiów nad chrystianizacją Pomorza Środkowego. In M. Dworaczyk, A. Kowalska, S. Moździoch & M. Rębkowski (eds) *Świat Słowian wczesnego średniowiecza*. Instytut Archeologii i Etnologii Polskiej Akademii Nauk, Szczecin-Wrocław: 647–655.

Chutnik, S. 2017. *Kobiety, które walczą. Rozmowy z zawodniczkami sportów walki*. Grupa Wydawnicza Foksal, Warszawa.

Clark, D. & Jóhanna Katrín Friðriksdóttir 2016. The Representation of Gender in Eddic Poetry. In C. Larrington, J. Quinn & B. Schorn (eds) *A Handbook to Eddic Poetry: Myths and Legends of Early Scandinavia*. Cambridge University Press, Cambridge: 331–348.

Clover, C.J. 1986. Maiden Warriors and Other Sons. *The Journal of English and Germanic Philology* 85(1): 35–49.

Clover, C.J. 1993. Regardless of Sex: Men, Women, and Power in Early Northern Europe. *Speculum* 68(2): 1–28.

Clover, C.J. 2005. Icelandic Family Sagas (Íslendingasögur). In C.J. Clover & J. Lindow (eds) *Old Norse-Icelandic Literature. A Critical Guide*. University of Toronto Press/Medieval Academy of America, Toronto-Buffalo-London: 239–315.

Clunies Ross, M. 2010. *The Cambridge Introduction to the Old Norse-Icelandic Saga*. Cambridge University Press, Cambridge.

Clunies Ross, M. 2014. The Role of the Horse in Nordic Mythologies. In T.R. Tangherlini (ed.) *Nordic Mythologies: Interpretations, Intersections, and Institutions*. North Pinehurst Press, Berkeley, Los Angeles: 50–70.

Coleman, N. 2014. Kvinnenamn. In N. Coleman & N. Løkka (eds) *Kvinner i vikingtid. Vikingatidens kvinnor*. Scandinavian Academic Press, Oslo: 288–322.

Coleman, N. & N. Løkka (eds) 2014. *Kvinner i vikingtid. Vikingatidens kvinnor*. Scandinavian Academic Press, Oslo.

Creutz, K. 2003. *Tension and Tradition. A Study of Late Iron Age Spearheads Around the Baltic Sea*. Stockholms Universitet, Stockholm.

Croix, S., P. Deckers & S. Sindbæk 2020. Recasting a Viking Warrior Woman from Ribe: 3D Digital Image Reconstruction Compared. *Journal of Archaeological Science: Reports* 32: 1–7.

Cubała, A. 2019. *Miłość '44. Prawdziwe historie powstańczej miłości*. Prószyński Media, Warszawa.

Damsholt, N. 1984. The Role of Icelandic Women in the Sagas and in the Production of Homespun Cloth. *Scandinavian Journal of History* 9: 75–90.

Davis-Kimball, J. 1997a. Warrior Women of the Eurasian Steppes. *Archaeology* 50(1): 44–48.

Davis-Kimball, J. 1997b. Chieftain or Warrior-priestess? *Archaeology* 1997 (September-October): 44–48.

Davis-Kimball, J. 1997–1998. Amazon Priestesses and Other Women of Status – Females in Nomadic Societies. *Silk Road Archaeology* 5: 1–50.

Davis-Kimball, J. 1998. Statuses of Eastern Iron Age Nomads. In M. Pearce & M. Tosi (eds) *Papers from the EAA Third Annual Meeting at Ravenna 1997. Volume I: Pre- and Protohistory*. Archaeopress, Oxford: 142–149.

Davis-Kimball, J. 2000. Enarees and Women of High Status: Evidence of Ritual at Tillya Tepe (Northern Afghanistan). In J. Davis-Kimball, L. Koryakova & L.T. Yablonsky (eds) *Kurgans, Ritual Sites, and Settlements: Eurasian and Bronze and Iron Age*. Archaeopress, Oxford: 223–239.

Davis-Kimball, J. 2001. Warriors and Priestesses of the Eurasian Nomads. In P. Biehl, F. Bertemes & H. Meller (eds) *The Archaeology of Cult and Religion*. Archaeolingua, Budapest: 243–259.

Davis-Kimball, J. 2002. *Warrior Women: An Archaeologist's Search for History's Hidden Heroines*. Warner Books, New York.

Dekker, R.M. & L.C. van de Pol 1989. *The Tradition of Female Transvestism in Early Modern Europe*. Macmillan Press, Houndmills, Basingstroke, Hampshire, London.

Deptuła, C. 2003. *Archanioł i Smok. Z zagadnień legendy miejsca i mitu początku w Polsce średniowiecznej*. Wydawnictwo Werset, Lublin.

Dillmann, F.-X. 1993. Seiður og shamanismi í Íslendingasögum. *Skáldskaparmál* 2: 20–33.

Dillmann, F.-X. 1994. Sejd og shamanisme i de islandske sagaer. In J.P. Schjødt (ed.) *Myt og ritual i det førkristne Norden: et symposium*. Odense University Press, Odense: 23–34.

Dobat, A.S. 2009. The State and the Strangers: The Role of External Forces in a Process of State Formation in Viking-Age South Scandinavia (c. AD 900–1050). *Viking and Medieval Scandinavia* 5: 65–104.

Dobat, A.S. (ed.) 2013. *Kongens borge: rapport over undersøgelserne 2007–2010*. Jysk Arkaeologisk Selskab, Højbjerg.

Dommasnes, L.H. 1979. Et gravmateriale fra yngre jernalder brukt til å belyse kvinners stilling. *Viking* 42: 95–114.

Dommasnes, L.H. 1982. Late Iron Age in Western Norway. Female Roles and Ranks as Deduced from an Analysis of Burial Customs. *Norwegian Archaeological Review* 15: 70–84.

Dommasnes, L.H. 1987. Male/Female Roles and Ranks in Late Iron Age Norway. In R. Bertelsen, A. Lillehammer & J.-R. Næss (eds) *Were They All Men? An Examination of Sex Roles in Prehistoric Society. Acts from a Workshop Held at Utstein Kloster, Rogaland 2.–4. November 1979. NAM-Forskningsseminar nr. 1*. Arkeologisk Museum i Stavanger, Stavanger: 65–77.

Dommasnes, L.H. 1991. Women, Kinship, and the Basis of Power in the Norwegian Viking Age. In R. Samson (ed.) *Social Approaches to Viking Studies*. Cruithne Press, Glasgow: 65–73.

Dommasnes, L.H. 1999. Kvinnearkeologi, feministisk arkeologi, genderarkeologi – fram og tilbake er like langt? *Arkeologiske Skrifter fra Universitetet i Bergen* 10: 27–41.

Downham, C. 2019. Von Æthelfleda bis Olga. Frauen und Kriegsführung. In J. Staecker & M.S. Toplak (eds) *Die Wikinger. Entdecker und Eroberer*. Propyläen/Ullstein Buchverlage, Berlin: 151–160.

Drozd, A. & A. Janowski 2007. Wczesnośredniowieczny topór inkrustowany z miejscowości Pień na ziemi chełmińskiej. In M. Bogacki, M. Franz & Z. Pilarczyk (eds) *Wojskowość ludów Morza Bałtyckiego. Materiały z II Międzynarodowej Sesji Naukowej Dziejów Ludów Morza Bałtyckiego. Wolin 4–6 sierpnia 2006*. Wydawnictwo Adam Marszałek, Toruń: 106–127.

Dubois, T. 1999. *Nordic Religions in the Viking Age*. University of Pennsylvania Press, Philadelphia.

Duczko, W. 1989. Runde Silberblechanhänger mit punziertem Muster. In G. Arwidsson (ed.) *Birka II:3. Systematische Analysen der Gräberfunde*. Kungl. Vitterhets Historie och Antikvitets Akademien, Stockholm: 9–18.

Dundes, A. (ed.) 1992. *The Evil Eye: A Casebook*. The University of Wisconsin Press, Wisconsin.

Durova, N. 1988. *The Cavalry Maiden: Journals of a Russian Officer in the Napoleonic Wars*. Indiana University Press, Bloomington.

Ebel, E. 1997. [Review] Jenny Jochens Women in Old Norse Society and Jenny Jochens Old Norse Images of Women. *Alvíssmál* 7: 108–112.

Edberg, R. & A. Söderberg 2018. Insignier, amuletter, krigsleksaker? Sigtunas miniatyryxor än en gång. *Situne Dei. Årsskrift för Sigtunaforskning och historisk arkeologi* 2018: 34–59.

Egeler, M. 2011. *Walküren, Bodbs, Sirenen. Gedanken zur religionsgeschichtlichen Anbildung Nordwesteuropas an den mediterranen Raum*. de Gruyter, Berlin and New York.

Eisenschmidt, S. 1994. *Kammergräber der Wikingerzeit in Altdänemark*. Habelt, Bonn.

Eisenschmidt, S. 2004. *Grabfunde des 8. bis 11. Jahrhunderts zwischen Kongea und Eider: Zur Bestattungssitte der Wikingerzeit im südlichen Altdänemark*. Wachholtz, Neumünster.

Ellis Davidson, H.R. 1998. *The Sword in Anglo-Saxon England: Its Archaeology and Literature*. The Boydell Press, Woodbridge.

Ellis, H.R. 1943. *The Road to Hel. A Study of the Conception of the Dead in Old Norse Literature*. Cambridge University Press, Cambridge.

Elsner, H. 1992. *Wikinger Museum Haithabu: Schaufenster einer frühen Stadt*. Wachholtz, Neumünster.

Engh, A.K. 2009. Rike importfunn i vikingtidsgraver. In J. Bergstøl (ed.) *Arkeologiske undersøkelser 2003–2004. Katalog og artikler*. Kulturhistorisk Museum/Fornminneseksjonen, Oslo: 147–165.

Eriksen, P., T. Egeberg, L. Helles Olesen & H. Rostholm (eds) 2009. *Vikinger i vest. Vikingetiden i Vestjylland*. Jysk Arkeologisk Selskab, Århus.

Eriksson, B.G. 2015. *Kungen av Birka. Hjalmar Stolpe – arkeolog och etnograf*. Atlantis, Stockholm.

Ewing, T. 2006. 'í litklœðum' – Coloured Clothes in Medieval Scandinavian Literature and Archaeology. In D. Ashurst, D. Kick & J. McKinnell (eds) *The Fantastic in Old Norse/Icelandic Literature. Sagas and the British Isles. Preprint Papers of the 13th International Saga Conference, Durham and York, 6th–12th August 2006*. Durham University, Durham: 223–230.

Falk, H. 1914. *Altnordische Waffenkunde*. Jacob Dybwad, Kristiania.

Falk, O. 2015. *The Bare-Sarked Warrior: A Brief History of Battlefield Exposure*. Arizona Center for Medieval and Renaissance Studies, Tempe, Arizona.

Farbregd, O. 1972. *Pilefunn fra Oppdalsfjella*. Det Kongelige Norske Videnskabers Selskab, Museet, Trondheim.

Fell, C.E. 1996. The First Publication of Old Norse Literature in England and its Relation to its Sources. In E. Roesdahl & P. Meulengracht Sørensen (eds) *The Waking of Angantyr: The Scandinavian Past in European Culture*. Aarhus University Press, Aarhus: 27–57.

Feveile, C. 2013. *Viking Ribe: Trade, Power and Faith*. Sydvestjyske Museer/Forlaget Liljeberget, Ribe.

Foote, P. & D.M. Wilson 1970. *The Viking Achievement*. Book Club Associates, London.

Fowler, C. 2004. *The Archaeology of Personhood. An Anthropological Approach*. Routledge, London and New York.

Fuglesang, S.H. 1989. Viking and Medieval Amulets in Scandinavia. *Fornvännen* 84: 15–25.

Fuglesang, S.H. 1999. Amulets as Evidence for the Transition from Viking to Medieval Scandinavia. In D.R. Jordan, H.

Montgomery & E. Thomassen (eds) *The World of Ancient Magic. Papers from the First International Samson Eitrem Seminar at the Norwegian Institute at Athens, 4–8 May 1997*. The Norwegian Institute at Athens, Bergen: 299–314.

Gade, K.E. 1985. Hanging in Northern Law and Literature. *Maal og minne* 1985: 159–183.

Gansum, T. 2002. Fra jord til handling. In K. Jennbert, A. Andrén & C. Raudvere (eds) *Plats och praxis. Studier av nordisk förkristen ritual*. Nordic Academic Press, Lund: 249–286.

Gansum, T. 2004. *Hauger som konstruksjoner – Arkeologiske forventninger gjennom 200 år*. Göteborgs Universitet, Göteborg.

Gapski, M.H. 2014. *Koń w kulturze polskiego średniowiecza. Wierzchowce na ścieżkach wyobraźni*. Wydawnictwo Nauka i Innowacje, Poznań.

Gardeła, L. 2008. Into Viking Minds. Reinterpreting the Staffs of Sorcery and Unravelling Seiðr. *Viking and Medieval Scandinavia* 4: 45–84.

Gardeła, L. 2009. A Biography of the Seiðr-Staffs. Towards an Archaeology of Emotions. In L.P. Słupecki & J. Morawiec (eds) *Between Paganism and Christianity in the North*. Wydawnictwo Uniwersytetu Rzeszowskiego, Rzeszów: 188–217.

Gardeła, L. 2010. Wszyscy należycie do Óðinn'a! Symbolika włóczni w epoce wikingów. In M. Bogacki, M. Franz & Z. Pilarczyk (eds) *Religia ludów Morza Bałtyckiego. Stosunki polsko-duńskie w dziejach. Materiały z V Międzynarodowej Sesji Naukowej Dziejów Ludów Morza Bałtyckiego Wolin 31 lipca-2 sierpnia 2009*. Wydawnictwo Adam Marszałek, Toruń: 77–101.

Gardeła, L. 2012a. What the Vikings Did for Fun? Sports and Pastimes in Medieval Northern Europe. *World Archaeology* 44(2): 234–247.

Gardeła, L. 2012b. Pies w świecie wikingów. In T. Borkowski & K. Ślipko-Jastrzębska (eds) *Człowiek spotyka psa*. Muzeum Miejskie Wrocławia, Wrocław: 11–22.

Gardeła, L. 2012c. *Entangled Worlds. Archaeologies of Ambivalence in the Viking Age*. University of Aberdeen (Unpublished PhD Thesis), Aberdeen.

Gardeła, L. 2012d. Entangled Worlds. Archaeologies of Ambivalence in the Viking Age. Summary. *Retrospective Methods Network Newsletter* 4: 229–233.

Gardeła, L. 2013a. The Dangerous Dead? Rethinking Viking-Age Deviant Burials. In R. Simek & L.P. Słupecki (eds) *Conversions: Looking for Ideological Change in the Early Middle Ages*. Fassbaender, Wien: 96–136.

Gardeła, L. 2013b. 'Warrior-women' in Viking Age Scandinavia? A Preliminary Archaeological Study. *Analecta Archaeologica Ressoviensia* 8: 273–339.

Gardeła, L. 2013c. Dead or Alive? Chamber Graves and their Inhabitants in the Old Norse Literature and Viking Age Archaeology. In S. Moździoch, B.M. Stanisławski & P. Wiszewski (eds) *Scandinavian Culture in Medieval Poland*. Institute of Archaeology and Ethnology of the Polish Academy of Sciences, Wrocław: 373–394.

Gardeła, L. 2013d. The Headless Norsemen. Decapitation in Viking Age Scandinavia. In L. Gardeła & K. Kajkowski (eds) *The Head Motif in Past Societies in a Comparative Perspective/Motyw głowy w dawnych kulturach w perspektywie porównawczej*. Muzeum Zachodniokaszubskie w Bytowie, Bytów: 88–155.

Gardeła, L. 2014a. *Scandinavian Amulets in Viking Age Poland*. Fundacja Rzeszowskiego Ośrodka Archeologicznego, Instytut Archeologii Uniwersytetu Rzeszowskiego, Rzeszów.

Gardeła, L. 2014b. Viking Death Rituals on the Isle of Man. In L. Gardeła & C. Larrington (eds) *Viking Myths and Rituals on the Isle of Man*. University of Nottingham/Centre for the Study of the Viking Age, Nottingham: 30–37.

Gardeła, L. 2015a. Uzbrojona kobieta z Truso. Nowe rozważania nad miniaturami tzw. walkirii z epoki wikingów. *Pruthenia* 10: 75–104.

Gardeła, L. 2015b. Vikings in Poland: A Critical Overview. In M.H. Eriksen, U. Pedersen, B. Rundberget, I. Axelsen & H.L. Berg (eds) *Viking Worlds: Things, Spaces and Movement*. Oxbow Books, Oxford: 213–234.

Gardeła, L. 2016a. Worshipping the Dead. Viking Age Cemeteries as Cult Sites? In M. Egeler (ed.) *Germanische Kultorte. Vergleichende, historische und rezeptionsgeschichtliche Zugänge*. Herbert Utz Verlag, München: 169–205.

Gardeła, L. 2016b. *(Magic) Staffs in the Viking Age*. Fassbaender, Wien.

Gardeła, L. 2016c. Wczesnośredniowieczne groby komorowe – lustra czy miraże życia? Rozważania nad praktykami funeralnymi na ziemiach polskich. In D. Błaszczyk & D. Stępniewska (eds) *Pochówki w grobach komorowych na ziemiach polskich w okresie wczesnego średniowiecza*. Instytut Archeologii Uniwersytetu Warszawskiego, Warszawa: 154–175.

Gardeła, L. 2016d. Amulety skandynawskie z Wolina i Truso. In J. Popielska-Grzybowska, J. Iwaszczuk & B. Józefów-Czerwińska (eds) *Meetings at the Borders. Studies Dedicated to Professor Władysław Duczko*. Pułtusk Academy of Humanities, Pułtusk: 99–105.

Gardeła, L. 2017a. Mujeres poderosas en la Era Vikinga. *Desperta Ferro: Arqueología & Historia* 13: 40–44.

Gardeła, L. 2017b. *Bad Death in the Early Middle Ages: Atypical Burials from Poland in a Comparative Perspective*. Fundacja Rzeszowskiego Ośrodka Archeologicznego, Instytut Archeologii Uniwersytetu Rzeszowskiego, Rzeszów.

Gardeła, L. 2017c. Amazons of the Viking World: Between Myth and Reality. *Medieval Warfare* 7(1): 8–15.

Gardeła, L. 2018a. Myths in Metal: Armed Females in the Art of the Viking Age. *Hugin and Munin* 3: 28–31.

Gardeła, L. 2018b. Amazons of the North? Armed Females in Viking Archaeology and Medieval Literature. In A. Bauer & A. Pesch (eds) *Hvanndalir – Beiträge zur europäischen Altertumskunde und mediävistischen Literaturwissenschaft*. de Gruyter, Berlin: 391–428.

Gardeła, L. 2018c. Lutomiersk Unveiled. The Buried Warriors of Poland. *Medieval Warfare* 8(3): 42–50.

Gardeła, L. 2019a. Czy w Polsce są groby wikingów? Skandynawskie praktyki pogrzebowe na ziemiach polskich we wczesnym średniowieczu. In M. Bogacki, A. Janowski & Ł. Kaczmarek (eds) *Wikingowie w Polsce? Zabytki skandynawskie z ziem polskich*. Muzeum Początków Państwa Polskiego/Wydawnictwo Triglav, Gniezno: 155–264.

Gardeła, L. 2019b. Tomboys and Little Vikings. *Current Anthropology* 60(6): 827–828.

Gardeła, L. 2019c. Death on Canvas. Artistic Reconstructions in Viking Age Mortuary Archaeology. In H. Williams, B.

Wills-Eve & J. Osborne (eds) *The Public Archaeology of Death*. Equinox Publishing, Sheffield: 96–112.

Gardeła, L. 2019d. Gegenseitige Einflüsse. Skandinavier und Westslawen. In J. Staecker & M.S. Toplak (eds) *Die Wikinger. Entdecker und Eroberer*. Propyläen/Ullstein Buchverlage, Berlin: 237–251.

Gardeła, L. 2019e. Lords of the Fjords: Viking Elites from Myklebostad, Norway. *Medieval Warfare* 9(4): 44–51.

Gardeła, L. 2019f. (Re)discovering the Vikings in Poland: From Nineteenth-century Romantics to Contemporary Warriors. In T. Birkett & R. Dale (eds) *The Vikings Reimagined: Reception, Recovery, Engagement*. de Gruyter, Berlin-Boston: 44–68.

Gardeła, L. 2019g. *Magia, kobiety i śmierć w świecie wikingów*. Wydawnictwo Triglav, Szczecin.

Gardeła, L. 2020a. Uncoiling the Serpent: Snake Figurines in the Viking Age. *Viking and Medieval Scandinavia* 16: 27–61.

Gardeła, L. 2020b. Viking Archaeology in Poland: Past, Present, and Future. In A. Pedersen & S. Sindbæk (eds) *Viking Encounters. Proceedings of the 18th Viking Congress*. Aarhus University Press, Aarhus: 547–564.

Gardeła, L. 2020c. The Slavic Way of Death. Archaeological Perspectives on Otherworld Journeys in Early Medieval Poland. In M. Egeler & W. Heizmann (eds) *Between the Worlds. Contexts, Sources and Analogues of Scandinavian Otherworld Journeys*. de Gruyter, Berlin-Boston: 207–252.

Gardeła, L. 2021. Amazonen, Walküren, Seherinnen. In M.S. Toplak (ed.) *Die Wikinger. Seeräuber und Krieger im Licht der Archäologie. Archäologie in Deutschland. Sonderheft*. Theiss, Darmstadt: 84–89

Gardeła, L. in press-a. Miniature Spears in the Viking Age: Small Symbols of Óðinn? *Religionsvidenskabeligt Tidsskrift*.

Gardeła, L. in press-b. Miniature Swords in the Viking Age. *Acta Archaeologica*.

Gardeła, L. in press-c. Women and Miniature Weapons in the Viking Age. In T. Kuusela (ed.) *The Feminine in Old Norse Mythology*. Brepols, Turnhout.

Gardeła, L. & Ł. Ciesielski 2012. Włócznie śmierci. Włócznie w obrzędowości pogrzebowej w epoce żelaza. In M. Franz & Z. Pilarczyk (eds) *Barbarzyńcy u bram. Monografia oparta o materiały z VI Międzynarodowej Sesji Naukowej Dziejów Ludów Morza Bałtyckiego. Wolin 05–07 sierpnia 2011*. Wydawnictwo Adam Marszałek, Toruń: 30–59.

Gardeła, L. & K. Kajkowski 2021a. Slavs and Snakes. Material Markers of Elite Identity in Viking Age Poland. *European Journal of Archaeology* 24(1): 108–130.

Gardeła, L. & K. Kajkowski 2021b. Slawische Krieger in der Wikingerwelt. In M.S. Toplak (ed.) *Die Wikinger. Seeräuber und Krieger im Licht der Archäologie. Archäologie in Deutschland. Sonderheft*. Theiss, Darmstadt: 29–38.

Gardeła, L. & K. Kajkowski in press. Bóg na ostrodze? Zachodniosłowiańskie oporządzenie jeździeckie z motywami antropomorficznymi. In P. Szczepanik & Ł. Kaczmarek (eds) *Słowianie Połabscy. Studia z zakresu archeologii, historii i językoznawstwa*. Wydawnictwo Uniwersytetu Mikołaja Kopernika, Toruń.

Gardeła, L., K. Kajkowski & Z. Ratajczyk 2019a. Ostrogi zoomorficzne z Ciepłego. Zachodniosłowiański model kosmosu? *Pomorania Antiqua* 28: 65–152.

Gardeła, L., K. Kajkowski, Z. Ratajczyk & S. Wadyl 2019b. Oporządzenie jeździeckie i elementy rzędu końskiego. In S. Wadyl (ed.) *Ciepłe. Elitarna nekropola wczesnośredniowieczna na Pomorzu Wschodnim*. Muzeum Archeologiczne w Gdańsku, Gdańsk: 139–164.

Gardeła, L., K. Kajkowski & B. Söderberg 2019c. The Spur Goad from Skegrie in Scania, Sweden: Evidence of Elite Interaction Between Viking Age Scandinavians and Western Slavs. *Fornvännen* 114(2): 57–74.

Gardeła, L. & K. Odebäck 2018. Miniature Shields in the Viking Age: A Reassessment. *Viking and Medieval Scandinavia* 14: 67–113.

Gardeła, L. & M.S. Toplak 2019. Walküren und Schildmaiden. Weibliche Krieger? In J. Staecker & M.S. Toplak (eds) *Die Wikinger. Entdecker und Eroberer*. Propyläen/Ullstein Buchverlage, Berlin: 137–151.

Gardeła, L. & M.S. Toplak 2020. Kleider und Krieg. Militaria bei Wikinger-Frauen. *Archäologie in Deutschland* (2)2020: 40–43.

Geibig, A. 1991. *Beiträge zur morphologischen Entwicklung des Schwertes im Mittelalter. Eine Analyse des Fundmaterials vom ausgehenden 8. bis. zum 12. Jahrhundert aus Sammlungen der Bundesrepublik Deutschland*. Wachholtz, Neumünster.

Gjerpe, L.E. (ed.) 2005a. *Gravfeltet på Gulli. E18-prosjektet Vestfold. Bind 1*. Kulturhistorisk Museum Fornminneseksjonen, Oslo.

Gjerpe, L.E. 2005b. De enkelte gravene. In L.E. Gjerpe (ed.) *Gravfeltet på Gulli. E18-prosjektet Vestfold. Bind 1*. Kulturhistorisk Museum Fornminneseksjonen, Oslo: 27–104.

Gjerpe, L.E. 2007. Haugbrottets konsekvenser for vikingtidsforskningen. *Viking* 70: 105–124.

Głosek, M. 1973. *Znaki i napisy na mieczach średniowiecznych w Polsce*. Ossolineum, Wrocław-Warszawa-Kraków-Gdańsk.

Głosek, M. 1984. *Miecze środkowoeuropejskie z X–XV w.* Wydawnictwa Geologiczne, Warszawa.

Głosek, M. & A. Nadolski 1970. *Miecze średniowieczne z ziem polskich*. Łódzkie Towarzystwo Naukowe, Łódź.

Górecki, J. 2001. *Gród na Ostrowie Lednickim na tle wybranych ośrodków grodowych pierwszej monarchii piastowskiej*. Muzeum Pierwszych Piastów na Lednicy, Lednogóra.

Graham-Campbell, J. 2013. *Viking Art*. Thames and Hudson, London.

Graham-Campbell, J. & C.E. Batey 1998. *Vikings in Scotland: An Archaeological Survey*. Edinburgh University Press, Edinburgh.

Gräslund, A.-S. 1980. *Birka IV. The Burial Customs. A Study of the Graves on Björkö*. Kungl. Vitterhets Historie och Antikvitets Akademien, Stockholm.

Gräslund, A.-S. 1998. A Princely Child at Birka. In A. Wesse (ed.) *Studien zur Archäologie des Ostseeraumes. Von der Eisenzeit zum Mittelalter. Festschrift für Michael Müller-Wille*. Wachholtz, Neumünster: 281–289.

Gräslund, A.-S. 2004. Dogs in Graves – a Question of Symbolism. In B. Santillo Frizell (ed.) *PECUS. Man and Animal in Antiquity: Proceedings of the Conference at the Swedish Institute in Rome, September 9–12, 2002*. The Swedish Institute in Rome, Rome: 167–176.

Gräslund, A.-S. 2005. Symbolik för lycka och skydd – vikingatida amuletthängen och deras rituella kontext. In K.A. Bergsvik

& A. Engevik (eds) *Fra funn til samfunn. Jernalderstudier tilegnet Bergljot Solberg på 70-årsdagen*. Arkeologisk Institutt, Universitetet i Bergen, Bergen: 377–392.

Gräslund, A.-S. 2006. Wolves, Serpents and Birds. Their Symbolic Meaning in Old Norse Belief. In A. Andrén, K. Jennbert & C. Raudvere (eds) *Old Norse Religion in Long-Term Perspectives. Origins, Changes and Interactions. An International Conference in Lund, Sweden, June 3–7, 2004*. Nordic Academic Press, Lund: 124–129.

Gräslund, A.-S. 2007. Some Viking Age Amulets – the Birka Evidence. In U. Fransson, M. Svedin, S. Bergerbrandt & F. Androshchuk (eds) *Cultural Interaction Between East and West – Archaeology, Artefacts and Human Contacts in Northern Europe*. Stockholm University, Stockholm: 90–96.

Gräslund, B. 2020. Swine, Swedes, and Fertility Gods. In I. García Losquiño, O. Sundqvist & D. Taggart (eds) *Making the Profane Sacred in the Viking Age. Essays in Honour of Stefan Brink*. Brepols, Turnhout: 228–242.

Grieg, S. 1947. *Gjermundbufunnet: en høvdingegrav fra 900-årene fra Ringerike*. Universitetets Oldsaksamling, Oslo.

Griffith, P. 2009. *The Viking Art of War*. Casemate, Philadelphia and Newbury.

Grøn, O., A. Hedeager Krag & P. Bennike 1994. *Vikingetidsgravpladser på Langeland*. Langelands Museum, Rudkøbing.

Guðrún P. Helgadóttir 1985. Kvinner og legekunst i den nørrone litteraturen. In R. Andersen, L.H. Dommasnes, Magnús Stefánsson & I. Øye (eds) *Kvinnearbeid i Norden fra vikingtiden til reformasjonen. Foredrag fra et nordisk kvinnehistorisk seminar i Bergen 3–7 august 1983*. Universitetet i Bergen, Bergen: 17–29.

Guldberg, G. 1901. Om skeletlevningerne af en kvinde fra vikingetiden begraven med vaaben og hest paa Nordre Kjølen i Aasnes. *Christiania Videnskabs-Selskabs Forhandlinger for 1901* 2(1901): 1–10.

Gunnell, T. 2017. Blótgyðjur, Goðar, Mimi, Incest, and Wagons: Oral Memories of the Religion(s) of the Vanir. In P. Hermann, S.A. Mitchell, J.P. Schjødt & A.J. Rose (eds) *Old Norse Mythology – Comparative Perspectives*. Harvard University Press, Cambridge, Massachusetts and London: 113–137.

Haavardsholm, J. 2004. *Vikingtiden som 1800-tallskonstruksjon*. Universitetet i Oslo, Oslo.

Hagberg, L. 1937. *När döden gästar. Svenska folkseder och svensk folktro i samband med död och begravning*. Wahlström & Widstrand, Stockholm.

Häggström, L. 2003. Den vardagliga kniven – om knivars terminologi och tolkning med småländska exempel. *In Situ* 2003: 43–58.

Häggström, L. 2005. *Den vardagliga kniven. Landskapsutnyttjande, bete och odling på Sydsvenska höglandet under äldre järnålder. Exemplet Öggestorp*. Goteborgs Universitet, Kristiansand.

Hall, M.A. 2016. Board Games in Boat Burials: Play in the Performance of Migration and Viking Age Mortuary Practice. *European Journal of Archaeology* 19(3): 439–455.

Hall, R. 2007. *Exploring the World of the Vikings*. Thames and Hudson, London.

Halpin, A. 2008. *Weapons and Warfare in Viking and Medieval Dublin*. National Museum of Ireland, Dublin.

Härke, H. 1990. Warrior Graves? The Background of the Anglo-Saxon Weapon Burial Rite. *Past and Present* 126: 22–43.

Härke, H. 1992a. Changing Symbols in a Changing Society. The Anglo-Saxon Weapon Burial Rite in the Seventh Century. In M. Carver (ed.) *The Age of Sutton Hoo*. The Boydell Press, Woodbridge: 149–166.

Härke, H. 1992b. *Angelsächsische Waffengräber des 5. bis 7. Jahrhunderts*. Rheinland–Verlag and Habelt, Cologne.

Härke, H. 1997. Material Culture as Myth: Weapons in Anglo-Saxon Graves. In K. Høilund Nielsen & C.K. Jensen (eds) *Burial and Society*. Aarhus University Press, Aarhus: 119–127.

Härke, H. 2014. Grave Goods in Early Medieval Burials: Messages and Meanings. *Mortality: Promoting the Interdisciplinary Study of Death and Dying* 19(1): 41–60.

Harrington, S. 2007. Stirring Women, Weapons and Weaving: Aspects of Gender Identity and Symbols of Power in Early Anglo-Saxon England. In S. Hamilton, R.D. Whitehouse & K.I. Wright (eds) *Archaeology and Women. Ancient and Modern Issues*. Left Coast Press, Walnut Creek: 335–352.

Harrison, S.H. & R. Ó'Floinn 2015. *Viking Graves and Grave-Goods in Ireland*. National Museum of Ireland, Dublin.

Hedeager, L. 2011. *Iron Age Myth and Materiality. An Archaeology of Scandinavia AD 400–1000*. Routledge, London and New York.

Hedenstierna-Jonson, C. 2002. A Group of Viking Age Sword Chapes Reflecting the Political Geography of the Time. *Journal of Nordic Archaeological Science* 13: 103–112.

Hedenstierna-Jonson, C. 2006a. Borre Style Metalwork in the Material Culture of the Birka Warriors. An Apotropaic Symbol. *Fornvännen* 101, 312–322.

Hedenstierna-Jonson, C. 2006b. *The Birka Warrior. Material Culture of a Martial Society*. Stockholm University, Stockholm.

Hedenstierna-Jonson, C. 2009. Rus', Varangians and Birka Warriors. In L. Holmqvist Olausson & M. Olausson (eds) *The Martial Society. Aspects on Warriors, Fortifications and Social Change*. Stockholm University, Stockholm: 159–178.

Hedenstierna-Jonson, C. (ed.) 2012. *Birka nu. Pågående forskning om världsarvet Birka och Hovgården*. Historiska Museet, Stockholm.

Hedenstierna-Jonson, C. 2015. To Own and be Owned: The Warriors of Birka's Garrison. In A. Klevnäs & C. Hedenstierna-Jonson (eds) *Own and be Owned. Archaeological Approaches to the Concept of Possession*. Stockholm University, Stockholm: 73–91.

Hedenstierna-Jonson, C. 2018. Women at War? The Birka Female Warrior and her Implications. *The SAA Archaeological Record. New Horizons in the Archaeology of the Viking Age* 18(3): 28–31.

Hedenstierna-Jonson, C. & A. Kjellström 2014. The Urban Woman. On the Role and Identity of Women in Birka. In N. Coleman & N. Løkka (eds) *Kvinner i vikingtid. Vikingatidens kvinnor*. Scandinavian Academic Press, Oslo: 186–208.

Hedenstierna-Jonson, C., A. Kjellström, T. Zachrisson, M. Krzewińska, V. Sobrado, N. Price, T. Günther, M. Jakobsson, A. Götherström & J. Storå 2017. A Female Viking Warrior Confirmed by Genomics. *American Journal of Physical Anthropology* 164: 853–860.

Heide, E. 2006a. Spinning seiðr. In A. Andrén, K. Jennbert & C. Raudvere (eds) *Old Norse Religion in Long Term Perspectives. Origins, Changes and Interactions. An International Conference in Lund, Sweden, June 3–7, 2004*. Nordic Academic Press, Lund: 164–170.

Heide, E. 2006b. Spirits Through Respiratory Passages. In D. Ashurst, D. Kick & J. McKinnell (eds) *The Fantastic in Old Norse/Icelandic Literature. Sagas and the British Isles. Preprint Papers of the 13th International Saga Conference, Durham and York, 6th–12th August 2006*. Durham University, Durham: 350–358.

Heide, E. 2006c. *Gand, seid og åndevind*. Universitetet i Bergen, Bergen.

Heindel, I. 1992. Äxte des 8. bis 14. Jahrhunderts im westslawischen Siedlungsgebiet zwischen Elbe/Saale und Oder/Neiße. *Zeitschrift für Archäologie* 26: 17–56.

Heller, R. 1958. *Die literarische Darstellung der Frau in den Isländersagas*. Max Niemeyer, Halle.

Helmbrecht, M. 2011. *Wirkmächtige Kommunikationsmedien. Menschenbilder der Vendel- und Wikingerzeit und ihre Kontexte*. Lunds Universitet, Lund.

Henriksen, M.B. & P.V. Petersen 2013. Valkyriefund. *Skalk* 2013(2): 3–10.

Hernæs, P. 1984. C22541a–g. Et gammelt funn tolkes på ny. *Nicolay* 43: 31–36.

Hernæs, P. 1985. *De østnorske sverdfunn fra yngre jernalder: en geografisk analyse*. Universitetet i Oslo (Unpublished MA Thesis), Oslo.

Hilczerówna, Z. 1956. *Ostrogi polskie z X–XIII wieku*. Państwowe Wydawnictwo Naukowe, Poznań.

Hjardar, K. & V. Vike 2016. *Vikings at War*. Casemate, Oxford and Philadelphia.

Hodder, I. 2012. *Entangled: An Archaeology of the Relationships between Humans and Things*. Wiley-Blackwell, Oxford.

Hofmann, A. 2015. The Reopening of Graves in Medieval Iceland. A Literary Analysis. In L. Gardeła & K. Kajkowski (eds) *Limbs, Bones and Reopened Graves in Past Societies*. Muzeum Zachodniokaszubskie w Bytowie, Bytów: 293–313.

Holck, P. 1984. Antropologisk kommentar ved lege Per Holck. *Nicolay* 43: 37–39.

Holck, P. 1986. *Cremated Bones. A Medical-anthropological Study of an Archaeological Material on Cremation Burials*. PhD Thesis. Anatomical Institute, University of Oslo, Oslo.

Holck, P. 1996. *Norsk folkemedisin: kloke koner, urtekurer og magi*. Cappelen, Oslo.

Holck, P. 2006. The Oseberg Ship Burial, Norway: New Thoughts on the Skeletons from the Grave Mound. *European Journal of Archaeology* 9(2–3): 185–210.

Holck, P. 2009. *Skjelettene fra Gokstad- og Osebergskipet*. Universitetet i Oslo, Oslo.

Holmquist, L. & S. Kalmring 2019. Birka. Seehandelsplatz und Hafenstruktur. In J. Staecker & M.S. Toplak (eds) *Die Wikinger. Entdecker und Eroberer*. Propyläen/Ullstein Buchverlage, Berlin: 127–136.

Holmqvist, W. 1960. The Dancing Gods. *Acta Archaeologica* 31: 101–127.

Hougen, B. 1940. Osebergfunnets billedvev. *Viking* 4: 85–124.

Hougen, B. 2006. Billedvev. In A.E. Christensen & M. Nockert (eds) *Osebergfunnet IV. Textilene*. Kulturhistorisk Museum, Universitetet i Oslo, Oslo: 15–139.

Íngunn Ásdísardóttir 2007. *Frigg og Freyja: Kvenleg goðmögn í heiðnum sið*. Hið íslenzka bókmenntafélag, Reykjavík.

Jagodziński, M.F. 2010. *Truso. Między Weonodlandem a Witlandem/Truso. Between Weonodland and Witland*. Muzeum Archeologiczno-Historyczne w Elblągu, Elbląg.

Jagodziński, M.F. 2015. *Truso – legenda Bałtyku/Truso – the Legend of the Baltic Sea*. Muzeum Archeologiczno-Historyczne w Elblągu, Elbląg.

Janowski, A. 2003. Misy brązowe męskim atrybutem wyposażenia? Groby z misami brązowymi na terenie ziem polskich we wczesnym średniowieczu. In W. Dzieduszycki & J. Wrzesiński (eds) *Kobieta – Śmierć – Mężczyzna*. Stowarzyszenie Naukowe Archeologów Polskich, Poznań: 331–347.

Janowski, A. 2006. Brązowe i srebrne trzewiki pochew mieczy z X–XIII w. z terenu Polski. Uwagi o proweniencji i datowaniu. *Acta Militaria Mediaevalia* 2: 23–50.

Janowski, A. 2007. Wczesnośredniowieczne okucia pochew mieczy tzw. trzewiki z terenu Pomorza, Warmii i Mazur. In M. Bogacki, M. Franz & Z. Pilarczyk (eds) *Wojskowość ludów Morza Bałtyckiego. Materiały z II Międzynarodowej Sesji Naukowej Dziejów Ludów Morza Bałtyckiego. Wolin 4–6 sierpnia 2006*. Wydawnictwo Adam Marszałek, Toruń: 150–177.

Janowski, A. 2014. Groby 558 i 1120 z Cedyni na tle wczesnośredniowiecznych zachodniopomorskich pochówków z mieczami. In P. Migdalski (ed.) *Civitas Cedene. Studia i materiały do dziejów Cedyni, tom 1*. Stowarzyszenie Historyczno-Kulturalne 'Terra Incognita'/Instytut Historii i Stosunków Międzynarodowych Uniwersytetu Szczecińskiego/Muzeum Regionalne w Cedyni, Chojna-Szczecin-Cedynia: 53–103.

Janowski, A. 2015. *Groby komorowe w Europie środkowo-wschodniej. Problemy wybrane*. Instytut Archeologii i Etnologii Polskiej Akademii Nauk, Ośrodek Archeologii Średniowiecza Krajów Nadbałtyckich, Szczecin.

Janowski, A. & T. Kurasiński 2002. The Graves with Bronze Bowls in the Area of Early-Piast Poland (10th/11th to 12th Century). Issues of Slavic-Scandinavian Contacts. *Archaeologia Historica* 28(3): 653–675.

Janowski, A. & T. Kurasiński 2009. Miecz i pochwa – razem i osobno. Wstęp do problematyki. In P. Kucypera, P. Pudło & G. Żabiński (eds) *Arma et Medium Aevum. Studia nad uzbrojeniem średniowiecznym*. Wydawnictwo Adam Marszałek, Toruń: 74–115.

Jażdżewski, K. 1951. Cmentarzysko wczesnośredniowieczne w Lutomiersku pod Łodzią w świetle badań z r. 1949. *Materiały Wczesnośredniowieczne* 1949(1): 91–191.

Jennbert, K. 2011. *Animals and Humans: Recurrent Symbiosis in Archaeology and Old Norse Religion*. Nordic Academic Press, Lund.

Jensen, B. 2010. *Viking Age Amulets in Scandinavia and Western Europe*. Archaeopress, Oxford.

Jensen, O.W. 2018. *På spaning efter det förflutna: en historia om arkeologiskt fältarbete i Sverige 1600–1900*. Vitterhetsakademien, Stockholm.

Jeppesen, J. 2005. Haldum. In A. Damm (ed.) *Viking Aros*. Moesgård Museum, Højbjerg: 72–75.

Jesch, J. 1991. *Women in the Viking Age*. Boydell & Brewer, Woodbridge.

Jesch, J. 2006. *The Nine Skills of Earl Rögnvaldr of Orkney. Inaugural Lecture Delivered in the University of Nottingham 1 March 2006*. Centre for the Study of the Viking Age, London.

Jesch, J. 2009. Constructing the Warrior Ideal in the Late Viking Age. In L. Holmquist Olausson & M. Olausson (eds) *The Martial Society: Aspects of Warriors, Fortifications and Social Change in Scandinavia*. Stockholm University, Stockholm: 71–78.

Jesch, J. 2014. Women and Identities. In N. Coleman & N. Løkka (eds) *Kvinner i vikingtid. Vikingatidens kvinnor*. Scandinavian Academic Press, Oslo: 268–286.

Jochens, J. 1995. *Women in Old Norse Society*. Cornell University Press, Ithaca and New York.

Jochens, J. 1996. *Old Norse Images of Women*. University of Pennsylvania Press, Philadelphia.

Jochens, J. 2002. Vikings Westward to Vínland. In S.M. Anderson & K. Swenson (eds) *Cold Counsel. Women in Old Norse Literature and Mythology*. Routledge, London and New York: 129–158.

Jordan, A. 2009. I Am No Man: A Study of Warrior Women in the Archaeological Record. *Field Notes: A Journal of Collegiate Anthropology* 1(1): 94–11.

Jørgensen, L. 2005. Hov og hørg ved Tissø. In T. Capelle & C. Fischer (eds) *Ragnarok. Odins verden*. Silkeborg Museum, Silkeborg: 131–142.

Jóhanna Katrín Friðriksdóttir 2009. Women's Weapons: A Re-evaluation of Magic in the Íslendingasögur. *Scandinavian Studies* 80: 409–436.

Jóhanna Katrín Friðriksdóttir 2010. *Hyginn og forsjál*. Wisdom and Women's Counsel in *Hrólfs saga Gautrekssonar*. In M. Arnold & A. Finlay (eds) *Making History: Essays on the Fornaldarsögur*. Viking Society for Northern Research/University College London, London: 69–84.

Jóhanna Katrín Friðriksdóttir 2012. From Heroic Legend to 'Medieval Screwball Comedy'? The Origins, Development and Interpretation of the Maiden-King Narrative. In A. Lassen, A. Ney & Ármann Jakobsson (eds) *The Legendary Sagas. Origins and Development*. University of Iceland Press, Reykjavík: 229–249.

Jóhanna Katrín Friðriksdóttir 2013. *Women in Old Norse Literature: Bodies, Words and Power*. Palgrave Macmillan, New York.

Jóhanna Katrín Friðriksdóttir 2020. *Valkyrie. The Women of the Viking World*. Bloomsbury Academic, London and New York.

Kajkowski, K. 2016. Depozyty zwierzęce na nekropoliach zachodniosłowiańskich. Kilka uwag do dyskusji nad genezą fenomenu grobu komorowego na obszarze wczesnośredniowiecznej Polski. In D. Błaszczyk & D. Stępniewska (eds) *Pochówki w grobach komorowych na ziemiach polskich w okresie wczesnego średniowiecza*. Instytut Archeologii Uniwersytetu Warszawskiego, Warszawa: 140–153.

Kajkowski, K. 2018. Symbolika wczesnośredniowiecznych depozytów szkieletów koni z ziem polskich. In S. Rosik, S. Jędrzejewska & K. Kollinger (eds) *Hierofanie, wierzenia, obrzędy... Kultura symboliczna w średniowieczu między pogaństwem a chrześcijaństwem*. Wydawnictwo Uniwersytetu Rzeszowskiego, Rzeszów: 121–157.

Kalmring, S. 2019. A New Throne-Amulet from Hedeby. First Indication for Viking-Age Barrel-Chairs. *Danish Journal of Archaeology* 8: 1–9.

Karpińska, K. 2018. Asche und Knochen. Vogelüberreste in wikingerzeitlichen Gräbern auf den Nordfriesischen Inseln und in Dänemark. *Arkæologi i Slesvig/Archäologie in Schleswig* 17: 115–131.

Kars, M. 2013. The Early-Medieval Burial Evidence and Concepts of Possession: Questioning Individual Identities. In B. Ludowici (ed.) *Individual and Individuality? Approaches Towards an Archaeology of Personhood in the First Millennium AD*. Niedersächsisches Landesmuseum Hannover, Hannover: 95–106.

Kastholm, O.T. 2015. Spydkvinden og den myrdede. Gerdrupgraven 35 år efter. *Romu: årsskrift fra Roskilde Museum* 2015: 63–85.

Kastholm, O.T. 2016. Afvigende normaler i vikingetidens gravskik? Dobbeltgraven fra Gerdrup 35 år efter. In J. Ulriksen & H. Lyngstrøm (eds) *Død og begravet – i vikingetiden*. Saxo-instituttet, Københavns Universitet, København: 63–74.

Kazakevičius, V. 1992. Sword Chapes from Lithuania. In A. Loit, E. Mugurēvičs & A. Caune (eds) *Die Kontakte zwischen Ostbaltikum und Skandinavien im frühen Mittelalter*. Almqvist & Wiksell International, Stockholm: 91–107.

Kazakevičius, V. 1996. Topory bojowe typu M. Chronologia i pochodzenie na ziemiach Bałtów. In Z. Kurnatowska (ed.) *Słowiańszczyzna w Europie średniowiecznej. Vol. 2: Miasta i rzemiosła*. Instytut Archeologii i Etnologii Polskiej Akademii Nauk, Wrocław: 233–241.

Kjellström, A. 2012. Projektet Människor i brytningstid: Skelettgravar i Birka och dess nära omland. In C. Hedenstierna-Jonson (ed.) *Birka nu. Pågående forskning om världsarvets Birka och Hovgården*. Historiska Museet, Stockholm: 69–80.

Kjellström, A. 2016. People in Transition: Life in the Mälaren Valley from an Osteological Perspective. In V. Turner (ed.) *Shetland and the Viking World. Papers from the Proceedings of the 17th Viking Congress 2013*. Shetland Amenity Trust, Lerwick: 197–202.

Kjesrud, K. & N. Løkka (eds) 2017. *Dronningen i vikingtid og middelalder*. Scandinavian Academic Press, Oslo.

Klevnäs, A. 2015. Overkill. Reopening Graves to Maim the Dead in Anglo-Saxon England. In L. Gardeła & K. Kajkowski (eds) *Limbs, Bones and Reopened Graves in Past Societies/Kończyny, kości i ekshumacje w dawnych kulturach*. Muzeum Zachodniokaszubskie w Bytowie, Bytów: 177–213.

Klevnäs, A. 2016. 'Imbued with the Essence of the Owner': Personhood and Possessions in the Reopening and Reworking of Viking-Age Burials. *European Journal of Archaeology* 19(3): 456–476.

Klos, L. 2006. Wanderer zwischen den Welten. Die Kriegerinnen der Eisenzeit. In E. Marold & U. Müller (eds) *Beretning fra femogtyvende tværfaglige vikingesymposium*. Hikuin, Aarhus Universitetet, Afdeling for Middelalder- og Renæssancearkæologi, Højbjerg: 25–43

Klos, L. 2007. Lady of the Rings: Järnålderns kvinnor mellan makt och kult. In I. Nordgren (ed.) *Kult, guld och makt: ett tvarvetenskapligt symposium i Götene*. Historieforum Västra Götaland, Skara: 70–86.

Koperski, A. 2004. Początki osadnictwa słowiańskiego i rozwój wczesnośredniowiecznego Przemyśla. In A. Koperski (ed.) *Dzieje Przemyśla. Tom I. Osadnictwo pradziejowe i wczesnośredniowieczne. Część II – Analiza źródeł i synteza*. Towarzystwo Przyjaciół Nauk w Przemyślu, Przemyśl: 77–216.

Kopytoff, I. 1986. The Cultural Biography of Things: Commoditization as a Process. In A. Appadurai (ed.) *The Social Life of Things: Commodities in Cultural Perspective*. Cambridge University Press, Cambridge: 64–91.

Kostrzewski, J. 1921. Cmentarzysko ze śladami kultury wikingów w Łubówku w pow. gnieźnieńskim. *Przegląd Archeologiczny* 1/3–4: 140–147.

Kotowicz, P.N. 2011. The Sign of the Cross on the Early Medieval Axes – A Symbol of Power, Magic or Religion? In L. Marek (ed.) *Weapons Bring Peace? Warfare in Medieval and Early Modern Europe*. Institute of Archaeology, University of Wrocław, Wrocław: 41–55.

Kotowicz, P.N. 2014. *Topory wczesnośredniowieczne z ziem polskich. Katalog źródeł*. Fundacja Rzeszowskiego Ośrodka Archeologicznego/Instytut Archeologii Uniwersytetu Rzeszowskiego/Muzeum Historyczne w Sanoku, Rzeszów.

Kotowicz, P.N. 2018. *Early Medieval Axes from the Territory of Poland*. Polish Academy of Arts and Sciences, Kraków.

Kovalenko, V. 2013. Scandinavians in the East of Europe: In Search of Glory or a New Motherland? In L. Bjerg, J.H. Lind & S. Sindbæk (eds) *From Goths to Varangians: Communication and Cultural Exchange Between the Baltic and the Black Sea*. Aarhus University Press, Aarhus: 257–294.

Kovalenko, V., A. Motsya & Y. Syty 2012. Kurgan s kamernym pogrebeniem iz raskopok 2006 g. In F. Androshchuk & V. Zotsenko (eds) *Scandinavian Antiquities of Southern Rus'. A Catalogue*. Ukranian National Committee for Byzantine Studies, Paris: 322–335.

Kovalev, R. 2012. Grand Princess Olga of Rus' Shows the Bird: Her 'Christian Falcon' Emblem. *Russian History* 39(4): 460–451.

Krappe, A.H. 1926. The Valkyries. *Modern Language Review* 21: 55–76.

Krause, W. 1926. *Die Frau in der Sprache der altisländischen Familiengeschichten*. Vandenhoeck & Ruprecht, Göttingen.

Kristján Eldjárn & Adolf Friðriksson 2000. *Kuml og haugfé. Ur heiðnum sið á Íslandi, 2 utgafa*. Fornleifastofnun Íslands/Mál og Menning/Þjóðminjasafn Íslands, Reykjavík.

Kristjánsson, J. 2007. *Eddas and Sagas. Iceland's Medieval Literature*. Hið íslenska bókmenntafélag, Reykjavík.

Kucypera, P., P. Pranke & S. Wadyl 2011. *Wczesnośredniowieczne toporki miniaturowe*. Wydawnictwo Adam Marszałek, Toruń.

Kuczkowski, A. 2008. Wolińska włócznia Juliusza Cezara – próba interpretacji. In M. Bogacki, M. Franz & Z. Pilarczyk (eds) *Kultura Ludów Morza Bałtyckiego. Tom 1. Starożytność i średniowiecze. Materiały z III Międzynarodowej Sesji Naukowej Dziejów Ludów Morza Bałtyckiego. Wolin 20–22 lipca 2007*. Wydawnictwo Adam Marszałek, Toruń: 408–421.

Kuhn, H. & G. Neckel (eds) 1983. *Die Lieder des Codex Regius nebst verwandten Denkmälern*. Carl Winter Universitätsverlag, Heidelberg.

Kulakov, V.I. & M.Y. Markovets 2004. Birds as Companions of Germanic Gods and Heroes. *Acta Archaeologica* 75: 179–188.

Kurasiński, T. 2004. Dziecko i strzała. Z problematyki wyposażania grobów w militaria na terenie Polski wczesnopiastowskiej (XI–XII wiek). In W. Dzieduszycki & J. Wrzesiński (eds) *Dusza maluczka a strata ogromna*. Stowarzyszenie Naukowe Archeologów Polskich, Poznań: 131–141.

Kurasiński, T. 2005. Topory typu M w grobach na terenie Polski wczesnośredniowiecznej – próba oceny znalezisk. In W. Dzieduszycki & J. Wrzesiński (eds) *Do ut des – dar, pochówek, tradycja*. Stowarzyszenie Naukowe Archeologów Polskich, Poznań: 199–224.

Kurasiński, T. 2008. Nie tylko broń. Drobne przedmioty codziennego użytku na wyposażeniu wczesnośredniowiecznego wojownika w świetle znalezisk grobowych z ziem polskich (X–XIII w.). In W. Świętosławski (ed.) *Nie tylko broń. Niemilitarne wyposażenie wojowników w starożytności i średniowieczu*. Łódzkie Towarzystwo Naukowe, Łódź: 27–49.

Kurasiński, T. 2014. Grotem w dół, grotem w górę. Deponowanie włóczni w grobach wczesnośredniowiecznych na ziemiach polskich. In T. Kurasiński & K. Skóra (eds) *Grób w przestrzeni, przestrzeń w grobie. Przestrzenne uwarunkowania w dawnej obrzędowości pogrzebowej*. Łódzkie Towarzystwo Naukowe, Łódź: 159–190.

Kurasiński, T. & K. Skóra 2016. *Cmentarzysko w Radomiu. Stanowisko 4*. Wydawnictwo Instytutu Archeologii i Etnologii Polskiej Akademii Nauk, Łódź.

Kyhlberg, O. 2012. *Den långa järnåldern. Sociala strategier, normer, traditioner*. Department of Archaeology and Ancient History, Uppsala.

Lassen, A. 2003. *Øjet og blindheden i norrøn litteratur og mytologi*. Museum Tusculanums Forlag, Copenhagen.

Lassen, A., A. Ney & Ármann Jakobsson (eds) 2012. *The Legendary Sagas. Origins and Development*. University of Iceland Press, Reykjavík.

Lauritsen, T. & O.T. Kastholm Hansen 2003. Transvestite Vikings? *Viking Heritage Magazine* 2003(1): 14–17.

Leahy, K. & C. Paterson 2001. New Light on Viking Presence in Lincolnshire. In J. Graham-Campbell, R. Hall, J. Jesch & D.N. Parsons (eds) *Vikings and the Danelaw. Select Papers from the Proceedings of the Thirteenth Viking Congress. Nottingham and York, 21–30 August 1997*. Oxbow Books, Oxford: 181–202.

Lia, Ø. 2004. Vikingtidsgravenes rituelle kompleksitet. In L. Melheim, L. Hedeager & K. Oma (eds) *Mellom himmel og jord. Foredrag fra seminar om religionsarkeologi. Isegran 31. Januar – 2. Februar 2002*. Instituttet for Arkeologi, Kunsthistorie og Konservering, Universitetet i Oslo, Oslo: 292–319.

Lie, R.O. 2016. Birkakrigere i Norge? *Spor* 2: 33–37.

Lindblom, C. 2016. Våbenfør kvinde i vognfading fra Oens – et bidrag til diskussionen om vognfadingsgrave med atypisk udstyr. In J. Ulriksen & H. Lyngstrøm (eds) *Død og begravet – i vikingetiden*. Saxo-instituttet, Københavns Universitet, København: 95–110.

Lindblom, C. & K. Balsgaard Juul 2019. Pokkers køn. *Tings Tale. Tidsskrift for Materiel Kultur* 1: 43–62.

Lindow, J. 2001. *Norse Mythology. A Guide to the Gods, Heroes, Rituals and Beliefs*. Oxford University Press, Oxford.

Linduff, K.M. & K.S. Rubinson (eds) 2008. *Are All Warriors Male? Gender Roles on the Ancient Eurasian Steppe*. AltaMira Press, Langham-New York-Toronto and Plymouth.

Liwoch, R. 2008. Zachodnioukraińskie miecze i trzewiki pochew mieczowych od X do połowy XIII w. *Acta Militaria Mediaevalia* 4: 39–59.

Løkka, N. 2014. Vikingtidskvinnen i ettertidens lys. In N. Coleman & N. Løkka (eds) *Kvinner i vikingtid. Vikingatidens kvinnor*. Scandinavian Academic Press, Oslo: 11–36.

Lower, W. 2015. *Furie Hitlera. Niemki na froncie wschodnim*. Wydawnictwo Czarne, Wołowiec.

Lund, A.B. 2016. *Women and Weapons in the Viking Age*. Aarhus University (Unpublished MA Thesis), Aarhus.

Lund, J. & M. Moen 2019. Hunting Identities: Intersectional Perspectives on Viking Age Mortuary Expressions. *Fennoscandia Archaeologica* 36: 142–155.

Lundström, I. & O. Foldøy 1995. Preface. In I. Lundström & G. Adolfsson (eds) *The Powerful Woman: From Volve to Witch*.

Arkeologisk Museum i Stavanger, Stavanger: 3.

Maixner, B. 2010. *Haithabu. Fernhandelszentrum zwischen den Welten*. Archäologisches Landesmuseum in der Stiftung Schleswig-Holsteinische Landesmuseen Schloss Gottorf, Schleswig.

Majchczack, B.S. 2016. The Current Model of Archaeological Metal Detecting and its Success in Schleswig-Holstein. In J. Martens & M. Ravn (eds) *Pløyejord som kontekst. Nye utfordringer for forskning, forvaltning og formidling. Artikkelsamling*. Portal Forlag og Kulturhistorisk Museum, Oslo: 89–100.

Malinowski, T. 2005. Wczesnośredniowieczne groby jeźdźców z Komorowa. In J. Dudek (ed.) *Europa Środkowo-Wschodnia. Ideologia, historia a społeczeństwo. Księga poświęcona pamięci Profesora Wojciecha Peltza*. Oficyna Wydawnicza Uniwersytetu Zielonogórskiego, Zielona Góra: 473–481.

Mäntylä, S. 2005. Broad-bladed Battle-axes, Their Function and Symbolic Meaning. In S. Mäntylä (ed.) *Rituals and Relations: Studies on the Society and Material Culture of the Baltic Finns*. Finnish Academy of Science and Letters, Saarijärvi: 105–130.

Marek, L. 2004. *Wczesnośredniowieczne miecze z Europy Środkowej i Wschodniej. Dylematy archeologa i bronioznawcy*. Wydawnictwo Uniwersytetu Wrocławskiego, Wrocław.

Marek, L. 2005. *Early Medieval Swords from Central and Eastern Europe. Dillemas of an Archaeologist and a Student of Arms*. Wydawnictwo Uniwersytetu Wrocławskiego, Wrocław.

Margeson, S. 1997. *The Vikings in Norfolk*. Norfolk Museums Service, Norwich.

Matczak, M.D. & W. Chudziak 2018. Medical Therapeutics and the Place of Healing in Early Medieval Culmen in Poland. *World Archaeology* 50(3), 434–460.

Mayburd, M. 2014. 'Helzt tottumk nu heima í millim...' A Reassessment of Hervör in Light of Seiðr's Supernatural Gender Dynamics. *Arkiv för nordisk filologi* 129: 121–164.

Mayburd, M. 2020. Objects and Agency in the Medieval North: The Case of Old Norse Magic Swords. *Średniowiecze Polskie i Powszechne* 12(16): 42–68.

Mayor, A. 2014. *The Amazons. Lives & Legends of Warrior Women Across the Ancient World*. Princeton University Press, Princeton.

McKinnell, J. 2002. Þorgerðr Hölgabrúðr and *Hyndluljóð*. In R. Simek & W. Heizmann (eds) *Mythological Women: Studies in Memory of Lotte Motz (1922–1997)*. Fassbaender, Wien: 265–290.

McKinnell, J. 2005. *Meeting the Other in Norse Myth and Legend*. D.S. Brewer, Cambridge.

McKinnell, J. 2014. Two Sex Goddesses: Þorgerðr Hölgabrúðr and Freyja in *Hyndluljóð*. In D. Kick & J.D. Shafer (eds) *Essays on Eddic Poetry. John McKinnell*. University of Toronto Press, Toronto Buffalo London: 268–291.

McLeod, S. 2019. Shieldmaidens in Anglo-Saxon England: Historical Possibility or Wishful Thinking? In P. Hardwick & K. Lister (eds) *Vikings and the Vikings. Essays on the Television's History Channel Series*. McFarland & Company, Inc., Publishers, Jefferson, North Carolina.

Meissner, R. 1921. *Die Kenningar der Skalden. Ein Beitrag zur skaldischen Poetik*. Schroeder, Bonn & Leipzig.

Meulengracht Sørensen, P. 1983. *The Unmanly Man: Concepts of Sexual Defamation in Early Northern Society*. Odense University Press, Odense.

Meylan, N. & L. Rösli (eds) 2020. *Old Norse Myths as Political Ideologies: Critical Studies in the Appropriation of Medieval Narratives*. Brepols, Turnhout.

Mihajlov, K.A. 2011. Chamber-Graves as Interregional Phenomenon of the Viking Age: From Denmark to Old Rus. In M. Rębkowski (ed.) *Ekskluzywne życie – dostojny pochówek. W kręgu kultury elitarnej wieków średnich*. Instytut Archeologii i Etnologii Polskiej Akademii Nauk, Wolin: 205–221.

Milek, K. 2006. *Houses and Households in Early Icelandic Society: Geoarchaeology and the Interpretation of Social Space*. Cambridge University (Unpublished PhD Thesis), Cambridge.

Milek, K. 2012. The Roles of Pit Houses and Gendered Spaces on Viking-Age Farmsteads in Iceland. *Medieval Archaeology* 56: 85–130.

Mitchell, S.A. 2020. Place-names, Periphrasis, and Popular Tradition: Odinic Toponyms on Samsø. In I. García Losquiño, O. Sundqvist & D. Taggart (eds) *Making the Profane Sacred in the Viking Age. Essays in Honour of Stefan Brink*. Brepols, Turnhout: 283–295.

MKP 1958. Województwo poznańskie. Góra, pow. Turek. *Z Otchłani Wieków* 24(6): 405–406.

Moen, M. 2011. *The Gendered Landscape. A Discussion on Gender, Status and Power in the Norwegian Viking Age Landscape*. Archaeopress, Oxford.

Moen, M. 2014. Women in the Landscape. In N. Coleman & N. Løkka (eds) *Kvinner i vikingtid. Vikingatidens kvinnor*. Scandinavian Academic Press, Oslo: 120–147.

Moen, M. 2019a. *Challenging Gender. A Reconsideration of Gender in the Viking Age Using the Mortuary Landscape. Vol 1*. Department of Archaeology, Conservation and History. University of Oslo, Oslo.

Moen, M. 2019b. Gender and Archaeology: Where Are We Now? *Archaeologies: Journal of the World Archaeological Congress* 15: 206–226.

Moen, M. 2019c. *Challenging Gender. A Reconsideration of Gender in the Viking Age Using the Mortuary Landscape. Vol 2*. Department of Archaeology, Conservation and History. University of Oslo, Oslo.

Moilanen, U. 2020. Theoretical and Methodological Approaches to Non-Normative Burials in Finland in the Eleventh-Thirteenth Centuries AD. In T.K. Betsinger, A.B. Scott & A. Tsaliki (eds) *The Odd, the Unusual, and the Strange. Bioarchaeological Interpretations of the Human Past: Local, Regional, and Global Perspectives*. University of Florida Press, Gainesville: 225–245.

Mokkelbost, M. 2007. *Sittegravbyggerne i Sandvika. En arkeologisk analyse av en lokal tradisjon i yngre jernalder på øya Jøa i Ytre Namdal*. NTNU, Trondheim.

Montgomery, J. 2000. Ibn Fadlān and the Rūssyyah. *Journal of Arabic and Islamic Studies* 3: 1–25.

Mørck, G. 1901. Indberetning om arkæologiske undersøgelser paa Nordre Kjølen, Aasnes pgd., Soløer. *Foreningen til Norske Fortidsmindesmærkers Bevaring. Aarsberetning for 1900*: 68–74.

Motz, L. 1975. The King and the Goddess. An Interpretation of the Svipdagsmál. *Arkiv för nordisk filologi* 90: 133–150.

Motz, L. 1980a. Sister in the Cave; the Stature and the Function of the Female Figures of the Eddas. *Arkiv för nordisk filologi* 95: 168–182.

Motz, L. 1980b. Old Icelandic völva: A New Derivation. *Indogermanische Forschungen. Zeitschrift für Indogermanistik und Allgemeine Sprachwissenschaft* 85: 196–206.

Motz, L. 1981. Giantesses and their Names. *Frühmittelalterliche Studien* 15: 495–511.

Motz, L. 1988. The Storm of Troll Women. *Maal og Minne* 1988: 31–41.

Motz, L. 1993. *The Beauty and the Hag. Female Figures of Germanic Faith and Myth*. Fassbaender, Wien.

Müller-Wille, M. 1969. Bestattung im Boot: Studien zu einer nordeuropäischen Grabsitte. *Offa* 25–26: 7–203.

Müller-Wille, M. 1972. Pferdegrab und Pferdeopfer im frühen Mittelalter. *Berichten van de Rijksdienst voor het Oudheidkundig Boemonderzoek* 20–21 1970/1971: 119–248.

Müller-Wille, M. 1985. Frühmittelalterliche Bestattungen in Wagen und Wagenkasten. *Archaeology and Environment* 4: 17–30.

Munch, G.S. 2003. Jet, Amber, Bronze, Silver and Gold Artefacts. In G.S. Munch, O.S. Johansen & E. Roesdahl (eds) *Borg in Lofoten. A Chieftain's Farm in North Norway*. Tapir Academic Press, Trondheim: 241–252.

Mundal, E. 1974. *Fylgjemotiva i norrøn literatur*. Universitetsforlaget, Oslo.

Mundal, E. & G. Steinsland 1989. Kvinner og medisinsk magi. In H. Hunneng (ed.) *Kvinnors rosengård – medeltidskvinnors liv og hälsa, lust och barnafödande*. Stockholms Universitet, Stockholm: 97–121.

Murphy, L.J. 2013. *Herjans dísir: Valkyrjur, Supernatural Femininities, and Elite Warrior Culture in Late Pre-Christian Iron Age*. University of Iceland (Unpublished MA Thesis), Reykjavík.

Nadolski, A. 1954. *Studia nad uzbrojeniem polskim w X, XI i XII wieku*. Zakład im. Ossolińskich we Wrocławiu, Łódzkie Towarzystwo Naukowe, Łódź.

Nadolski, A. 1955. Pochwa miecza znaleziona w osadzie miejskiej z XI wieku w Gdańsku. *Wiadomości Archeologiczne* 22(2): 186–192.

Nadolski, A., A. Abramowicz & T. Poklewski 1959. *Cmentarzysko z XI w. w Lutomiersku pod Łodzią*. Łódzkie Towarzystwo Naukowe, Łódź.

Næss, J.-R. 1974. Kvinner i vikingtid. *Frá Haug ok Heidni* 1974: 124–139.

Næss, J.-R. 1994. Kvinneliv i Sagatiden: En statusrapport sett fra arkeologies ståsted og synspunkter på fremtidige forskningsoppgaver. In O. Foldøy (ed.) *Frøyas Hus: Rapport fra fagseminaret 'Kvinne- og dagliv i sagatid', som ble holdt på Hamar 28.-29. april 1994*. Arkeologisk Museum i Stavanger, Stavanger: 13–47.

Næss, J.-R. 2006. Prolog. Kvinne – arkeolog – kvinnearkeolog gjennom 45 år. Om og til Gro. In R. Barndon, S. Innselset, K.K. Kristoffersen & T. Lødøen (eds) *Samfunn, symboler og identitet. Festskrift til Gro Mandt på 70-årsdagen*. Arkeologisk Institutt, Universitetet i Bergen, Bergen: 15–26.

Näsström, B.-M. 1995. *Freyja – the Great Goddess of the North*. University of Lund, Lund.

Näsström, B.-M. 1996. Freyja and Frigg – Two Aspects of the Great Goddess. In J. Pentikäinen (ed.) *Shamanism and Northern Ecology*. de Gruyter, Berlin and New York: 81–96.

Ney, A., Armann Jakobsson & A. Lassen (eds) 2009. *Fornaldarsagaerne. Myter og virkelighed. Studier i de oldislandske fornaldarsögur Norðurlanda*. Museum Tusculanums Forlag/Københavns Universitet, København.

Nicolaysen, N. 1882. *Langskibet fra Gokstad ved Sandefjord*. Cammermeyer, Kristiania.

Nielsen, B.H. 1991. Langbladsøksen. *Skalk* 1991(2): 9–13.

Nilsson Stutz, L. & S. Tarlow (eds) 2013. *The Oxford Handbook of the Archaeology of Death and Burial*. Oxford University Press, Oxford.

Nilsson, T. 1992. Stentinget. *Skalk* 1992(4): 3–9.

Nordberg, A. 2002. Vertikalt placerade vapen i vikingatida graver. *Fornvännen* 97: 15–24.

Nordberg, A. 2003. *Krigarna i Odins sal. Dödsföreställingar och krigarkult i fornnordisk religion*. Stockholms Universitet, Stockholm.

Nordeide, S.W. 2006. Thor's Hammer in Norway. A Symbol of Reaction Against the Christian Cross? In A. Andrén, K. Jennbert & C. Raudvere (eds) *Old Norse Religion in Long-Term Perspectives. Origins, Changes and Interactions. An International Conference in Lund, Sweden, June 3–7, 2004*. Nordic Academic Press, Lund: 218–223.

Nordeide, S.W. 2011. *The Viking Age as a Period of Religious Transformation: The Christianisation of Norway from AD 560–1150/1200*. Brepols, Turnhout.

Nordeide, S.W. & S. Brink (eds) 2013. *Sacred Sites and Holy Places: Exploring the Sacralisation of Landscape through Time and Space*. Brepols, Turnhout.

Norderval, L.W. 2006. *Skandinaviske jomfruer eller andre skeivinger? – et blikk på kjønn i vikingtid*. Norges Teknisk-naturvitenskaplige Universitet, Trondheim (Unpublished MA Thesis).

Nordström, N. 2006. From Queen to Sorcerer. In A. Andrén, K. Jennbert & C. Raudvere (eds) *Old Norse Religion in Long-Term Perspectives. Origins, Changes and Interactions. An International Conference in Lund, Sweden, June 3–7, 2004*. Nordic Academic Press, Lund: 399–404.

Norrman, L.E. 2000. Woman or Warrior? The Construction of Gender in Old Norse Myth. In G. Barnes & M. Clunies Ross (eds) *Old Norse Myths, Literature and Society. Proceedings of the 11th International Saga Conference, 2–7 July 2000 University of Sydney*. Centre for Medieval Studies, University of Sydney, Sydney: 375–385.

Norrman, L.E. 2004. Visual and Verbal Art: Weaving and Poetry in Classical Greek and Old Norse Narratives. *Cosmos. Journal of the Traditional Cosmology Society* 20: 121–151.

Norrman, L.E. 2005. Weaving Meaning: Micro Narratives in the Nordic Oral Tradition. *Viking and Medieval Scandinavia* 1: 137–162.

Norrman, L.E. 2008. *Viking Women. The Narrative Voice in Woven Tapestries*. Cambria Press, Amherst, New York.

Nygaard, S. & L.J. Murphy 2017. Processioner i førkristen nordisk religion. *Religionsvidenskabeligt Tidsskrift* 66: 40–77.

Nylén, E. & J.P. Lamm 2003. *Bildstenar*. Gidlunds, Värnamo.

O'Donoghue, H. 2004. *Old Norse-Icelandic Literature. A Short Introduction*. Blackwell, Oxford.

O'Meadhra, U. 2018. Unfinished and Unused. A New Look at Two Iconic Antler Finds from Sigtuna, the 'Mammen' Sword-guard and the 'Sigtuna Viking'. *Situne Dei. Årsskrift för Sigtunaforskning och historisk arkeologi* 2018: 6–33.

Oakeshott, E. 1991. *Records of the Medieval Sword*. The Boydell Press, Woodbridge.

Oakeshott, E. 1999. *The Archaeology of Weapons: Arms and Armour from Prehistory to the Age of Chivalry*. The Boydell Press, Woodbridge.

Odebäck, K. 2018. 'Krigare' i graven? Praktik, ideal och iscensättning under skandinavisk vikingatid. *Primitive Tider* 20: 65–80.

Oestigaard, T. 2015. Changing Rituals and Reinventing Tradition: The Burnt Viking Ship at Myklebostad, Western Norway. In J.R. Brandt, M. Prusac & H. Roland (eds) *Death and Changing Rituals: Function and Meaning in Ancient Funerary Practices*. Oxbow Books, Oxford: 357–377.

Ohlmarks, Å. 1939a. *Studien zum Problem des Schamanismus*. Lunds Universitet, Lund.

Ohlmarks, Å. 1939b. Arktischer Schamanismus und altnordischer seiðr. *Arkiv für Religionswissenschaft* 36: 171–180.

Orchard, A. 2002. *Cassell's Dictionary of Norse Myth and Legend*. Cassell, London.

Orrling, C. 2008. Schwedens Wikingerzeit. In U. Löber (ed.) *Die Wikinger*. Landesmuseum Koblenz, Koblenz: 21–37.

Owen, O. & M. Dalland 1999. *Scar: A Viking Boat Burial on Sanday, Orkney*. Tuckwell Press/Historic Scotland, East Linton.

Parker Pearson, M. 2003. *The Archaeology of Death and Burial*. The History Press, Sparkford.

Paterson, C., A.J. Parsons, R.M. Newman, N. Johnson & C.H. Davis 2014. *Shadows in the Sand: Excavation of a Viking-Age Cemetery at Cumwhitton, Cumbria*. Oxford Archaeology North, Lancaster.

Paulsen, P. 1939. *Axt und Kreuz bei den Nordgermanen*. Ahnenerbe-Stiftung-Verlag, Berlin.

Paulsen, P. 1953. *Schwertortbänder der Wikingerzeit. Ein Beitrag zur Frühgeschichte Osteuropas*. Kohlhammer, Stuttgart.

Paulsen, P. 1956. *Axt und Kreuz in Nord- und Osteuropa*. Habelt, Bonn.

Paulsen, P. 1966. *Drachenkämpfer, Löwenritter und die Heinrichsage. Eine Studie über die Kirchentür von Valthjofsstad auf Island*. Böhlau Verlag, Köln, Graz.

Pearl, F.B. 2014. The Water Dragon and the Snake Witch: Two Vendel Period Picture Stones from Gotland, Sweden. *Current Swedish Archaeology* 22: 137–156.

Pedersen, A. 1997. Weapons and Riding Gear in Burials – Evidence of Military and Social Rank in 10th Century Denmark? In A.N. Jørgensen & B.L. Clausen (eds) *Military Aspects of Scandinavian Society in a European Perspective, AD 1–1300*. National Museum, Copenhagen: 123–135.

Pedersen, A. 2009. Amulette und Amulettsitte der jüngeren Eisen- und Wikingerzeit in Südskandinavien. In U. von Freeden, H. Friesinger & E. Wamers (eds) *Glaube, Kult und Herrschaft. Phänomene des Religiösen im 1. Jahrtausend n. Chr. in Mittel- und Nordeuropa. Akten des 59. Internationalen Sachsensymposions und der Grundprobleme der frühgeschichtlichen Entwicklung im Mitteldonauraum*. Habelt, Bonn: 287–302.

Pedersen, A. 2014a. *Dead Warriors in Living Memory. A Study of Weapon and Equestrian Burials in Viking-Age Denmark, AD 800–1000*. University Press of Southern Denmark and the National Museum of Denmark, Copenhagen.

Pedersen, U. 2014b. Kaupangs kvinner. In N. Coleman & N. Løkka (eds) *Kvinner i vikingtid. Vikingatidens kvinnor*. Scandinavian Academic Press, Oslo: 166–185.

Pedersen, U. 2016. *Into the Melting Pot: Non-ferrous Metalworkers in Viking-period Kaupang. Kaupang Excavation Project Publication Series. Volume 4*. Aarhus University Press, Aarhus.

Pentz, P. 2018. Viking Art, Snorri Sturluson and Recent Metal Detector Finds. *Fornvännen* 113: 17–33.

Pentz, P., M. Panum Baastrup, S. Krag & U. Mannering 2009. Kong Haralds vølve. *Nationalmuseets Arbeidsmark 2009*: 215–232.

Pesch, A. 2018. Gotterthrone und ein gefahrlicher Stuhl: Bemerkungen zum 'Odin aus Lejre'. In A. Bauer & A. Pesch (eds) *Hvanndalir – Beiträge zur europäischen Altertumskunde und mediävistischen Literaturwissenschaft*. de Gruyter, Berlin: 463–496.

Pestell, T. 2013. Imports or Immigrants? Reassessing Scandinavian Metalwork in Late Anglo-Saxon East Anglia. In D. Bates & R. Liddiard (eds) *East Anglia and its North Sea World in the Middle Ages*. The Boydell Press, Woodbridge: 230–255.

Petersen, J. 1919. *De norske vikingesverd. En typologisk-kronologisk studie over vikingetidens vaaben*. Jacob Dybwad, Kristiania.

Petersen, J. 1928. *Vikingetidens smykker*. Arkeologisk Museum i Stavanger, Stavanger.

Petersen, J. 1951. *Vikingetidens redskaper*. Videnskaps-Akademi, Oslo.

Petersen, P.V. 1992a. Danefæ. In R.A. Sekretariat (ed.) *Arkæologiske udgravninger i Danmark 1991*. Det Arkæologiske Nævn, København: 208–218.

Petersen, P.V. 1992b. Valkyrier i Ribe. *By, Marsk og Geest* 1992: 41–46.

Petersen, P.V. 2005. Odins fugle, valkyrier og bersærker – billeder fra nordisk mytologi fundet med metaldetektor. In T. Capelle & C. Fisher (eds) *Ragnarok. Odins verden*. Silkeborg Museum, Silkeborg: 57–86.

Petersen, P.V. 2010. Valkyrier og bersærker. Mytologien i smykkekunsten. In M. Andersen & P.O. Nielsen (eds) *Danefæ. Skatte fra den danske muld*. Gyldendal, København: 134–138.

Petersson, K.G. 1958. Et gravfynd från Klinta, Köpings sn., Öland. *Tor* 4: 134–150.

Petrenko, V.G. 1995. Scythian Culture in the North Caucasus. In J. Davis-Kimball (ed.) *Nomads of the Eurasian Steppes in the Early Iron Age*. Zinat Press, Berkeley: 5–26.

Petrenko, V.G., V.E. Maslov & A.R. Kantorovich 2004. Pogrebenie znatnoi skifyanki iz mogilnika Novozavedennoe-II (predvaritelnaya publikatia). In L.T. Yablonsky (ed.) *Arkheologicheskie pamyatniki rannego zheleznogo veka Uga Rossii*. IA RAN-Press, Moscow: 179–210.

Poklewski, T. 1961. *Misy brązowe z XI, XII, XIII wieku*. Łódzkie Towarzystwo Naukowe, Łódź.

Poole, R. 1991. *Viking Poems on War and Peace. A Study in Skaldic Narrative*. University of Toronto Press, Toronto.

Poppe, A. 1992. Once Again Concerning the Baptism of Olga, Archontissa of Rus. *Dumbarton Oaks Papers* 46: 271–277.

Præstgaard Andersen, L. 1982. *Skjoldmøer – en kvindemyte*. Gyldendal, Viborg.

Præstgaard Andersen, L. 2002. On Valkyries, Shield-Maidens and Other Armed Women – in Old Norse Sources and Saxo Grammaticus. In R. Simek & W. Heizmann (eds) *Mythological Women: Studies in Memory of Lotte Motz, 1922–1997*. Fassbaender, Wien: 291–318.

Price, N.S. 2002. *The Viking Way. Religion and War in Late Iron Age Scandinavia*. Department of Archaeology and Ancient History, Uppsala University, Uppsala.

Price, N.S. 2006. What's in a Name? An Archaeological Identity Crisis for the Norse Gods (and Some of their Friends). In A. Andrén, K. Jennbert & C. Raudvere (eds) *Old Norse Religion in Long-Term Perspectives. Origins, Changes and Interactions*.

An International Conference in Lund, Sweden, June 3–7, 2004. Nordic Academic Press, Lund: 179–183.

Price, N.S. 2008a. Bodylore and the Archaeology of Embedded Religion: Dramatic Licence in the Funerals of the Vikings. In D.S. Whitley & K. Hays-Gilpin (eds) *Belief in the Past. Theoretical Approaches to the Archaeology of Religion.* Walnut Creek: 143–165.

Price, N.S. 2008b. Dying and the Dead: Viking Age Mortuary Behaviour. In S. Brink & N. Price (eds) *The Viking World.* Routledge, London and New York: 257–273.

Price, N.S. 2010a. Heathen Songs and Devil's Games. In M. Carver, A. Sanmark & S. Semple (eds) *Signals of Belief in Early England. Anglo-Saxon Paganism Revisited.* Oxbow Books, Oxford: xii–xvi.

Price, N.S. 2010b. Passing into Poetry: Viking-Age Mortuary Drama and the Origins of Norse Mythology. *Medieval Archaeology* 54: 123–156.

Price, N.S. 2012a. Wooden Worlds. Individual and Collective in the Chamber Graves of Birka. In C. Hedenstierna-Jonson (ed.) *Birka nu. Pågående forskning om världsarvet Birka och Hovgården.* Historiska Museet, Stockholm: 81–93.

Price, N.S. 2012b. Mythic Acts. Material Narratives of the Dead in Viking Age Scandinavia. In C. Raudvere & J.P. Schjødt (eds) *More than Mythology. Narratives, Ritual Practices and Regional Distribution in Pre-Christian Scandinavian Religions.* Nordic Academic Press, Lund: 13–46.

Price, N.S. 2013a. The Way of the Warrior. In G. Williams, P. Pentz & M. Wemhoff (eds) *Viking.* Nationalmuseet, Copenhagen: 116–117.

Price, N.S. 2013b. Belief & Ritual. In G. Williams, P. Pentz & M. Wemhoff (eds) *Viking.* Nationalmuseet, Copenhagen: 162–195.

Price, N.S. 2014. Nine Paces from Hel: Time and Motion in Old Norse Ritual Performance. *World Archaeology* 46(2): 178–191.

Price, N.S. 2015. From Ginnungagap to the Ragnarök. Archaeologies of the Viking Worlds. In M.H. Eriksen, U. Pedersen, B. Rundberget, I. Axelsen & H.L. Berg (eds) *Viking Worlds: Things, Spaces and Movement.* Oxbow Books, Oxford: 1–10.

Price, N.S. 2016. Pirates of the North Sea? The Viking Ship as Political Space. In L. Melheim, H. Glørstad & Z. Tsigaridas Glørstad (eds) *Comparative Perspectives on Past Colonisation, Maritime Interaction and Cultural Integration.* Equinox, Sheffield-Bristol: 149–176.

Price, N.S. 2019. *The Viking Way: Magic and Mind in Late Iron Age Scandinavia.* Oxbow Books, Oxford and Philadelphia.

Price, N.S., C. Hedenstierna-Jonson, T. Zachrisson, A. Kjellström, J. Storå, M. Krzewińska, T. Günther, V. Sobrado, M. Jakobsson & A. Götherström 2019. Viking Warrior Women? Reassessing Birka Chamber Grave Bj. 581. *Antiquity* 93(367): 181–198.

Price, T.D., C. Arcini, I. Gustin, L. Drenzel & S. Kalmring 2018. Isotopes and Human Burials at Viking Age Birka and the Mälaren Region, East Central Sweden. *Journal of Anthropological Archaeology* 49: 19–38.

Price, T.D., K.M. Frei, A.S. Dobat, N. Lynnerup & P. Bennike 2011. Who Was in Harold Bluetooth's Army? Strontium Isotope Investigations of the Cemetery at the Viking Age Fortress at Trelleborg, Denmark. *Antiquity* 85: 476–489.

Pritchard, F. 2014. Textiles from Dublin. In N. Coleman & N. Løkka (eds) *Kvinner i vikingtid. Vikingatidens kvinnor.* Scandinavian Academic Press, Oslo: 224–240.

Raffield, B. 2014. 'A River of Knives and Swords': Ritually Deposited Weapons in English Watercourses and Wetlands during the Viking Age. *European Journal of Archaeology* 17: 517–538.

Raffield, B. 2019. Playing Vikings: Militarism, Hegemonic Masculinities, and Childhood Enculturation in Viking Age Scandinavia. *Current Anthropology* 60(6): 813–835.

Raffield, B., C. Greenlow, N.S. Price & M. Collard 2016. Ingroup Identification, Identity Fusion and the Formation of Viking Warbands. *World Archaeology* 48: 35–50.

Rajewski, Z. 1937. Wielkopolskie cmentarzyska rzędowe okresu wczesnodziejowego. *Przegląd Archeologiczny* 6: 28–65.

Rajewski, Z. 1975. Koń w wierzeniach u Słowian wczesnośredniowiecznych. *Wiadomości Archeologiczne* 39: 516–521.

Ramskou, T. 1950. Viking Age Cremation Graves in Denmark. *Acta Archaeologica* 21: 137–182.

Randsborg, K. 1980. *The Viking Age in Denmark: The Formation of a State.* Duckworth, London.

Ratajczyk, Z. 2013. Jednak ostrogi – brązowe okucia typu lutomierskiego w świetle najnowszych badań na cmentarzysku w Ciepłem, gm. Gniew. *Slavia Antiqua* 54: 287–305.

Ratajczyk, Z. 2016. Groby komorowe z wczesnośredniowiecznego cmentarzyska w Ciepłem, gm. Gniew, woj. pomorskie. In D. Błaszczyk & D. Stępniewska (eds) *Pochówki w grobach komorowych na ziemiach polskich w okresie wczesnego średniowiecza.* Instytut Archeologii Uniwersytetu Warszawskiego, Warszawa: 90–101.

Redon, A. 2017. *Female Warriors of the Viking Age: Fact or Fiction?* University of Iceland (Unpublished MA Thesis), Reykjavik.

Reichborn-Kjennerud, I. 1928. *Vår gammle trolldomsmedicin. Vol. I.* Jacob Dybwad, Oslo.

Resi, H.G. 2013. Nebeneinander, gleichzeitig, doch sehr unterschiedlich. Was davon ist Individualität. In B. Ludowici (ed.) *Individual and Individuality? Approaches Towards an Archaeology of Personhood in the First Millennium AD.* Niedersächsisches Landesmuseum Hannover, Hannover: 117–122.

Révész, L. 2014. The Era of the Hungarian Conquest. In L. Révész (ed.) *The Era of the Hungarian Conquest. Permanent Exhibition of the Hungarian National Museum.* Hungarian National Museum, Budapest: 7–105.

Reynolds, A. 2009. *Anglo-Saxon Deviant Burial Customs.* Oxford University Press, Oxford.

Ringstedt, N. 1997. *The Birka Chamber-Graves. Economic and Social Aspects. An Analysis Based on Quantitative Methods.* Stockholm University, Stockholm.

Rittershaus, A. 1917. *Altnordische Frauen.* Huber, Frauenfeld.

Robbins, H. 2004. *Seated Burials at Birka: A Select Study.* University of Uppsala (Unpublished MA Thesis), Uppsala.

Roesdahl, E. 1975. Eastern Imports at the Viking Fortress of Fyrkat, Denmark. In B. Chropovský (ed.) *Rapports du IIIe Congres International d'Archéologie Slave.* Veda, Bratislava: 665–669.

Roesdahl, E. 1977. *Fyrkat. En jysk vikingeborg. II. Oldsagerne og gravpladsen.* Det kgl. nordiske Oldskriftselskab, København.

Roesdahl, E. & P. Meulengracht Sørensen (eds) 1996. *The Waking of Angantyr: The Scandinavian Past in European Culture.* Aarhus University Press, Aarhus.

Rosengren, E. 2010. Miniatyren – ingen småsak. En presentation av en alternativ tolkning till vapen- och redskapsminiatyrer i

Uppåkra. In B. Hårdh (ed.) *Uppåkrastudier 11. Från romartida skalpeller till senvikingatida urnesspännen. Nya materialstudier från Uppåkra*. Lunds Universitet, Lund: 201–212.

Rubinson, K.S. 2008. Tillya Tepe: Aspects of Gender and Cultural Identity. In K.M. Linduff & K.S. Rubinson (eds) *Are All Warriors Male? Gender Roles on the Ancient Eurasian Steppe*. AltaMira Press, Langham-New York-Toronto and Plymouth: 51–63.

Rundkvist, M. & H. Williams 2008. A Viking Boat Grave with Amber Gaming Pieces Excavated at Skamby, Östergötland, Sweden. *Medieval Archaeology* 52: 69–102.

Rygh, O. 1885. *Norske oldsager*. Cammermeyer, Christiania.

Sankiewicz, P. & A.M. Wyrwa (eds) 2013. *Topory średniowieczne z Ostrowa Lednickiego i Giecza/Medieval Axes from Lednica Holm and Giecz*. Muzeum Pierwszych Piastów na Lednicy, Lednica.

Sankiewicz, P. & A.M. Wyrwa (eds) 2018. *Broń drzewcowa i uzbrojenie ochronne z Ostrowa Lednickiego, Giecza i Grzybowa*. Muzeum Pierwszych Piastów na Lednicy, Lednica.

Sanmark, A. 2014. Women at the Thing. In N. Coleman & N. Løkka (eds) *Kvinner i vikingtid. Vikingatidens kvinnor*. Scandinavian Academic Press, Oslo: 88–105.

Sarnowska, W. 1955. Miecze średniowieczne w Polsce. *Światowit* 21: 276–323.

Sawicki, T. 1990. Wczesnośredniowieczna nakładka głowicy miecza z Gniezna. *Gniezno. Studia i Materiały Historyczne* 3: 223–236.

Sayer, D., E. Sebo & K. Hughes 2019. A Double-edged Sword: Swords: Bodies, and Personhood in Early Medieval Archaeology and Literature. *European Journal of Archaeology* 22(4): 542–566.

Sayer, D. & H. Williams (eds) 2009. *Mortuary Practices and Social Identities in the Middle Ages. Essays in Burial Archaeology in Honour of Heinrich Härke*. University of Exeter Press, Exeter.

Schetelig, H. 1905. Gravene ved Myklebostad paa Nordfjordeid. *Bergen Museums Aarbok 1905* No. 7: 1–54.

Schetelig, H. 1911. En miniatyrøks av bronse fra vikingetiden. *Bergen Museums Aarbok 1911(13)*: 1–18.

Schetelig, H. 1912. Fortegnelse over de til Bergen Museum i 1910 indkomne saker ældre end reformationen. *Bergens Museums Aarbok* 1911(8): 1–40.

Schröder, F.R. 1941. *Skadi und die Götter Skandinaviens*. Verlag von J.C.B. Mohr, Tübingen.

Schultze, H. 1987. Köpings socken. In M. Beskow Sjöberg (ed.) *Ölands järnåldersgravfält I*. Riksantikvarieämbetet/Statens Historiska Museum, Stockholm: 21–138.

Seiler, A. & O. Magnell 2017. Til árs ok friðar – gårdsnära rituella depositioner. In *at Upsalum – människor och landskapande. Utbyggnad av Ostkustbanan genom Gamla Uppsala*. Arkeologerna. Statens historiska museer, Stockholm: 189–208.

Sellevold, B.J., U.L. Hansen & J.B. Jørgensen 1984. *Iron Age Man in Denmark. Prehistoric Man in Denmark. Vol. III*. Det Kongelige Nordiske Oldskriftselskab, København.

Shelach, G. 2008. He Who Eats the Horse, She Who Rides It? Symbols of Gender Identity on the Eastern Edges of the Eurasian Steppe. In K.M. Linduff & K.S. Rubinson (eds) *Are All Warriors Male? Gender Roles on the Ancient Eurasian Steppe*. AltaMira Press, Langham-New York-Toronto and Plymouth: 93–109.

Shetelig, H. 1912. *Vestlandske graver fra jernalderen*. A/S John Griegs Boktrykkeri, Bergen.

Short, W.R. 2014. *Viking Weapons and Combat Techniques*. Westholme Publishing, Yardley.

Sigurðsson, J.V. 2017. *Skandinavia i vikingtiden*. Pax Forlag, Oslo.

Sikora, J. 2014. Groby wojowników, groby z bronią. Uwagi o wczesnośredniowiecznym rytuale deponowania uzbrojenia w grobach. In W. Dzieduszycki & J. Wrzesiński (eds) *Królowie i biskupi, rycerze i chłopi – identyfikacja zmarłych*. Stowarzyszenie Naukowe Archeologów Polskich, Poznań: 297–311.

Sikora, M. 2003–2004. Diversity in Viking Age Horse Burial: A Comparative Study of Norway, Iceland, Scotland and Ireland. *The Journal of Irish Archaeology* 12–13: 87–109.

Sikora, P. 2001. Dolne okucia pochew mieczy (tzw. trzewiki) z terenu północnej Słowiańszczyzny we wczesnym średniowieczu – katalog źródeł. *Materiały i Sprawozdania Rzeszowskiego Ośrodka Archeologicznego* 22: 107–132.

Simek, R. 2002. Goddesses, Mothers, Dísir. Iconography and Interpretation of the Female Deity in Scandinavia in the First Millennium. In R. Simek & W. Heizmann (eds) *Mythological Women. Studies in Memory of Lotte Motz*. Fassbaender, Wien: 93–124.

Simek, R. 2006. *Dictionary of Northern Mythology*. D.S. Brewer, Cambridge.

Simek, R. 2016. *Vinland! Wie die Wikinger Amerika Entdeckten*. C.H. Beck, München.

Simek, R. & W. Heizmann (eds) 2002. *Mythological Women: Studies in Memory of Lotte Motz (1922–1997)*. Fassbaender, Wien.

Simek, R. & H. Pálsson 2007. *Lexikon der altnordischen Literatur. Die mittelalterliche Literatur Norwegens und Islands*. Alfred Kröner, Stuttgart.

Skaarup, J. 1976. *Stengade II. En langelandsk gravplads med grave fra romersk jernalder og vikingetid*. Langelands Museum, Rudkøbing.

Skov, H. 2005. Aros 700–1100. In A. Damm (ed.) *Viking Aros*. Moesgård Museum, Højbjerg: 15–39.

Skre, D. (ed.) 2007. *Kaupang in Skiringssal, Kaupang Excavation Project Publication Series. Volume 1*. Aarhus University Press, Aarhus.

Skre, D. (ed.) 2008. *Means of Exchange: Dealing with Silver in the Viking Age. Kaupang Excavation Project. Publication Series. Volume 2*. Aarhus University Press, Aarhus.

Skre, D. (ed.) 2011. *Things from the Town: Artefacts and Inhabitants in Viking-Age Kaupang. Kaupang Excavation Project. Publication Series. Volume 3*. Aarhus University Press, Aarhus.

Słupecki, L.P. 1998. *Wyrocznie i wróżby pogańskich Skandynawów. Studium do dziejów idei przeznaczenia u ludów indoeuropejskich*. Instytut Archeologii i Etnologii Polskiej Akademii Nauk, Warszawa.

Smirnov, K.F. 1989. Savromatskaya i rannesarmatskaya kultury. In A.I. Melyukova (ed.) *Stepi evropeiskoi chastii SSSR v skifo-sarmatskoe vremya. Arkheologiya SSSR*. Nauka, Moscow: 165–177.

Smith, A. 2016. *Danger Close. My Epic Journey as a Combat Helicopter Pilot in Iraq and Afghanistan*. Atria Books, New York, London, Toronto, Sydney and New Delhi.

Söderberg, B. 2014. *Väg E6 Trelleborg-Vellinge: Område 6:1. Järnåldersgårdar i dösmiljö. Skåne, Trelleborgs kommun, Skegrie socken, Skegrie 39:1, fornlämning Skegrie 39*. Riksantikvarieämbetet, Lund.

Sognnes, K. 1988. *Iron Age Arrow-Heads from Hordaland, Norway. Testing a Classification System*. Universitetet i Trondheim Vitenskapsmuseet, Trondheim.

Solberg, B. 1984. *Norwegian Spear-heads from the Merovingian and Viking Periods*. Universitetet i Bergen, Bergen.

Solberg, B. 2003. *Jernalderen i Norge: Ca. 500 f. Kr – 1030 e. Kr.* Cappelen Akademisk Forlag, Oslo.

Solli, B. 1998. Odin – the *Queer*? Om det skeive i norrøn mytologi. *Universitetets Oldsaksamling Årbok* 1997–1998: 7–42.

Solli, B. 1999a. Odin the Queer? Om det skeive i norrøn mytologi. In I. Fuglestvedt, T. Gansum & A. Opedal (eds) *Et hus med mange rom: vennebok til Bjørn Myhre på 60-årsdagen*. Arkeologisk Museum i Stavanger, Stavanger: 393–427.

Solli, B. 1999b. Odin the *Queer*? On *ergi* and Shamanism in Norse Mythology. In A. Gustafson & H. Karlsson (eds) *Gylfer och arkeologiska rum – en vänbok till Jarl Nordbladh*. University of Göteborg, Göteborg: 341–349.

Solli, B. 2002. *Seid. Myter, sjamanisme og kjønn i vikingenes tid*. Pax Forlag, Oslo.

Solli, B. 2008. Queering the Cosmology of the Vikings: A Queer Analysis of the Cult of Odin and the 'Holy White Stones'. *Journal of Homosexuality* 53(1–2): 192–208.

Sołtysiak, A. 2003a. The Number Nine in the Tradition of the Norsemen. In M.S. Ziółkowski & A. Sołtysiak (eds) *Między drzewem życia a drzewem poznania. Księga ku czci profesora Andrzeja Wiercińskiego*. Uniwersytet Warszawski, Warszawa and Kielce: 231–242.

Sołtysiak, A. 2003b. Dziewiątka w kulturze Normanów. In A. Sołtysiak (ed.) *Antropologia religii. Wybór esejów, t. 3*. Warszawa: 167–184.

Soma, R. 2007. *Haugbrott og herskermakt. Om gravrøveri som ritual*. Universitetet i Oslo (Unpublished MA Thesis), Oslo.

Sørensen, M.L.S. 2004. *Gender Archaeology*. Polity Press, Cambridge.

Sørheim, H. 1997. *En høvdings gård – en høvdings grav. En vikingtids båtgrav på Egge i Steinkjer, Nord-Trøndelag*. Norges teknisk-naturvitenskapelige universitet Vitenskapsmuseet, Trondheim.

Sørheim, H. 2011. Three Prominent Norwegian Ladies with British Connections. *Acta Archaeologica* 82: 17–54.

Sørheim, H. 2014. Female Traders and Sorceresses. In N. Coleman & N. Løkka (eds) *Kvinner i vikingtid. Vikingatidens kvinnor*. Scandinavian Academic Press, Oslo: 121–147.

Speed, G. & P. Walton Rogers 2004. A Burial of a Viking Woman from Adwick-le-Street, South Yorkshire. *Medieval Archaeology* 48: 51–90.

Stalsberg, A. 1987. The Interpretation of Women's Objects of Scandinavian Origin from the Viking Period Found in Russia. In R. Bertelsen, A. Lillehammer & J.-R. Næss (eds) *Were They All Men? An Examination of Sex Roles in Prehistoric Society. Acts from a Workshop Held at Utstein Kloster, Rogaland 2.–4. November 1979. NAM-Forskningsseminar nr. 1*. Arkeologisk Museum i Stavanger, Stavanger: 89–100.

Stalsberg, A. 1991. Women as Actors in North European Viking Age Trade. In R. Samson (ed.) *Social Approaches to Viking Studies*. Cruithne Press, Glasgow: 75–83.

Stalsberg, A. 2001. Visible Women Made Invisible: Interpreting Varangian Women in Old Russia. In B. Arnold & N. Wicker (eds) *Gender and the Archaeology of Death*. Altamira Press, Walnut Creek: 65–79.

Stalsberg, A. & O. Farbregd 2011. Why so Many Viking Age Swords in Norway. *Studia Universitas Cibiniensis, Series Historica, Supplementum No. 1*: 47–52.

Steinforth, D.H. 2015a. *Die skandinavische Besiedlung auf der Isle of Man. Eine archäologische und historische Untersuchung zur frühen Wikingerzeit in der Irischen See*. de Gruyter, Berlin and Boston.

Steinforth, D.H. 2015b. *Die Wikingergräber auf der Isle of Man*. Archaeopress, Oxford.

Steinsland, G. 1985. Kvinner og kult i vikingtid. In R. Andersen, L.H. Dommasnes, Magnús Stefánsson & I. Øye (eds) *Kvinnearbeid i Norden fra vikingtiden til reformasjonen. Foredrag fra et nordisk kvinnehistorisk seminar i Bergen, 3–7 august 1983*. Universitetet i Bergen, Bergen: 31–42.

Steinsland, G. 1991. *Det hellige bryllup og norrøn kongeideologi. En analyse av hierogami-myten i Skírnismál, Ynglingatal, Háleygjatal og Hyndluljóð*. Solum, Larvik.

Steinsland, G. 1996. Husfruer, gydjer og volver – den skjulte tradisjon i norrøn religion. In G. Sæter (ed.) *HUN – en antologi om kunnskap fra kvinners liv*. Spillerom, Oslo: 81–92.

Stenvik, L.F. 2005. Sosjale forskjeller. In I. Bull, O. Skevik, K. Sognnes & O.S. Stugu (eds) *Trøndelags historie. Bind 1. Landskapet blir landsel. Fram til 1350*. Tapir Akademisk Forlag, Trondheim: 147–153.

Storm, G. 1885. Om Thorgerd Hölgebrud. *Arkiv för nordisk filologi* 2: 124–135.

Stoumann, I. 2009. *Ryttergraven fra Grimstrup og andre vikingetidsgrave ved Esbjerg*. Sydvestjyske Museer, Ribe.

Strand, B. 1980. *Kvinnor och män i Gesta Danorum*. Historiska institutionen, Göteborgs Universitet, Göteborg.

Straubhaar, S.B. 2002. Ambiguously Gendered: The Skalds Jórunn, Auðr and Steinunn. In S.M. Anderson & K. Swenson (eds) *Cold Counsel. Women in Old Norse Literature and Mythology. A Collection of Essays*. Routledge, New York and London: 261–271.

Ström, F. 1942. *On the Sacral Origin of the Germanic Death Penalties*. H. Ohlssons boktryckeri, Lund.

Ström, F. 1973. Nid och ergi. *Saga och Sed* 1973: 27–47.

Ström, F. 1974. *Nið, ergi and Old Norse Moral Attitudes*. Viking Society for Northern Research, London.

Strömbäck, D. 1935. *Sejd. Textstudier i nordisk religionhistoria*. Gebers, Stockholm.

Strömbäck, D. 2000. *Sejd och andra studier i nordisk själsuppfattning*. Gidlunds Förlag, Hedemora.

Strömberg, M. 1951. Schwertortbänder mit Vogelmotiven aus der Wikingerzeit. *Meddelanden från Lunds Universitets Historiska Museum* 1950–1951: 221–243.

Stylegar, F.-A. 2007. The Kaupang Cemeteries Revisited. In D. Skre (ed.) *Kaupang in Skiringssal, Kaupang Excavation Project Publication Series, Volume 1*. Aarhus University Press, Aarhus: 65–101.

Suchodolski, S. 2015. The Obol of the Dead. In *Bodzia. A Late Viking-Age Elite Cemetery in Central Poland*. Brill, Leiden and Boston: 313–340.

Sulej, K. 2014. Ścięty warkoczyk. In U. Jabłońska (ed.) *Walka jest kobietą*. Dom Wydawniczy PWN, Warszawa: 174–193.

Svanberg, F. 2003. *Death Rituals in South-East Scandinavia AD 800–1000. Decolonizing the Viking Age Vol. 2*. Almqvist & Wiksell International, Lund.

Szczepanik, P. 2017. Early Medieval Bronze Sheaths with Zoo- and Anthropomorphic Ornamental Fittings from Poland – Mythical

Pictures and their Content. In F. Biermann, T. Kersting & A. Klammt (eds) *Religion und Gesellschaft im nördlichen westslawischen Raum. Beiträge der Sektion zur slawischen Frühgeschichte der 22. Jahrestagung des Mittel- und Ostdeutschen Verbandes für Altertumsforschung in Chemnitz, 29.–31. März 2016*. Beier & Beran. Archäologische Fachliteratur, Langenweissbach: 169–178.

Szymczak, J. 2018. *Rycerz i jego konie*. Polskie Towarzystwo Heraldyczne/Edition La Rama/Wydawnictwo DiG, Bellerive-sur-Allier.

Świętosławski, W. 1990. *Strzemiona średniowieczne z ziem Polski*. Polska Akademia Nauk Instytut Historii Kultury Materialnej, Łódź.

Świętosławski, W. 2001. Rola Awarów w rozpowszechnieniu w Europie azjatyckich form uzbrojenia. *Acta Universitatis Lodziensis. Folia Archaeologica* 23: 75–85.

Świętosławski, W. 2006. *Ślady koczowników Wielkiego Stepu z X, XI, XII wieku w dorzeczach Wisły i Odry*. Instytut Archeologii i Etnologii Polskiej Akademiii Nauk, Łódź.

Talbot, A.-M. & D.F. Sullivan (eds) 2005. *The History of Leo Deacon: Byzantine Military Expansion in the Tenth Century*. Dumbarton Oaks Research Library and Collection, Washington DC.

Tedlock, B. 2005. *The Woman in the Shaman's Body: Reclaiming the Feminine in Religion and Medicine*. Bantam Books, New York.

Thålin-Bergman, L. 1986a. Übersicht über die Schwerter von Birka. In G. Arwidsson (ed.) *Birka II:2: Systematische Analysen der Gräberfunde*. Almqvist & Wiksell International, Stockholm: 11–14.

Thålin-Bergman, L. 1986b. Die Waffengräber von Birka. In G. Arwidsson (ed.) *Birka II:2: Systematische Analysen der Gräberfunde*. Almqvist & Wiksell International, Stockholm: 5–10.

Thompson, T. (ed.) 2015. *The Archaeology of Cremation: Burned Human Remains in Funerary Studies*. Oxbow Books, Oxford.

Thomsen, B. 2014. Kvinder og klær. In N. Coleman & N. Løkka (eds) *Kvinner i vikingtid. Vikingatidens kvinnor*. Scandinavian Academic Press, Oslo: 210–223.

Thorvildsen, K. 1957. *Ladby-skibet*. Det Kongelige Nordiske Oldskriftselskab, København.

Þóra Pétursdóttir 2007. *'Deyr fé, deyja frændr'. Re-animating Mortuary Remains from Viking Age Iceland*. Faculty of Social Sciences, University of Tromsø (Unpublished MA Thesis), Tromsø.

Thunmark-Nylén, L. 1998–2006. *Die Wikingerzeit Gotlands*. Kungl. Vitterhets Historie och Antikvitets Akademien, Stockholm.

Thunmark-Nylén, L. 2006. *Die Wikingerzeit Gotlands. IV: 1. Katalog*. Kungl. Vitterhets Historie och Antikvitets Akademien, Stockholm.

Tilley, C. 1994. *A Phenomenology of Landscape: Places, Paths and Monuments*. Berg, Oxford/Providence.

Toler, P.D. 2019. *Women Warriors: An Unexpected History*. Beacon Press, Boston.

Tolley, C. 2009. *Shamanism in Norse Myth and Magic. Volume 1*. Suomalainen Tiedeakatemia/Academia Scientiarum Fennica, Helsinki.

Tomiccy, J.R. 1975. *Drzewo życia. Ludowa wizja świata i człowieka*. Ludowa Spółdzielnia Wydawnicza, Warszawa.

Tomicki, R. 1976. Słowiański mit kosmogoniczny. *Etnografia Polska* 20(1): 47–95.

Toplak, M.S. 2016. *Das Wikingerzeitliche Gräberfeld von Kopparsvik auf Gotland. Studien zu neuen Konzepten sozialer Identitäten am Übergang zum christlichen Mittelalter*. Universität Tübingen, Tübingen.

Toplak, M.S. 2019a. The Warrior and the Cat: A Re-Evaluation of the Roles of Domestic Cats in Viking Age Scandinavia. *Current Swedish Archaeology* 27: 213–245.

Toplak, M.S. 2019b. Brennende Schiffe und blutige Zeremonien. Die Bestattungssitten. In J. Staecker & M.S. Toplak (eds) *Die Wikinger. Entdecker und Eroberer*. Propyläen/Ullstein Buchverlage, Berlin: 45–60.

Toplak, M.S. in press. Equestrian Burials on Viking Age Gotland: Between Mounted Warriors and Totemic Animals. In L. Gardeła & K. Kajkowski (eds) *Animals and Animated Objects in the Early Middle Ages*. Brepols, Turnhout.

Trotzig, G. 1985. An Axe as a Sign of Rank in a Viking Community. *Archaeology and Environment* 4: 83–87.

Trotzig, G. 1991. *Craftsmanship and Function: A Study of Metal Vessels Found in Viking Age Tombs on the Island of Gotland*. Statens Historiska Museum, Stockholm.

Trupinda, J. (ed.) 2004. *Pacifica Terra. Prusowie-Słowianie-Wikingowie u ujścia Wisły. Katalog wystawy*. Muzeum Zamkowe w Malborku, Malbork.

Tschan, F.J. (ed.) 2002. *The History of the Archbishops of Hamburg-Bremen*. Columbia University Press, New York.

Tsigaridas, Z. 1998. Fra gård til grav: langhauger, kvinneroler og reproduksjon av samfunnet. *Primitive Tider* 1998: 1–20.

Tulinius, T. 2005. Sagas of Icelandic Prehistory. In R. McTurk (ed.) *A Companion to Old Norse-Icelandic Literature and Culture*. Blackwell, Oxford: 447–461.

Ulriksen, J. 2011. Spor af begravelsesritualer i jordfæstegrave i vikingetidens Danmark. *KUML* 2011: 161–245.

Ulriksen, J. 2018. A Völva's Grave at Roskilde, Denmark? *Offa* 71/72, 2014/2015: 229–240.

van Hamel, A.G. 1934. The Game of the Gods. *Arkiv för nordisk filologi* 50: 218–242.

Varberg, J. 2011. Odin's Valkyries. In H. Skov & J. Varberg (eds) *Aros and the World of the Vikings. The Stories and Travelogues of Seven Vikings from Aros*. Højbjerg: 81–83.

Vésteinn Ólason 2005. Family Sagas. In R. McTurk (ed.) *A Companion to Old Norse-Icelandic Literature and Culture*. Blackwell, Oxford: 101–118.

Vierck, H. 2002. Zwei Amulettbilder als Zeugnisse des ausgehenden Heidentums in Haithabu. In C. Radtke (ed.) *Berichte über die Ausgrabungen in Haithabu 34. Das archäologische Fundmaterial VII*. Wachholtz, Neumünster: 9–67.

von Schweringen, G.F. 1909. Women in the Germanic Hero-Sagas. *Journal of English and Germanic Philology* 8: 501–512.

Vretemark, M. 2018. Birds of Prey as Evidence for Falconry in Swedish Burials and Settlements (550–1500 AD). In K.-H. Gersmann & O. Grimm (eds) *Raptor and Human – Falconry and Bird Symbolism throughout the Millennia on a Global Scale*. Wachholtz Murmann, Kiel-Hamburg: 827–839.

Wadyl, S. (ed.) 2019. *Ciepłe. Elitarna nekropola wczesnośredniowieczna na Pomorzu Wschodnim*. Muzeum Archeologiczne w Gdańsku, Gdańsk.

Walsch, M.J., M. Moen, S. O'Neill, S.H. Gullbekk & R. Willerslev 2020. Who's Afraid of the S-word? Deviants' Burials and Human Sacrifice. *Norwegian Archaeological Review* 2020: 1–9.

Wamers, E. 2017. Miniaturwaffen-Amulette. In S. Holst, L. Jørgensen & E. Wamers (eds) *Odin, Thor und Freyja: Skandinavische Kultplätze des 1. Jahrtausends n. Chr. und das Frankenreich. Eine Ausstellung des Archäologischen Museums Frankfurt und des Dänischen Nationalmuseums Kopenhagen.* Schnell Steiner, Frankfurt: 67.

Warming, R.F., R. Larsen, D.V.P. Sommer, L. Ørsted Brand & X. Pauli Jensen 2020. Shields and Hide – On the Use of Hide in Germanic Shields of the Iron Age and Viking Age. *Bericht der Römisch-Germanischen Kommission* 97: 155–225.

Weigand, M.E. 2008. *Die Pferde der Wikingerzeit. Herkunft, Typendifferenzierung und kulturelle Bedeutung des frühmittelalterlichen Pferdes in Nordwesteuropa.* Verlag Dr. Kovac, Hamburg.

Wenn, C.C. 2020. What Happened at Langeid? Understanding Reopened Graves after Time has Taken its Toll. In A. Klevnäs, E. Aspöck & N. Müller-Scheeßel (eds) *Grave Disturbances.* Oxbow Books, Oxford and Philadelphia: 137–156.

Wheeler, R.E.M. 1927. *London and the Vikings.* Lancaster House, London.

Wicker, N. 1998. Selective Female Infanticide as Partial Explanation for the Dearth of Women in Viking Age Scandinavia. In G. Halsall (ed.) *Violence and Society in the Early Medieval West.* Boydell & Brewer, Woodbridge.

Wicker, N. 2020. Humans and Animals: The Changing Corpus of Danish Viking Art. In A. Pedersen & S. Sindbæk (eds) *Viking Encounters. Proceedings of the 18th Viking Congress.* Aarhus University Press, Aarhus: 413–425.

Wickholm, A. 2006. 'Stay Where You Have Been Put!' The Use of Spears as Coffin Nails in Late Iron Age Finland. In H. Valk (ed.) *Etnos Ja Kultur. Uurimusi Silvia Laulu auks.* Tartu Ülikool, Arheoloogia õppetool/Tallinna Ülikooli, Ajaloo Instituut, Tartu-Tallinn: 193–205.

Williams, D. 1997. *Late Saxon Stirrup-Strap Mounds: A Classification and Catalogue. A Contribution to the Study of Late Saxon Ornamental Metalwork.* Council for British Archaeology, York.

Williams, G. 2013. Warfare & Military Expansion. In G. Williams, P. Pentz & M. Wemhoff (eds) *Viking.* Nationalmuseet, Copenhagen: 76–115.

Williams, H. (ed.) 2003. *Archaeologies of Remembrance. Death and Memory in Past Societies.* Springer, New York.

Williams, H. 2006. *Death and Memory in Early Medieval Britain.* Cambridge University Press, Cambridge.

Williams, H. 2016. Viking Mortuary Citations. *European Journal of Archaeology* 19(3): 400–414.

Williams, H. & M. Giles (eds) 2016. *Archaeologists and the Dead: Mortuary Archaeology in Contemporary Society.* Oxford University Press, Oxford.

Williams, H. & D. Sayer 2009. 'Halls of Mirrors': Death and Identity in Medieval Archaeology. In D. Sayer & H. Williams (eds) *Mortuary Practices and Social Identities in the Middle Ages. Essays in Honour of Heinrich Härke.* University of Exeter Press, Exeter: 1–22.

Williams, H., B. Wills-Eve & J. Osborne (eds) 2019. *The Public Archaeology of Death.* Equinox Publishing, Sheffield.

Wilson, D.M. 2008. *The Vikings in the Isle of Man.* Aarhus University Press, Aarhus.

Wojtasik, J. 1967. *Cmentarzysko wczesnośredniowieczne na Wzgórzu 'Młynówka' w Wolinie.* Muzeum Pomorza Zachodniego, Szczecin.

Wolf, K. 1996. Amazons in Vínland. *Journal of English and Germanic Philology* 95: 469–485.

Wolf, K. 1997. Transvestism in the Sagas of Icelanders. In J.R. Hagland, J. Sandnes, G. Foss & A. Dybdahl (eds) *Sagas and the Norwegian Experience. 10th International Saga Conference. Trondheim 3–9 August 1997. Preprints.* NTNU, Trondheim: 675–684.

Wolf, K. 2006. The Color Blue in Old Norse-Icelandic Literature. In D. Ashurst, D. Kick & J. McKinnell (eds) *The Fantastic in Old Norse/Icelandic Literature. Sagas and the British Isles. Preprint Papers of the 13th International Saga Conference, Durham and York, 6th–12th August 2006.* Durham University, Durham: 1071–1080.

Wrzesiński, J. 1998. Groby z mieczami na terenie Polski wczesnopiastowskiej (X–XIII wiek). *Prace i Materiały Muzeum Archeologicznego i Etnograficznego w Łodzi* 40: 7–46.

Wrzesiński, J. 2000. Noże żelazne w grobach na wczesnośredniowiecznym cmentarzysku w Dziekanowicach. *Studia Lednickie* 6: 91–124.

Wrzesiński, J. 2007. Pole bitwy na dnie jeziora? *Z Otchłani Wieków* 62(1–4): 16–21.

Wrzesiński, J. 2011. Groby z toporami w państwie Piastów. In O. Ławrynowicz, J. Maik & P.A. Nowakowski (eds) *NON SENSISTIS GLADIOS. Studia ofiarowane Marianowi Głoskowi w 70. rocznicę urodzin.* Instytut Archeologii Uniwersytetu Łódzkiego/Instytut Archeologii i Etnologii Polskiej Akademii Nauk, Oddział w Łodzi/Stowarzyszenie Naukowe Archeologów Polskich, Oddział w Łodzi/Łódzkie Towarzystwo Naukowe, Łódź: 463–486.

Wyrwa, A.M., P. Sankiewicz & P. Pudło (eds) 2011. *Miecze średniowieczne z Ostrowa Lednickiego i Giecza.* Muzeum Pierwszych Piastów na Lednicy, Dziekanowice-Lednica.

Zappatore, F. 2017. *Shieldmaidens in the Gesta Danorum (I–IX): The Collectvie Literary Imaginary and History.* Università di Bologna (Unpublished MA Thesis), Bologna.

Zeiten, M.K. 1997. Amulets and Amulet Use in Viking Age Denmark. *Acta Archaeologica* 68: 1–74.